# SOCIAL CONTRACTS
# UNDER STRESS

# SOCIAL CONTRACTS UNDER STRESS

The Middle Classes of America,
Europe, and Japan at the Turn
of the Century

*Edited by Olivier Zunz, Leonard
Schoppa, and Nobuhiro Hiwatari*

*Russell Sage Foundation*
*New York*

## The Russell Sage Foundation

The Russell Sage Foundation, one of the oldest of America's general purpose foundations, was established in 1907 by Mrs. Margaret Olivia Sage for "the improvement of social and living conditions in the United States." The Foundation seeks to fulfill this mandate by fostering the development and dissemination of knowledge about the country's political, social, and economic problems. While the Foundation endeavors to assure the accuracy and objectivity of each book it publishes, the conclusions and interpretations in Russell Sage Foundation publications are those of the authors and not of the Foundation, its Trustees, or its staff. Publication by Russell Sage, therefore, does not imply Foundation endorsement.

**Library of Congress Cataloging-in-Publication Data**

Social contracts under stress : the middle classes of America, Europe, and Japan at the turn of the century / edited by Olivier Zunz, Leonard Schoppa, and Nobuhiro Hiwatari.
    p. cm.
  Includes bibliographical references and index.
    1. Middle class—Europe—History—20th century. 2. Middle class—United States—History—20th century. 3. Middle class—Japan—History—20th century. I. Zunz, Olivier. II. Schoppa, Leonard J. (Leonard James), 1962– III. Hiwatari, Nobuhiro, 1955–

HT690.E73 S63 2002
305.5'5'09049—dc21

2001055714

RUSSELL SAGE FOUNDATION
112 East 64th Street, New York, New York 10021
10 9 8 7 6 5 4 3 2 1

*For Henri Mendras*

# Contents

### Part III   VANISHING BORDERS AND THE SOCIAL CONTRACT

# Contributors

**Olivier Zunz** is Commonwealth Professor of History at the University of Virginia and is president of the Tocqueville Society.

**Leonard Schoppa** is associate professor in the Woodrow Wilson Department of Government and Foreign Affairs at the University of Virginia.

**Nobuhiro Hiwatari** is professor of Japanese and comparative politics at the Institute of Social Science at the University of Tokyo.

**Maurice Aymard** is director of studies at the École des hautes études en sciences sociales and director of the Maison des sciences de l'homme in Paris.

**Arnaldo Bagnasco** is professor of sociology at the University of Turin.

**Christophe Charle** is professor of modern history at the Université de Paris-I Panthéon-Sorbonne and director of the Institut d'histoire moderne et contemporaine (CNRS Ecole normale supérieure).

**Patrick Fridenson** is director of studies at the École des hautes études en sciences sociales.

**Andrew Gordon** is professor of history at Harvard University and director of the Edwin O. Reischauer Institute of Japanese Studies.

**Derek Hoff** is a doctoral candidate in American history at the University of Virginia.

**Meg Jacobs** is assistant professor of history at the Massachusetts Institute of Technology.

**Ira Katznelson** is Ruggles Professor of Political Science and History at Columbia University.

**William W. Kelly** is professor of anthropology and the Sumitomo Professor of Japanese Studies at Yale University.

**Bo Öhngren** is a researcher at the Swedish Council for Research in the Humanities and Social Sciences.

**Mari Osawa** is professor of social policy at the Institute of Social Science at the University of Tokyo and a member of the Japanese Council for Gender Equality of the Prime Minister.

**Chiara Saraceno** is professor of sociology at the University of Turin.

**Mike Savage** is professor and head of the Department of Sociology at Manchester University.

**Hannes Siegrist** is professor of modern comparative history of Europe at the Institut für Kulturwissenschaften at the University of Leipzig.

**Margaret Weir** is professor of sociology and political science at the University of California at Berkeley and a nonresident senior fellow at the Brookings Institution.

# Acknowledgments

The idea for this project emerged from a conversation I had with Maurice Aymard in the spring of 1997. We both felt the time had come to bring together historians and social scientists from Japan, the United States, and several European countries to review and compare the state of our social contracts. To ensure a strong East Asian component, I asked the political scientists Leonard Schoppa and Hiwatari Nobuhiro to join me in organizing a working group. Together we recruited exceptional scholars who met to prepare this volume first in Paris in January 1998, then in Tokyo in June 1999, and finally in Charlottesville, Virginia, in April 2000.

The Paris meeting was funded by the Maison des Sciences de l'Homme (MSH), with the Japan Foundation responsible for the travel of Japanese participants and the Russell Sage Foundation for that of the Americans. We assembled as a group in the newly built and splendid Maison de la Culture du Japon and also the Maison Suger, the conference center and guest house of the MSH, where Director Jean-Luc Lory extended to us his usual warm hospitality.

A generous grant from the Center for Global Partnership of the Japan Foundation allowed us to meet again in Tokyo a year and a half later. Professor Hirowatari Seigo welcomed us at the Institute of Social Science of the University of Tokyo (Shaken) and graciously made its facilities available to us.

The third and last meeting, funded by the Russell Sage Foundation, took place at the Miller Center of Public Affairs of the University of Virginia. Russell Sage Foundation President Eric Wanner, a staunch supporter of this project since its inception, joined us for this last round of discussions.

Assembling a volume of this sort, with authors from seven countries across three continents, was no simple task. In addition to the help received from the institutions already mentioned, a great deal of assistance was provided by the University of Virginia's Bankard Fund for the Study of Political Economy, which made it possible for Leonard Schoppa and I to work together in the summer of 1999 after the Tokyo meeting, and by the University of Virginia East Asia Center.

A number of people were especially important in helping us bring the volume to fruition. Miura Mari and Maire Murphy worked out the complex mechanics of making local arrangements in Tokyo and Charlottesville, respectively. Bonnie J. Ford expertly oversaw the disbursement of funds. Derek Hoff prepared the manuscript for publication with his usual energy and attention to detail. Charlie Feigenoff, a senior independent editor in Charlottesville, loaned us his extraordinary critical skills and culture in working out the final version of the chapters with each author. At Russell Sage, Suzanne Nichols and Cindy Buck have upheld the foundation's tradition of excellence in publication. We are deeply indebted to them all.

Olivier Zunz
*Paris, Tokyo, Charlottesville*
Summer 2001

# Introduction: Social Contracts Under Stress

## Olivier Zunz

When the British philosopher R. G. Collingwood set out in the midst of World War II to define a postwar "social contract" of "free participation in a joint enterprise," he stressed first his cherished ideas of political consent. Calling his 1942 book *The New Leviathan,* he juxtaposed Hobbes's consciousness of freedom against the imminent threat of German "barbarism." Collingwood's purpose was to reinvigorate the ideas of popular sovereignty and freedom inherited from the Enlightenment and combine them with the more recent commitments to social welfare and the reduction of inequality. After reestablishing a postwar order based on political consent, one had to reduce "gross disparities in the riches of individual members" of society. Thus, a new "social contract" would finally synthesize liberty and equality, the two great, but almost defeated, overlapping trends of modern history, and restore their viability.[1]

Collingwood's ideals were echoed by policymakers throughout the Allied world. In the British policy circles of these war years, concern about want stimulated William Beveridge and others to outline the contours of the welfare state.[2] In Washington, Franklin Roosevelt and his advisers, although they had abandoned their early New Deal attempt to repair the structural flaws of capitalism, placed the power of the state behind market-based redistributive mechanisms as a way to ensure the widespread diffusion of postwar prosperity throughout American society. Many voices in other Allied quarters contributed to imagining the postwar social contract. When the young French philosopher Simone Weil joined General de Gaulle in London, her reflections on the French national defeat led her to define a new postwar

1

social "doctrine" that emphasized individual obligations toward the community rather than universal rights.[3]

What was important in these numerous and often conflicting blueprints was their emphasis on a shared will that would create and maintain new institutionalized patterns of social cohesion. Restore freedom first, then foster the democratization of wealth by facilitating access to the market, as most liberal American policymakers saw it, or by institutionalizing social protection, a course advocated by most Europeans. Regardless of policy, institutional arrangements were to be balanced with renewed individual commitments to the communal well-being.

Restoring and strengthening democracy required proactive policies that promoted social advancement. The social contracts of the postwar years stimulated middle-class expansion in the advanced industrialized nations, dramatically accelerating the American prewar trend of merging the working and middle classes into a huge, albeit differentiated middle class. Through a great variety of mechanisms of wealth redistribution and market expansion, the middle class of the United States, Europe, and Japan grew significantly larger, absorbing a large part of the working class by blurring the collar line. The challenge of this book is to recognize this large historical transformation as it took place in these regions, understand the social change it generated, identify its fault lines, assess its limits, and determine the extent to which postwar social contracts have come under pressure in recent decades.

Social contracts are works in progress and reflect the prevailing goals of the era in which they were formulated. In the first half of the twentieth century, they were merely ameliorative or "progressive." They were designed to ease the excesses of laissez-faire and to bring the working class more fully into the mainstream. They raised the standard of living of some groups and pushed social policies to serve individual freedom, but their influence was uneven. They did not lead to a political consensus or a global class redefinition, nor were they intended to. By contrast, postwar social contracts, however flawed, were meant to be universalist. Although they were not implemented everywhere at once and some people remained excluded, postwar social contracts were designed with sweeping goals, in victorious nations as well as in nations that had lost the war. Despite their limitations, they were largely effective. In the span of one postwar generation in Japan and other parts of Asia, in Western Europe, and in North America, people of widely different cultural and national traditions, as well as of different wealth, status, and power, including workers, came to see themselves as belonging to a broad middle class in a society that was predominantly middle-class.

The phenomenon has been not only widespread but in some cases extreme. From the mid-1960s on, about 90 percent of the citizens of Japan have categorized themselves as middle class.[4] If there is a similarity among advanced societies today, it is that most of their citizens identify themselves as members of the middle class. Even large numbers of British workers, who have held out the longest, no longer hesitate to think of themselves as middle class. How did the various social contracts encourage this change of identity? How many diverse trajectories and prescriptions did it take? And why has this self-identification been so widespread? As this volume makes clear in its first part, the policies and emphases have varied significantly among nations and national blocs. But when national policies are laid out side by side, as they are here, their cumulative effect is inescapable.

As a descriptive statement of modern history, this assertion of great middle-class expansion is true, yet it has certainly not affected everyone equally or at the same pace. Much has been achieved, as we recognize, but the touted universalism has remained elusive. Cold war politics has complicated social policies at every turn in Germany and Japan. Moreover, middle-class expansion and social inclusiveness are not the same. As it has often been said, much of the old working-class life has been repackaged into middle-class identities. Racial inequality has proved incredibly resilient, especially in the United States, even after the "Second Reconstruction" of the civil rights movement. New gender relations have been formulated but have affected middle-class mores only partly.

We examine these problems in part II as we address the limits of the postwar social contracts in Asian and European countries as well as in the United States. This is where we note that postwar middle-class social contracts are not merely under stress but have also generated large social fractures of their own. In the United States, the middle class gave only reluctant support to minority rights in the 1960s. In fact, the exclusion of minorities from postwar prosperity motivated John Rawls to revive the debate on the social contract in *A Theory of Justice* (1971). As a philosopher, Rawls stayed above the fray, constructing his dialogue mostly with other philosophers as he sought to update Hobbes, Locke, Rousseau, and Kant for the 1960s and 1970s. But Rawls went further. In the midst of the civil rights movement, he saw civic disobedience as a social good to obtain justice.[5] Other nations experienced the limits of middle-class expansion and inclusiveness. Everywhere in the 1960s, middle-class values were questioned.

Grassroots challenges to postwar social contracts climaxed in 1968 as the new fault lines became highly visible.

If the middle classes of advanced nations have been complacent toward those excluded from their social bargain, they have felt the pinch of slowing growth themselves, beginning with the oil shock of 1973 and continuing into the early 1990s. Moreover, while economic growth was slowing, the rules of the economic game were changing. International trading regimes and regional economic pacts have disrupted social contracts at both national and local levels. Even as economic growth returned in the 1990s, competition among the advanced economies under the new condition of globalization and regionalization continued to transform the terms of social bargains everywhere. This is the problem we take up in the third and most speculative and forward-looking part of the book. Here we seek to understand how new institutions and practices, which are encroaching on national sovereignty, are redefining the options that policy-makers and grassroots movements exercise in defining the social contracts.

## National Paths to Middle-class Formation

Such factors as greater access to education, higher levels of inter-generational upward mobility, a significant rise in the standard of living of workers through rising wages and collective bargaining, wide access to consumption, and the sharing by all of a new "middlebrow" culture helped make the postwar social contract a middle-class contract. At a different pace and under different conditions, all these mechanisms materialized in the countries studied here. The social distance separating the old independent entrepreneurs or the new professionals and upper managerial ranks from the huge working classes persisted, but the distinction between manual and nonmanual labor lost much of its significance for determining class identity. New class identities were renegotiated at the collar line, with the result that beginning in the 1950s, the collar line loosened dramatically, setting in motion a complex process of class redefinition.

Individual countries, each retaining distinct lessons from its own past, created their own variety of this postwar middle-class contract. To highlight national trends, the authors in part I analyze the factors favorable to middle-class expansion as well as the factors that deterred it in Germany, the United Kingdom, France, Japan, and the United States. They pay special attention to the surviving influences of older political cultures, to class conflicts, and to recurrent threats to middle-class social contracts by radical alternatives from both the left and the right. While making no attempt to be comprehensive, they take up one or more of these problems within a larger national history. The result is a description of the diversity and contradictions in middle-class social contracts over three continents.

We begin with Germany, the country where building an inclusive postwar middle class in response to Collingwood's call for a return to political consent was most urgent. In his chapter, Hannes Siegrist gives us a comprehensive analysis of middle-class re-formation in Germany. He examines the re-creation of the idea of the middle class in the immense "social flux" of the postwar years. He looks at its redefinition as an inclusive "imagined community" in the context of the abandonment of old ideas of status (which traditionally used a multiplicity of terms to represent a more hierarchical society). Siegrist describes this phenomenon in both postwar Germanys. Under the supervision of the Allies, the West German middle classes became "a republican and democratic class," with the clear project of preventing the emergence of a Communist regime. At the same time, East Germany turned its middle class into a service class to serve the general interest of the working class and the socialist state. Siegrist then describes the difficult encounter of the West German middle class with the vestiges of the East German "upper service class" after the surprise reunification in 1990. As a result, while the middle classes of other countries are currently worrying about their future in the global economy, the middle classes in Germany are concerned about the extension of their postwar social contract to the former East Germany. They are, in effect, the first to work out the terms of the social integration of the former Soviet Union into Western Europe.

The British, Mike Savage argues, although citizens of the oldest parliamentary democracy, never thought of themselves as creating a large middle class until very recently. Savage explains the paradox of this old democracy holding on to a low level of middle-class identification and a high level of working-class pride. In the United Kingdom, a widely acknowledged and distinctive middle-class practice of emulating the gentry has kept the more prosperous members of the working class from aspiring to the middle class. Because the British aristocracy and the new "middle classes" refused for so long to carry the banner for democratic rights, it was the working class that took on this role and thereby forged an enduring cultural association between itself and the democratic tradition. As many as 64 percent of British citizens considered themselves members of the working class in 1991 and asserted that they were proud of its democratic heritage. A comparatively low level of middle-class identity has persisted despite the loss of industrial jobs that England has experienced along with other advanced economies in the last decade. Still, with fewer workers to integrate into its ranks, the middle class is finally opening up, resulting in considerable class and political ambiguity. As a result, England is considering the possibilities of a middle-class contract under the unexpected leadership of a "labour party," which is awkwardly assuming a new middle-class identity under an old name.

France represents something of a distinct case: the middle classes have remained fragmented and refused to adopt a group identity. Christophe Charle tells the intriguing story of French political labels masking rather than revealing social identities. As he explains, the values of the nineteenth-century middle classes—work, economy, and the cult of individual entrepreneurship—were not fully consolidated into the Republican model of instruction, solidarity, and promotion. Class identities continued to be fought over in the political arena, where they split between right and left. In the Third Republic, the idea of a middle-class party was even so strange that it became known as the "radical" party, but it could never arbitrate for very long between political extremes. There were temporary alliances of smaller groups and moments of national unity, but a strong political center did not materialize. When some French leaders sought a national *rassemblement,* as successfully inspired by de Gaulle, they adopted a populist rhetoric, not one of middle-class identity.[6] A social center could survive only if it was made up of many different political groups and thought of itself in "semantic ambiguity." Hence the French habit of spelling "middle classes" in the plural; this was not a matter of linguistic preference but the result of a misfit between class and politics. As Charle puts it, "the middle classes, lacking distinct social boundaries and in search of social mobility," have adopted a rhetoric of extremes, only occasionally leaving space for inclusiveness.

This history makes the ultimate convergence of the French social structure toward a broader middle class all the more remarkable. One way to understand it is to recognize its peculiar French makeup, fractured by the many sociological and organizational barriers that Patrick Fridenson describes as persisting to some extent even within the new middle class. Thus, a large number of public servants (over 5 million in 1999) have retained something of the corporate order of the old regime in the face of Europeanization. They prefer to perpetuate their own privileged arrangements rather than allow the creation of a market-based, middle-class society of the American model. Subcategories of civil servants have even worked out their own institutional arrangements within the larger French social safety net. This is but one of the many obstacles to the formation of a broad middle

6

class that Fridenson points to, yet both Fridenson and Charle see a larger middle class emerging in France, one freer from the ideology and allegiances of left and right and more willing to face the challenges of globalization and Europeanization, to which we turn in closing the volume.

Middle-class social contracts were clearly a postwar innovation in Japan even if there too we find some prewar antecedents. As in Germany, the old Japanese middle classes were tainted for having failed democracy. But unlike in Germany, only a marginal Japanese middle class existed before the war, and its members, dubbed "Western clothes paupers," were often in a precarious position.

The experience of war and defeat, Andrew Gordon argues, had "a powerful homogenizing effect" as all Japanese strove to achieve a new life. Yet not until the late 1950s and the 1960s did "middle-class life" as both a mass experience and the self-identified status of the vast majority of people come to characterize Japanese society. By the late 1950s, a significant weakening of the collar line was well under way as the effects of mass education, the nuclear family structure, suburbanization, and the weight of new large-scale, bureaucratic, and commercial institutions were felt everywhere. By the 1960s, it hardly seemed possible to identify a separate Japanese working class. National issues had become, by definition, middle-class issues.

The Japanese constructing their own version of a middle-class contract could be seen as the ultimate victory of the Americans, if only the American middle-class consensus had been as solid as it seemed. Already in the 1830s, Tocqueville had posited the United States as the quintessential middle-class country of the future, but the large-scale industrialization of the late nineteenth century had been a serious obstacle.[7]

It took a long time for a modern mass middle class to form. To late-nineteenth-century adherents of laissez-faire, "social contract" still sounded like an oxymoron; Herbert Spencer denounced it as "baseless," and his American disciple William Graham Sumner exposed "the absurd effort to make the world over."[8] Yet the trend was clearly toward the blending of the collar line. High industrial incomes, as Werner Sombart observed in his 1906 comparative analyses of workers' wages, eventually helped support a widely shared American standard of living.[9] Hard-earned collective contractual agreements and social legislation increasingly contributed to a higher family wage. As these factors combined with high levels of consumption and intensified in the postwar era in the United States, a class structure bulging at the center and with an income distribution resembling a bell-shaped curve struck analysts as an important and desirable

American phenomenon. David Potter recorded the moment in his famous 1954 essay *People of Plenty*.[10] The American working class had finally made the notion of collective contract acceptable. New Deal guarantees had become the norm, and consensus scholars were celebrating a new era of conservative unionism and labor-management comprehensive agreements, which greatly fostered middle-class expansion.

But the consensus rested on a fragile alliance, as Meg Jacobs explains in chapter 6 of this volume. A large part of the middle class comprised those industrial workers supported by presumably inflationary wages earned at the bargaining tables. High wages for some brought the fear of rising prices and declining purchasing power for others. By examining "middle-class" class strife when conservative unionism was at its apex at the height of postwar economic expansion—two factors otherwise favorable to a relaxing of the collar line—Jacobs teaches us how little it took for the American middle class to feel insecure about its status and to turn on the institutions that had eased the entry of the working class into the middle class. A few wage-price maladjustments were enough to pit the middle and working classes against one another. In the midst of the so-called consensus of abundance, the language of politics prevailed over that of class (not unlike in France) as Republicans denounced union demands as inflationary. Jacobs shows that the politics of the bargaining table, under the right circumstances, retained the potential to obstruct class inclusion.

## Constituencies in Conflict

After having documented the ways in which large middle classes have increasingly come to define new social contracts in the postwar years, we then turn more systematically in part II to the problem of inclusion in the middle classes. The institutions of mass society, which promoted the rise of the middle class, also promoted a form of middle-class homogeneity that was shaped by gender and racial biases.

This middle-class conformity of the postwar years has been thoroughly discussed by the social critics of the 1950s and 1960s, who denounced the stifling homogenizing effects of a new "mass society."[11] These critics exposed the pressures that markets and politics applied to make people conform to average expectations. Although, retrospectively, they overestimated the agency of institutions and underestimated the agency of individuals, they were clearly correct in showing how difficult it was to make a mass society democratic. Even though it may not be surprising that the drive to create a large, uniform middle class would incorporate—or at least leave unchallenged—popular and ingrained prejudices, the authors in part II show how long-standing prejudices, whether toward women or minorities, became reinforced and perpetuated by the middle-class social contracts. The presence of these older discriminatory practices in a sense strengthened social contracts for a while by making it easier for the mass of people to adjust to the new dominant norms—a need felt by new middle-class people on an unprecedented scale.

The hegemonic effects of this posture were clearly visible: the male-dominated nuclear family structure was built into the welfare states, and ethnic minorities had to assimilate to share in the distribution of resources. Many excluded groups would attack the social contracts and turn them into battlegrounds. We therefore examine the ways in which policies that in theory at least were meant to ensure the universalist nature of social contracts were biased against women and minorities. All of the contributors to the book address this important issue, but the authors in this part give it special attention.

That the mass middle-class contracts have not been universalist is all too clear in the politics of race, especially in the United States, where the term "mass society" first rose to prominence. But the United States was also the first country to discredit the term, which fell out of favor in the 1970s, precisely because racial politics exposed the segregationist underside of a benign pluralism of white males. At best, the American middle class stood aloof, leaving policy elites and the disadvantaged to haggle over the fragile terms of integration. At worst, middle-class expansion and minority rights clashed head-on.

Two studies of the politics of race in the United States ably develop these points. Ira Katznelson uncovers the political mechanisms through which the racial politics of the Democratic South, in the New Deal and postwar years, systematically undercut the universal pretensions of the middle-class social contracts. As Katznelson looks at the exclusionary tactics used by southern politicians, he finds that they tinkered with presumably universalistic policies (like the GI Bill) in such a way as to deepen rather than mitigate the racial divide. Katznelson's theme is the missed opportunity of these postwar years; he describes "the former Confederacy" using the federal political system to exclude blacks from citizenship and full access to civil society. As he puts it, a Democratic Party partnership of "strange bedfellows" obviously produced a series of "strange deals" that, together, constituted a program of affirmative action not for blacks but instead for whites "granted privileged access to state-sponsored economic mobility."

If there is one endeavor ideologically at the heart of a universal middle-class contract of inclusion, it is education. To borrow John Dewey's expression, education is the "democratic password" and the key to upward mobility for all.[12] If there were to be racial inclusion, it would happen as a result of education, which at least in theory was a central element of the social contract. Education has not, however, been an effective means of furthering racial inclusion in the postwar years, as Margaret Weir shows in chapter 8. The problem has partly been one of historical circumstances. In these postwar years, inclusion in the productive forces of large-scale industry rather than education was the principal means of attaining middle-class status through social mobility. African Americans, like other Americans, therefore improved their situation by taking well-paid blue-collar jobs that required little formal training. But the situation has changed. Now that the number of well-paid blue-collar jobs is rapidly declining in the United States, education has taken on added importance while African Americans' access to quality education has remained limited. Washington's general retrenchment has left the states, traditionally responsible for the education budgets, with seemingly too many other responsibilities to allow them to expand their educational programs. States have abandoned their great investment in schooling, and racial integration, which depends largely on the fragile politics of affirmative action, is again in danger.

Equality for women is also a divisive issue. In the United States, where women have made significant headway in redefining the social contract, there have been major contradictions and setbacks: the effort to pass an Equal Rights Amendment was abandoned, and old-fashioned tests of moral rectitude have been kept in welfare legislation longer and more fully than in other nations.[13] Women throughout much of Europe, especially when employed outside the home, have also gained significant recognition of their needs, but not uniformly. As Chiara Saraceno details here, the Scandinavian countries, France, and Belgium have put the power of the state behind support for working mothers. But Germany, Austria, the Netherlands, and Luxembourg have been significantly more timid. In the United Kingdom, retrenchment has superseded the more generous spirit that characterized the Beveridge plan of the war years. The lowest level of benefits persists in the Mediterranean countries, which continue to insist on an established division of labor between men and women.

Instead of treating women uniformly as dependent on a man to gain access to the benefits of the welfare state, European countries have recognized, in varying degrees, the right of women to be independent participants in social contracts. The purpose remains that of balancing, as Saraceno puts it pithily, "the need and right to be cared for, the need and right to care for, and the need and right not to be crushed by caring obligations."

For caring obligations can indeed be crushing for Japanese women—to the point that, as William Kelly shows in chapter 10, their weight may very well be too heavy for the postwar idea of a "mainstream" to survive much longer. Few groups have experienced a greater transformation since the war than Japanese women, who were especially targeted for equality in the new constitution. Yet old gender hierarchies die hard. As Kelly retraces its history, "New Middle-class" Japan emerged after the war and benefited a generation not responsible for the war. With accomplishment returned pride, wide recognition, and a huge increase in the national standard of living. But with time and aging, more Japanese question mutually exclusive gender roles and no longer believe in the supposed "fairness of educational outcomes." Two key ideological tenets of the mainstream are collapsing. Nowadays, Kelly concludes, the cultural and institutional web that has created "unifying frames for people's experiences" is not equal to the domestic and international challenges of a post-catch-up, post-bubble era. Not only is demand for greater individual self-expression being felt more, but an aging population is less able to participate in the national project while increasing global competition makes the educational system more elitist, hence less consensual.

Moreover, as both Osawa Mari and Kelly show, gender inequality is being increasingly challenged. Osawa, who retraces the legislative measures affecting gender through carefully constructed social statistics, shows that reforms undertaken during the 1980s, whether by big companies or the state, have failed to reverse the gendered division of labor in Japan or provide adequate benefits that would free working women. Persisting structural inequality, in a society that prides itself on equality, makes Japanese women less willing participants in a social contract not adapted to their aspirations. Kelly concurs by pointing out that Japanese women, by questioning their status, may be putting an end, if not to male domination, at least to the old mainstream consensus. More Japanese women are postponing marriage and devoting themselves to moving ahead with their own careers. They are no longer willing to be caught between a work environment biased against them and home responsibilities that include both child raising and care for the elderly.

## Vanishing Borders and the Social Contract

How effectively each country tinkers with its own social contracts has been increasingly dependent on events in the larger world. The much freer movement of capital across borders during the last two decades is transforming labor markets in the United States, Japan, and Europe. Moreover, the European Economic Union (EEU), a generation in the making, is affecting national sovereignty in countless ways, with consequences for social contracts. At the same time, the slow but unmistakable integration of Eastern Europe into the Western orbit is changing European society. We examine the social consequences of globalization in the third and concluding part. With shifting economic relationships vastly reshaping the middle-class contracts that have characterized the last fifty years, we are entering the most speculative part of our book.

First among global problems is the obvious difficulty that national governments have in preserving the more generous promises of their postwar social contracts. A major reason for this failure is the need to keep inflation in check, the topic of Hiwatari Nobuhiro's important study on the comparative monetary policies of the United Kingdom, the United States, France, Italy, Germany, and Japan. Hiwatari's point of departure is simple: since "high inflation cannot be tolerated in a world of global mobile capital," the increasing volume of capital flow has "forced" governments with inflation rates higher than those of their trading partners to carry out disinflationary policies. To survive in the global economy, it has become imperative to reduce expenditures that cause inflationary deficits, even at the cost of unemployment. The ability to do this depends on political systems. Hiwatari sets up an elaborate model of the interaction between electoral systems and economic policy and shows how distinct political traditions have shaped the responses to the inflationary crisis of the 1970s and 1980s. He explains that the British and U.S. governments, operating within the context of high-inflation, majoritarian democracies, have fought inflation with adversarial measures. They have "mobilized pro-market forces by making them beneficiaries of tax cuts, privatization, and deregulation, while confronting the unions and targeting public assistance and employment programs to reduce the budget deficit." Moreover, the United States, facing persistent trade deficits, pressured trade-surplus partners like Germany and Japan (as well as Taiwan and Korea in the mid-1980s) to "appreciate their currencies and enact fiscal stimulus packages to increase domestic consumption." In Hiwatari's scheme, conservative politics takes on a new meaning in the context of anti-inflation policies. We also understand better why the determination of Ronald Reagan and Margaret Thatcher to cut welfare and regulation survived their administrations and found a second wind in Bill Clinton's welfare reforms and Tony Blair's "welfare-to-work" policies.

France and Italy, also high-inflation countries, have sought cooperation rather than take adversarial measures. They have worked on agreements on deflation across party lines and between capital and labor. But they too have had to put a significant brake on employment security and cut back on welfare. Germany and Japan, low-inflation "consensus democracies," have retrenched less because they had less inflation. But on the whole, Hiwatari maintains, the "inability" of all these governments to "guarantee employment and social protection" in the face of the necessities of global economic relationships has put the postwar social contract under stress and weakened the sense of security and entitlement among the middle classes.

Moreover, income inequality has been rising again in all advanced societies, undermining one of the goals of the postwar social contract of removing causes of friction between groups. In his famous 1955 presidential address to the American Economics Association, Simon Kuznets demonstrated that income inequality in the industrialized nations had been significantly reduced since 1929, despite widening during the early years of industrial capitalism.[14] The leveling in Kuznets's curve became almost a law of economics for advanced middle-class societies and a basic tenet of the social contract. But as workers are being "substituted for each other" across national boundaries, and the old Fordist model of production becomes a vestige of the past, a significant wave of inequality is overtaking advanced societies. Leonard Schoppa addresses this problem in detail. He documents the extent to which well-paid, low-skilled workers in the different rich countries are losing work to low-wage workers in the developing world. In essence, global inequality is now more likely to be seen on a national level. Taking this perspective, Schoppa compares the current wave of globalization with the preceding one (1870 to 1913) and analyzes several data sets, including one assembled especially for this volume by Derek Hoff (see appendix). Schoppa concludes that, although globalization is driving "a wedge through the middle classes of the advanced economies, pushing less-skilled workers down and more-skilled workers up out of a middle class that had for a few decades been home to both," European countries have proven more efficient than the United States and Japan in stemming the tide of greater inequality. The mix of activist state policies at the heart of European postwar social contracts has proven more effective at holding out against the effects of globalization. In contrast, "the rapid increases in inequality in the United States, Britain, and Japan suggest that approaches that rely on consumption-led growth and convoy capitalism have *not* proven sufficient to maintain previous levels of equality."

But Europe may not be ahead much longer. Pressures to create a regional and probably less generous system of social benefits are increasingly felt. Opening economic borders and adopting a single currency may well be a prelude to a larger but less generous European social contract. Bo Öhngren, who takes up this question, argues that European welfare states cannot shield themselves in a fortress Europe. In fact, as Öhngren sees it, the forces for change lie within Europe itself. The countries of northern Europe, which provide the most copious benefits, have been reluctant European partners precisely for fear of having to reduce the level of their services to citizens, especially middle-class citizens, if they are forced to adopt a pan-European mean. In Sweden, the middle class stands behind transfers of income to government, which amount to about 40 percent of disposable household income. There is no middle-class consensus on social policy in the other welfare systems that Öhngren describes. "Compared with the broad Scandinavian notion of social policy as redistributive policies based on social rights irrespective of one's position in the labor market, the European debate taking place under the rubric of social policy is more concerned with industrial relations than with the making of a European social citizenship."

Moreover, as both Maurice Aymard and Hannes Siegrist powerfully show, if a new European social contract is to emerge, it will also have to make room for the countries of the former Soviet Union now joining an enlarged Europe. Hannes Siegrist opens this question in chapter 1 with his reflection on the effects of German reunification on the middle classes in both halves of the country. Reunification left large segments of the East German middle classes with little opportunity to participate in the privatization process. In chapter 15, Maurice Aymard enlarges the discussion to encompass the entire Eastern bloc in the midst of "an apparently peaceful but deeply revolutionary context" of social change. Aymard argues that the former Communist regimes generated genuine middle classes, even though they never bore that name. Their members had "education, qualification, and skills" even if they enjoyed less professional autonomy and personal freedom than their Western counterparts and were subject to severe restrictions on consumption. They too must be included in the new social contracts.

We are not attempting to predict how these issues will be resolved within new social contracts. But there are already limited models that suggest new departures. Arnaldo Bagnasco tells in chapter 16 the remarkable story of the resurgence of individual entrepreneurship in northern Italy. He describes an old provincial middle class regaining control of its political and economic destiny. In the last twenty-five years, the northern Italian middle class has created numerous small firms, as well as a new kind of civil society, by aligning social, political, and economic ends. Small northern Italian entrepreneurs have drawn strength from a powerful mix of creative organizational capabilities and reliance on intense social relations. As a result, there are sixty-eight industrial enterprises in Italy today for every one thousand inhabitants, against thirty-five in France, forty-six in the United Kingdom, and thirty-seven in Germany. The new entrepreneurial middle classes have pushed Italy to the rank of fourth industrial producer in the world. Although Bagnasco sees difficulties in translating this model to a national scale, it nonetheless shows that under the right circumstances, a dynamic mix of economic efficiency, social cohesion, and political liberty can revitalize entire regions. The northern Italian revival came as a "post-Fordist surprise" and stands in sharp contrast with the economy of the politically regulated south. Bagnasco sees the Italian middle class, otherwise aloof between government action and the market, as capable of building institutions that generate efficiency and also guarantee democratic freedom.

Such is the range of our contributions. In gathering our multinational working group, we never intended to provide rigorously systematic comparisons or prescriptions, but to show, on the basis of a wide range of existing expertise, that the great postwar expansion of middle classes has been both an agent and an outcome of social contracts in the countries under study. By retracing competing trajectories to these social contracts and highlighting similarities and differences, we have documented the ways in which these countries have experimented with partnerships between business, labor, and government to improve the standard of living, create safety nets, guarantee social peace, and ensure political stability. As a result, they have expanded their middle classes and sustained the democratization of wealth for almost half a century. Despite these impressive results, however, many forms of income, gender, and race gaps have tenaciously persisted and are made all the more objectionable by the universalist claims of middle-class social contracts. But in taking stock of these broken promises and articulating the need for solutions, we are well aware that the richer countries' ability to improve, or simply maintain, their existing social contracts is being challenged by the shifting boundaries of our political economy, as the chapters on globalization show. As it turns out, these new global economic relationships may be limiting social policy options in the countries studied in this volume while expanding them, at least partly, in less developed countries, including the new European partners. Altogether, keeping the middle classes open and inclusive will require a renewed level of cross-national collective will. This book's ambition is to frame the issues for such an effort.

## Notes

1. R. G. Collingwood, *The New Leviathan, or Man, Society, Civilization, and Barbarism*, edited by David Boucher (1942; rev. ed., Oxford: Clarendon, 1992), 133, 238–39, 258.
2. Jose Harris, *William Beveridge: A Biography* (Oxford: Clarendon, 1997).
3. Simone Weil, *L'enracinement* [1943], in *Œuvres* (Quarto), edited by Florence de Lussy (Paris: Gallimard, 1999), 1025–1218. Simone Weil died in London at age thirty-four. Although she would never meet de Gaulle and opposed some of his proposals, her views of postwar France had come to resemble spiritually those of the general. See Simone Pétrement, *La vie de Simone Weil* (Paris: Fayard, 1973), 654; and André-A. Devaux, "'Une certaine idée de la France . . .': Simone Weil and Charles de Gaulle," *Cahiers Simone Weil* 21(December 1988): 301–27.
4. See Kelly (this volume).
5. John Rawls, *A Theory of Justice* (Cambridge: Belknap Press of Harvard University Press, 1971). Although Rawls makes only a passing reference to Martin Luther King Jr. (364n), civil disobedience plays an important part in his attempt to resolve the tension between justice and goodness.
6. See Annie Kriegel, "De Gaulle, populiste et tragique," *Tocqueville Review* 13(1, 1992): 63–71.
7. Alexis de Tocqueville, *Democracy in America*, vols. 1 [1835] and 2 [1840], translated by Henry Reeve, revised by Francis Bowen, and further revised by Phillips Bradley, with an introduction by Daniel J. Boorstin (New York: Vintage Books, 1990), especially 1: 177–78, 213.
8. Herbert Spencer, "The Man *Versus* the State" [1884], in *Political Writings*, edited by John Offer (Cambridge: Cambridge University Press, 1994), 146; William Graham Sumner, "The Absurd Effort to Make the World Over" [1894], in *On Liberty, Society, and Politics: The Essential Essays of William Graham Sumner*, edited by Robert C. Bannister (Indianapolis: Liberty Fund, 1992), 251–62.
9. Werner Sombart, *Why Is There No Socialism in the United States?* [1906], translated by Patricia M. Hocking and C. T. Husbands, edited and introduced by C. T. Husbands, foreword by Michael Harrington (White Plains, N.Y.: M. E. Sharpe, 1976).
10. David Morris Potter, *People of Plenty: Economic Abundance and the American Character* (Chicago: University of Chicago Press, 1954).
11. See, for example, David Riesman, in collaboration with Reuel Denney and Nathan Glazer, *The Lonely Crowd: A Study of the Changing American Character* (New Haven: Yale University Press, 1950), and Dwight MacDonald, *Against the American Grain* (New York: Random House, 1962); see also *The Essential Frankfurt School Reader*, edited by Andrew Arato and Eike Gebhardt (New York: Urizen Books, 1978).

12. John Dewey, *The School and Society* [1899], edited by Jo Ann Boydston, with a preface by Joe R. Burnett (Carbondale: Southern Illinois University Press; London: Feffer & Simons, 1980), 38.
13. Linda Gordon, *Pitied but Not Entitled: Single Mothers and the History of Welfare, 1890–1935* (New York: Free Press, 1994), 49.
14. Simon Kuznets, "Economic Growth and Income Inequality," *American Economic Review* 45(March 1955): 1–28.

# Part I

---

# NATIONAL PATHS TO MIDDLE-CLASS FORMATION

# 1

## From Divergence to Convergence: The Divided German Middle Class, 1945 to 2000

*Hannes Siegrist*

After the defeat of the Nazi Reich, the German middle classes were targeted by the Allies for de-Nazification, demilitarization, and decartelization. They were disqualified from social, economic, political, and cultural leadership, having proven themselves incapable of guaranteeing prosperity, democracy, human rights, and peace. During the Weimar Republic, they had shown a lack of republican political virtues and the foresight needed to balance particular and general interests for the good of society. During the Nazi Reich, they had either belonged to the ruling party or lent their services to its totalitarian and brutal program. Accordingly, the Western Allies decided to remake the German middle classes in a republican mold and to limit class antagonism. They accomplished this end through mediation, the rule of law, and support for the rise of an inclusive middle class that would embody legal and democratic values and be able to act as a mediating class between different interests and cultures. The West German path led to the rise of the middle classes and the construction of the so-called leveled middle-class society.

In Eastern Germany, the Soviet military administration and the Communists took a different approach, restricting the influence and power of individuals, social groups, and institutions that they regarded as "bourgeois" and "petty bourgeois." The East German path led, on the one hand, to the cultural discrimination against and economic expropriation, social and political marginalization, and even physical expulsion of those middle-class groups that had been labeled reactionary and imperialist. On the other hand, it led to a new definition of the functional and professional elites: in the socialist hierarchy of power and prestige, the party-affiliated nomenclatura were at the top, the upper service class of the professions were in the middle, and the lower employees were in the administrative sector at the bottom. This approach was based on the Marxist-Leninist notion that the bourgeoisie had to be replaced by the progressive working class and that the working class was represented by the Communist Party, which would build the classless socialist society.

In the late 1940s, it became clear that the middle classes in the two German states had a common past but a diverging future. In 1990, with the reunification of Germany, two German states and their middle classes ceased to follow separate courses, and the institutions and values of the capitalist and democratic Federal Republic of Germany (FRG) were transferred to the territory of the centralized and state-socialist East Germany, the former German Democratic Republic (GDR). This merger led to the expansion of the Western social contract and to the need to constitute a new post-socialist middle class in the Neue Bundesländer (Brandenburg, Sachsen, Sachsen-Anhalt, Mecklenburg-Vorpommern, and Thüringen). The East Germans had to adjust themselves to the West German functions and meanings of being middle-class.

The history of the 1990s has raised new questions not only for East Germans but for all Germans, and even Europeans. In the course of transforming the Neue Bundesländer, West German patterns have been not only emulated but adapted. These new forms and meanings, in their turn, have affected ideas about the middle class throughout Germany. In united Germany, the political and institutional processes generally still support the existence and identity of the middle classes as they were constituted in the postwar period, and they confirm the Western postwar social contracts in principle. At the same time, economic, social, and cultural processes are reshaping the middle classes and eroding the social basis of the contracts. Some of these processes are not particular to Germany. In the 1990s, the challenges for the German middle classes were in many respects the same as, for example, the French and Swedish middle classes. They resulted from the end of state socialism and from European integration and globalization, all forces that threatened the existing regional and national middle-class agreements. In some senses then, the German example, while undoubtedly unique in many respects, reflects the situation across Europe.

The postwar history of the middle classes in Germany shows clearly that "middle-class" continues to be a political, economic, social, cultural, and legal construction that must be studied on both the symbolic and social levels. I do not approach the middle classes as just a statistical aggregate but as a collective social actor in order to analyze the discourses, terms, and memories that filter and mediate in specific situations the perception, interpretation, and social action of the middle classes.

To trace this process in detail, I look first at the history of the meanings, uses, and functions of the term "middle-class" and related terms in Germany in different historical, social, and political settings. In the following section, I begin my comparison of the two paths, examining the history of the West German middle classes and bringing into focus the social conditions, mentalities, organizations, perspectives, and programs of diverse middle-class groups. The next section presents a short history of the middle class, the nomenclatura, the intelligentsia, and the service class in East Germany from 1945 to the 1990s. The concluding section discusses the middle-class policies of the political parties in the social context of the late 1990s—especially the Social Democratic program of the "New Center"—and highlights the tensions between more and less inclusive concepts of middle-class.

## Meanings and Narratives of "Middle-class"

In Germany, the meaning and function of the term *middle-class* have changed profoundly since 1945. The same holds true for the wide spectrum of terms referring to middle-class formations and subgroups—namely, bourgeoisie (Bürgertum), middle estates of small business and trades (Mittelstand), white-collar employees (Angestellte), professionals (liberale Berufe, freie Berufe), civil servants (Beamte), and qualified workers (Facharbeiter).

In the decades after 1945, the German term "Bürgertum" was used in three different ways. It referred to the "capitalist bourgeoisie" in the Marxian sense—that is, the economic class of the owners of capital, self-employed entrepreneurs, and the top managers. It also was used to refer to the "modern bourgeoisie," a more encompassing sociocultural formation constituted of owners or holders of material and cultural capital, both self-employed and employed by others, characterized by specific conditions, values, and attitudes and integrated by common interests, social practices, and cultural styles.[1] Finally, Bürgertum designated a political milieu affiliated with the so-called modern bourgeoisie and petty bourgeoisie—in other words, the social basis of nonsocialist parties like the Christian Democratic Union (CDU) and the Liberal Democratic Party (FDP).

Before the Second World War, "Bürgertum" and "bürgerlich" designated a relatively exclusive social formation composed of entrepreneurs and small businessmen, "rentiers" (persons of independent means), landlords, self-employed professionals, higher civil servants, managers, and higher white-collar employees. This categorization changed in the first years after World War II. A "society" (as a relatively stable system of position and status) did not then exist in Germany. Many had lost their position and income, and there had been a mass immigration of millions of people from the eastern territories of the former German Reich. This instability produced enormous uncertainty about who belonged to the Bürgertum. In this situation, a vague and encompassing notion of the middle classes, which were labeled "Mittelschichten," seemed to be more appropriate.[2] The labels "bourgeoisie" and "bourgeois" were then often used in a rather vague and polemical way by the adversaries of the bourgeoisie. Even those who had traditionally considered themselves bourgeois preferred terms like "free entrepreneurs," "liberal professions" (freie Berufe), and "middle-class" in the sense of middle strata (Mittelschichten) or middle estates (Mittelstand). These terms in important respects were congruent with "bourgeoisie," but they helped to avoid the negative connotations associated with this term.[3]

"Mittelstand" referred to small businessmen, self-employed craftsmen, and retail traders.[4] Owing to the economic situation and the politics of decartelization in the decade after World War II, small and mid-size businesses and trades played a strategic role in the reconstruction of the German economy. The meanings of "Mittelstand" dated from the late nineteenth and early twentieth centuries. "Stand" (estate) hinted at the fact that many of these middling groups were organized in compulsory organizations and that qualification, access, and type of work were regulated by laws and supervised by the relatively autonomous administrative bodies of these organizations.

Originally, the Mittelstand was regarded as the "old middle class," as distinct from the modern "industrial bourgeoisie" (Industriebürgertum). Today "Mittelstand," or "mittelständisch," designates the firms, owners, and managers of small- and mid-size enterprises (crafts and industrial enterprises up to 250, 500, or 1,000 workers, depending on the categories of the national and supra-national census).

This Mittelstand can also be compared with the new Mittelstand. From the late nineteenth century to the 1960s, employees or white-collar workers (Angestellte) in the private sector were regarded as the "new middle estates" (neuer Mittelstand).[5] Today the employees of the industrial, commercial, and banking sectors are sometimes called "old urban middle class" (städtische Mittelschichten) because they differ from the professionals and employees in the technologically most advanced industries of information and communication.

Traditionally, the professionals who had studied at a university were a very important subgroup of the middle classes or modern bourgeoisie. Doctors, lawyers, Protestant clergy, professors, and high school teachers formed the sociocultural milieu that, until 1970, was called the "Akademikerstand" or the "Bildungsbürgertum" (highly educated bourgeoisie).[6] This middle-class milieu was differentiated into many subgroups and professional organizations. Each group had its particular entitlements, customs, and forms of work, employment, and income.

In Germany, the professionals employed as higher civil servants (Beamte) traditionally had more prestige than those who were self-employed. Self-employed professionals belonged to the "free professions," or "liberal professions," and enjoyed a relatively high degree of professional autonomy and self-government. In the first half of the twentieth century, the position and reputation of the higher civil servants were undermined—first by their disloyalty to the Weimar Republic, and second by their willingness to serve the Nazi regime.[7]

As diverse and fragmented as these subgroups were, they could all claim to be the bearers of specific bourgeois or middle-class virtues and to have a mission in service to the general welfare of the nation. In Germany, the concept of "bourgeois virtue" traditionally referred to work, social honor, lifestyle, morality, and individual culture (Bildung) more than to political republicanism. "Bourgeois" (bürgerlich) designated the culture of an exclusive middle class and a national elite rather than the culture of sovereign citizens. During the first half of the twentieth century, "middle-class" was associated with social closure and exclusivity, economic protectionism, the legalization of social privileges, political authority, and cultural hegemony in a national society characterized by cleavages and tensions with regard to class, religion, and region. A strong fear of crisis, decline, and catastrophe was combined with a weak sense of compromise, free exchange, and mobility. These traits proved problematic after 1945, when a functionally differentiated economy and society needed a political class capable of mediating interests and acting for the common good.

Under the supervision of the Allies, the German middle classes became a republican and democratic middle class.[8] They realized both the classic middle-class project—governing a society without an aristocratic or plutocratic upper class—and the modern, Western middle-class project—preventing the emergence of a Communist regime. They also learned to mediate between the rich and poor, and between different interests and cultures.

Accordingly, in the second half of the twentieth century, the meaning of "middle-class" became more inclusive, fluid, and optimistic. In the so-called middle-class society, middle-class increasingly has been regarded as a heterogeneous social and cultural field, a fluid stratum and milieu in a dynamic, meritocratic, pluralist, and open society. Middle-class is seen less as an "estate" and more as a social construction, a voluntary association, and an imagined community that has specific values and styles and is open to those who want to join it. A higher degree of acceptance of the market has been combined with a higher acceptance of democratic values, social solidarity, and justice. The culture of the middle classes has become less static, less elitist, less nationalist, and less homogeneous. Change is not primarily regarded as decline but as a challenge or opportunity. The discourses of crisis, which have accompanied the cyclical economic crises from the late 1960s to our own day, may use the same words, symbols, and phrases used in previous periods, but the meanings of the words have changed, in keeping with a long period of relative stability, prosperity, and inclusiveness of the middle classes.

As a result, by the 1960s traditional designations for the middle classes had begun to lose their meaning. The wealthy and highly educated middle classes dreamed of reconstructing a more elitist bourgeoisie, but in fact they seldom used that term.[9] When the term "bourgeoisie" was rediscovered in the 1960s by leftist circles, it was used to designate the liberal-conservative establishment of the Federal Republic. The sociology of class and social stratification was on the rise in the 1970s and 1980s. Its theoretical and empirical analyses of the middle classes as a whole oscillated between theoretical deductions, formal classifications, findings about correlations among single variables, and loose descriptions. A few studies insisted on the persistence of the bourgeoisie, but the majority agreed that class in the economic sense was less important than social stratification with regard to status and income, educational level, cultural styles, profession, and status groups.[10]

In the 1970s and 1980s, historians started to study more thoroughly the history of the middle classes from about 1750 to the 1930s. One of their initial conclusions was that the modern bourgeoisie (Bürgertum) was a historically and culturally specific construction of the economic and cultural middle classes and typical of the nineteenth century and of a few western and central European societies like Germany, France, Switzerland, and Italy. According to

Jürgen Kocka, the Bürgertum as a socioeconomic and cultural formation became diluted and finally dissolved in the decades after World
War I.[11] There are good reasons for this thesis, which relativizes the
Bürgertum in its historical and cultural context, yet it is not confirmed by empirical research on the twentieth century. In fact, the
phenomenology of the middle classes after 1945 shows many conti-
nuities between nineteenth- and twentieth-century constructions, as
well as adaptations of the old discourses and sociocultural practices
to new needs and conditions, even though some of the old designations lost their currency.[12]

During the late 1990s, journalists, politicians, and social scientists
have once again turned to the word "Bürgertum."[13] After the optimistic turn in the German middle classes after the end of the GDR, and
in a period of neoliberalism[14] and deregulation, the word is no longer
taboo. Before 1990, GDR propaganda had identified the Federal Republic with an aggressive type of capitalist bourgeoisie, and in West
Germany the historical bourgeoisie was generally suspect. Today all
the parties, including Social Democrats and Greens—and in some respects even the post-Communists—praise the entrepreneurial and innovative spirit of highly educated and achievement-oriented citizens,
the erstwhile bourgeoisie. Those who are able and willing to invest
human and financial capital in Germany are applauded. With the
growing distance from the historically repressive bourgeoisie, the
younger generations glorify the bourgeoisie's entrepreneurial spirit
and idealize its respect for the individual—as long as these qualities
are combined with respect for democracy, social justice, solidarity,
and progress.[15]

In the past fifty years, the German middle classes have developed a
more pragmatic style of confronting the continual change, uncertainty, and ambivalence that constitute modernity. Most middle-class
Germans have learned to balance tradition and progress and accept
the fact that change means transition and risk not only for the lower
classes but also for themselves. They have become more self-reflexive
and developed or adapted discourses for understanding and handling
the dynamics of economy, society, politics, and culture more effectively. In certain situations, they may still use the traditional vocabulary of estates and the defensive rhetoric of the bourgeois elites of
the nineteenth and early twentieth centuries, but their postwar experience has taught them that the concept "middle-class" is relative
and subject to change and that they are not destined to decline and
vanish. Their approach to reflecting and representing their past and
future is still governed by two master narratives: the narrative of rise,
success, and progress, on the one hand, and the narrative of decline

and tragedy on the other. In the postwar period, the success story has finally prevailed.

## From Crisis to Prosperity, from Exclusivity to Inclusivity: West Germany, 1945 to the 1990s

The postwar history of the German middle classes started with the deepest political, economic, social, and cultural crisis they had ever faced. The middle classes, which ideologically and functionally had supported the racist and totalitarian Nazi regime, were delegitimized and lost position, status, power, and cultural influence. At the same time, small groups of antifascists and liberals began efforts to revitalize pre-1933 concepts of middle-class like the Bürgertum and the Mittelstand and to preserve laws that privileged middle-class interests and the particular interests of professionals, civil servants, entrepreneurs, and small-business people and tradespeople.[16] The reference to pre-1933 concepts was more than pure opportunism, since the Nazi regime had formally enlarged the legal privileges of the professions, civil servants, and the trades but had in fact reduced their influence and power.

After a first wave of harsh de-Nazification and reeducation, the Western Allies' middle-class policy became more benevolent. This was a pragmatic decision, given the urgent need for functional expertise and entrepreneurial spirit.[17] Moreover, the Allies planned to win the middle classes over to further their goals. These aims contrasted sharply with the ostensibly classless society idealized in East Germany, which marginalized and oppressed the middle classes, regarding them as relics of the bourgeoisie, National-Socialists, and adherents of an aggressive nationalism and imperialism.[18]

In West Germany, many of the changes in the lot of the middle classes were determined by Allied measures directed at big corporations. Monopolies and cartels were dissolved, and the politics of international free trade influenced decisionmaking.[19] Big businesses were at first controlled directly by the Allies, then later co-managed, with workers participating in decisionmaking.[20] Workers and their trade unions participated on the supervisory boards and the directorates of the big steel and iron companies, a right that was later extended to workers in large companies in other sectors.

After 1945, members of the professions, joined by groups of higher civil servants, worked to reconstruct an exclusive middle class that would be seen as the legitimate successor of the Bürgertum. Until the 1960s, they cultivated an elitist version of middle- and upper-middle-class characterized by support for economic protectionism, skepticism toward democracy, and a conservative, nationalist attitude opposed to materialist Western "civilization," "Americanization," and "mass society."[21] They criticized the lack of what their German "Kulturkritik" called inner values, high culture, and the individual's duty to pursue self-cultivation.

Postwar history demonstrates that the West German professions succeeded in gaining traditional entitlements, laws governing the professions, market monopolies, and self-administration that were reminiscent of those available to them before 1933.[22] Around 1960, they opened themselves in limited ways to the market and became more pro-democratic. They did away with traditional antimarket ideologies, but the elitist attitudes of a traditional civil service class survived longer.[23] The professions even accepted the reforms in higher education, which, after the so-called Sputnik shock, led to more open access to the university and the professions. The general rise of incomes and the greater need for professional services, furthered by welfare state measures, helped to restore the professions to their old social status. Secure in this status, West German professionals did not find the 1980s overcrowding of some professions, including teaching, law, history, and sociology, to be a profound crisis. The old image of the closed Bildungsbürgertum or Akademikerschaft had faded even among its members. Eventually, overcrowded professions ceased to be a problem when many young West German professionals joined the new functional elites in the Neue Bundesländer after reunification.

The situation for the small-business middle classes of crafts and trades (Mittelstand) was slightly different. They had supported the National Socialist Party in the 1930s because it promised them protection against big industry and large retailing companies (department stores and consumer cooperatives).[24] After 1945, self-employed Mittelstand enjoyed favorable economic circumstances but faced a number of problems. The U.S.-military government abolished protectionist measures and regarded the legal privileges of the crafts and trades as "illiberal." In 1948 the U.S. administration rejected the compulsory crafts-guilds and abolished the "full professional certificate for crafts-masters" (grosser Befähigungsausweis), which since its introduction in 1935 had been the necessary prerequisite for starting a business in many crafts. In the British and French occupation zones, however, the traditional German laws and rules survived, and in 1953 the Parliament of the Federal Republic approved the Statute for the Crafts (Handwerksordnung), which confirmed the traditional system and introduced a limited co-determination of the workers. Even the Social Democrats, who in earlier programs had predicted that small businesses would vanish and therefore deserved no help, voted for the law. They regarded the small business as a bulwark against impersonal capitalism. Moreover, they wanted to snatch the Mittelstand away from the influence of what they considered bourgeois, antisocialist, and antidemocratic circles.[25]

In the 1950s and 1960s, the governing Christian Democrats and Liberals vigorously pursued legislation to preserve the Mittelstand. In the 1970s, the governing Social Democrats and Liberals were equally active in enabling the Mittelstand to adapt itself to the new challenges of the dynamic market economy.[26] This policy was itself adopted by the conservative-liberal government from 1982 to 1998. In the interests of smoothing the process of unification, politicians and representatives of the middle class declared that hundreds of thousands of small businesses would make the East German economy boom within a very short time. Today the Social Democratic–Green majority supports the Mittelstand throughout Germany, regarding it as the backbone of the labor market and economy.

The most decisive change in the postwar history of the Mittelstand came from within the group itself, which shifted during the 1960s away from a traditionalist and protective mentality and embraced the entrepreneurial spirit and capitalism.[27] Small businesses profited from the economic boom of those years. The average size, investment in capital equipment, and annual turnover of the average craft or trade business were growing. The increase of incomes of craft-masters and self-employed retailers was higher than for many other social groups. The majority of them owned their house, and a much higher percentage of them owned durable goods, such as refrigerators, telephones, and cars, than was the case among the working class.[28] In a culture of abundance, economic success became more important than traditional ideology. The Mittelstand increasingly regarded the democratic state as its own.

White-collar workers (Angestellte) also experienced a change in attitude during the postwar years. In the early twentieth century, white-collar workers in private industry, banking, trade, and insurance companies were traditionally seen as belonging to the lower-middle classes.[29] They were distinct, however, from the workers. In 1911 this difference was underlined by the Employees Insurance Law (Angestellten-Versicherungsgesetz), which distinguished white-collar workers from blue-collar workers and gave them some privileges. The Conservative-Liberals behind the law wanted to stiffen the loyalty of an unstable middle-class group and erect a bulwark against the socialist working class. In the early Weimar Republic, some groups of white-collar workers joined with trade unions and Social Democrats, but after 1929 conservative groups gained in strength. The Nazi government vacillated between equalizing white-collar workers with blue-collar workers and privileging them.

After 1945, white-collar workers succeeded in conserving their particular insurance rights and their general legal status. During the long economic boom of the 1950s and 1960s, the gap between blue- and white-collar workers diminished, though not because of any loss of status or income by white-collar workers. Rather, blue-collar workers improved their situation. A coalition of left-wing Christian Democrats and Social Democrats succeeded in improving the legal status of blue-collar workers and bettering their working conditions.[30] Ultimately, the upper levels of the working class began to regard themselves as (lower-) middle-class.

The blurring of the collar line can be observed in the union activities of white-collar workers. After World War II, the traditional special trade unions and associations of employees were refounded and united in the Trade Union of Employees (Deutsche Angestellten-Gewerkschaft [DAG]). The majority of white-collar workers, however, opted for the industrial trade unions belonging to the Federation of German Unions (DGB). These were the traditional organizations of the working class. As the polarized industrial-class society faded after the 1960s,[31] the concept of "employees" lost its original meaning and its function of separating the working population into loyal, pro-capitalist liberal-conservative employees, on the one hand, and anti-capitalist, socialist workers, on the other. Class distinctions were less useful, if not obsolete, in a society that saw itself as middle-class.

Since the 1970s, the growing proportion of white-collar occupations in industry has further reduced the social and legal distance between workers and employees and between their respective trade unions.[32] Relations between the Federation of German Trade Unions and the Trade Union of Employees have become more amicable, and their cooperation has intensified. In 1999 their leaders even celebrated May Day together. A common trade union of all employees in both the private and public sectors was founded in 2001.

At the same time that the notion of a white-collar worker has blurred, new social distinctions both within and outside the middle classes have arisen. These include the distinction between those with regular work contracts and those with time contracts.[33] Furthermore, recent studies about the effects of globalization and new technologies and systems of information management suggest that the middle classes are divided into winners and losers. Urban professionals in the information and communication business have developed specific styles of work and consumption and formed a new sociocultural milieu distinct from that of the classic middle classes, which have a stronger local and national orientation. Peter Noller states that in Frankfurt am Main the middle classes are polarized between those who represent the international culture and profit from the global city and those who represent the local urban culture. According to Noller, there is an "increasing economic, cultural, and ideological distance between the traditional middle class and the new cosmopolitan service class."[34] The research about such trends is still rather impressionistic. The empirical basis is not very impressive, and the theoretical framework is primarily inspired by a sociological tradition that identifies urban middle-class groups as "rootless" trend-setters breaking up the unity of the middle class. These divisions in the broad middle class are quantitatively and qualitatively less important than the long-term alliance of employees and workers as part of the general postwar project of constructing a broad, inclusive, and leveled middle class.

The notion of the "broad" or "leveled" middle class became popular around 1960.[35] Since then, many sociologists have characterized this development by describing such variables as position, status, income, wealth, way of life, level of consumption, qualification, working conditions, housing, social security, access to high culture, use of cultural goods, and so on.[36] These studies show that the middle class remains a social and material reality in certain respects. Equally important, the broad middle class is also a representation, a way of thinking, feeling, and acting. The broad middle class was a sociocultural movement adopted by the majority of Germans who opposed their so-called middle-class values to the threat of communism. The aim of this inclusive middle-class project was to reanimate the liberal and democratic German traditions and construct an encompassing national middle-class society that would include broad strata of the German people.[37] It motivated and included skilled workers, employees, civil servants, professionals, self-employed businesspeople and entrepreneurs, and even farmers. It was also the means of social and cultural integration for many millions of Germans who had fled the former German territories and East Germany.

This vision of the middle class was repeatedly attacked by those who praised the virtues of exclusivity and warned against the risks and perils of including the lower-middle classes in the middle-class project. The complaints of the nineteenth and twentieth centuries against the materialism of the masses were revived, as were predictions of the decline of a society lacking an elite that combined honor with strong individualism and was capable of taking responsibility for the masses (including the lower-middle classes). Despite the efforts of these critics, the general economic, political, social, and cultural trend favored the inclusive middle-class society. That project was motivated by Social Democratic, Christian Democratic, and Social-Liberal visions of political and social citizenship. It was supported by concepts of the welfare state, a socially responsible market economy (soziale Marktwirtschaft), and last but not least, the nation as a community of destiny. After the war, the state was responsible not only for the welfare of the lower classes but also for that of the widows and children of middle-class soldiers and refugees who had lost their property and position but not their pretensions to being middle-class. The assumption that a member of the middle class had to be able to live on the fruits of his or her own work or capital was contested by the new realities.

Furthermore, the project of the inclusive middle class was reinforced by the democratic, social, and humanist German traditions that were revived after 1945 with the support of the occupying powers. It converged with the broader contemporary Western middle-class project that aimed to prevent sharp class tensions and conflicts, which in the interwar period had led to the rise of dictatorial and totalitarian regimes. That project was justified by the experience of the Weimar Republic, which was torn by the extremism of the Right and the Left and ruined by the panic of the old, exclusive middle classes. The concept of the broad and leveled middle class as the bearer of society and state was furthered by a cultural and institutional transfer from the United States and France, which exported their republican, democratic, and social notions of middle-class to Germany.

Initially, the broad middle-class project was pursued by a small German elite that included democrats, socialists, liberals, and antifascists who, after having been persecuted, exiled, and imprisoned during the Nazi regime, were willing to cooperate across classes. In the beginning, the objectives of the movement were primarily republicanism, human rights, and peace in Germany and Europe. From the mid-1950s onward, the notion of a leveled middle class became entwined with ideas of social welfare, increasing wealth, and the modern consumer culture.[38] In the following decades, the project was gradually extended to include individual rights and the idea of social citizenship. It was furthered by the steady growth of incomes, reduced work time and more spare time, increases in mobility, higher standards of living, new lifestyles, and finally, the dissolution of class cultures, traditional sociocultural milieus, and old gender divisions. The reforms of schools and universities in the 1960s and 1970s opened access to higher education. Starting in the 1970s, the socialist and left-liberal movement for socioculture (Soziokultur) democratized access to cultural institutions, events, and goods.[39]

Ultimately, the goal of the postwar middle-class project was to integrate West German society. This unified society became a political, social, material, and cultural reality, as well as a true community with regard to experiences, narratives, and myths. Nonetheless, fear for the collective decline of the middle class or of single groups remained. The middle-class discourses reflect that risk in many ways. Middle-class groups reacted immediately when cyclical or structural crises called into question their status, position, and beliefs.[40]

## The East German Middle Classes Between 1945 and the 1990s: Death and Rebirth

The German Democratic Republic was for forty years the stage for a radical social experiment directed against the traditional middle classes and everything for which they stood.[41] The state was ruled by the Socialist Unity Party (Sozialistische Einheitspartei Deutschlands [SED]), which also controlled all of East German society. The small elite of party and state supervised the functional-political elite, that is, the nomenclatura (Nomenklatura) and the Kader, the members of which were both highly qualified and homogenized by ideological training.[42] The Kader comprised managerial positions throughout the hierarchy, from the foreman to the top position of the state. It also included specialists. Everyone who occupied one of these positions, which were regarded as crucial for state and society, plus all the candidates for such positions, were listed in a central file.[43] The next level down was the intelligentsia, which was composed of groups that in the West included professionals, higher civil servants, and white-collar workers. In the 1980s, the intelligentsia made up about 15 percent of the working population.[44]

The East German intelligentsia was not conceived as a middle class, but as either an upper service class (Dienstklasse) or a section of the working class. Its official aim and duty was to serve the general interest of the working class and the socialist state.[45] The professionals and members of the intelligentsia had no right to organize separately or to assert their professional autonomy. They were integrated into the "mass organizations" of party and state. There was an endless ideological, political, and sociological debate about their relationship with the working class and their place in both capitalist and socialist society. They were not regarded as part of the "antagonistic" class of the bourgeoisie as long as they were cooperative SED members—or at least followers of the so-called bloc parties forced into line by the SED state.

The program for replacing the traditional middle classes with a new socialist service class was started immediately after the war. The teachers and lawyers who either had been members of the National Socialist Party and other Nazi organizations or were regarded as followers of reactionary bourgeois or petty bourgeois ideologies were socially and politically cleansed. Quite a few "bourgeois" and a not-insignificant number of former Nazi Party members survived in niche areas because the state urgently needed their specific know-how. The old middle-class culture survived in groups of physicians in private practice, professors on medicine and natural sciences faculties, Protestant clergy, and engineers with specialized and essential training.[46] They retained a few material and symbolic privileges at the price of being loyal to the system and acting as disinterested experts and humanists. Some of them used symbols of the bourgeois middle class to distinguish themselves. A few cultivated an old-fashioned middle-class style, which the Communists both rejected and sometimes admired.

To become more independent from the bourgeois element in the service class as well as the intelligentsia, the socialist state planned to create new elites by mobilizing the children of urban and rural workers to pursue secondary and university education. From the early 1950s to the 1960s, the new intelligentsia and the service class were recruited to a remarkable degree from lower-class families. For children of entrepreneurs and professionals (Akademiker), access to higher education and the professions was limited, even closed with regard to some professions. This higher education and professional qualification policy was accompanied by a cultural policy that specifically opened access to high culture to workers and developed the creativity and cultural capacities of industrial and rural workers. Writers and artists were given incentives to develop a nonbourgeois culture and to promote socialism, the state, and the working class.

The second fundamental decision of the GDR with regard to the bourgeoisie and the middle classes was to abolish private enterprise and to marginalize the small-business middle class of crafts and retail trade. The first targets of expropriation, nationalization, and collectivization were the owners of big industrial and financial corporations and large agricultural estates, especially if they were former Nazi leaders or Nazi Party members. With the attempt to create a stratum of small "New Farmers" on redistributed land on the verge of failure, the GDR started to collectivize small and mid-size farms, an initiative completed around 1960.[47] Initially, mid-size farmers who had entered the agricultural cooperatives (Landwirtschaftliche Produktionsgenossenschaften [LPG]), whether voluntarily or by coercion, were able to conserve informally their traditional rural–middle-class prestige and to exert their influence on the board of their cooperative.

When the cooperatives were later merged into more centralized units, however, they lost their position and prestige.

The long process of deprivatizing small and mid-size private industrial enterprises was started in 1952 and completed in 1972. The industrial and business middle class was gradually discouraged, discriminated against, marginalized, forced to retire, or expelled.[48] For a long time, the ruling party vacillated between declaring the convergence of interests of the small business (which was mainly engaged in the consumer goods industry) and the working class, on the one hand, and denouncing the small business as an exploitative capitalist class. In 1963 the SED reclassified the small business as an "active crafts" (werktätige Handwerker) rather than as Mittelstand. In 1972 the small and mid-size private industrial enterprises were forced to offer their shares to the state.[49] The enterprises were merged with the big state-owned Kombinate—the large-scale and horizontally integrated corporations. Only a limited number of self-employed craftspeople managed to attain a relatively favorable economic position in the niches of the planned economy. Their function was to compensate the inadequacy of the centralized planned economy.

Although GDR society was relatively homogenous, specific mechanisms produced and reproduced particular forms of inequality. The closure of the party elite and the nomenclatura, for instance, gave rise to what critical contemporary observers called the "new class," which controlled the deprivatized and nationalized resources without being subject to a functioning system of checks and balances. In the last two decades of the GDR, it became common knowledge that the first-generation intelligentsia and service class monopolized the higher ranks and that their children were overrepresented among the new generations of the service class and intelligentsia.[50]

From an ideological perspective, to be sure, the GDR was very dissimilar from West Germany, which consciously celebrated middle-class society. Yet while some authors have called the GDR a working-class society, others suggest that it was a special kind of "broad and leveled middle-class society, composed of qualified workers, employees, and specialists" who were all employed by the state.[51] In addition, in a society that remained in close communication by radio and television and through family relations with Western culture, the patterns of Western middle-class life influenced the socialist way and view of life. One explanation for the German unification in 1990, then, is that East Germans wanted to become middle-class in the Western style. They no longer found plausible the ritualistic declarations in the GDR media and by GDR politicians that the Western middle classes were economically declining and morally corrupt and that their economic system was in a fatal crisis. As Christian Welzel observes, the motives of the GDR intelligentsia and service class in opposing their own regime were "postmaterialist values, democracy, and participation," while the motives of the rest of the population were materialist values and the hope of obtaining a Western standard of consumption.[52] The younger generations of the intelligentsia and service class, which were blocked at the lower and middle ranks, together with self-confident workers and some intellectuals, finally diagnosed a permanent and paralyzing crisis in their classless society. The targets of their discourse of crisis and decline were the state and the Communist Party. The option of adopting the values of West German middle-class society promised a way out of that crisis.

The language of nation building and anticommunism, which dominated in the process of German unification, has obscured the fact that unification was mainly motivated by the desire of East Germans to have the advantages of the Western middle class. Despite some disillusionment in the 1990s, the majority of East Germans still aspire to the middle-class ideal, although they vacillate between an inclusivist and an exclusivist version of this vision. The majority have an inclusivist vision of the middle class: they believe in relatively equal and open social, cultural, and political citizenship.[53] They also believe that those who have problems maintaining status and position should receive support from the state.

A substantial minority—especially owners and managers of small and mid-size enterprises and self-employed professionals—favor the concept of an exclusive middle class. Sociological studies of the elites in the Neue Bundesländer have shown that East German managers and professionals hold values similar to those of their West German counterparts.[54] These eastern groups believe that the upper level of the middle class should lead society.[55] Those who advocate an exclusive middle class tolerate a high degree of social polarization, and they remind the inclusivists that the conditions for including everybody in the middle class are especially unfavorable in eastern Germany, which has been radically deindustrialized and must compete with neighboring low-labor-cost regions such as the Czech Republic and Poland. The inclusivists, on the other hand, use the language of national solidarity, the welfare state, and regionalism. They "territorialize" their arguments by stressing the right to equal regional development in the national state and in the European Union.

Attitudes in the Neue Bundesländer about the future vary according to status. A closer look at middle-class divisions today would be helpful. The post-unification middle class in the Neue Bundesländer is made up of employees in the private sector, who profited from the tertiarization of the economy and privatization in the banking, insurance, communication, and media industries; the owners and managers of small and mid-size enterprises in industry and crafts, which are either newly founded or the privatized units of former big, state-owned corporations; civil servants in the public sector; and self-employed professionals, who voluntarily or involuntarily profited from the privatization of legal, financial, health, and engineering services. It is also possible to include in the new middle class the skilled workers who have long been accorded de facto middle-class status and retirees, many of whom took an early retirement for economic and political reasons and now receive relatively high old-age pensions that enable them to attain the status of a (lower-) middle-class consumer.

There is quite a lot of empirical research on the constitution, recruitment, and characteristics of those middle-class groups that now constitute the elite of the Neue Bundesländer and on how they have changed with unification. These studies show that the central element of the transformation of the GDR economy and society was the evolution of a new middle class from its Communist-era starting point.

Much of this change has been driven by economic reality. As industry has retrenched, the number of managerial positions has decreased. At the same time, the number of self-employed professionals and small-business owners has risen sharply. In the last years of the GDR, 99 percent of physicians and pharmacists, 96 percent of dentists, and 90 percent of attorneys were employed in working units of the state. In the early 1990s, the majority of them became self-employed, independent practitioners. The total number of self-employed professionals rose from about 16,000 in 1990 to 64,000 in 1992 (the same number as in 1952!).

In 1989, 90 percent (3.3 million) of workers in the industrial sector of the GDR were employed by the 270 complex and integrated corporations called the Kombinate, which had up to 70,000 workers each.[56] Between 1989 and 1998, the percentage of self-employed persons of all classes rose from 2 to 7 percent. Among them was a small share of almost 4,000 small and mid-size businesses that were returned to either the former proprietor or that person's family.[57] By comparison, the percentage of self-employed in the West German regions was 9 percent.[58]

Nonetheless, the opportunities available to former East Germans have their limits. Sociological research shows that East Germans are proportionally underrepresented in higher positions in state administration, the military, private companies, and trade unions throughout Germany. They are even underrepresented in administration, in the judiciary, and on university faculties of law, economics, sociology, and history.[59] In essence, these data confirm the colonization thesis. However, East Germans dominate other areas in the Neue Bundesländer. Among self-employed professionals and small-business owners, East Germans are the overwhelming majority, except in some new professions like tax consulting and auditing.[60] Most of the professionals in the health and education sectors are of East German origin. Overall, 70 to 80 percent of the new self-employed in the Neue Bundesländer are former GDR citizens.[61]

The majority of the current East German elite are former members of the old professional sub-elites and the GDR service class who have requalified and adapted themselves to new conditions. According to Heike Solga, the groups with the best chance of preserving their upper-service-class position between 1989 and 1993 were professional specialists, including women and the younger generations. The diverse studies about the new regional elites in the Neue Bundesländer demonstrate that between 50 and 80 percent of the actual managerial elite came from the old elite and service class.[62] For those who had occupied executive positions within the Socialist Unity Party and the state before 1990, the probability of holding or assuming a position in management or in the professions was much lower. The majority were either dismissed or forced to retire.

In general, the professional middle classes in the Neue Bundesländer express a high degree of satisfaction with their professional situation and chances. They feel uplifted by the acceptance of their individuality and by the high prestige of being self-employed. At the same time, they feel constricted by laws and regulations imported from West Germany. The members of the liberal professions, on the other hand, feel that they are important bearers of the political system and that they have come out winners in the political turn of events.[63] They have not only adopted Western norms and values but assumed the same classic fears and uncertainties of the self-employed everywhere. The small-business middle class feels threatened by large West German or foreign enterprises. They feel the burden of relatively high financial investments in their new business, and they often have marketing problems. Members of the health professions are afraid that their fees will be lowered by national health policies. Entrepreneurs and professionals dislike the demands of indigenous workers and employees to receive salaries comparable to the West German level. In general, they reject such demands. Many of them undermine the collective contract system, which has been one of the pillars of Western middle-class society and was imported to the Neue Bundesländer.

The census data show that wealth and income in East Germany are still lower than in West Germany but are on the rise. The trend for the upper and middle classes is convergence.[64] Many East Germans advocate an inclusivist middle-class concept, which is supported by a positive memory of GDR lower-middle-class egalitarianism. There are also vocal partisans of a crudely meritocratic, neoliberal, and exclusive middle class. Both groups vacillate between the discourse of crisis and that of optimism. The conditions of the East German middle class are carefully observed all over Germany, because the West Germans have realized that German unity has consequences for themselves as well, and that one of these consequences could be the decline of some middle-class groups.

## Conclusions and Perspectives

The history of the German middle classes in the twentieth century has shown that "middle-class" is not only a statistical aggregate, a social category, and an economic class, but also a political and cultural construction that is pivotal to both the dynamics and the balance of modern societies. Although the concept of middle-class was central to the reconstruction of West Germany, it was officially erased from the GDR blueprint. The unification of the two German states made it necessary to build in short order a middle class in the Neue Bundesländer. The state-sponsored "rise of the East" (Aufschwung Ost) was heavily based on the premise that the economy would be buoyed by small businesses and self-employed professionals. In effect, the idea was to emulate the reconstruction in the West after 1945; it was an attempt to repeat this success story and to confirm the myths of the origin of the modern middle class and of civil society.

As in the years after 1945, the second construction of a middle class was not the work of radical German nationalists. The process of unification, initiated by the East Germans and led by the West Germans, was strongly influenced by universal Western values and supported by other nation-states and supra-national institutions. Thus, we can expect that the German middle classes will not fall back into the types of nationalism that characterized German middle classes until 1945. The German middle classes are as Europeanized as their economy. On the level of institutions and values, the ongoing process of German unification follows the same trends of deregulation, liberalization, and self-help that have influenced the European integration.

These developments have put the topic of the middle class back on the agenda of the political parties and the media in new ways. In principle, all the German political parties agree that there is a need to have a dynamic, achievement-oriented middle class. Although the professional and small-business class had long been one of the central issues of the program of the Liberal Democratic Party, the Christian Democratic parties have always declared that they represent both the exclusive and the inclusive middle class.

Finally, in 1998, the Social Democrats, in order to win that year's elections, presented their vision of a "new middle-class society," or "New Center" (Neue Mitte). The New Center aims to reconcile the inclusive vision of middle-class with the interests and ambitions of the meritocratic elites to shape a social and national unity in Germany. The principles of freedom, social justice, solidarity, and performance are to be combined in new ways. According to the party program, solidarity and justice are the basis of the "broad middle class." Achievement-oriented workers and trade unions, professionals, managers, entrepreneurs, and self-employed craftsmen and retailers together form the New Center of society. Nonetheless, party organizers insist that "justice requires more equality of distribution of income, property, and the right for equal chances. . . . Solidarity is necessary for expanding the chance of the individual for self-realization."[65] Economy, work, welfare, and the tax system have to be changed to encourage small and mid-size businesses, which are regarded as the "backbone" of the German and European economies because they employ the majority of people and their share in economic performance is still higher than that of the big corporations.

The program of the Social Democratic Party (SPD) argues against "unsupportable forms of polarization" in society and aims at creating a broad middle class with equal rights and chances and an effective middle stratum of entrepreneurs and professions who should be supported so that they can compete in a Europeanized and global economy. Yet the program of the Social Democratic Party, like the programs of the other parties (including the Greens and the East German post-Communists), includes an offer for the self-employed middle classes and a declaration of the values of the European and cosmopolitan middle class.

The middle-class programs of the political parties aim at winning elections,[66] while the different social strata, milieus, and groups are trying to reformulate their self-definitions in order to gain more cohesion and strength in promoting their social interests. The boundaries between the old subgroups and the exclusive and inclusive notions of middle-class are blurred by new economic, social, and cultural trends. The middle classes are using cosmopolitan, nationalist, regionalist, and gendered discourses in new ways. While traditional middle classes use national and regional discourses, the more dynamic middle classes define themselves as European or cosmopolitan.

## Notes

1. Jürgen Kocka, "Das europäische Muster und der deutsche Fall," in *Einheit und Vielfalt Europas*, vol. 1: *Bürgertum im 19: Jahrhundert*, edited by Jürgen Kocka (Göttingen: Vandenhoeck & Ruprecht, 1995), 9–84; Jürgen Kocka, "The Middle Classes in Europe," *Journal of Modern History* 67(December 1995): 783–806; Hannes Siegrist, "Ende der Bürgerlichkeit?: Die Kategorien 'Bürgertum' und 'Bürgerlichkeit' in der westdeutschen Gesellschaft und Geschichtswissenschaft in der Nachkriegsperiode," *Geschichte und Gesellschaft* 20(1994): 549–83.
2. Helmut Schelsky, "Die Bedeutung des Schichtungsbegriffs für die Analyse der gegenwärtigen Gesellschaft," in *Auf der Suche nach der Wirklichkeit*, edited by Helmut Schelsky (Düsseldorf: Diederichs, 1965); Hans Braun, "Helmut Schelskys Konzept der 'nivellierten Mittelstandsgesellschaft' und die Bundesrepublik der 50er Jahre," *Archiv für Sozialgeschichte* 29(1989): 199–223.
3. Siegrist, "Ende der Bürgerlichkeit?"; Hannes Siegrist, "Der Wandel als Krise und Chance: Die westdeutschen Akademiker 1945–1965," in *Wege zur Geschichte des Bürgertums: vierzehn Beiträge*, edited by Klaus Tenfelde and Hans-Ulrich Wehler (Göttingen: Vandenhoeck & Ruprecht, 1994), 289–314; Hannes Siegrist, "Der Akademiker als Bürger: Die westdeutschen gebildeten Mittelklassen 1945–1965 in historischer Perspektive," in *Biographien in Deutschland: Soziologische Rekonstruktionen gelebter Geschichte*, edited by Wolfram Fischer-Rosenthal and Peter Alheit (Opladen: Westdeutscher Verlag, 1995), 118–36.
4. Heinrich-August Winkler, *Zwischen Marx und Monopolen: der deutsche Mittelstand vom Kaiserreich zur Bundesrepublik Deutschland* (Frankfurt am Main: Fischer Taschenbuch, 1991).
5. Jürgen Kocka, *Die Angestellten in der deutschen Geschichte, 1850–1980: vom Privat beamten zum angestellten Arbeitnehmer* (Göttingen: Vandenhoeck & Ruprecht, 1981).
6. Werner Conze and Jürgen Kocka, eds., *Bildungsbürgertum im 19. Jahrhundert* (Stuttgart: Klett-Cotta, 1985).
7. Konrad H. Jarausch, *The Unfree Professions: German Lawyers, Teachers, and Engineers, 1900–1950* (New York: Oxford University Press, 1990); Geoffrey Cocks and Konrad H. Jarausch, eds., *German Professions, 1800–1950* (New York: Oxford University Press, 1990).
8. For the concept of republicanism, republican virtues, and the middle class, see John G. A. Pocock, *The Machiavellian Moment: Florentine Political Thought and the Atlantic Republican Tradition* (Princeton: Princeton University Press, 1975); Barbara Weinmann, "Der Weg in die andere Bürgergesellschaft" (Ph.D. diss., Free University, Berlin, 1999); Ronald M. Glassmann, *The Middle Class and Democracy in Sociohistorical Perspective* (Leiden: Brill, 1995).
9. Siegrist, "Ende der Bürgerlichkeit?"; Siegrist, "Der Wandel als Krise und Chance."
10. Braun, "Helmut Schelskys Konzept der 'nivellierten Mittelstandsge-

sellschaft'"; Stefan Hradil, "Individualisierung, Pluralisierung, Polarisierung: Was ist von den Klassen und Schichten geblieben?" in *Die Bundesrepublik Deutschland: Eine historische Bilanz*, edited by Robert Hettlage (Munich: C. H. Beck, 1990), 111–38.

11. Kocka, "Das europäische Muster und der deutsche Fall."

12. Siegrist, "Ende der Bürgerlichkeit?"; Siegrist, "Der Wandel als Krise und Chance"; Siegrist, "Der Akademiker als Bürger"; Klaus Tenfelde, "Stadt und Bürgertum im 20. Jahrhundert," in Tenfelde and Wehler, *Wege zur Geschichte des Bürgertums*, 317–53.

13. "Der Göttinger Parteienforscher Franz Walther über die Kampfgemeinschaft CDU, rechte Konkurrenz und die Zukunft der Union," *Der Spiegel* 9(2000): 37–38; "Der Freiburger Politikwissenschaftler Wilhelm Hennies über die Spendenaffäre, das System Kohl und den Wildwuchs des Parteienstaates," *Der Spiegel* 5(2000): 32–33.

14. The terms "liberal" and, more often, "neoliberal" are increasingly used in Europe to describe policies that Americans label "conservative."

15. Heinz Bude and Stephan Schleissnig, eds., *Junge Eliten: Selbständigkeit als Beruf* (Stuttgart: Kohlhammer, 1997).

16. Jarausch, *The Unfree Professions*; Siegrist, "Der Wandel als Krise und Chance"; Siegrist, "Der Akademiker als Bürger."

17. Lutz Niethammer, "War die bürgerliche Gesellschaft in Deutschland 1945 am Ende oder am Anfang?" in *Bürgerliche Gesellschaft in Deutschland*, edited by Lutz Niethammer (Frankfurt am Main: Fischer-Taschenbuch, 1990), 515–32.

18. Sigrid Meuschel, *Legitimation und Parteiherrschaft in der DDR* (Frankfurt am Main: Suhrkamp, 1992).

19. Volker Berghahn, *Unternehmer und Politik in der Bundesrepublik* (Frankfurt am Main: Suhrkamp, 1995); Hervé Joly, *Grossunternehmer in Deutschland: Soziologie einer industriellen Elite, 1933–1989* (Leipzig: Leipziger Universitäts-Verlag, 1998).

20. Paul Erker, "Amerikanisierung der westdeutschen Wirtschaft?: Stand und Perspektiven der Forschung," in *Amerikanisierung und Sowjetisierung in Deutschland 1945–1970*, edited by Konrad Jarausch and Hannes Siegrist (Frankfurt am Main: Campus, 1997), 137–45; Harm Schröter, "Zur Übertragbarkeit sozialhistorischer Konzepte in die Wirtschaftsgeschichte: Amerikanisierung und Sowjetisierung in deutschen Betrieben 1945–1975," in Jarausch and Siegrist, *Amerikanisierung und Sowjetisierung in Deutschland*, 147–65.

21. Ralf Dahrendorf, *Gesellschaft und Demokratie in Deutschland* (Munich: Piper, 1965); Siegrist, "Ende der Bürgerlichkeit?"; Siegrist, "Der Akademiker als Bürger"; Michael Ermarth, "Amerikanisierung und deutsche Kulturkritik 1945–1965: Metastasen der Moderne und hermeneutische Hybris," in Jarausch and Siegrist, *Amerikanisierung und Sowjetisierung in Deutschland*, 315–34.

22. For the civil servants, see Udo Wengst, *Beamtentum zwischen Reform und Tradition: Beamtengesetzgebung in der Gründungsphase der Bundesrepublik Deutschland 1948–1953* (Düsseldorf: Droste-Verlag, 1988). For the professions, see Jarausch, *The Unfree Professions*; Siegrist, "Ende der Bürgerlichkeit?"; Siegrist, "Der Wandel als Krise und Chance"; Siegrist, "Der Akademiker als Bürger."

23. Dahrendorf, *Gesellschaft und Demokratie in Deutschland*.

24. Winkler, *Zwischen Marx und Monopolen.*
25. Ibid., 111.
26. Ibid.
27. Kurt Schmücker, "Der gewerbliche Mittelstand in Deutschland," in *Der Mittelstand in der Wirtschaftsordnung heute: Die Akten des internationalen Mittelstandskongresses von Madrid,* edited by Arthur-Fridolin Utz (Heidelberg: F. H. Kerle, 1959), 294–302; Winkler, *Zwischen Marx und Monopolen.*
28. Abdolreza Scheybani, "Vom Mittelstand zur Mittelschicht?: Handwerk und Kleinhandel in der Gesellschaft der früheren Bundesrepublik Deutschland," *Archiv für Sozialgeschichte* 35(1995): 131–95.
29. Kocka, *Die Angestellten in der deutschen Geschichte;* Michael Prinz, "Wandel durch Beharrung: Sozialdemokratie und 'neue Mittelschicht,'" *Archiv für Sozialgeschichte* 24(1989): 35–76; Mario König, *Die Angestellten unterweg: vom Berufsstand zur modernen Gewerkschaft 1890 bis 1990* (Cologne: Bund-Verlag, 1991).
30. Prinz, "Wandel durch Beharrung," 73.
31. Josef Mooser, *Arbeiterleben in Deutschland 1900–1970: Klassenlagen, Kultur, und Politik* (Frankfurt am Main: Suhrkamp, 1980).
32. König, *Die Angestellten unterwegs.*
33. The percentage of German working people who were employed on the basis of a standard work contract sank from 84 percent in 1975 to 68 percent in 1995. Ulrich Beck, *Schöne neue Arbeitswelt: Vision: Weltbürgergergesellschaft* (Frankfurt am Main: Campus, 1999), 94, 107.
34. Peter Noller, *Globalisierung, Stadträume, und Lebensstile: Kulturelle und lokale Repräsentationen des globalen Raums* (Opladen: Leske & Budrich, 1999), 132, 185.
35. Braun, "Helmut Schelskys Konzept der 'nivellierten Mittelstandsgesellschaft'"; Siegrist, "Ende der Bürgerlichkeit?"
36. Bernhard Schäfers and Wolfgang Zapf, eds., *Handwörterbuch zur Gesellschaft Deutschlands* (Opladen: Leske & Budrich, 1998); Rainer Geissler, *Die Sozialstruktur Deutschlands: zur gesellschaftlichen Entwicklung mit einer Zwischenbilanz zur Vereinigung* (Bonn: Bundeszentrale für Politische Bildung, 1996); Gerhard Schulze, *Die Erlebnisgesellschaft: Kultursoziologie der Gegenwart* (Frankfurt am Main: Campus, 1992).
37. Axel Schildt, "Für die breiten Schichten des Volkes: Zur Planung und Realisierung des 'Sozialen Wohnungsbaus' in der Bundesrepublik Deutschland (1950–1960)," *Comparativ* 6(3, 1996): 24–48.
38. Gerhard A. Ritter, *Über Deutschland: die Bundesrepublik in der deutschen Geschichte* (Munich: C. H. Beck, 1998), 77–128; Christoph Klessmann, *Zwei Staaten, eine Nation: Deutsche Geschichte 1955–1970* (Bonn: Bundeszentrale für politische Bildung, 1988); Michael Wildt, "Die Kunst der Wahl: Zur Entwicklung des Konsums in Westdeutschland in den 1950er Jahren," in *Europäische Konsumgeschichte: zur Gesellschafts- und Kulturgeschichte des Konsums (18. bis 20. Jahrhundert),* edited by Hannes Siegrist, Hartmut Kaelble, and Jürgen Kocka (Frankfurt am Main: Campus, 1997), 307–26; Axel Schildt, "Freizeit, Konsum, und Häuslichkeit in der 'Wiederaufbau'-Gesellschaft: zur Modernisierung von Lebensstilen in der Bundesrepublik Deutschland in den 1950er Jahren," in Siegrist, Kaelble, and Kocka, *Europäische Konsumgeschichte,* 327–48.

39. Norbert Sievers, ed., *Bestandsaufnahme Soziokultur: Beiträge, Analysen, Konzepte; Dokumentation des gleichnamigen Forschungsprojektes der Kulturpolitischen Gesellschaft e.V.* (Stuttgart: Kohlhammer, 1992).

40. Hans Hartwig Bohle, "Armut trotz Wohlstand," in *Was treibt die Gesellschaft auseinander?* edited by Wilhelm Heitmeyer (Frankfurt am Main: Edition Suhrkamp, 1997), 118–55.

41. Meuschel, *Legitimation und Parteiherrschaft in der DDR*; Ritter, *Über Deutschland*, 129–93.

42. Michael C. Schneider, *Bildung für neue Eliten: Die Gründung der Arbeiter-und-Bauern-Fakultäten in der SBZ/DDR* (Dresden: Hannah-Arendt-Institut für Totalitarismusforschung, 1998); Arnd Bauerkämper et al., *Gesellschaft ohne Eliten?: Führungsgruppen in der DDR* (Berlin: Metropol, 1990).

43. Stefan Hornbostel, "Die geplante Elite: Erste Ergebnisse aus der Analyse der Kaderdatenspeicher des Ministerrates," *Potsdamer Bulletin für Zeithistorische Studien* 10(July 1997): 56.

44. Ritter, *Über Deutschland*, 161.

45. Heike Solga, "Der Elitenimport nach Ostdeutschland: Transformationstypen und Veränderungen in der Elitenrekrutierung," in *Zwischenbilanz der Wiedervereinigung, Strukturwandel, und Mobilitäten im Transformationsprozess*, edited by Martin Diewald (Opladen: Leske & Budrich, 1996), 89–109; Heike Solga, "The Fate of the East German Upper Service Class After 1989: Types of System Transformations and Changes in Elite Recruitement," in *Eliten, politische Kultur und Privatisierung in Ostdeutschland, Tschechien und Mittelosteuropa*, edited by Ilja Srubar (Konstanz: Universitätsverlag Konstanz, 1998), 97–117.

46. Ralph Jessen, *Akademische Elite und kommunistische Diktatur: Die ostdeutsche Hochschullehrerschaft in der Ulbricht-Ära* (Göttingen: Vandenhoeck & Ruprecht, 1999); Anna-Sabine Ernst, "Die beste Prophylaxe ist der Sozialismus": Ärzte und medizinische Hochschullehrer in der SBZ/DDR, 1945–1961 (Münster: Waxmann, 1997); Christoph Klessmann, "Relikte des Bildungsbürgertums in der DDR," in *Sozialgeschichte der DDR*, edited by Hartmut Kaelble, Jürgen Kocka, and Hartmut Zwahr (Stuttgart: Klett-Cotta, 1994), 254–70; Dolores L. Augustine, "Frustrierte Technokraten: Zur Sozialgeschichte des Ingenieurberufs in der Ulbricht-Ära," in *Die Grenzen der Diktatur: Staat und Gesellschaft in der DDR*, edited by Richard Bessel (Göttingen: Vandenhoeck & Ruprecht, 1996), 49–75.

47. Arnd Bauerkämper, "Kontinuität und Auflösung der bürgerlichen Rechtsordnung: Landwirtschaftliches Bodeneigentum in Ost- und Westdeutschland (1945–1990)," in *Eigentum im internationalen Vergleich (18.–20. Jahrhundert)*, edited by Hannes Siegrist and David Sugarman (Göttingen: Vandenhoeck & Ruprecht, 1999), 109–34; Arnd Bauerkämper, *"Junkerland in Bauernhand"?: Durchführung, Auswirkungen, und Stellenwert der Bodenreform in der Sowjetischen Besatzungszone* (Stuttgart: Steiner, 1996).

48. Ina Merkel, *Utopie und Bedürfnis: die Geschichte der Konsumkultur in der DDR* (Cologne: Böhlau, 1999), 38.

49. Ibid., 71–74.

50. Solga, "Der Elitenimport nach Ostdeutschland."

51. Meuschel, *Legitimation und Parteiherrschaft in der DDR*, 12.

52. Christian Welzel, "Rekrutierung und Sozialisation der ostdeutschen Elite: Aufstieg einer demokratischen Gegenelite?," in *Eliten in Deutschland: Rekrutierung und Integration*, edited by Wilhelm Bürklin and Hilke Rebenstorf (Opladen: Leske & Budrich, 1997), 85.

53. Their attitude toward democracy in general is more ambivalent. Industrial workers appreciate mediation procedures between the managers and workers of a firm. According to Lohr, the transfer of institutionalized mechanisms and Western industrial relations has worked well because both sides have a common interest in modernizing companies, thus enabling them to survive. Katrin Lohr, "Interaktionsmuster zwischen Management und Belegschaft im Prozess der Transformation," in Srubar, *Eliten, politische Kultur und Privatisierung*, 325–40. In addition, some elements of the former GDR attitude toward work and cooperation support the transfer. See Peter Hübner and Klaus Tenfelde, eds., *Arbeiter in der SBZ-DDR* (Essen: Klartext, 1999).

54. Viktoria Kaina, "Wertorientierungen im Eliten-Bevölkerungsvergleich: vertikale Distanzen, geteilte Loyalitäten, und das Erbe der Trennung," in Bürklin and Rebenstorf, *Eliten in Deutschland*, 351–89.

55. Welzel, "Rekrutierung und Sozialisation," 201–37.

56. Wolf Klinz, "Stand und Perspektiven der mittelständischen Industrie in den NBL," in *Mittelstand im Aufbau: Reden und Diskussionsbeiträge auf dem Tag des industriellen Mittelstandes am 25. April 1991 im Gewandhaus zu Leipzig*, edited by BDI (Cologne: Industrie-Förderung GmbH, 1991), 27–38.

57. Friedrich Kaufmann et al., *Die Situation der reprivatisierten Unternehmen in den neuen Bundesländern* (Bonn: Institut für Mittelstandsforschung, 1997).

58. Michael Thomas, "'Neue Selbständige': Eigenarten und Grenzen der Akteurkonstitution im Transformationsprozess," in Srubar, *Eliten, politische Kultur und Privatisierung*, 303–24.

59. Welzel, "Rekrutierung und Sozialisation," 201–37; Solga, "Der Elitenimport nach Ostdeutschland"; Jürgen Kocka, ed., *Wissenschaft und Wiedervereinigung: Disziplinen im Umbruch, Interdisziplinäre Arbeitsgruppe Wissenschaften und Wiedervereinigung* (Berlin: Akademie-Verlag, 1998).

60. Wilhelm Oberlander, "Zwischen Markt und Staat: eine sozialstrukturelle und berufssoziologische Betrachtung der Freien Berufe in den neuen Bundesländern" (Ph.D. diss., Universität Erlangen-Nürnberg, 1995).

61. Thomas, "'Neue Selbständige,'" 303–24, 305.

62. Markus C. Pohlmann and Hans-Joachim Gergs, "Manager in Ostdeutschland: Reproduktion oder Zirkulation einer Elite?" *Kölner Zeitschrift für Soziologie und Sozialpsychologie* 49(1997): 540–62; Solga, "The Fate of the East German Upper Service Class After 1989," 97–118; Solga, "Der Elitenimport nach Ostdeutschland."

63. Oberlander, "Zwischen Markt und Staat," 8.

64. Schäfers and Zapf, *Handwörterbuch zur Gesellschaft Deutschlands*.

65. SPD-Vorstand, ed., *Wir sind bereit: Fünf sichere Zeichen: Arbeit, Innovation, und Gerechtigkeit: SPD-Wahlprogramm für die Bundestagswahl 1998 and Grundsatzprogramm der Sozialdemokratischen Partei Deutschlands* (Bonn: SPD , 1998).

66. See Charle (this volume) on France and Savage (this volume) on England.

# 2

## Individuality and Class: The Rise and Fall of the Gentlemanly Social Contract in Britain

### Mike Savage

In 1949, towards the end of the postwar Labour government, which was popularly credited with introducing wide-ranging reforms that consolidated the welfare state, researchers associated with David Glass, professor of sociology at the London School of Economics, carried out a survey of popular attitudes to class. No fewer than 75 percent of the sample stated that they were working-class.[1] Fifteen years later, in the first national survey on voting behavior in Britain, 63 percent of the sample claimed to be working-class.[2] Nearly thirty years later, in 1991, the British Social Attitudes Survey found that 64 percent thought of themselves as working-class.[3]

These surveys remind us of the strikingly enduring nature of working-class identity in Britain. Being "working-class" has a resonance and appeal that is remarkably resilient, while middle-class identities have never been popular amongst people who see them as embodying claims to social exclusiveness. Despite profound social change in Britain since the Second World War, the proportion of the population claiming to be working-class has changed hardly at all. Even though the proportion of the workforce involved in manual employment fell from 62 percent in 1961 to 41 percent in 1991, there was no shift in the number of people thinking of themselves, however loosely, as working-class.[4] The rise in middle-class jobs has not led to a rise in middle-class identities.

The aim of this chapter is to interpret this stability as it relates to the distinctively British "gentlemanly social contract" that was formed in the early nineteenth century and reached its apogee in the mid-twentieth century.[5] In developing this idea of a gentlemanly social contract, I draw on the work of Peter Cain and Eric Hopkins, who argue that British economic development was premised on a form of "gentlemanly capitalism."[6] They see the sectors linked to Britain's imperial role—trading, financial, and service—as the key dynamic force in shaping British social development in the nineteenth and early twentieth centuries. In this chapter, I adapt this idea to show that the key feature of this gentlemanly social contract was a standoff between manual labor and the professional middle class in which historically it was working-class idioms that were associated with notions of individuality. I show that such a contract underpinned the complex tension between tradition and modernity that has characterized twentieth-century British history. It explains how class relations in Britain remained stable even as major social and economic change was taking place, and how a society in which class had always played a defining role could modernize. My aim is therefore to argue against those who regard Britain simply as a "traditional" society that has failed to modernize itself.[7]

In the first section, I show that the years between 1945 and 1970 marked the high point of a gentlemanly social contract whose historical roots dated to the early nineteenth century. I show that this social contract depended on defining the growing middle classes of professionals and senior managers as a gentlemanly group whose claims to high status depended on conceding the claim that it was members of the working class who were ordinary, democratic, male individuals and citizens. I argue that the cultural field organized by this class distinction had a major impact on early- and mid-twentieth-century developments. In the second part of this chapter, I argue that this gentlemanly social contract has come under increased stress, owing to changes in both working-class and middle-class formation. This stress has eroded the centrality of the gentlemanly social contract in British society as a whole, but I argue that no alternative cultural framework has yet replaced class as key organizing features of British culture.

## The Formation of the British Gentlemanly Social Contract

In Britain, as in many other countries, social stability in the period after 1945 was based on growing economic prosperity and a commitment to economic redistribution. Trends in the distribution of income and wealth between 1945 and the later 1970s indicated a shift towards economic equality.[8] This trend was particularly marked between the early 1960s and the late 1970s, when the real incomes of poor households rose by over half,[9] and in relative terms rose faster than the income of rich households. The development of social welfare provision, however, was the clearest indication of the significance of a social settlement based on the provision of social citizenship rights.[10] The expansion of public education services, the provision of universal, free health care, and the increase in good-quality public housing and transport testified to the development of social rights that (especially in the case of the National Health Service) seemed to advance common citizenship rights so that they encompassed social as well as political and legal rights.

The social contract of these years was one that spanned classes and invoked new kinds of citizenship rights. Also encoded within this social contract, however, was the long history of British class relations. The working classes played a key role in defining the meaning of modern British citizenship, whereas the middle classes were defined, like the upper classes, as an exclusive class. For our understanding of the origins of this cultural framework, we are still indebted to E. P. Thompson's *The Making of the English Working Class*, in particular his emphasis on the role of the working class in bearing the democratic tradition.[11] Thompson argues that at the critical moment for the development of democracy in Britain, in the radical agitation leading up to the Reform Act of 1832, the working class organized and led popular protest. Thompson's writings have been much criticized for confusing a radical populist culture with working-class culture in the years after 1832.[12] Critics note that there was no developed language of class that defined class relationships as fundamental to politics. Rather, radical discourse continued to embrace a strong populist culture in which the anger of radicals was directed against political corruption.

Although these critics are generally right to point out the limits of class awareness in nineteenth-century radical politics, in some respects this is precisely Thompson's main point. Because the aristocracy and the "middle classes" refused to carry the banner for democratic rights, it was the working class that took on this role and thereby forged an enduring cultural association between the working classes and the democratic tradition. Because other social classes ultimately failed to support the democratic project, it was left to diverse groups of workers to "nurture the liberty tree" (to use Thompson's own phrase) and transform the historical discourse of the freeborn Englishman into modern claims for citizenship. Recent historiography on the English middle classes amply testifies to the acuity of Thompson's judgment. Dror Wahrman has examined the ways in which the idea of the middle class was articulated in political discourse between the 1790s and 1830s, the critical period during which the concept of class became a mainstay in social and political discourse in Britain.[13] Wahrman claims that there was no strong, self-identified, middle-class interest group proclaiming its own rights. Rather, phrases such as the "middling sort" were more popular.[14] As the "middle class" became a feature of political discourse, it was defined variously and used by diverse interest groups to define a constituency for competing political projects. Between 1793 and 1815, some political leaders claimed the middle class as a force supporting the Napoleonic war, while others defined it as a force opposing that conflict. Central to this construction of the "middle class" was the idea that the middle classes existed as intermediaries between two visible and preexisting social and political forces: radical popular forces, on the one hand, and the landed establishment, on the other. In effect, the middle classes were formed in a cultural space already occupied by these two powerful and opposed social forces. The middle classes became identified in opposition to a powerful radical and popular (even "working-class") bloc that commanded center stage in defining what it was to be an "ordinary" citizen. Assertions of middle-class status therefore marked a claim to some kind of cultural distinction and elevation above the culture of manual labor.

Wahrman's other main contention concerns the articulation of class in the agitation leading to the Great Reform Act of 1832. He argues that hitherto haphazard references to the middle class became more consistent during this period, and that the passage of the reform act was critical in renewing old status distinctions within a new class discourse. The Great Reform Act did not openly admit the legitimacy of democratic principles but continued to refer to older, corporate, and interest group–based defenses of restricted parliamentary representation. Debate centered on the question of whether there was a legitimate interest group that had expanded and had no representation in the existing political system. Thus, the effect of the reform act was to admit the middle classes, as a distinctive status and interest group, into the polity. (Not only was the franchise extended to the propertied middle class, but electoral redistricting gave a greater number of seats in the House of Commons to new urban areas.) By these means, the middle classes came to be recognized as a distinctive status group *within the established social and political order* that did not pose a challenge to that order.

Wahrman shows that the new middle classes could be accommodated within a traditional, status-based social and political system. In this way, the middle classes became a "gentlemanly" middle class.

That class developed its own claims to status in a hierarchical, gentlemanly culture, and these claims relied on the overall legitimacy of aristocratic culture as the guarantor of the status system as a whole. Yet the gentlemanly middle class also needed to challenge the upper-class monopoly of status to emphasize its own distinct place within the status system. This it did primarily by defining the new cities as its territorial power bases in a parallel way to the aristocracy's territorial relationship to its country seats, and also by championing the claims of intellectual merit and expertise. Intellectual merit was seen, however, as the product of social upbringing, and thus of a specific form of class culture, rather than as a reflection of individual talent.

In this way, the middle classes were formed in complex tension with the upper and working classes. With respect to the former, the middle classes challenged their definition of status while at the same time relying on the validation of status as a whole.[15] With respect to working-class culture, Ross McKibbin has shown that the Tory Party mobilized middle-class sentiment in interwar Britain by rallying the middle-class "public" against the expanding and increasingly visible Labour movement.[16] Given the inevitable diversity of middle-class life, fractured along occupational, religious, and cultural lines, the best way of uniting the middle class lay in defining it against the working class.

Middle-class formation in Britain reacted against the world of manual labor and the working classes. It depended on creating social and cultural distance between manual work and various modes of "middle-class" employment. The most important device was to seize upon traditional professional identities as supports for new and expanding forms of middle-class identification. Professional power in Britain was long established,[17] but during the nineteenth century the professions were restructured when credentialist routes were developed to place graduates of leading universities in professional jobs. David Cannadine has shown that the reform of the professions was linked to the declining presence of aristocratic and gentry forces within them. (Traditionally, the professions, and especially the church and the law, had been a major occupational destination for the younger sons of the landed classes.)[18] Professional reforms allowed the middle classes both to become more self-recruiting and to form around traditional status identities.

The welfare state of postwar Britain marked the culmination of this process of professional dominance. A crucial feature of the social contract was the settling of accounts between professional bodies and the Labour government. As part of the reforms leading to the development of the National Health Service in 1948, doctors (represented by the British Medical Association) forced the Labour government to respect their professional autonomy and also managed to gain agreement to allow the secret payment of bonuses to senior doctors.[19] The state also underwrote the elitist character of higher education. University students not only had their fees paid but were also allowed a maintenance grant that allowed them to study full-time, without needing to work. Oxford and Cambridge colleges were able to rely on higher-than-average payments from the public purse through special government grants. The expansion of the welfare state also involved the emergence of the regulatory professions of social work. The Civil Service itself became one of the centers of this gentlemanly culture. The Northcote-Trevelyan reforms of the 1850s divided this work into "intellectual" and "mechanical" wings and also divided intellectual work into three classes. Moving into the senior ranks of the Civil Service became a major aspiration of Oxbridge graduates.

The crystallization of this kind of professional dominance is illuminated in Noel Annan's autobiography.[20] Annan, one of the most senior British University administrators in the post-1945 period, writes of how the privately educated, Oxbridge elite put their stamp on postwar British society. Strikingly, he notes that a highly integrated elite, which depended strongly on considerable face-to-face recognition and bonds cultivated at the two dominant universities, was able not only to survive but also to take advantage of the new opportunities opened up by the expansion of the state. The British Broadcasting Company (BBC) was an excellent example of how a gentlemanly culture could be at once traditional and modern. It defined its public-service mission in elitist terms (educating the general public) and in the process pioneered radio and television services in Britain. It recruited predominantly from Oxford and Cambridge.[21] It was not until the 1980s that challenges to gentlemanly power within the BBC became marked.

The social contract in postwar Britain was therefore one in which gentlemanly professionals held sway. But the contract was more complex than the idea of professional dominance would suggest, since, as I have already noted, there was also widespread recognition that the working class played a central role in British society. The postwar settlement in fact marked a particular kind of class compromise in which gentlemanly professional dominance could coexist with plebeian working-class culture. Manual work cultures in Britain relied strongly on the persistence of handicraft practices. As is now well known, British industrial growth in the nineteenth century relied on labor-intensive processes as employers focused on having skilled laborers work more effectively.[22] Until the middle years of the twentieth century, workers took responsibility for their own training, usually through variants of apprenticeship; as a result, gaining craft skills was seen as synonymous with achieving male independence and autonomy.[23] There were similarities in the cultures of skilled manual work and professionalism that allowed both groups to respect the other.[24] Both saw the acquisition of skills as a process that took place early in adult life, and the gaining of a degree (profession) or of articles (skilled work) as a rite of passage to male adulthood. Both shared the idea that once trained, the adult male could be left in charge to do his work autonomously and responsibly. Both also endorsed the view that organization—whether in a trade union or a professional association—was necessary to protect trade interests and ensure the independence of workers from their employers. The cultures of the male, skilled, independent worker and the gentleman professional could coexist given this recognition of separate spheres and non-intervention. Managerial, bureaucratic intervention was seen as inimical to the interests of both groups, and as a violation of work norms and values.

Within this cultural framework, the world of management was seen by both skilled workers and gentlemen professionals as "polluted." Senior management within the private sector was dominated by private family interests allied with professional specialists (such as company secretaries, solicitors, and accountants).[25] The growth of professional management was stunted in Britain until well into the twentieth century.[26] Junior managers and administrators, whose expansion played a key role in the bureaucratization of British society on which the postwar settlement depended, were defined "liminally"—that is, they were not given full admission into the middle class. Whereas in the United States managers tended to be credentialed and could claim full membership in the middle class, in Britain most managerial employment was regarded as of relatively low status. As firms expanded in the early and mid-twentieth century, and as a limited degree of bureaucratization took place, the positions of managers, supervisors, and clerks were not attractive to the established professional middle classes. Most managerial and supervisory positions were filled from below, often from the shop floor. (Professional workers sought to be hired for only the most senior managerial positions.) Studies of occupational mobility in Britain show that until at least the 1970s, two very different kinds of middle-class mobility patterns were associated with professionals and managers. Professionals were educated at universities (often having been to private or grammar schools) and moved directly into professional employment in their early twenties. Managers were unlikely to have been highly educated (until at least the 1970s) and tended to have commenced work on the shop floor or in routine white-collar work, from which they were internally promoted.[27]

The British middle class therefore developed as an essentially fractured class that made a strong distinction between professional and managerial workers, with little interplay between those two wings. This middle-class formation seems to be different from the situation found in the United States, as well as in other European countries, where managers were more likely to be credentialed. This is one reason the American ideal of a middle-class society in which most people can aspire towards middle-class status had much less currency in Britain. Both skilled workers and professionals could take pride in their "trade" and look with a degree of disdain at managers, who had moved away from the world of autonomous, independent labor yet were not fully accepted as members of the established, gentlemanly middle class.

David Glass's social mobility study revealed this cultural tension in an interesting way. Glass reported that fathers generally wished their sons to move into two types of jobs: the majority of the population favored skilled manual work (which was linked to the idea of apprenticeship and being a time-served man), and those from middle-class backgrounds primarily wanted their sons to choose professional employment. Being a clerk, manager, or supervisor in a bureaucratic setting was not a common aspiration. It seems that these jobs were seen as culturally degraded positions in which a man was neither "one thing nor the other." Interestingly, significant numbers of managers and supervisors wanted their sons to become either skilled workers or professionals.[28] The idea of being a manager had little cultural appeal in British society. This marked the cultural basis of the postwar settlement, which allowed class differences to coexist, up to a point, with shared values and cultures.

Within this social settlement, a further distinctive role was played by gender, which became an axis of social closure within most areas of the labor market. Both skilled manual workers and professionals excluded women from entry into their trades. Women in Britain were often employed specifically on female grades and formally barred from promotion.[29] They tended to be excluded from professional education and found it difficult to enter career-track jobs until after World War II (outside the female professional ghettos of nursing and teaching). The deployment of women in subordinate capacities allowed the older gentlemanly career to be retained even as bureaucracies expanded.

Finally, consumer culture played a significant role in the postwar

settlement. Olivier Zunz has shown that a central feature of the social contract in the United States lay in the ability of the middle
classes to demonstrate their inclusion in the American mainstream
by the purchase of new consumer products.[30] General Motors in particular encouraged upward mobility by offering a graduated selection
of automobile products that allowed it to maintain its relationship
with the consumer even as the consumer's aspirations changed. In
Britain, this form of consumerism did not develop during the postwar
settlement. It is noteworthy that Britons did not commonly possess
televisions, motor cars, and telephones until the 1970s, whereas from
at least the 1950s these products were staples of middle-class American life. In Britain, what was culturally important was not the mere
fact of the purchase of products, but rather the ways in which such
products were used and consumed. Thus, in Britain owning a television was not a marked cultural signifier. What did signify, however,
was whether people watched BBC (and especially BBC2, which was
developed in the 1960s specifically to be an intellectual channel) or
the commercial channel ITV, which had a more popular appeal. Furthermore, suburbanization, a major force in the United States behind
the creation of middle-class aspirations, played out differently in the
Britain postwar settlement: local and central governments encouraged the suburbanization of working-class populations. In many British cities, public housing for low-income groups was provided in large
suburban estates. Thus, whereas in the United States leaving the city
for the suburbs might be a marker of having acquired middle-class
status, in Britain this was not necessarily so. Similarly, moving into
a new house in Britain was a marker of social deprivation rather
than social mobility. In short, consumer culture never mapped onto
class divisions in a neat way in Britain. New forms of consumption—
such as the TV—were appropriated into older modes of cultural
distinction.

## Contemporary Challenges to the Gentlemanly Social Contract

I now turn to recent changes to the social contract in Britain. It is, of
course, something of a commonplace to regard the period since the
early 1970s as marking a breakdown in established, stable patterns of
social relationships in most Western countries.[31] There is a general
acceptance of the view that "globalization," in which the command
of the global (rather than the national or continental) market becomes
crucial for the economic success of major multinational firms, marks
a fundamental break from previous arrangements.[32] Such changes
might be supposed to impinge on professional dominance, since the

expertise of professionals is being defined internationally and is less regulated by the nation-state.[33] My argument here, however, is that although we should not underestimate the dramatic nature of global social change, we need to recognize that it is mediated from specific locations. Social change in Britain is not just a response to exogenous factors linked to the restructuring of the global economy. Nor is it simply a product of the changing political climate introduced by Margaret Thatcher following her election in 1979. Social change, I argue, should also be seen as the unraveling of the social tensions underlying the gentlemanly British social contract. The idea of independence and autonomy that lay at the heart of the gentlemanly social contract and bound together professionals and manual workers in a complex embrace has been undercut by subtle alterations in the situations of both groups.

The key point here is that the central role of male manual labor in British claims to true individuality and citizenship has weakened. Part of the reason for this is simply the numerical decline of manual employment in Britain since the 1960s, and especially since 1980: fewer than one-third of British employees were manual workers by the 1990s. This trend began in the 1960s, intensified in the early 1980s, and has continued ever since. Even during the late 1980s and early 1990s—a time seen by some as the period of the "white-collar recession"—it was manual workers who continued to be more likely to be made redundant, and income polarization between the middle and working classes continued to increase.[34]

More significantly, however, the cultural meaning of manual work has changed: it is no longer the chief repository for values of individuality. There are four reasons for this. First, the apprenticeship system collapsed during the 1980s. Whereas in the 1960s there had been more apprentices than university students, by the late 1980s apprenticeship was largely defunct as a means of training skilled manual workers and socializing them into the values of older working-class men. Although apprenticeship was reinvented in the 1990s, it took a very different form, with vocational skills being taught in specialized educational institutes rather than on the shop floor.[35] Second, the age profile of manual work changed. Rather than representing the prized job for independent, skilled adult men, manual work increasingly became the domain of young workers, who take on these jobs early in their careers, when they are still likely to be living in their parents' home. The association between manual work and notions of male adult independence was thus eroded.[36] Third, some skilled manual workers were incorporated into internal labor markets and thereby lost their formerly cherished "independence," while others worked on an increasingly casual basis.[37] Fourth, trade unionism, traditionally one of the main vehicles for sustaining values of independence and solidarity, was severely weakened among manual workers, especially in the private sector, with the result that unionism became disproportionately associated with public-sector professional workers rather than manual labor. The result of all these trends is that manual labor, traditionally the repository for the positive cultural values of independence, autonomy, and mastery, has become increasingly defined as a mode of servile employment.

The eclipse of manual labor as a key cultural motif in British society allows a subtle reworking of the professional model. Professionalism itself no longer depends on a relational contrast with the manual working class to gain its cultural visibility, and increasingly notions of individuality and independence that have historically been associated with manual work can be reworked through professional motifs. The traditional, gentlemanly, professional career anchored the middle classes to the ascriptive devices of gender and the life course rather than to notions of individuality and autonomy. Since the 1980s, there has been a rapid increase in the number of women in professional and managerial occupations.[38] Moreover, the relative pay disparities between middle-aged and younger professionals and managers have declined significantly.[39] These changes betoken a cultural shift in the meaning of middle-class professionalism, away from its associations with status (in the form of middle-aged men from privileged backgrounds) and towards associations with ideas of ambition, competition, and entrepreneurship.

A good example of this shift can be found in the banking sector, which had exemplified the traditional gentlemanly career.[40] Male bank clerks were recruited from grammar schools and could expect regular promotion and a "job for life." As banks expanded and recruited women to fill the subordinate clerical positions, men were able to continue having good promotion prospects.[41] In the words of one bank clerk, "In those days [the 1970s], if you came from the right background, if you know what I mean, a professional background, then you got in and had a job for life. This seemed to matter more than qualifications."[42] Or as another man put it, "I had been to a grammar school. . . . I had a nice family background. I didn't do anything silly. . . . I didn't really think too far ahead . . . it all virtually just happened. I can't say I ever made any decision that has affected my job or career because those sorts of things are made, they are quite honestly made for you." In the traditional banking system, a clerk lost his individuality and freedom when he was promoted to a managerial position and took on more responsibility. "It was explained to me that you can't go from being one of the lads . . . to being a manager in the same branch. It was felt to be a hurdle to get over, in terms of being one of the boys to being accountable, making decisions, giving instructions and so forth."

As banking has restructured, there has been a significant reworking of managerial identities.[43] Women are now no longer formally barred from management posts, and the number of women in management has increased remarkably—from 1 percent in 1980 to around 28 percent in the later 1990s. Competition for promotion is hence more intense. Management itself has been redefined as managers are rewarded according to whether they meet targets. Managers are expected to apply for jobs rather than be "selected" for them by their seniors, as well as to take responsibility for enhancing their own skills. They are expected to move rapidly between specialist areas rather than confine their jurisdiction to one particular functional area. Managers have also lost their immunity to redundancy: following the 1987 financial crash, managers were for the first time laid off in large numbers. In short, the management career has been redefined as a "risky" one in which rewards are linked more specifically to performance.

This particular case study indicates that gentlemanly professionalism has been remade as its traditional appeal—based on its claims to distance and status compared with the manual working class—fades away. In contrast, a new model of individuality has been championed by corporate enterprise. In describing the transformation of retailing, Paul Du Gay notes that managers are now expected to be "entrepreneurial" and "competitive." [44] Similar developments can be found in much of the public sector. The middle classes can still expect to do well, but their career routes are defined less in terms of steady rewards and more in terms of risk and enterprise. Rather than occupying a liminal, marginalized location between the cores of manual labor and the professions, management has taken on increasing prominence. Challenges to the traditional autonomy of professionals undermine their intrinsic status claims and put pressure on them to achieve certain outcomes, as measured by performance indicators.[45] The position of professionals has also been affected by more skeptical popular attitudes to professionally regulated modes of service delivery and a growing interest in "alternative" forms of provision (for instance, in health care).[46]

The result has been that with relatively little resistance, the status and conditions of service associated with the traditional public-sector professions (education, health, and welfare) have declined, and graduates have become more interested in taking up jobs in the newer finance-related and corporate professions.[47] This change indicates a shifting relationship between the established traditional middle classes and the public and private sectors. Politically, the transformation of the Labour Party under Tony Blair's leadership is significant: from having clear roots in manual work cultures and the trade union movement, Labour is now the party of the professional middle classes. Whereas voting patterns continued to be affected by class membership throughout the 1980s, the evidence of the 1997 general election shows a marked weakening of this link: unprecedented numbers of middle-class voters supported the Labour Party.[48] In the past, professionals have been loyal supporters of the Conservative Party, but they have become increasingly disillusioned with the Conservatives. Today doctors, social workers, and teachers tend to be Labour or Liberal Democrat supporters.[49]

## Conclusion: Contemporary Idioms of Class and Culture

Let me now return to the key concerns of this chapter. My argument has been that the British have traditionally relied on a way of representing themselves as being "ordinary" and "average" individuals through the language of the working classes. Historically, this was a precondition for a gentlemanly social contract that allowed professionals to represent themselves as properly privileged by distancing themselves from the world of manual labor. Therefore, gentlemen professionals were best able to define their political and cultural leadership when they existed in tension with the working class: as this latter group has faded from view, so the meaning of the middle classes has also become diffuse and ambivalent, and professional dominance itself less sure.

What do we make of this situation? Here are the views of one man with whom I spoke in Manchester in 1997.

MS: Is Britain becoming "classless"?
RESPONDENT: That's a tough one. In many ways, yes. In the sense that I think many of the old boundaries of class distinctions or the mechanisms that held the class system in place are being eroded by education, by change in the way we live, by other factors. But I think those things change very slowly. I think a lot of the change may be superficial. . . . My perception is that people who are middle-class or above would seem to like to hold on to something. That's a bit of a generalization, . . . but in conversation, when you scratch beneath the surface, sometimes you pick out people wanting to have this sense of "Well, we've

moved on," . . . and I like to pursue that quite often in conversation just to see what people mean.

MS: How do they react when you do pursue it?

RESPONDENT: Sometimes . . . when they realize that you're on the hunt for something, [with] denial—"Oh, no, that's not what I meant" kind of thing, and sometimes just by being quite . . . defensive about it, you know, sort of, "Yeah, sure," you know, "Why shouldn't one be proud of x, y, and z," you know. So, yes, it's being eroded. I think the class structure has been and is being eroded, but there is, I think, an undercurrent of class which is probably still there.

MS: Do you think of yourself as belonging to a particular class?

RESPONDENT: No. I was going to say I didn't. . . . I'm working-class by background and upbringing, and I'm still working, so in that sense I'm still working-class. I find [it] a difficult area to make distinctions in. Again, it's a scale or criteria that I prefer not to use, so I don't find it helpful or meaningful.[50]

We find here a number of interesting themes. The identification of the middle classes with elitist values can easily be traced, even though the respondent emphasizes that the class system has changed. We also find marked defensiveness and ambivalence in the discussion of class. In some ways the respondent is fascinated by class, and in other ways he finds it repugnant. And what is ultimately most striking is that once he has registered all of his ambiguities and doubts, it is still a hesitant working-class identification that he favors above others. No other model of popular identification has arisen to challenge the residual appeal of the working class, though it is striking that this appeal to residual working-class values has a nostalgic air.

We should not read too much into one man's views, but I do want to suggest that they help lay out the continued, nostalgic visibility of the working class in British culture and media. His views conjure up a view of the autonomous individual rather than the risk-taking, ambivalent individual associated with the new kinds of professional and managerial imagery. It is not coincidental that British culture has been preoccupied with portraying the working class for much of the twentieth century; it is, after all, the argument of this chapter that the working-class presence has been a key feature of the gentlemanly social contract. The historical association between "realist" soap operas and films and the depiction of working-class life was especially strong as recently as the 1960s.[51] Recent years have seen a growing number of TV shows focusing on aspects of middle-class professional life (especially tracing the lives of doctors, nurses, teachers, and lawyers as well as the traditionally popular police officers).[52] Nonetheless, residual images of the working classes retain remarkably enduring appeal. There has been a striking revival of realist films during the 1990s (notably in the work of Ken Loach and Mike Leigh), and a number of British soap operas and thrillers continue to evoke the world of the working class as their key reference point.[53] In a similar way, British politicians still seek to legitimize their appeal by emphasizing their working-class "roots."

The collapse of the gentlemanly social contract allows notions of individuality to float free of their historical ties to the working class. This change allows significantly more mobility in notions of the individual, which no longer need to be tied to independent, adult men. As a result, the middle classes become increasingly fractionalized as they cease to gain their common identity by contrast with the working class. However, it remains striking that historical working-class ideals based in democratic, popular, and egalitarian motifs are still nostalgically evoked. We might legitimately worry that in the absence today of genuine social and political forces to defend these values and interests, they have become less secure.

## Notes

1. David Glass, *Social Mobility in Britain* (London: Routledge, 1954). It should be noted that this was a national sample but it was carried out in two locations, Greenwich and Hartford, that may have been somewhat skewed towards a working-class population.
2. David Butler and Donald E. Stokes, *Political Change in Britain* (London: Macmillan, 1969).
3. Keith Young, "Class, Race, and Opportunity," in *British Social Attitudes: The Ninth Report*, edited by Social and Community Planning Research (Aldershot: Dartmouth, 1992, 175–93). See the further discussion in Mike Savage, *Class Analysis and Social Transformation* (Milton Keynes: Open University Press, 2000).
4. Figures taken from Manuel Castells, *The Rise of the Network Society* (Oxford: Blackwell's, 1996), table 4.20, 307. Manual employment is taken to mean "craft and operators, semi-skilled service workers and semi-skilled transport workers" (table 4.20).
5. This chapter synthesizes fuller arguments I have made elsewhere. Although little primary evidence is cited here, readers can find fuller references to empirical research supporting the claims in Savage, *Class Analysis*.
6. Peter J. Cain and Anthony G. Hopkins, *British Imperialism*, 2 vols. (London: Longmans, 1992).
7. The best presentations of the classic argument remain Perry Anderson, "Origins of the Present Crisis," *New Left Review* 23(January–February 1964): 26–53; and Tom Nairn, "The Nature of the Labour Party," *New Left Review* 27(September–October 1964): 38–65, and 28(November–

December 1964): 33–62. This argument continues to inform much of the political debate, especially espousals of "Third Way" politics—for instance, the influential arguments of Will Hutton, *The State We're In* (London: Cape, 1995).

8. Guy Routh, *Occupation and Pay in Great Britain, 1918–1979* (London: Macmillan, 1980); Joseph Rowntree Foundation, *Inquiry into Income and Wealth*, vols. 1 and 2 (York: Joseph Rowntree Foundation, 1995).

9. Rowntree Foundation, *Inquiry*, 2:28, table 14.

10. The classic argument to this effect is, of course, Thomas Marshall, *Citizenship and Social Class, and Other Essays* (Cambridge: Cambridge University Press, 1950).

11. Edward P. Thompson, *The Making of the English Working Class* (London: Gollancz, 1963).

12. See, for example, Patrick Joyce, *Visions of the People* (Cambridge: Cambridge University Press, 1990); Eugenio Biagini, *Liberty, Retrenchment, and Reform: Popular Liberalism in the Age of Gladstone* (Cambridge: Cambridge University Press, 1992); Eugenio Biagini and Alistar Reid, eds., *Currents of Radicalism: Popular Radicalism, Organized Labor, and Party Politics* (Cambridge: Cambridge University Press, 1991); Gareth Stedman Jones, *Languages of Chartism* (Cambridge: Cambridge University Press, 1983).

13. Dror Wahrman, *Imagining the Middle Class: The Political Representation of Class in Britain*, c. 1780–1840 (Cambridge: Cambridge University Press, 1994); Asa Briggs, "The Language of Class in Early Nineteenth Century England," in *Essays in Labor History in Memory of G. D. H. Cole*, edited by Asa Briggs and John Saville (London: Macmillan, 1960); Harold Perkin, *The Origins of Modern English Society, 1780–1880* (London: Routledge, 1969).

14. Bob Harris, "Praising the Middle Sort?: Social Identity in British Nineteenth Century Newspapers," in *The Making of the British Middle Class: Studies of Regional and Cultural Diversity Since the Eighteenth Century*, edited by Alan Kidd and David Nicholls (Stroud: Sutton, 1998), 1–19.

15. This interpretation is indebted to the arguments of Pierre Bourdieu, *Distinction: A Social Critique of the Judgment of Taste* (Cambridge: Harvard University Press, 1984).

16. Ross McKibbin, *The Ideologies of Class: Social Relations in Britain, 1880–1950* (Oxford: Clarendon, 1990).

17. Penelope Corfield, *Power and the Professions in Britain, 1700–1850* (London: Routledge, 1995).

18. David Cannadine, *The Decline and Fall of the British Aristocracy* (New Haven: Yale University Press, 1990).

19. Charles Webster, *The Health Services Since the War* (London: Her Majesty's Stationery Office, 1996).

20. Noel Annan, *Our Age: The Generation That Made Postwar Britain* (London: Fontana, 1991).

21. Tom Burns, *The BBC: Public Institution and Private World* (London: Macmillan, 1977).

22. Raphael Samuel, "The Workshop of the World: Steam Power and Hand Technology in Mid-Victorian Britain," *History Workshop* 3(Spring 1977): 6–72; Richard Biernacki, *The Fabrication of Labor: Germany and Britain, 1640–1914* (Berkeley: University of California Press, 1995).

23. Charles More, *Skill and the English Working Class* (London: Croom Helm, 1980); Mike Savage and Andrew Miles, *The Remaking of the British Working Class, 1830–1914* (London: Routledge, 1994); Savage, *Class Analysis.*

24. John Garrard and Vivienne Parrott, "Craft, Professional, and Middle-class Identity: Solicitors and Gas Engineers, c. 1850–1914," in Kidd and Nicholls, *The Making of the British Middle Class*, 148–68.

25. On the significance of family interests in British firms, see Alfred Chandler, *Scale and Scope: The Dynamics of Industrial Capitalism* (Cambridge, Mass.: Belknap Press of Harvard University Press, 1990). On family interests in the recruitment of senior managers, see John Quail, "From Personal Patronage to Public School Privilege: Social Closure in the Recruitment of Managers in the United Kingdom from the Late Nineteenth Century to 1930," in Kidd and Nicholls, *The Making of the British Middle Class*, 169–85.

26. Mike Savage et al., *Property, Bureaucracy, and Culture: Middle-class Formation in Contemporary Britain* (London: Routledge, 1992).

27. See, variously, Savage et al., *Property, Bureaucracy, and Culture*; Anthony Stewart, Kenneth Prandy, and Robert Blackburn, *Social Stratification and Occupations* (London: Macmillan, 1980); Colin Mills, "Managerial and Professional Work Histories," in *Social Change and the Middle Classes*, edited by Timothy Butler and Michael Savage (London: UCL Press, 1995), 95–116.

28. Glass, *Social Mobility*. See also the fuller discussion in Savage, *Class Analysis*, ch. 6.

29. Mike Savage, "Career Mobility and Class Formation: British Banking Workers and the Lower Middle Classes," in *Building European Society: Occupational Change and Social Mobility in Europe, 1840–1940*, edited by Andrew Miles and David Vincent (Manchester: Manchester University Press, 1993), 196–216; Anne Witz, *Patriarchy and Professions* (London: Routledge, 1992); Meta Zimmeck, "Marry in Haste, Repent at Leisure: Women, Bureaucracy, and the Post Office, 1870–1920," in *Gender and Bureaucracy*, Sociological Review Monograph, edited by Mike Savage and Anne Witz (Oxford: Blackwell's, 1992), 65–93.

30. Olivier Zunz, *Why the American Century?* (Chicago: University of Chicago Press, 1998).

31. This idea has been explored within regulation theory under the guise of debates about the transition from Fordist to post-Fordist regimes of accumulation; see, for example, Robert Boyer, *The Regulation School: A Critical Introduction* (New York: Columbia University Press, 1990). See also Scott Lash and John Urry, *The End of Organized Capitalism* (Oxford: Polity, 1987) and their discussion of the shift from organized to disorganized capitalism, as well as various debates about the rise of postmodernism. Krishan Kumar, *From Postindustrial to Postmodern Society* (Oxford: Blackwell's, 1995), offers one of the best critical overviews.

32. See the debate in Paul Hirst and Graham Thompson, *Globalization in Question: The International Economy and the Possibility of Governance* (Cambridge: Polity, 1996).

33. Yves Dezaly and David Sugarman, *Professional Competition and Professional Power: Lawyers, Accountants, and the Social Construction of Markets* (London: Routledge, 1995); Nikolas Rose, *Powers of Freedom* (Cambridge: Cambridge University Press 1999).

34. Savage, *Class Analysis*, ch. 3.
35. Howard Gospel, "The Revival of Apprenticeship Training in Britain," *British Journal of Industrial Relations* 36(September 1998): 435–57.
36. Muriel Egerton and Mike Savage, "Age Stratification and Class Formation: A Longitudinal Study of the Social Mobility of Young Men and Women," *Work, Employment, and Society* 14(March 2000): 23–50. See, more generally, Sarah Irwin, *Rites of Passage* (London: UCL Press, 1995).
37. Savage, *Class Analysis*, chs. 3 and 6.
38. Rosemary Crompton and Kate Sanderson, *Gendered Jobs and Social Change* (London: Hutchinson, 1990); Susan Halford, Mike Savage, and Anne Witz, *Gender, Careers, and Organizations* (Basingstoke: Macmillan, 1997).
39. Savage, *Class Analysis*, ch. 3.
40. See Paul Thompson, "Snatching Defeat from the Jaws of Victory: The Last Post of the Old City Financial Elite, 1945–1995," in Kidd and Nicholls, *The Making of the Middle Classes*, 228–46.
41. Katherine Stovel, Mike Savage, and Peter Bearman, "Ascription into Achievement: Career Systems in Lloyds Bank, 1880–1940," *American Journal of Sociology* 102(September 1996): 358–99; Rosemary Crompton, "Women in Banking," *Work, Employment, and Society* 3(June 1989): 141–56.
42. This and subsequent quotes are from a research project I conducted with Susan Halford and Anne Witz, funded by the Economic and Social Research Council (ESRC)(ref. R00023277301); see Susan Halford, Mike Savage, and Anne Witz, *Gender, Careers, and Organizations: Current Developments in Banking, Nursing, and Local Government* (Basingstoke: Macmillan, 1997).
43. Andrew Leyshon and Nigel Thrift, "The Restructuring of the U.K. Financial Services Industry in the 1990s: A Reversal of Fortune?" *Regional Studies* 9(May 1989): 223–41.
44. Paul du Gay, *Consumption and Identity at Work* (London: Sage, 1996).
45. See generally Nikolas Rose, "Government, Authority, and Expertise in Advanced Liberalism," *Economy and Society* 22(August 1993): 283–99.
46. See, for instance, Sarah Cant and Ursula Sharma, "The Reluctant Profession: Homeopathy and the Search for Legitimacy," *Work, Employment, and Society* 9(December 1995): 743–62.
47. Since the early 1980s, accountancy has been the most popular occupational destination for university graduates. Anthony Adonis and Stuart Pollard, in *A Class Act: The Myth of Britain's Classless Society* (London: Penguin, 1997), have shown that graduates of Oxford University, Britain's highest-status university, have become less likely to go into teaching and other kinds of public-sector professionalism and tend to seek employment in the City or in "blue-chip" firms. This trend marks a very radical departure from traditional modes of elite formation.
48. Geoff Evans and Pippa Norris, *Critical Elections: British Parties and Voters in Long-term Perspective* (London: Sage, 1999). See also the papers in Geoff Evans, ed., *The End of Class Politics?* (Oxford: Clarendon, 1999).
49. Anthony Heath and Mike Savage, "Political Alignments Within the Middle Classes, 1972–1989," in Butler and Savage, *Social Change and the Middle Classes*, 275–92.

50. This quote is taken from Mike Savage, Gaynor Bagnall, and Brian Long-hurst, "Ordinary, Ambivalent, and Defensive: Class Identities in the Northwest of England," *Sociology* (August 2001).
51. Stuart Laing, *Representations of Working-class Life, 1957–1964* (Basingstoke: Macmillan, 1986).
52. Examples of British soap operas and thrillers depicting these middle-class occupations include *Peak Practice, Casualty, This Life,* and *Hope and Glory.*
53. Examples include *The Royle Family* and the perennially popular "working-class" soap operas *Coronation Street* and *Brookside.*

# 3

# The Middle Classes in France: Social and Political Functions of Semantic Pluralism from 1870 to 2000

## Christophe Charle

In French, the term "classes moyennes" (middle classes) is semantically peculiar. In its commonly used plural form, the term serves to unite a multiplicity of middle classes. This does not hold true in other languages. For instance, in English the singular and plural forms have rival meanings, depending on the context, while in German (Mittelstand, Kleinbürgertum) the singular form is dominant. The French singular form (classe moyenne) was also dominant during the first half of the nineteenth century, when it was generally equivalent to the notion of "bourgeoisie." This term also referred to the "grande bourgeoisie," a concept similar to the original use of "middle class" in Great Britain to refer to the new industrial and economic bourgeoisie (denied suffrage until 1832), as opposed to the oligarchy of the gentry and the nobility.[1]

The special use of the term "middle classes" has a more complex significance and function. Through a study combining an analysis of the representation and variable significance of the term in light of the major social changes that have occurred since the last third of the nineteenth century, I defend the following theses:

- The plural form was particularly suited to, and even necessary in, a country where the middle classes held greater sway than elsewhere. Their influence was a result of the Third Republic's parliamentary democracy and unique balance of powers. Because of its ambiguity, this form of government facilitated consensus and tacitly contained several of the disparate elements of the "republican compromise": individualism, faith in social mobility and fluidity, attachment to small property (industrial, rural, and commercial), and hostility toward the privileged.

- Compared with English or German social dynamics, the French social dynamic accentuates (at least in its mythified representations) aspiration toward equality—especially equality of opportunity. Such aspiration is manifested through a well-known system of upward mobility in recognized channels. The term "middle classes" asserts and reifies this equality.[2]

During periods of uncertainty, the discourse surrounding the term "middle classes" has been more concrete and precise. This was the case during the interwar period and at the end of the 1950s, when France faced rapid social change. Recently, globalization has called into question the accomplishments of the new middle classes during the "Thirty Glorious Years." During periods of prosperity and widening social mobility (the 1960s and 1970s, for instance), we return to vague and ambiguous definitions. To map out these cycles, I discuss three distinct periods of time: (1) the beginning of the Third Republic, when the modern sense of the plural form was defined; (2) the period of growing corporatism (roughly 1900 to 1970), when the management of political crises required multiple meanings of the term "middle class"; and (3) the period since the 1970s, when the changing economic climate, the growing demand for access to secondary and higher education, and the increasing number of women in senior positions have once again raised sensitive social and political questions regarding the middle classes, which are trapped within increasingly dated rhetoric.

The old definition of the middle class persists despite the fact that today's French society has little in common with that of the interwar years. The current public debates are marked by confusion and an inability to produce a new common project that is neither nostalgic nor limited to a particular segment of society.

## The Middle Classes and the Republic: 1870 to 1900

*The New Social Strata*

A lexicographical study based in the transitional period between 1869 and 1872 shows that the term "middle classes" in the sense of "bourgeoisie" disappeared with the appearance of an "intermediate class" linking the bourgeoisie and the common people.

In 1870 the economist Paul Leroy-Beaulieu, heir to the great liberal Orleanist bourgeoisie, wrote that "the bourgeoisie or middle class has two qualities that make it the pivotal point of society: it carries the spirit of tradition and the spirit of initiative."[3] A year earlier, the conservative Count of Falloux recognized the multiplicity of middle-class groups, writing that "the advent of the middle or popular classes is simply logical."[4] Falloux foreshadowed the famous formula that Léon Gambetta would espouse on September 26, 1872, in his discourse in Grenoble on the "new social strata." As the head of the Republican Party, Gambetta proposed a scheme to justify the appointment of a new political staff who would reflect the political power of the intermediate groups:

> Haven't we seen the workers of the cities and the country (this working world that owns the future) make their entry into political affairs? Is this not the characteristic warning that the country—after having tried many forms of government—wants to charge a different social group with the project of experimenting upon the republican form. . . . Indeed! I have a premonition, I feel, I announce the arrival and the presence, within the political sphere, of a new social formation . . . which has been in power for the past eighteen months, and which is surely far from falling inferior to its predecessors.[5]

Gambetta maintained that classes no longer existed in a democracy; thus, there were neither middle classes nor any other classes (working or upper class). The only distinguishing characteristic of this broad group was that its members were workers, a fact that placed them in opposition to the notables and the rich who had previously held power. In this view, Gambetta's "workers" had much the same significance as the old singular term "middle class," defined simply as the group between the nobility and the common people. What was new was the emphasis on individual merit rather than on property or heredity, and on merit demonstrated by talent, academic credentials, economy, and civic engagement. As Gambetta put it: "Where do we see, aside from in Democracy, the economy resulting in assuring the future generations, children, relatives, and even your factory workers and employees an education, without which one is useless in this nineteenth-century world, where intelligence and science are allpowerful?"[6]

By assigning the new republican trilogy (work, economy, education) not only to the new social strata of the middle classes but also to its employees, Gambetta indicates that he had a very clear notion that his audience was broad and included owners of small businesses, small-scale shopkeepers, and craftsmen, all of whom could have had employees.

This new formulation gained its strength from its close ties with the first republican reforms: educational reform, freedom of the press, development of regional public office, and the democratization of the corps of noncommissioned officers and officers.[7] The image of a mobile society also corresponded to a number of transformations described by social historians: the growth of intermediate categories (employers, employees, professionals); the diminution of the poorest categories of the peasant society; and professional mobility accelerated by the diffusion of instruction and networks based on merit.[8] This discourse was optimistic in tone, in direct contrast to middle-class attitudes during the era of the notables or the attitudes of the upper classes or popular classes, which were often defensive or pessimistic. Gambetta's comments on the virtues of the middle classes set the tone for a perspective that would last until the 1950s.[9]

With the power of the most revolutionary elements in the working class checked for fifteen years by the collapse of the Commune, the moderate republicans shored up their power base in their struggle against the heirs of the notables by formulating this new broad thematic of the middle classes. They based it on a catch-all strategy—attracting a comprehensive electoral body from otherwise rather diverse milieus. The republican peasantry of the east and southeast, the popular classes of the large cities, the new wage-earning classes, elements of the bourgeoisie, and the most open-minded professionals all found common ground in this formulation.[10]

### The Challenge of Socialism and French Specificity in Europe

After 1885, the Republicans, increasingly tied up in scandals, faced attacks from both the extreme left and the extreme right and were subjected to the same criticism leveled at their Orleanist predecessors. In 1840 the socialists and legitimists had denounced the bourgeois oligarchy, and between 1885 and 1895 the literary pamphleteers would take out their anger on the bourgeois republic and the new feudality of the business republic.[11] For socialists like Jean Jaurès, these new charges highlighted the social decline of the "classe moyenne." His return to the use of the singular form has a militant connotation, in contrast to the assuaging tone of the plural. From his vantage point, the distinctions between groups that could be classified as middle class were insignificant:

French society, and European society in general are composed of three classes: the proletariat, the middle class and the capitalist class. These three classes communicate among themselves through intermediaries; they are perfectly distinct from one another. . . . The middle class is composed of all those who, having a limited amount of capital, live much less off this capital than off the activities they do to raise the capital. Within this class, there are small-scale entrepreneurs, small shopkeepers, small-scale industrialists, and store-owners who have established themselves and who have loyal customers. . . . The middle class still includes all the farming landowners that have a large enough domain in which to live with their families.[12]

With observations similar to Gambetta's, Jaurès announced not the coming of the new social classes, but a "continuous oppression of the middle class by the capitalist class" and the new oligarchy, which had been appropriated by the Republic.[13]

In Belgium and Germany, a negative discourse developed for the same reasons, but in a different political and social context.[14] It is important to note that in these contexts a unified terminology was used ("petite bourgeoisie" in Belgium, "Mittelstand" in Germany), homologous to that used by the other political groups in conflict. In Germany, the absence of a plural form of "Mittelstand" and the growing diversity of the groups defined by this term obliged commentators to introduce qualitative distinctions, such as "old" and "new" Mittelstand. The former term covered the independent middle class, which included small-business owners, small-scale shopkeepers, and craftsmen. The latter term encompassed the wage-earning middle class (employees). This classification resisted the social-democratic representation that turned the bourgeoisie into a minority group faced with a growing working class.[15]

The French plural form, used for political ends by Gambetta, can be ascribed to the weak organization of social groups in France, both the middle classes themselves and other classes. At the end of the nineteenth century, neither the employers nor the working class nor the peasantry formed a unified group, and none of their discourses about class carried the degree of legitimacy or diffusion needed to qualify as political discourse. In a society based on universal suffrage and individual liberty, political discourse is the only way to describe and define the social world and to secure transactions between groups. As Gambetta was well aware, he was compelled not only to be universalistic but to transcend classes simply for electoral reasons.

These discursive constraints are accentuated in France by the choice of district-based suffrage, which tends to undercut the power of individual groups. In such a system, the constituent elements of modern industrial society are mostly underrepresented, except in certain parts of the large cities. There are few places in fact where there are enough peasants, workers, or intermediate groups to mobilize in favor of a candidate and ensure his election.

Accordingly, what some republicans or radicals justify as a so-called objective analysis of French society is in fact a rationalization of their electoral strategies. Appealing to the middle classes broadly defined offers all those who do not speak the vocabulary of a unified class a common identity. This label, however, imposes none but the most minimal obligations: to vote rather than organize, and to choose among political programs elaborated by others rather than devise a rigorous and coherent strategy that might exert decisive influence.

## Between Corporatism and Politicization: 1900 to 1970

As the twentieth century advanced, electoral outcomes shifted often enough in France to give a working space to all voters and groups uncertain about their will and their identities—a characterization particularly appropriate to the plural form "middle classes"—that was more efficient and fluid than the cumbrous system of pressure groups found in other countries. Under such systems, the discourse on the middle class, or the petite bourgeoisie, is engaged much more clearly in classic social conflict. At the same time, the plural form remained dominant during this period because the political elites (mainly recruited from the professions) adopted it. These elites, descended from those whose professional skills (rather than wealth) had made them eligible for office (the "capacités" of the July Monarchy), and the middle classes shared in many respects a common worldview. Both groups were wary about the state, valued individualism, and devoted themselves to personal interests.[16]

Between the end of the nineteenth century and the 1970s, the term "middle classes" would again find currency and convey multiple and ambiguous identities. The same discourses and social realities returned, not because the realities of the Republican period persisted, but because the semantic plural form authorized a culture of ambiguity and constant adaptability.

### Generalized Corporatism

One could argue that the shifting electoral results that characterized most of the century were primarily an expression of the objective situation of the middle classes and their passage through favorable or unfavorable times, as social and political circumstances dictated. What is impressive is the persistence of this formulation despite social transformation far more rapid than that of the nineteenth century. According to the census results, the percentage of employers in industry and commerce (mostly small-business owners) declined by less than 2 percent between 1886 and 1931 (from 13.9 percent to 12 percent of the active male population), but then dropped by 5 percent between 1936 and 1982 (from 13.2 percent to 8.2 percent).[17] Theorists, ideologists, and defenders of the petite bourgeoisie, as well as socialist analysts and centrist political figures, continue to adhere to the vocabulary of the late nineteenth century to describe the intermediate categories, even though these groups were affected by extensive socioprofessional change. It is during this period that the independent middle classes gave up their place of privilege to the wage-earning middle classes; that women entered the intermediate professions in large numbers; and that the family, at the core of the middle classes in the nineteenth century, experienced its strongest shock. It is also a period in which the rising academic accomplishment of all classes made rigid classification difficult.[18]

The paradox is less severe than it appears to be when we note that it was precisely the diversity and multiplicity of the middle-class groups (a classification that varies with time) that made adherence to the republican terminology a logical course of action. Unlike the alternative socialist or communist rhetoric, based on a social vision of the ultimate oneness of each class (the working class, the bourgeoisie, the petite bourgeoisie, the middle class), only a loose pluralist terminology offers a vision of a social world adapted to groups that do not recognize themselves within it and feel they are arbitrarily grouped together. The term "middle classes" conveys much of its original heritage—the Gambetta-inspired republicanism that arose from the perception of an independent lower-middle class composed of craftsmen, merchants, small-scale landowners, and manufacturers.[19] The term is also marked by its indirect heritage—a liberal centrist vision favored by old or new professionals and other technicians who want to express their social autonomy.[20]

*Contrasting Political Customs*

The term "middle classes" is highly adaptable. It can be used by the center Left as part of a republican-inspired defense against "upper-class" privilege.[21] It can also be used by the center Right in the corporatist defense against the state, downward mobility, and the threat of the working class.[22] Not inclined to organize themselves, the middle classes of the interwar period preferred to follow the party that best expressed their diverse interests. The rhetoric of the middle classes equally suited alliances with the Left and with the Right. These alliances were always justified as in the interest of the middle classes, or the "average Frenchman." Two prominent leaders, Édouard Herriot and Édouard Daladier, were masters of this type of discourse.[23]

The left-wing alliance at the time of the Popular Front needed to attach the middle classes to the Left to combat the fascist threat. According to contemporary analyses, the goal was to prevent the middle classes from slipping toward the extreme right, as they had done in Germany.[24] The deflation and austerity measures passed by the right-wing government made it possible to rally the middle classes to the Socialist and Communist Left. Thus, on June 18, 1935, the primary promoter of the alliance, Daladier, categorized his support of the Popular Front under the auspices of a "fraternal accord between the middle classes and the proletariat in the republican battle."[25] His party was reputed to be the representative of the middle classes, whereas the Socialist and Communist Parties of the proletariat. The alliance was first and foremost promoted as a political defense of the Republic that transcended class interests.

The other political parties—including the dissident neo-Socialists, the center Right parties, and even the Communist Party, which proposed a moderate program to the SFIO (the Socialist Party) to facilitate the support of the radicals—also sought to curry favor from middle-class groups before the election of 1936.[26] Just after an electoral victory that revealed weakness among the radicals and a muted enthusiasm among SFIO voters, a Socialist representative took the initiative to found a "parliamentary defense group" for small and mid-size businesses. Daladier united the left-wing and right-wing representatives and attempted to bring back into balance governmental policies that, since the Matignon Accords, had essentially been used to benefit the workers and, to a lesser degree, the peasants. In October 1936, this initiative was superseded, outside of Parliament, by the founding of a defense league for the middle classes. This league would be the first in a long series of associations designed to pressure the right wing of the majority. The Communists did not stop there: they took advantage of their nonparticipation to lay out a series of bills favoring the middle classes, which they had formerly spoken of disdainfully as the "petite bourgeoisie."[27]

Left-wing activism in all domains, however, had the unintended effect of alarming the middle-class associations, which grew increasingly hostile to the Popular Front between October 1936 and July 1937. When Popular Front social policies undermined the prosperity of the middle class, its spokesmen were ready to switch allegiance, though without changing the essential terms they used to describe themselves. They adopted the tone of complaint that the associations used from 1936 to 1937 and sometimes assumed leadership of those associations. Thus, during their 1937 assembly, certain "radicals" asked themselves, in the words of Salomon Hirsch at the Congress of Biarritz:

> Will we allow the slow disappearance of the small French business owners whose economic spirit, whose bitter and unremitting labor, and whose moderate and calm mentality provided the moral stability and the social equilibrium of the country? Or, as of now, is it admitted that between the working class, represented by the CGT and the tycoons of commerce and industry, of which the General Confederation of French Production is representative, there is no more room for the small-business owners or for the craftsmen who represent infinitely more laborers and employees than the big bosses.[28]

Thus, the middle classes, which used the plural term as an expression of their weakness and their independence, saw themselves victimized by two unified class juggernauts.

## The Weight of Words

It is not by chance that the climax of the realist political discourse coincided with the Fourth Republic, a system based on proportional representation.[29] Such a voting system encourages the formation of associations directly from the social groups that intervene in the political sphere. This process is illustrated by the success of the CGPME, which represented small-business owners in the 1951 elections, and by the rapid growth and relative electoral success of the Poujade movement (1953 to 1956).[30] That movement clearly presented itself as an expression of the merchants, artisans, and independent middle classes who were threatened by the modernization of the economy. This political organization emerged directly from the UDCA, its professional association.[31]

In returning to a system based on a majority of the popular vote by district, the Fifth Republic favored the formation of coalitions among disparate groups. It cultivated an increasingly unified discourse in which the middle classes, as most broadly defined, could take back their conciliatory role. This occurred first on the right, within the Gaullist movement. Charles de Gaulle and his supporters elevated the notion of national union (rassemblement), which they cherished over class concerns. A new emphasis on coalition building was also apparent in the center, with the presidency of Valéry Giscard d'Estaing, and on the left, with the renovation of the Socialist Party after 1971.[32]

These coalitions endowed themselves with strong corporate organizations capable of influencing the new balance of powers in the technocratic state. Under the Third Republic, parliamentary lobbies promoted middle-class interests in the political sphere, and durable autonomous organizations were viewed as superfluous, except in times of crisis. As Patrick Fridenson (this volume) explains, since the Liberation the middle classes had practiced modes of collective action similar to those of the wage-earners within the framework of the emerging French welfare state. The peasant confederations represented the rural middle bourgeoisie.[33] The CGPME defended small-business owners at least as much against big business as against the government. It attempted regularly to form large alliances of the different middle classes and to pressure political candidates.[34] The federations of civil servants and teachers succeeded, at least until the 1970s, in unionizing a greater percentage of wage-earners than the worker unions.[35] The federations of engineers and managers monitored the diverse financial structures (retirement funds, medical insurance, and so on) associated with the establishment of a welfare state, while the medical unions and the Order of Doctors had a direct stake in the permanency of Social Security and in the control of the quota system at the start of their studies that guaranteed them social status and stable revenue.[36]

## The 1970s to the Present: Middle Classes and Political Crisis

Striking a balance between the social and political domains has become a higher priority since the end of the 1970s. This period has witnessed the decline of Marxism, even within the most left-wing factions of the political spectrum. It has also seen the weakening of all types of unions with the rise of underemployment and the demographic decline of certain segments of the middle classes. It follows that the question of the place and future of the middle classes has come once again to the forefront of political debate.

The growing instability resulting from shifts in electoral outcomes (1981, 1986, 1988, 1993, 1995, 1997) marks the dissatisfaction of increasingly numerous factions of voters. This mood is in marked contrast to the situation at the beginning of the Fifth Republic. The Fifth Republic was built on two inverse principles: continuity (due to the division of opposition parties) and an absence of opposition between the president of the Republic and the Parliament (due to the existence of a dominant political formation, the Gaullist Party). This stability was also facilitated by the prosperity that coincided with the Republic's years of strong expansion under de Gaulle and Pompidou (1958 to 1974). It allowed the most serious conflicts to be defused through a redistribution of benefits.

*Dual Failure: From Guizot-Giscard to . . .*

Political scientists interpreted the first reflux of Gaullism after Pompidou's death as a reflection of the desire to liberate the wage-earning middle classes from an over-interventionist state, a promise that seemed to take shape in the beginning of Giscard d'Estaing's seven-year term. With a view to the 1978 elections, the recently elected president wrote in his book:

> The current evolution, far from driving toward the face-to-face meeting of two strongly contrasted and antagonistic classes, the bourgeoisie and the proletariat, translates into the expansion of an immense, shadily outlined central group, which possesses the aptitude, by its exceptionally rapid numeric expansion, by its ties with every other category of society, by its open quality to which it largely offers access, and by its modern values, to progressively and pacifically integrate the entire French society in itself.[37]

Although written in 1976—two years after the start of economic difficulties—this analysis nevertheless reflects the optimism of the Thirty Glorious Years and of the technocratic vision dominant in the 1960s and 1970s, when France was fascinated by the American model of the middle class.[38] Still believing that they were facing a short-term crisis, the new president and his team were searching above all to ease the difficulties of the most fragile groups, which included the workers as well as the immigrants in the least competitive sectors. The immigrants were encouraged to return to their countries of origin. This plan to advance the middle classes (a "central group," to use a modern term that emphasizes their unity)[39] is a departure from the idea of a "France divided in two," as it was conceptualized in the era of the "union of the Left," with its strongly neo-Marxist common plan of government. As it turned out, the two coalitions based their grouping strategies on equally fallacious diagnoses. The middle classes, as demonstrated by all sociological inquiries, certainly formed a growing electoral base for the Gaullist, centrist, and Socialist parties, but they remained particularly divided along many lines that coincided with traditional Left-Right divisions.[40] Thus, certain societal reforms, like the law permitting abortion, were finally achieved when an alliance between leftists and post-1968 middle-class liberals overcame a party of the conservative majority, which is always attached to those among the traditional middle classes who are Catholic or particularly strong advocates of familial values.

### . . . to Mitterrand-Gambetta

The spectacular rise to prominence of the Socialist Party after 1971 rested heavily on these proliferating social groups[41] that were aligned with neither traditionally left-wing parties nor any of those on the right. The center had been absorbed by the conservative majority in the elections of Pompidou and Giscard d'Estaing.

This transformation of the discourse and the political configuration, out of sync with the transformations of social structures (what Henri Mendras called "the Second French Revolution"), occurred over a paradox. The rejuvenated Socialist Party returned to Marxism to justify its alliance with the Communist Party, whose support was needed to overcome the barriers associated with the voting system of the Fifth Republic. In the process, the Socialist Party became a party of the wage-earning middle classes and of the superior fringe of the popular classes.[42] The notion of a "Front of the Wage-Earning Class," a phrase large and vague enough to reconcile old and new Socialist voters, played the same role as the "new social strata" envisioned by Gambetta. The denunciation of "monopolies" (common in Communist discourse, though more often associated with the working class) was in effect an allusion to the traditional mythology of the Left since the 1880s, as well as that of the Popular Front, which saw itself uniting the common people against the privileged "two-hundred families."[43]

Nevertheless, the analogy with the "republican Republic" of the 1880s quickly encountered limits. The success of 1981 was very short-lived. In three years the fissures led to a rupture between Socialist and Communist headquarters. The electoral body of the united Left was demobilized. The new voters of the Left returned to the Right, while the ensuing confusion and dissatisfaction brought on an outburst of extreme right-wing activity in 1983 and 1984.[44] To explain these political difficulties, the Left invoked external factors: international economic constraints limiting its margin of action; American hostility toward Communist ministers; the domination of the media by large capitalist interests; and the inequalities of political representation induced by different voting systems. It could go no further in its self-analysis, however, since its directors had interpreted the 1981 success as a mandate for change in society.

In fact, the fraction of voters (notably from the middle classes) who tipped the balance in favor of Mitterrand on May 10, 1981, voted against an incumbent president finishing a term because he had not held to his promises and had underestimated the crisis. According to a poll taken in August 1981, 61 percent of small-business owners and craftsmen and 60 percent of mid-size business managers disapproved of Giscard d'Estaing's agenda.[45] Seven years of economic difficulties and the failure of the economic policies meant to address them began to produce political effects that resembled those of the 1930s: the rise of corporatism, the deregulation of social-protection mechanisms while unemployment was on the rise, and loss of faith in the technocratic elites in power. In the short run, social discomfort facilitated the change in the party in power, but immediately afterward it played against the alliance that claimed to be the incarnation of the Left. As unemployment progressed during the 1970s, voters increasingly favored the Left, but ultimately in the 1980s they never subscribed to a united Left. Social groups split between those exposed to unemployment and declassification and those protected from underemployment by their status.

Rather than easing these schisms, the measures taken during the first months of Mitterrand's presidency reinforced them. Nationalization, justified by the struggle against unemployment and the goal of preserving national independence, affected the most concentrated sectors. Large businesses generally were the most generous with their employees in matters of employment, working conditions, and compensation for dismissal. Employees of the small and mid-size businesses (particularly women and youths), on the other hand, benefited only from the reevaluation of the SMIC (minimum wage) and the shortened workday (by one hour). This latter group was hit hard by the economic errors of the first years of leftist power and, later, by the un-pegging of wages and prices designed to prepare the way for a European monetary union and reduce exterior deficits.

Under pressure from the traditional middle classes, the government withdrew its plan to nationalize private education in 1984. This move had a doubly negative effect. First, the proposal itself led to the mobilization of the independent and right-oriented middle classes—those most attached to the old style of education—who, with the support of the opposition, won their first great political success since February 6, 1934. Second, the retreat from this initiative embittered the teachers' corps, one of the pillars of the Socialist electoral body and a breeding ground of the Socialist Party[46]—that is to say, a segment of the middle classes that had progressed substantially in strength and in societal importance during the Thirty Glorious Years and had made a substantial contribution to the Socialist success of 1981.[47] The Left thus paid, by its miscues, for the fragility of its ideological and political bases. It also paid for its unrealistic expectation that the interests of the classes it hoped to unite would themselves converge. In fact, their efforts only exacerbated the many existing internal conflicts.

The Right has had a similar experience. Witness the persistent vulnerability of the conservatives in power, their growing divisions, and the continuous rise during the 1990s of the extreme Right, which attracted a growing number of new voters as well as older right-wing and even left-wing voters. The Right's relative success in the 1986 legislative elections was undermined by the rise of the student movement of November 1986. The measures that were meant to undo the policies put in place by the Left, such as the suppression of taxes on large fortunes and the attribution of nationalized societies to groups close to power, backfired and led to the Right's complete failure in 1988.

### Political Crisis, Social Crisis, and the Crisis of the Middle Classes

Understanding this dual process of rapid and repeated rejection of the two main political camps returns us to our general interpretive scheme. Political discourse in France for more than ten years now has been increasingly unable to find an inclusive rhetoric that permits a durable alliance of the privileged classes, the middle classes, and the segments of the popular classes, whether on the left or the right. This sort of alliance characterized the stable era of the Fifth Republic. Without such a collective representation, which allowed the mobilization of its members for major elections, a majority system with multiple political parties, like that in France, cannot function.

Of all the comparable countries in Europe, France is without doubt the one whose political model is most dysfunctional. It holds to an underlying division that its politicians, themselves either uncertain of their options or simply prone to tactical ambiguity, are not able to control coherently. The segment of the middle classes that support a neoliberal,[48] non-interventionist option are in fact accustomed to being supported by the state in a way that ensures their social and academic permanence. This situation goes back, not to the Liberation, as it is often said, but to the end of the nineteenth century. Such protectionism characterized efforts to preserve small businesses and small farms in the face of international competition during the 1890s, the politics of development and academic unification during the past century, the formation of a European agricultural market, and the expansion of medical insurance since the Liberation.[49]

When French right-wing leaders followed Margaret Thatcher's example and in 1986 applied a true neoliberal, non-interventionist political program, they found themselves opposed not only by the established interests of the rather traditionally left-oriented middle classes tied to the state but also, to their surprise, by a large fraction of the rather right-oriented middle classes of the private sector, and even by certain elites close to the state.[50] In fact, the growing perception by all members of the middle classes of the importance of state-controlled education doomed efforts to reform the high schools and universities. In the reduced social circumstances caused by the unemployment of the 1980s and 1990s, they feared that any change of rules would lead to leveling, loss of status, or exclusion of their children in the future.[51]

The laboriously reached compromise of the Fifth Republic on private education reflected the contradictions within the middle classes that were so difficult to incorporate into any ideological agenda. The faction of the middle classes that is hostile to too much state intervention in education and uses private education in a preferential manner to educate its children plays on both sides of the issue. This faction takes advantage of an education imbued with its moral and social values without having to pay the true price because that education is largely subsidized.[52] On the other side are the segments of the middle classes attached to public education. Their children are overrepresented in the literary and legal curricula and attend the universities where all neoliberal attempts to limit government's role have been blocked.

For similar reasons, the middle classes abandoned many social projects, refusing to foot the bill. The rising level of the social costs associated with the underemployment crisis could not be met by the left-wing governments for one fundamental reason: the French Left does not have at its disposal the modes of social mobilization inherent in strong and united unions and an appealing, broad-based party ideology.[53] After the reform attempts of 1981, the Left was once again stymied by exterior constraints (particularly the dictates of European free trade). In the end, it charged the fraction of the middle classes that traditionally supported it with the cost of supporting the most fragile elements of society. As a result, these classes, longtime victims of unemployment and deteriorating working conditions,[54] no longer provide anything but intermittent electoral support for the Left. This lack of support has been compounded by the Communist Party's diminished influence, the rise of abstention from voting in the popular strata, the younger generation's disinterest in politics, and the growing appeal of the extreme Right in certain regions and neighborhoods where the low standard of living and broken promises promote xenophobic demagogy. In 1993 the definitive electoral defeat of the Left resulted from the growing discontent among the middle classes tied to the state. These individuals were weary of paying the increasing cost of social measures designed to combat unemployment and, among blue-collar workers, fed up with inefficient politics that catered to contradictory interests without satisfying anyone.[55] The Right, during its unexpected defeat of 1997, experienced the same poor luck for partly similar reasons.

## An End to the Discourse on National Reunion

The inability to find a consensual discourse and a coherent strategy about and for the middle classes is understandable. These classes are marked by critical contradictions that make it impossible to employ the strategies based on the rhetoric of balance and ambiguity that have served for over a century. It is even more unfortunate that the presidential election is undermined by this problem. The goal would be to find a rhetoric that surmounts the antagonisms between the diverse segments of the middle classes without antagonizing more than a small fraction of the popular classes or the privileged classes. This is what must be done if a candidate is to aspire to be the president of all French people. It is necessary, for example, to promise both lower taxes (since the middle classes pay the most income tax and have the least effective means of escaping controls) and more state intervention.

During the presidential election of 1995, it seemed that a double negative vote prevailed over a positive vote: those who supported the Socialist Lionel Jospin in the second round did so to knock out the competition, Jacques Chirac. During the first round, by contrast, nearly half of the voters on the Left had opted for other leftist candidates. Similarly, on the Right Chirac managed to defeat his rival, Prime Minister Edouard Balladur. Chirac's demagogic discourse on social divisions and his critique of technocrats allowed him to recoup voters on the right who were dissatisfied with the measures that had been taken by Balladur. Because of both his existing responsibilities and his personal technocratic tendencies, the outgoing prime minister could not join in the already surreal critique of technocracy. At the same time, Chirac collected more votes among young voters, many of whom were equipped with good academic training but nervous about their future considering the diminution of job prospects that affected graduates during this period.[56] They voted not so much for Chirac as against Jospin. This phenomenon of negative votes is even more concentrated in the popular classes than in the middle classes tied to the state. Despite everything, these middle classes remain more faithful to the Left because they are wary of the supposedly liberal Right and because any Socialist government would at least augment public employment, of which they would be the first beneficiaries.[57]

Far from finding a consensual magic formula, the French political discourse on society (outside of elections) is increasingly marked by an obsession with unemployment, the risk of France losing status as international competition accelerates, the deepening income inequality within the framework encouraged by the "new economy" and internationalization, and the unequal distribution of sacrifices by age cohort and sex. The political discourse is dominated by a rhetoric of extremes that recalls, whether in academic or impoverished populist form, the primitive Marxist-leftist themes and populist currents of the Right in the 1930s. Both the employed and the unemployed engage in this discourse.[58] The middle classes, lacking distinct social boundaries and in search of social mobility, have found no place in this rhetorical construction. They simply claim that they are becoming an endangered species. Insurmountable tension has resulted between the old rhetoric of inclusiveness, necessary for the presidential election, and the new rhetoric of differences, used mostly for territorial legislative or European elections. As a result of these constant oscillations, political discourse has lost credibility.

## Conclusion

Today in France what we can call the "crisis of the middle classes" is perhaps above all a recognition that the hundred-year-old republican rhetoric is no longer effective. This rhetoric withstood fluctuations in the political climate because, unlike in other countries, it could be adjusted to fit the particularly diverse and fluid middle classes and because regional differences were strong until the 1960s. This allowed for a large margin of political maneuvering and the manipulation of the middle classes through contradictory messages. The construction of the welfare state, the opening of France to the world, and all the social changes of the past thirty years have reinforced the national character of these social divisions and the interdependence of sectional politics. This interdependence and the shrinkage of maneuvering room for France's traditional national state diminished the credibility of the old dual discourses on the middle classes and society in general. The antagonism between the two types of government and the two approaches to managing the crisis of the welfare state since the 1980s (the Anglo-American, neoliberal version and the toned-down, Nordic, social-democratic version) is felt among all political, administrative, and intellectual elites[59] and among all social classes.[60]

We have thus produced a society defined by multiple antagonisms, frequent elections, and a rhetoric of mutual fear. The nineteenth-century values of the middle classes (work, economy, the cult of individual entrepreneurship), as well as those of the republican, Gambetta-inspired model (instruction, solidarity, promotion), were perpetuated by the school system on all social levels.[61] To reconcile these two sets of values in a coherent plan, today's politicians need to find an inclusive, mobilizing, and universalistic discourse like the Gaullist or republican platforms. However, confronted with globalization, neither the old cult of the nation nor the weakly supported movement for a unified Europe have thus far succeeded in accomplishing this goal.[62] There is little hope of doing so in the short term in light of the aging and squabbling of the political class. Nevertheless, the new growth and improvement in the job market hold out hope that politicians may yet find a new agenda for the twenty-first century.

## Acronyms

CGT: Confédération générale du travail (the main workers' trade union)

CGPME: Confédération générale des petites et moyennes entreprises (general confederation of small and mid-sized entrepreneurs)

SFIO: Section française de l'Internationale ouvrière (affiliated with the Socialist Party)

SMIC: salaire minimum interprofessionnel de croissance (minimum wage)

UDCA: Union de défense des commerçants et artisans (Union for the Defense of Shopkeepers and Master Artisans)

---

Translated from the French by Alicia Fagen.

## Notes

1. See Savage (this volume) for a full discussion of middle-class-ness in Great Britain. See also Eric Hobsbawm, "The Example of the English Middle Class," in *Bourgeois Society in Nineteenth-Century Europe*, ed-

ited by Jürgen Kocka and Allan Mitchell (Oxford: Providence, 1993),
127–50; Werner Conze, "Mittelstand," in *Geschichtliche Grundbegriffe*,
vol. 4, edited by Otto Bruner, Werner Conze, and Reinhart Koselleck
(Stuttgart: Klett, 1984), 49–92; Désirée Nisard, *Les classes moyennes en
Angleterre et la bourgeoisie en France* (Paris: Lévy, 1850).

2. Christophe Charle, *A Social History of France in the Nineteenth Century* (Oxford: Berg, 1993).

3. Paul Leroy-Beaulieu, *La question ouvrière au XIXème siècle* (Paris:
Charpentier, 1872), 242. Originally published as Paul Leroy-Beaulieu,
"La question ouvrière au XIXè siècle: IV Le rôle de la bourgeoisie dans la
production," *Revue des deux mondes* (July 15, 1870): 451–76, quoted in
Jean Dubois, *Le vocabulaire politique et social en France de 1869 à 1872*
(Paris: Larousse, 1962), 252.

4. Comte Armand de Falloux, *Des élections prochaines* (Paris, 1869), 15,
quoted in Dubois, *Le vocabulaire politique et social en France*, 19.

5. Léon Gambetta, "Discours de Grenoble, 26 septembre 1872," in *Discours et plaidoyers politiques*, vol. 3 (Paris: Charpentier, 1880), 88–120.

6. Léon Gambetta, "Discours de Chambéry, 22 septembre 1872," in *Discours et plaidoyers politiques*, 39.

7. Marc Martin, *Médias et journalistes de la République* (Paris: O. Jacob,
1996); William Serman, *Les Officiers français dans la nation, 1848–1914*
(Paris: Aubier, 1982); Jean-Noël Luc and Alain Barbé, *Des normaliens:
Histoire de l'École normale supérieure de Saint-Cloud* (Paris: Fondation
nationale des sciences politiques, 1982); Jean-Pierre Briand and Jean-
Michel Chapoulie, *Les collèges du peuple: Histoire de l'enseignement
primaire supérieur* (Paris: Belin, 1992); Jean-François Chanet, *L'école ré-
publicaine et les petites patries* (Paris: Aubier, 1996).

8. Charle, *Social History of France*; Olivier Marchand and Claude Thélot,
*Deux siècles de travail en France*, rev. ed. (Paris: Nathan, 1997); Jacques
Dupâquier and Denis Kessler, eds., *La société française au XIXè siècle:
Tradition, transition, transformations* (Paris: Fayard, 1992).

9. Sylvie Guillaume, *La confédération générale des petites et moyennes entreprises: son histoire, son combat, un autre syndicalisme, 1944–1978* (Bordeaux: Presses universitaires de Bordeaux, 1987).

10. Philip Nord, *The Republican Moment: Struggles for Democracy in Nineteenth Century France* (Cambridge, Mass.: Harvard University Press,
1995).

11. Jean Garrigues, *La république des hommes d'affaires* (Paris: Aubier,
1997); Zeev Sternhell, *La droite révolutionnaire, 1885–1914: Les ori-
gines françaises du fascisme*, rev. ed. (Paris: Éditions du Seuil, 1984).

12. Jean Jaurès, *Études socialistes* (Paris: Rieder, 1931), 14–15. Originally
published as "La classe moyenne," *La dépêche de Toulouse*, March 3,
1889.

13. Jaurès, *Études socialistes* (March 10, 1889), 17.

14. David Blackbourn, "Between Resignation and Volatility: The German
Petty Bourgeoisie in the Nineteenth Century," in *Populists and Patri-
cians*, edited by David Blackbourn (London: Allen and Unwin, 1987),
84–113; Geoffrey Crossick and Heinz-Gerhard Haupt, *The Petite Bourgeoisie in Europe, 1780–1914: Enterprise, Family, and Independence*
(London: Routledge, 1995); Geoffrey Crossick, "Formation ou invention
des 'classes moyennes'?: Une analyse comparée: Belgique-France-

Grande-Bretagne (1880–1914)," *Revue belge d'histoire contemporaine* 26(3–4, 1996): 105–34; Ginette Kurgan van Hentenryk and Serge Jaumain, *Aux frontières des classes moyennes: La petite bourgeoisie belge avant 1914* (Bruxelles: Éditions de l'Université de Bruxelles, 1992).

15. Geoff Eley, *Reshaping the German Right: Radical Nationalism and Political Change After Bismarck* (New Haven: Yale University Press, 1980); Jürgen Kocka, *Les employés en Allemagne, 1850–1980: Histoire d'un groupe social,* French ed. (Paris: Éditions de l'École des Hautes Études en Sciences Sociales, 1989). See also Siegrist (this volume).

16. Pierre Guillaume, *Le rôle social du médecin depuis deux siècles, 1800–1945* (Paris: Association pour l'étude de l'histoire de la sécurité sociale, 1996); Christophe Charle, "Légitimités en péril: Éléments pour une histoire comparée des élites et de l'État en France et en Europe occidentale, XIXè–XXème siècle," *Actes de la recherche en sciences sociales* 22(March 1997): 39–52; Christophe Charle, "La bourgeoisie de robe en France au XIXème siècle," *Le mouvement social* 181(October–December 1997): 52–72; Lucien Karpik, *Les avocats: Entre l'État, le public, et le marché, XIIIè–XXè siècles* (Paris: Gallimard, 1995); Christian Delporte, *Les journalistes en France, 1880–1950* (Paris: Éditions du Seuil, 1998).

17. Marchand and Thélot, *Deux siècles de travail en France,* 182.

18. Pierre Bourdieu, *La distinction: Critique sociale du jugement* (Paris: Minuit, 1979). Published in English as *Distinction: A Social Critique of the Judgment of Taste* (Cambridge, Mass.: Harvard University Press, 1984).

19. Nonna Mayer, *La boutique contre la gauche* (Paris: Fondation nationale des sciences politiques, 1986); François Gresle, "La notion de classe moyenne indépendante," *Vingtième siècle* 10 (January–March 1993): 35–43; Sylvie Guillaume, *Les classes moyennes au coeur du politique sous la IVè République* (Bordeaux: Éditions de la Maison des sciences de l'homme d'Aquitaine, 1997); Jean Ruhlmann, *Ni bourgeois ni prolétaires: La defense des classes moyennes en France au xxème siècle* (Paris: Éditions du Seuil, 2001).

20. At its founding in March 1920, the Confederation of Intellectual Workers claimed 220,000 members and 220 professional unions. See Alain Chatriot, "La notion de 'chômeur intellectuel' et l'action de la CTI Confédération des travailleurs intellectuels en France pendant les années 30" (mémoire de maîtrise, Masters directed by Christophe Charle and Rosemonde Sanson, Université de Paris-I, 1996); Guillaume, *Le rôle social du médecin depuis deux siècles, 1800–1945;* Karpik, *Les avocats;* Gilles Le Béguec, "Prélude à un syndicalisme bourgeois: L'association de défense des classes moyennes, 1907–1939," *Vingtième siècle* 10(January–March 1993): 93–104; Delporte, *Les journalistes en France.*

21. Pierre Birnbaum, *Le peuple et les gros: Histoire d'un mythe* (Paris: Hachette, 1995).

22. Le Béguec, "Prélude à un syndicalisme bourgeois"; Ruhlmann, *Ni bourgeois ni prolétaires,* chapter 1.

23. Édouard Herriot was the son of a lieutenant of modest origins, a former student of the École normale supérieure, a professor of letters, and the son-in-law of a doctor; Édouard Daladier was the son of a baker, and he was also a secondary-school teacher. See Élizabeth Du Réau, *Édouard Daladier, 1884–1970* (Paris: Fayard, 1993). Herriot lived in a large com-

mercial and industrial city (Lyons), and Daladier in a small middle town of the south (Carpentras). As we would expect from what we know of the sociology of the radical party, they were in close contact with the petit bourgeois groups without quite being a part of the professionals and civil service to which they owed their upward social mobility. See Serge Berstein, *Édouard Herriot ou la République en personne* (Paris: Fondation nationale des sciences politiques, 1985); Serge Berstein, *Histoire du parti radical*, vol. 1 (Paris: Fondation nationale des sciences politiques, 1982).

24. Raymond Aron, "Une révolution antiprolétarienne: Idéologie et réalité du national-socialisme," in *Inventaire: La crise sociale et les idéologies nationales*, edited by Elie Halévy et al. (Paris: Alcan, 1936), 24–55; Heinz-Gerhard Haupt, "La petite bourgeoisie en France et en Allemagne dans l'entre-deux-guerres," in *Gefährdete Mitte?: Mittelschischten und politische Kultur zwischen den Weltkriegen: Italien, Frankreich, und Deutschland*, edited by Horst Möller, Gérard Raulet, and Andreas Wirsching (Sigmaringen: Beihefte der Francia, Jan Thorbecke Verlag, 1993), 38–40.
25. Quoted in Berstein, *Histoire du parti radical*, 1:368.
26. Ruhlmann, *Ni bourgeois, ni prolétaires*, 182–3.
27. Arthur Havez, "Le bilan du groupe parlementaire communiste en faveur des classes moyennes," *Cahiers du bolchévisme* (July 1937): 574–600, quoted in Ruhlmann, *Ni bourgeois, ni prolétaires*, 183.
28. Quoted in Berstein, *Histoire du parti radical*, 1:468.
29. For examples of political texts, see Sylvie Guillaume, *Les classes moyennes au coeur du politique sous la IVè République* (Bordeaux: Éditions de la Maison des sciences de l'homme d'Aquitaine, 1997).
30. Guillaume, *La confédération générale*, 42–44.
31. Dominique Borne, *Petits bourgeois en révolte?: Le mouvement Poujade* (Paris: Flammarion, 1977).
32. Georges Lavau, Gérard Grunberg, and Nonna Mayer, eds., *L'univers politique des classes moyennes* (Paris: Fondation nationale des sciences politiques, 1983).
33. Sylvain Maresca, *Les dirigeants paysans* (Paris: Minuit, 1983).
34. Guillaume, *La confédération générale*.
35. Jeanne Siwek-Pouydesseau, *Les syndicats de fonctionnaires depuis 1948* (Paris: PUF, 1989); Véronique Aubert et al., *La forteresse enseignante: La Fédération de l'éducation nationale* (Paris: Fayard, 1985).
36. Guillaume, *Le rôle social du médecin depuis deux siècles*.
37. Valéry Giscard d'Estaing, *Démocratie française* (Paris: Fayard, 1976), 56.
38. Luc Boltanski and Pierre Bourdieu, "La production de l'idéologie dominante," *Actes de la recherche en sciences sociale* 2(June 1976): 4–73.
39. Giscard d'Estaing (*Démocratie française*, 57) wrote that "the sociological center of our nation was already a real unit and it assembles, according to observable data, much more than half of the population."
40. Bourdieu, *La distinction*; François de Singly and Claude Thélot, *Gens du privé, gens du public: La grande différence* (Paris: Dunod, 1988).
41. Henri Mendras, *La Seconde révolution française, 1965–1984*, rev. ed. (Paris: Gallimard, 1994).
42. The atypical regions, where the SFIO disputed at one time or another the preeminence of the Communist Party (the Nord, Pas-de-Calais, and Mar-

seille regions), were particularly shaken by the economic crisis. The Socialists, in contrast, made progress in regions that lacked a strong leftist tradition (like Brittany and Alsace) and in newly urbanized zones, such as the dormitory suburbs of the large cities or the mid-size cities that were expanding owing to industrial decentralization and the development of tertiary employment. See Alain Bergounioux and Gérard Grunberg, *Le long remords du pouvoir: Le parti socialiste français, 1905–1992* (Paris: Fayard, 1992), 384.

43. Birnbaum, *Le peuple et les gros.*
44. According to electoral inquiries, the groups that voted again for the Right after having turned briefly to the Left in 1981 were middle managers of the private sector (in general, former electors of Giscard d'Estaing), who were anxious about the effects of left-wing politics after 1982. The sudden breakout of the National Front rested above all on the shifting to the extreme right of a fraction of the independent middle classes (a majority of whom are traditionally on the right). This fraction was hostile to the European Community (which was supported by both the socialist Left and the traditional Right) and was shocked by what it perceived as the government's overly liberal cultural and social agenda and its "lax" attitude toward immigrants. These latter issues also resonated on the extreme Right with those population subgroups that were in decline: among first-time voters for the National Front in the European elections in 1984, 23 percent were inactive or retired, 30 percent were workers, and 9 percent were small-business owners. Mayer, *La boutique contre la gauche,* 322–23. For complementary analysis, consult Bernard Lacroix, "Ordre politique et Ordre social," in *Traité de science politique,* vol. 1, edited by Madeleine Grawitz and Jean Leca (Paris: PUF, 1985), 554–73.
45. Mayer, *La boutique contre la gauche,* 334.
46. In May–June 1981, 161 elected Socialist deputies were teachers, as were fifteen members of the Mauroy government. See Aubert et al., *La forteresse enseignante,* 210.
47. Antoine Prost, *Éducation, société, et politique: Une histoire de l'enseignement en France de 1945 à nos jours* (Paris: Éditions du Seuil, 1992), 169–87.
48. The terms "liberal" and, more often, "neoliberal" are increasingly used in Europe to describe policies that Americans label "conservative."
49. See Fridenson (this volume).
50. Pierre Bourdieu and Lauretta C. Clough, *The State Nobility: Elite Schools in the Field of Power* (Stanford: Stanford University Press, 1996); Michel Bauer and Bénédicte Bertin-Mourot, *Les 200: Comment devient-on un grand patron?* (Paris: Éditions du Seuil, 1990).
51. Jean-Jacques Becker and Pascal Ory, *Crises et alternances 1974–1995* (Paris: Éditions du Seuil, 1998).
52. According to the Fauroux report, 91 percent of education spending was controlled by the state in France in 1992, as opposed to 75 to 77 percent in the United States, Japan, and Germany. Roger Fauroux, *Pour l'école: Rapport de la commission présidée par Roger Fauroux* (Paris: Calmann-Lévy–La Documentation française, 1996), 232.
53. Bergounioux and Grunberg, *Le long remords du pouvoir.*
54. Pierre Bourdieu et al., *La misère du monde* (Paris: Éditions du Seuil, 1993).

55. The Socialist Party, which received above-average support in 1988 from professionals, intellectuals, and members of the working class, lost ground among these groups in 1993. It also lost ground among craftsmen and small-business owners. Philippe Habert, Pascal Perrineau, and Colette Ysmal, *Le vote sanction les élections législatives des 21 et 28 mars 1993* (Paris: *Figaro* Department of Political Studies and Fondation nationale des sciences politiques, 1993), 212.

56. Ibid., 230–31.

57. Pascal Perrineau and Colette Ysmal, eds., *Le vote de crise: L'élection présidentielle de 1995* (*Figaro* Department of Political Studies and Fondation nationale des sciences politiques, 1995), 202–4.

58. Pierre-Noël Giraud, *L'inégalité du monde: Économie du monde contemporain* (Paris: Gallimard, 1996), 300; Alain Lipietz, *La société en sablier: Le partage du travail contre la déchirure sociale, suivi de 1998: L'audace après l'enlisement?* (Paris: La Découverte, 1998).

59. For the controversy among intellectuals about the social movement of 1995, see Julien Duval et al., *Le "décembre" des intellectuels français* (Paris: Liber-Raisons d'agir, 1998). On the differences between welfare states, see Ohngren (this volume).

60. As sociologists show, these divisions are even doubled in terms of generation, sex (given the workforce inequalities between men and women regarding their sectors and qualifications), and national origins (French of a more or less recent date). See Fridenson (this volume); Christian Baudelot and Roger Establet, *Avoir trente ans en 1968 et en 1998* (Paris: Éditions du Seuil, 2000).

61. According to a post-electoral poll in 1997, the majority in every social category (the working class and farmers included) consider themselves members of the "classes moyennes." *Le Monde*, 23 December 1997, 19.

62. Bruno Théret, ed., *L'État, la finance, et le social: Souveraineté nationale et construction européenne* (Paris: La Découverte, 1995).

# 4

## Could Postwar France Become a Middle-class Society?

*Patrick Fridenson*

Like many other industrial nations, France has undergone extensive social change since the end of World War II. Its population almost doubled (from 37 million to 60 million), through internal growth as well as through immigration. The tertiary sector expanded considerably and now accounts for 70 percent of the working population. The size of the working class peaked in the late 1960s and subsequently declined in relative, then in absolute, terms. All of the old industrial regions suffered major economic and social crises. Since 1960, women have become wage-earners in greater and greater proportions. Given the scope of these changes, a number of sociologists, political scientists, economists, and historians have repeatedly heralded "the end of the French exception" and the coming dominance of the middle class in France.

Indeed, there is additional evidence corroborating such a prognosis. The collar line, which earlier in the century had never been as pronounced as in Germany, became even thinner, and new levels of social mobility were attained. France entered an age of mass consumption in the 1950s. "Distinction"—as Pierre Bourdieu calls it[1]—divided the members of each social group according to their tastes and practices as consumers of material and cultural goods rather than their economic or social standing. From the 1960s onward, new social movements centered on gender, urban life, and ecological issues developed as they did in other industrial nations, and the resulting changes tended to benefit the middle class.[2] Finally, the privatization of state-owned enterprises, starting in 1986 and continuing today, not only weakened an exceptionally strong central state but also destroyed a major element of the postwar social settlement, opening the way for British and American institutional investors to acquire 40 percent of the capital of large-scale French companies.[3] These trends were reinforced when France built and participated in the European Common Market (1958), and later in the European Union (1993).

Nonetheless, history dealt several major blows to those prophets who saw French social life converging with the American model of a mass society. One such blow came with the mass strikes of students, workers, cadres, and civil servants in May and June 1968. Dealing another blow were the mass strikes in November and December 1995 of students, civil servants, and wage-earners of the remaining public and nationalized enterprises, widely supported in demonstrations and opinion polls by private-sector wage-earners. The expansion of the middle classes was a reality, but it never was accepted as an inclusive project, nor did it generate universal support.[4]

Although it is true that since World War II class boundaries in France have changed, sometimes becoming less visible, they have not entirely disappeared, contrary to the expectations of many analysts of "the affluent society" and Americanization.[5] To understand this phenomenon, we have to be more specific and distinguish between two different periods. The first, between 1945 and 1974, is characterized by the preservation of most social distances in an era of high growth (of the economy as well as of the middle class). The more general achievement of stability in Europe after the "two great, destructive wars" was a complex process, and the American historian Charles Maier lucidly underscores its importance: "In fact, stabilization is as challenging a historical problem as revolution. . . . Stabilization, moreover, does not preclude significant social and political change, but often requires it."[6] The second period, between 1975 and the turn of the century, has featured an opposite combination: an acceleration of change in an era of slow economic growth that might ultimately lead to a middle-class society. This contrast between the two periods makes more sense than the traditional view of French uniqueness. But it should not lead us to believe that the pace of the French and world economies was the sole factor molding the growing middle class during these two periods. Actors and institutions, learning the rules of the postwar game and finding ways to modify its dynamics, also played an important part.

## Preserving Most Social Distances in an Era of High Growth: 1945 to 1974

In this first period, our problem is to analyze how and why, after the disastrous shocks of World War II, French society maintained most class boundaries during the long ensuing wave of economic growth.

We suggest three lines of possible interpretation of this state of affairs: the institutional barriers evolved but remained solid; the middle class itself changed and became more inclusive, but only slowly and not in significant ways; and the newly erected bridges from blue-collar to middle-class status were used by only a limited number of people. The influences of these factors often continued to be felt during the second period under discussion, and in fact some still shape social change today.

## The Relative Stability of the Institutional Barriers

Like all the other barriers, institutional barriers between classes are historical constructions. It is not surprising that a good many were erected before World War II. But despite the proclaimed ideal of the French Resistance movements and the Liberation governments, quite a few were established after the war ended. As Luc Boltanski showed in *The Making of a Class*, a number of the prewar barriers were suggested or built by the upper classes to keep middle-class wage-earners away from the workers, whereas most of the postwar barriers were requested by the middle classes themselves.[7] Indeed, their postwar catchwords were "specificity" and "difference," whether at work, in social protection, in higher education, or in consumer culture.

*The Separateness of the Middle Class at Work*  A majority of middle-class cadres showed a preference for distinctive institutions addressing their problems at work. They wanted a separate voice in the trade unions, both in collective bargaining agreements and in voting sections. Many formed their own unions.

France had experimented with collective agreements since at least the 1870s (in the building trades), but only on a small scale because of the reluctance of most employers to participate. Only in 1936, under the pressure of blue-collar sit-down strikes, were they generalized. Ever since, in each branch of commerce and industry where a deal is signed, there are different agreements for middle-class cadres and for workers. The same duality appears whenever agreements are reached on the company or plant level. In the 1960s, some trade unions attempted to secure a unified framework for the determination of all wages, from laborer to engineer (a demand that had its counterpart among Japanese blue-collar workers in the steel industry after the end of World War II). These efforts met with considerable resistance from both employers' associations and a majority of middle-class cadres.[8] Even the rational classification of all the jobs in the French metallurgy industry, achieved in 1975 after seven years of bargaining between the employers' association and the trade unions, took the shape of two distinct agreements.[9]

Various laws also granted cadres specific voting sections in companies. Voting in the workplace had been a long-standing demand of both republican politicians and labor as an expression of wage-earners' citizenship. Whenever middle-class wage-earners obtained from the legislature the right to vote in the workplace, it was to be practiced in specific voting sections. This was true of labor courts (1907) and shop stewards (1936), but also of works committees (1945). So voting further substantiated differentiation.

Unionization itself was another path that cadres used to reinforce their individuality. In the interwar years, several associations or small unions of engineers were created to foster an ideology of autonomy and to dissuade cadres from affiliating with the Confédération générale du travail (CGT, the French trade union confederation). Just after World War II, a specialized trade union of cadres was formed: the Confédération générale des cadres (CGC). It soon dominated the federations of cadres affiliated with the three main trade union confederations with which it competed from 1948 onward. It also fought against the influence of blue-collar unions. It rejected communism and, more generally, class struggle. Under the aegis of Roger Millot, it promoted a convergence of different middle-class movements, gathering farmers, doctors, and so on, under the rubric of continued growth and political equilibrium.[10] By its weight and initiatives, it played a significant part in the final shaping of the welfare state.

*Not Just One Welfare State*   This search for specific organizations is equally apparent in the institutions of the welfare state, as it was called after World War II on the basis of the British model. In France, it is in fact not at all a unified system but rather a heterogeneous series of various structures (the "régimes") that have at least some principles in common (redistribution and safety), most of them defined or reworked in the Liberation years.

This pluralism is path-dependent. It takes into account the earlier initiatives—workers' friendly societies, employers' welfare institutions, civil servants' pension schemes, and the interwar social insurance funds regulated by the state—and endeavors to improve and coordinate them. It also assumes as a goal an increase in solidarity between the various groups of French society.[11]

However, the various segments of the middle classes refused the homogenization of the new welfare state. The civil servants insisted on maintaining their own social security system and pension plan. In fact, they staged several mass demonstrations during the interwar years to support these issues.[12] In addition, they established their own friendly societies, first for car insurance (the teachers' MAIF [Mutuelle d'assurance des instituteurs de France] was founded in 1934), then for complementary health allowances. (The postal service's Mutuelle générale de la poste was founded in 1945, and the teachers' MGEN [Mutuelle générale de l'éducation nationale] 1947.) Such societies not only improved the civil servants' safety net but reinforced their unique collective identity. The farmers also wanted a specific social security "régime" and supplemented it with a friendly society, the Mutualité sociale agricole. Many cadres agitated for distinct schemes under the encouragement of the CGC trade union and soon got what they wanted. They reached two successive agreements with the employers, one in 1947 creating a pension fund that complemented the pensions of the social security (AGIRC, Association pour la gestion interprofessionnelle de la retraite des cadres), and another in 1958 creating a specific section in the new funds for unemployment insurance (ASSEDIC, Associations pour l'emploi dans l'industrie et le commerce). Thus, their specific identity in relation to other wage-earners was preserved. It should be noted that the continuously growing numbers of civil servants and cadres strengthened all of these special institutions.[13]

A final element of the diversity in these institutions calls for attention. It was not until 1967 that most cadres and civil servants made a contribution to social security allowances in proportion to their total income. Until then, they and blue-collar workers had paid up to the same income ceiling. Thus, redistribution was limited, and the governments that attempted to extend it had to overcome the counterattacks of most associations and unions of cadres.

*Two Types of Higher Education*   The distinct identity of the middle-class cadres was preserved in the institutions of higher education. Here too there have been two different tracks.

The special schools, most of them outside French universities, were first established for state engineers and top teachers in the eighteenth century, then for private engineers and managers in the nineteenth century, and finally for high-ranking civil servants in the twentieth century. (The most powerful one, École nationale d'administration [ENA], was born in 1945 after many earlier projects had failed.) A dual system thus arose. In other countries, there are differences among universities and a hierarchy of prestige and quality, but in France the differences are between the special schools and the universities. The special schools are considered superior. Despite some obvious nuances in prestige among the "grandes écoles" themselves, and between them and the "petites écoles," the social and geographic recruitment of these schools largely manages to preserve the social and cultural elites, though in a diversified way according to institutions and periods.[14]

Various attempts to unify French higher education have been debated, yet defeated by the successive lobbies of the alumni of the grandes écoles. In 1965 a special committee of the General Planning Commission studied ways to overcome the French weakness in management education. Some of its members first contemplated the idea of a national school of business administration, open to alumni of schools of commerce and engineering who wished to complete their education, but the project did not prevail. A public foundation for management education was created in the heyday of May 1968.[15] Its role was to send students to the United States and Canada to earn an M.B.A. or D.B.A. and to help French universities and schools develop this field. The scheme resurfaced ten years later under a different guise. In 1978 the government created the Institut Auguste Comte in Paris in the former buildings of the École Polytechnique; its purpose was to provide further training for the crème de la crème of the alumni of the grandes écoles.[16] The Left's assumption of power in 1981 killed this cradle of a new hyper-meritocracy, yet it did not change the rules of the game; French society had to preserve "the barrier and the level," as the French sociologist Edmond Goblot so aptly put it in 1925.[17]

*Specific Channels for Consumption and Leisure*  Since the early nineteenth century, French workers and small employees, like their counterparts in other industrial nations, have created and developed their own institutions to improve their range of consumption: the consumer co-ops. Since the 1930s, and especially since the late 1940s, the same groups have fostered specific associations for leisure under the rubric of social tourism.[18]

From the 1950s onward, such institutions did not grow to include the other types of wage-earners. It was not simply that the co-ops were unable to adjust to changes in taste, cycles in fashion, or that political divisions plagued social tourism. Managers and professionals in France deliberately built their own institutions for leisure and consumption: first the Club Med in 1950, then the FNAC (Fédération nationale d'achat des cadres) in 1954.

Paradoxically, these typical middle-class institutions were created by men who belonged to the Left. The founder of Club Med, Gérard Blitz, was a Socialist, and was soon joined by Gilbert Trigano, a for-

mer Communist. The two founders of FNAC, André Essel and Max
Théret, came to their new enterprise from Trotskyism.[19] For some
time, neither institution posed as a business enterprise. Club Med,
specializing in tourism, was organized as a membership club. For a
long time it banned money—colored beads were the currency of
choice. It abolished signs of status with the "vision not so much of a
classless society as of a society in which everyone was equal in the
sight of things." FNAC, which began by selling cameras at discount,
then records, books, and computers, was a "national federation for
cadres as buyers."

Yet the clientele and the values of these two organizations were
unmistakably middle-class. These organizations even participated in
the renovation of middle-class lifestyles. Club Med grew first, from
ten thousand members in 1955 to four hundred thousand in 1967.
Although it also attracted members of other social groups and many
foreigners, its clientele was predominantly from middle-class salaried
sectors. (Over time it "became older and financially better off.") Club
Med emphasized a "closed and controlled environment," thus delin-
eating "a space for redrawing social and cultural hierarchies rather
than abolishing them." Similarly, FNAC openly fought for the diffusion of culture, criticized large corporations that refused to grant it
rebates, and adopted the position of defender of every consumer.[20] In
fact, most of its customers were middle-class. Club Med mildly shook
conventions, promoting "relaxation, play, and the sun, the language
of the self and of individual pleasure." The FNAC's emphasis on au-
diovisual material, modern and pop-rock music, paperbacks, foreign
authors, and comics was similarly "crucial for the cultural consolidation of a new middle class." These two organizations eclipsed co-ops
and popular tourism. Their tremendous growth, while opening un-
heard-of possibilities to individuals, finally (like other aspects of consumer culture) redefined social distinctions.

## Non-institutional Barriers to a More Inclusive Middle Class

Another reason the middle class remains distinct in France is that
non-institutional barriers have limited access by nontraditional
groups. These barriers were clearly visible in 1945, when a significant
portion of middle-class wage-earners were French and male, were paid
monthly, and had been taught in private schools. It is obvious that,
over the years, such characteristics have changed a great deal, but the
distinctive features of the middle class have only been modified, not
replaced.

*Reducing the Gender Imbalance*   Since 1945, women have joined the ranks of middle-class wage-earners in large numbers. Until 1960, however, they mostly entered the civil service, which brought them neither the best wages nor the highest prestige, especially at the levels to which they could aspire. Only after 1960 did they reach private-sector management positions in larger numbers. Even there, however, most women were paid less than their male counterparts and remained their subordinates.

Several scholars argue that attempts to improve the status of women in the workplace have produced (despite spectacular progress) less significant effects for middle-class wage-earners than for workers. A 1982 government report, confirming these views, was followed in 1983 by a law on the equality of wages and hierarchical positions. Another government report in 1998 showed that the gender gap had been relatively diminished since passage of the law of 1983, but that many companies had not yet equalized wages and bonuses between women and men, as prescribed by the law. This report paved the way for yet another law on professional equality, which was passed in 2001. The progress achieved has led middle-class wage-earning women to judge the remaining gaps even more unacceptable.[21]

*The Stubborn Nationality Criterion*   The second distinctive characteristic of the middle class, nationality, has proven even more resistant to change than gender inequality. To be sure, there have always been a minority of foreigners among the members of the middle classes in France. Their numbers and proportion have increased for several reasons: the spread of European Common Market rules of equal access of all Europeans to most French civil service jobs and some professions; the establishment of multinational subsidiaries in France; the new internationalism in higher education and research; and the spread of international secondary schools for the children of foreigners, which have proven to be incubators for training people for managerial jobs.[22]

Despite these trends, the middle class is still predominantly French, and thus remains in striking contrast with the working class, whose ranks, especially in the least-skilled jobs, have been swelled by immigration.

*The Generalization of the Monthly Paycheck*   The third barrier—monthly pay—was long both a status symbol and a source of multiple inequalities. Middle-class wage-earners used to receive monthly paychecks; other groups were paid every other week, every week, or even daily. A monthly paycheck was seen as a status symbol and a sign of job security. Workers' unions repeatedly struggled from the 1950s onward to achieve equal status. But it was only after the mass sit-down strikes of May and June 1968 that their demand was taken up by the Gaullist candidate in the ensuing presidential campaign. After Georges Pompidou had been elected, his administration promoted collective bargaining for a monthly payment of wages, and that practice was soon generalized. Thus, with the obvious exception of temporary workers, that element of the collar line disappeared thirty years ago.[23]

Two qualifications should be added. The government proclaimed that the end of this barrier would erase other divisions, but this did not prove true. One reason was that at the very time blue-collar workers obtained a monthly payment of their wages, their number, as already mentioned, ceased to grow and even began to decline. At the same time, the use of interim cadres started to spread. They would reach a total of seven thousand by the turn of the century, and half would be women.[24]

*The Affirmation of Private Secondary Education*   Traditionally, private secondary schools were primarily Catholic and educated mostly children of the middle class. After the end of World War II, parents' associations from private schools struggled in the political arena to affect legislation (for instance, by convincing families not to pay their taxes and by supporting the legislative candidates who endorsed their demands). They wanted laws that gave private schools access to public funding (for teachers, scholarships, and buildings) while retaining their distinctive characteristics: their religious character, their right to hire teachers, and their insistence on more flexible methods. They secured this financing by a series of laws in 1951, 1959, 1971, and 1977. When the left-wing government tried to repeal these laws after the elections of 1981 and tried to integrate the private schools into the public service, the parents' associations, supported by the Catholic hierarchy and all of the conservative parties, called for mass demonstrations in 1984. The government yielded, and the bill was abandoned.

The laws of the 1950s and the 1970s thus delineate a power relation that is much more favorable to private education than it was before the war. For secondary schools especially, the laws give middle-class families a free choice between public education with a diverse group of children and private education with middle-class children.

In absolute terms, the number of pupils grew, together with the increase of the French population and the growing popularity of secondary schooling. In 1999, private secondary schools attracted 2.238 million pupils.[25]

In relative terms, with the democratization of secondary education, the private schools' share of the total secondary school age population declined by half, from 41 percent in 1950 to 20 percent in 1975, a level that has remained stable ever since. However, not all the pupils have remained middle-class: secondary private schools have gained the status of an alternative schooling system for pupils who cannot adjust to the rigidity of public education. Without limiting the analysis to the Jesuits' colleges or to the famous École des Roches, more recent as it was founded in 1898 by followers of the Catholic engineer Frédéric Le Play, with the personal support of the conservative sociologist of the crowd, Gustave Le Bon, it should be added that the upper strata of the middle class still mostly send their children to very select and exclusive secondary private schools, especially in the provinces.[26]

### The Limitations of the Bridges Above the Collar Line

The idea of social bridges was embedded in Republican ideology. It could find support in tradition: the access of self-taught people to management positions used to be quite significant in French industry and services, as in most other European nations. After World War II, French social actors and governments thought it necessary to build other bridges: the social promotion of labor, continuous education, and internal promotion systems in the civil service. The limited success of these efforts and others is one reason the middle classes have retained their distinctive identity.

*The Shrinking Pool of Self-taught People*   As late as 1975, it was still true that some 30 percent of the engineers and managers in the metalworking industries were self-taught.[27] In a society in which degrees and titles have become a central obsession (as Pierre Bourdieu argues), such a proportion could only diminish, not just in that sector but, similarly, in others. The most striking example, however, has been in banking, not in industry. The advent of the computer and the changes in the functions of financial institutions have transformed the banks. Formerly the domain of self-taught people, banking is now dominated by those with titles and degrees.[28]

Thus, the traditional bridges have been supporting fewer and fewer passengers. Because of their decreasing influence, their most vocal proponents have disappeared. This shift has also had a qualitative impact. Self-taught cadres were long a counterweight to the social origins, the abstract orientation, and the generalist approach of most alumni of the grandes écoles. With the shrinking of this population, that balance was lost—a consequence that clearly raised the question of how to build other bridges.

*The Social Promotion of Labor*  At the same time that individual means of bridging the collar line became ineffective, the state created an alternative method. It did not, however, become as successful as was hoped.[29]

Shortly after the Liberation, the French Ministry of Labor made it possible for people to take special classes, organized under its aegis, to improve their chances of entering the stratum of middle-class wage-earners. This political design, in keeping with the Republican tradition, was also part and parcel with the continuing rivalry about education between that ministry and the Ministry of National Education, which the former suspected of identifying itself with the visions of teachers rather than addressing the wishes of citizens or the needs of society.

This system was revised and became more important during the Gaullist years, under the influence of Prime Minister Michel Debré, who was then minister of finance. Two laws initiated by him in 1959 (grants and subsidies for further vocational training) and 1966 (paid leave for wage-earners looking for social and technological mobility) overcame the reluctance of both teachers in the Ministry of National Education and high-ranking civil servants in the Department of the Budget. By the time the second bill was passed in 1966, the projected system of special classes had become too complex and inflexible. It ignored some of the new trends at work in French society, such as the appeal of higher education and cultural autonomy. The new opportunities ultimately attracted only a limited number of wage-earners.

*Continuous Education Circumscribed*  Nonetheless, the rationale behind these two laws—to overcome the lack of skilled labor and of middle managers and to give a second chance to those who left school early—was so strong that it soon prompted French organizations to move again, but in a different direction.

In 1970 a national agreement negotiated by the employers' confederation (CNPF, Conseil national du patronat français) and the three trade union confederations, followed by a 1971 law, granted all types of wage-earners a certain amount of paid time in their career to update or upgrade their skills.

Similar measures materialized in other industrial nations during the same period. Official statistics, however, proved that this opportunity was much more often used by middle-class wage-earners than by blue-collar workers. Management would thus continue to climb the wage ladder within the middle classes while only a small contingent of workers benefited from the opportunity to bridge the collar line.

The same outcome occurred twenty years later. On July 20, 1992, a law prepared by two successive Socialist ministers was passed that made it possible for present or former wage-earners to offer their job experience as a way of meeting part of their university requirements. But a number of academics were reluctant to enforce the law. Only small numbers take advantage of it (four thousand people each year), and most are already in the middle class.[30]

*Civil Service Mechanisms*   The same distance between intentions and their consequences has characterized the evolution of the promotion system within the civil service.

Traditionally there had been very few French civil servants who could enjoy, like the postmasters from 1945 to 1990, a unified career framework and move without significant difficulty from employee to middle-class status.[31] In response to union demands to rectify this situation, various governments established mechanisms for internal promotion. These mechanisms proved so rigid, however, that they were applied to only a small proportion of the possible applicants, especially those whose personal values were already close to those of the upper stratum of civil servants.

This very selective promotion system was epitomized by the second track of admission to the École nationale d'administration (ENA), which, since 1945 (and again at the impetus of the Republican Gaullist Michel Debré), is reserved for civil servants who have already been on the job for at least five years. Consequently, this promotion system did not democratize the process for filling high-ranking positions. Thus, when the Left returned to government in 1981 after twenty-three years, it immediately created a more open third path for admission. The resistance of a majority of civil servants, however, notably the alumni association, was so strong that the new government could enforce only a miniaturized version of the decree.[32]

In sum, national and local governments recognized the problem of internal promotion both inside the civil service and in companies, but they were unable to design truly adequate solutions to this stubborn issue. Indeed, top managers often did no better in their own companies.

## The Recent Acceleration of Change in an Era of Slow Growth

After 1974, the middle class kept growing. As in other industrial nations, the rise of an information society and a service economy in France prompted the recruitment of numerous white-collar workers, both in industry and in the services. At the same time, the number of civil servants increased, in local as well as central administrations, and reached 5 million in 1999. This is unique to France.

Concurrently, the number of blue-collar workers underwent a relative, then absolute decline. Blue-collar workers were 37.7 percent of the working population at their peak in 1968 (an often forgotten dimension of the mass strikes during that year). By 1993 they had fallen to 28.5 percent, then to 26.0 in 1997.[33]

These two trends combined brought about a new configuration. In some sectors, the proportion of employees, mostly middle-level and upper managers, now exceeds the percentage of workers, whose absolute number has declined. This phenomenon was seen first in oil and aerospace, then in computer hardware and software, and now it has become apparent in the automobile industry.[34] Of course, changes in not only technology, communication facilities, and bureaucratization but in product lines and layoffs have all prompted this evolution, which has not occurred to the same extent in all sectors. At the same time, as the civil service grew, its social structure changed in the same direction as that of companies: those civil servants ranked as cadres or middle-class came to represent much higher proportions of the total.

However, a series of factors accelerated social change. Most important, French economic growth, which had long been the base of the expansion of the middle class, slowed down from the mid-1970s to 1996. Consequently, as in most other countries, mass unemployment surged. Simultaneously, most major institutions that had supported the postwar social settlement became bureaucratized and weakened. The number of students increased considerably as young people sought to gain higher skills and avoid unemployment. These various trends seem to have diminished the differences and distances between the middle classes and the rest of French society.

## The Consequences of Slow Growth

The slower pace of economic growth had inescapable effects on middle-class wage-earners. Like blue-collar workers, they gradually became accustomed to new working conditions in industry and services—mass unemployment, short-time contracts for younger employees, and compulsory early retirement for older ones. They also faced more intensive working environments, less certain careers, and stagnant wages. Like blue-collar workers, they began to fear a decline of social security allowances and a shake-up of the delicate pension system by repartition, which had been remodeled after 1945. Like blue-collar workers, a fraction of cadres campaigned for part-time work or against excessively long working hours. Finally, no quick fix could be found in the creation of new firms; start-ups declined slightly, from 294,181 in 1994 to 266,447 in 1998.[35]

Blue-collar workers faced similar conditions. The slowdown of economic growth, the difficult relationship between trade unions and political parties, and the decay of major ideologies converged to bring about a sharp decline in the membership of French trade unions. Membership fell to one of the lowest levels in Europe. Thus, the rate of unionization of middle-class wage-earners, which traditionally had been low, became much closer to that of workers. Unionization (and by extension, a propensity to strike) remained higher in the civil service, but it too experienced a significant decline. One after the other, the main unions had to change their strategy to adjust to the new context and their diminished forces.

The stable wage relation complemented by medical insurance, pension funds, and family allowances—called the "Fordist régime" by French economists of the régulation school—was therefore called into question. It too could no longer rely on strong, unchallenged institutions, whether in industrial relations or in social security.[36]

## The New Position of Universities

Political, social, and economic change has also influenced how the French public regards institutions of higher learning. To be sure, since the early 1970s the government and the chambers of commerce have allowed the grandes écoles (and the petites) to recruit a slightly higher number of students. This number was almost nothing, however, compared with the increased enrollment of universities. By 1999 it had reached 1.506 million students. Let us review the main consequences of this tremendous social change.

The graduates of the university system spilled out beyond the civil service, which, as Luc Boltanski has shown, was their principal destination until 1975.[37] They invaded the territory of the large-scale corporations and even, much more gradually, that of the small and mid-size enterprises. By 1999 these enterprises accounted for 57 percent of the hirings of new cadres.[38] The traditional pattern of segregation between the alumni of universities and of the écoles tended therefore to be superseded by a pattern of domination of the vast masses of former students by the écoles' graduates.

The universities also became the main vehicle that women could use to increase their access to the middle classes. Although today the proportion of women in the écoles is much higher than in the past, the number of women enrolled in these institutions is still inferior to the number attending the universities.

Nowhere has the change in the consequences of university education been so striking as in the production of engineers. Owing to a
policy advanced by left-wing governments and universities in the
early 1980s, the proportion of French engineers educated in universities and holding the title of "ingénieur diplômé," according to the
law of 1934,[39] has risen to 50 percent of a growing total. This level of
involvement by universities, which has been constant for the past six
years, brings France closer to the other industrial nations. French universities, as elsewhere, have become the main suppliers of the expanding middle class, though they have not become the major incubators for CEOs and ministry directors.

*Separate Identity Versus Integration*

It is still possible to identify the middle class according to traditional
signifiers such as rate of ownership of country residences, computers,
and multimedia material and access to culture. Yet in other areas,
middle-class identity has been undermined by members of the middle
class who have opted for greater integration into society.

At the last election of the French labor courts, on December 10,
1997, the CFDT (Confédération française démocratique du travail)
trade union, which has long advocated close relationships between
cadres and other wage-earners, garnered the largest number of voters
for the first time. The Confédération générale des cadres (CGC),
which has identified itself exclusively with the cadres for fifty years
and views middle-class prerogatives as due to status, not position,
lost its traditional dominance and entered into a state of crisis. The
results suggest that a sizable number of French cadres have decided to
adopt a new view in the face of so intense a social change as the one
that is now under way. In turn, this shift may be related to the rise in
the number of cadres who are women and university graduates.

The same alternative emerged in 1998–99 with the first law prepared by Socialist Minister Martine Aubry, and especially in early
2000 with the application to the cadres of Aubry's second law, on the
thirty-five-hour week. The CFDT called for a limited number of qualifications for the cadres, and the CGC and other unions called for a
variety of specific rules. What was at stake was no less than the integration of the cadres into a France that was finally becoming a middle-class society.

## Conclusion

The fifty-five-year evolution of French society and the quick pace of
transformations of all kinds in the past ten years have created two

paradoxes for French middle-class wage-earners. Their importance at work and in the marketplace has kept growing, but they have experienced no parallel increase in power—whether in the workplace or in shareholders' assemblies (despite the spread of stock ownership and stock-option plans). The old class boundaries, though much weaker than they were in 1945, still exist, despite their relative loss of relevance. History does not vanish into thin air, and institutional change lags behind economic and cultural change.

The proportion of holders of a university or école degree among the middle class has also kept growing, but, as the sociologist Edmond Goblot recognized as early as 1925, degrees and titles coined for a minority do not necessarily keep their value when attained by a majority. No longer do they automatically open the gates of the upper elites—or even sometimes the gates of the middle class. This has been the experience of many women in the middle class in particular.

These paradoxes point to a further contradiction. Even if historians are not so good at extrapolations, it seems logical to think that in the near future the middle class may constitute the majority of the working population of France. Its dominant experience in the past twenty years, however, has been destabilization: the middle class increasingly experienced flexible working conditions and uncertain careers and adopted the union and party preferences more common among the rest of French society.[40]

This is not to say that because France has become more of a middle-class society it will follow the American model. To be sure, since 1983 the functions of both state and local governments have shrunk, the private sector is offering more and more services that compete with or replace those of state institutions, and the penetration of multinationals and foreign investors keeps growing. Moreover, France has felt the spread of innovative values that focus less on obedience, conformity, and social hierarchies and more on creativity and voluntary cooperation. Yet the yearning for distinctive characteristics and differentiation in society remains strong. The old French way of working and living together that was framed in the eighteenth century still enjoys some support in the changing France of today.[41] This vision of society promotes a logic of honor, strongly differentiates noble tasks from vile ones, and legitimate from nonlegitimate methods of command, and depreciates so-called parvenus. In this society, the state rather than contractual links still determines rank. Indeed, the percentage of civil servants in the French middle class remains higher than in a number of industrial nations. Even if some members of the French middle class have adopted the new values and are sensitive to the constraints of globalization, most call for specific adaptations of the French civil service, that is, for incremental change. Even taking into consideration the potential impact on French society of the aging of its population—especially on the middle class, which enjoys a longer life expectancy—they have not lost their deep-seated belief in the necessity of regulation. Thus, there may be an unexpected survival of the "French exception." Although it may look like a hybrid of transatlantic and British values and methods, the French exception will not be exactly aligned with these forms.

## Notes

1. Pierre Bourdieu, *Distinction: A Social Critique of the Judgment of Taste* (Cambridge, Mass.: Harvard University Press, 1984).
2. Françoise Picq, *Libération des femmes: Les années-mouvement* (Paris: Éditions du Seuil, 1993); Michelle Durand and Yvette Harff, *La qualité de la vie: Mouvement écologique, mouvement ouvrier* (Berlin: W. de Gruyter, 1977); Pierre Lascoumes, *L'éco-pouvoir: L'environnement entre nature et politique* (Paris: La Découverte, 1994).
3. Franck Bancel, "Directions in French Corporate Governance Since 1945," *Entreprises et histoire* 8(June 1999): 29–43.
4. Patrick Fridenson, "Le conflit social," in *Histoire de la France*, rev. ed., vol. 5, edited by André Burguière and Jacques Revel (Paris: Éditions du Seuil, 2000): 381–495.
5. Richard F. Kuisel, *Seducing the French* (Berkeley: University of California Press, 1993); Jonathan Zeitlin and Gary Herrigel, eds., *Americanization and Its Limits* (Oxford: Oxford University Press, 2000).
6. Charles Maier, *In Search of Stability: Explorations in Historical Political Economy* (Cambridge: Cambridge University Press, 1987), 154.
7. Luc Boltanski, *The Making of a Class: Cadres in French Society* (Cambridge: Cambridge University Press, 1987).
8. Claude and Michelle Durand, *De l'OS à l'ingénieur: Carrière ou classe sociale* (Paris: Éditions ouvrières, 1972); Andrew Gordon, *The Wages of Affluence: Labor and Management in Postwar Japan* (Cambridge, Mass.: Harvard University Press, 1998), 26–35.
9. Éric Pezet, "La négociation des classifications dans la métallurgie 1968–1975: Contexte, acteurs, et méthode d'une innovation sociale" (DEA thesis, École des Hautes Études en Sciences Sociales, 1997).
10. Guy Groux, *Les cadres* (Paris: La Découverte, 1983); Boltanski, *The Making of a Class*; Sylvie Guillaume, ed., *Les classes moyennes au cœur du politique sous la IVe République* (Bordeaux: Éditions de la Maison des sciences de l'homme d'Aquitaine, 1997); Hélène Olivier, "Roger Millot (1903–1973) et l'avènement des classes moyennes" (Ph.D. diss., Université de Dijon, 1995).
11. Pierre Laroque, *Au service de l'homme et du droit* (Paris: Association pour l'étude de l'histoire de la Sécurité sociale, 1993); Susan Pedersen, *Family, Dependence, and the Origins of the Welfare State: Britain and France, 1914–1945* (Cambridge: Cambridge University Press, 1993).
12. Élise Feller, "L'entrée en politique d'un groupe d'âge: La lutte des pensionnés de l'État dans l'entre-deux-guerres et la construction d'un 'mo-

dèle français de retraite,'" *Le mouvement social* 40(January–March 2000): 33–59.

13. Gilles Heuré, *Histoire de la MGPTT 1945–1990* (Paris: Éditions Racines mutualistes, 1995).

14. Pierre Bourdieu and Loretta C. Clough, *The State Nobility: Elite Schools in the Field of Power* (Stanford: Stanford University Press, 1996); Jean-Pierre Nioche and Monique de Saint Martin, eds., "Former des gestionnaires," *Entreprises et histoire* 6(June 1997, special issue); André Grelon and Françoise Birck, eds., *Des ingénieurs pour la Lorraine XIXé–XXé siècles* (Metz: Éditions Serpenoise, 1998).

15. Marie Chessel and Fabienne Pavis, *Le technocrate, le patron et le professeur* (Paris: Belin, 2001).

16. Roger Martin, *Patron de droit divin* (Paris: Gallimard, 1984).

17. Edmond Goblot, *La barrière et le niveau* (1925; reprint, Paris: Gérard Monfort, 1984).

18. A good deal of this section relies on the work of Ellen Furlough. See her *Consumer Cooperation in France: The Politics of Consumption, 1834–1930* (Ithaca: Cornell University Press, 1991); Ellen Furlough and Carl Strikwerda, eds., *Consumers Against Capitalism?: Consumer Cooperation in Europe, North America, and Japan, 1840–1990* (Oxford: Rowman and Littlefield, 1999); Ellen Furlough, "Packaging Pleasure: Club Méditerranée and French Consumer Culture, 1950–1968," *French Historical Studies* 18(Spring 1993): 65–81; Ellen Furlough, "Genealogies of Leisure and Work," *Comparative Studies in Society and History* 40(April 1998): 247–86. Also Alain Ehrenberg, *Le culte de la performance* (Paris: Calmann-Lévy, 1991), 97–168.

19. See two autobiographies: André Essel, *Je voulais changer le monde* (Paris: Stock, 1985); Gilbert and Serge Trigano, *La saga du Club* (Paris: Grasset, 1998). Also an obituary: François Bostnavaron, "Gilbert Trigano," *Le Monde*, February 6, 2001.

20. Jean-Louis Pétriat, *Les années FNAC de 1954 à après-demain* (Paris: Fayard, 1991).

21. Margaret Maruani, ed., *Les nouvelles frontières de l'inégalité entre hommes et femmes sur le marché du travail* (Paris: La Découverte, 1998).

22. Anne-Catherine Wagner, *Les nouvelles élites de la mondialisation: Une immigration dorée en France* (Paris: Presses Universitaires de France, 1998).

23. Jean Bunel, *La mensualisation: Une réforme tranquille* (Paris: Éditions Ouvrières, 1973).

24. "Le boom de l'intérim des cadres," *Le Monde* (economic supplement), 11 April 2000.

25. Marcel Launay, *L'Église et l'École en France XIXé–XXé siècles* (Paris: Desclée, 1988), 108–15, 143–58; Direction de la Programmation et du Développement, *Les grands chiffres de l'Éducation Nationale* (Paris: Ministère de l'Éducation Nationale, de la Recherche et de la Technologie, 2000), 1.

26. Bourdieu and Clough, *The State Nobility*; Michel and Monique Pinçon, *Sociologie de la bourgeoisie* (Paris: La Découverte, 2000), 87–91. Gabriel Langouët and Alain Léger, *Le choix des familles. École publique ou école privée?* (Paris: Fabert, 1997).

27. Luc Boltanski, "Cadres et ingénieurs autodidactes," in *L'ingénieur dans*

*la société française,* edited by André Thépot (Paris: Éditions Ouvrières, 1985), 127–34.

28. Yves Grafmeyer, *Les gens de la banque* (Paris: PUF, 1992).

29. Guy Thuillier, *La promotion sociale,* 2nd ed. (Paris: PUF, 1969); Colette Bec, *L'assistance en démocratie* (Paris: Belin, 1998), 64; Pierre Benoist, *La formation professionnelle dans le bâtiment et les travaux publics 1950–1990* (Paris: L'Harmattan, 2000), 213–24.

30. Information kindly supplied by the Direction de la Programmation et du Développement (of the French Ministry of Education) in March 2000.

31. Odile Join-Lambert, *Le receveur des Postes, entre l'État et l'usager (1944–1973)* (Paris: Belin, 2001).

32. François de Singly and Claude Thélot, *Gens du privé, gens du public: La grande différence* (Paris: Dunod, 1988); Arnaud Teyssier, "L'ENA comme symbole de tous les maux," *Les Cahiers de l'ENSPTT* 4(October 1999): 31–34; Irène Bellier *L'ENA comme si vous y étiez* (Paris: Éditions du Seuil, 1993).

33. Michel Verret, *Chevilles ouvrières* (Paris: Éditions de l'Atelier, 1995); Paul Bouffartigue and Charles Gadea, *Sociologie des cadres* (Paris: La Découverte, 2000), 38.

34. See, for instance, Yvette Lucas, *Le vol du savoir* (Villeneuve d'Ascq: Presses Universitaires de Lille, 1989).

35. Virginie Malingre, "Lionel Jospin offre de nouvelles aides aux créateurs d'entreprise," *Le Monde,* April 12, 2000.

36. Pierre Karila-Cohen and Bernard Wilfert, *Leçon d'histoire sur le syndicalisme en France* (Paris: PUF, 1998).

37. Boltanski, *The Making of a Class.*

38. "Les PME, premiers recruteurs de jeunes diplômés," *Le Monde* (economic supplement), April 11, 2000.

39. See Charle (this volume).

40. Paul Bouffartigue, ed., *Cadres: la grande rupture* (Paris: La Découverte, 2001).

41. Philippe d'Iribarne, *La logique de l'honneur* (Paris: Éditions du Seuil, 1989); Mairi Maclean, "Corporate Governance in France and the United Kingdom: Long-term Perspectives on Contemporary Institutional Arrangements," *Business History* 41(January 1999): 88–116.

# 5

## The Short Happy Life of the Japanese Middle Class

### Andrew Gordon

A provocative headline lament—"Sayonara, Middle-Stream Consciousness!"—greeted readers of the Sunday "Weekend Economy" page of the *Asahi* newspaper on November 13, 1997. The reporter argued that the prolonged recession and corporate restructuring had made once-secure jobs unreliable, while crashing land and stock prices and microscopic interest rates had eroded the assets of the middle-class population. The article related the nightmare of the forty-nine-year-old Mr. A., employed at a company that sold electronic equipment. He had been transferred to the "market development section," a posting widely understood by coworkers to be a dead-end dumping ground for those targeted by the company for "voluntary retirement." Explicitly told by his boss that he should volunteer for early retirement, Mr. A. was discouraged, angry, and humiliated. He had worked for this company for thirteen years and had just taken out a loan to pay for a new four-bedroom home that he would be paying off until age seventy. He and his wife, who worked part-time in a real estate sales office, faced college preparation and tuition costs for their three teenage children. Mr. A. had not yet had the courage to tell her honestly how intensely he was being pressured to resign. He asked, "Can my ever-so-average lifestyle be so easily snatched away from me?" Angry at the company's "insincerity" and determined to fight to keep his job, he had recently joined the Tokyo Managerial Employees Union, but his future on his job was uncertain.

The goal of this chapter is to place this tale of a common man's despair in a historical perspective. It would be hasty and misleading to take this article at face value and conclude that a long-standing state of Japanese middle-class stability suddenly evaporated in the prolonged recession of the 1990s. Reversing the historian's old saw that in the long sweep of modern European history the middle class is always rising, the Japanese middle class appears to have been forever declining, from the moment it appeared in the accounts of historians and contemporaneous observers.

As early as 1907, for example, two of Japan's early socialists, Sakai Toshihiko and Morichika Unpei, wrote in their "Socialist Platform":

> Today's middle-level [chūtō] society includes many salary earners in addition to independent small-scale enterprisers. Those in its upper reaches serve as the teeth and claws of the great capitalists. They belong to the class of pure gentlemen. Those at the lower end include government clerks, office workers, and schoolteachers. Even if they nominally belong to middle-level society, they are in fact no more than wage laborers. The youths of middle-level society have the opportunity to acquire considerable education. Although they should be able to choose a respectable occupation, it is virtually impossible for them to carry on independent businesses. They must scrounge and race after salaried positions. In truth, most of the unemployed today are not so much the children of the lowest strata of the poor; they are rather the youths of middle-level society with a fair education. Even if they find a salaried position, they are dominated by the laws of the wage market, and their salaries are not even as high as the wages of a skilled manual laborer. The living standards of policemen, prison guards, and elementary school teachers are actually lower than those of the rickshaw pullers or longshoremen whom they so despise.[1]

This is a rather complex and provocative analysis of the state of Japan's modern middle class in its infancy. It stresses poor job prospects and low wages for those seeking middle-class occupations. This understanding, which was a fairly typical view at the time and has remained so, has not been limited to socialists with a bias for exaggerating the prospect for social collapse. Their declaration describes the middle class as a heterogeneous mix of social types and levels, and it suggests that education rather than property was the ticket to membership. These two views of the middle class were also typical of the time and of later decades as well. The final sentence points to tension between those at the lower end of the middle class and the archetypal lower-class types, the rickshaw puller and the longshoreman. It suggests that education, occupation, and a certain sensibility, rather than income itself, defined membership in the middle class and the appeal of belonging to it.

Certainly the structure of Japanese society has changed vastly over the twentieth century. But we see in both the "Socialist Platform" and the *Asahi* analysis of Mr. A.'s plight a similar tone of anxiety over the prospects for preserving one's status as a member of the nation's middle class. In this chapter, I stress the centrality of such anxieties as I trace the story of the Japanese middle class in the twentieth century, devoting particular attention to the mix of changes and continuity in its social history, on the one hand, and its cultural or intellectual history, on the other.

In the realm of middle-class social history, one important continuity since roughly the start of the century has been the centrality of education and occupation, rather than property or family background, as the socioeconomic gateways to middle-class life. But we will see that changes have been dramatic. Membership in the middle class of the early twentieth century was a decidedly minority experience. Any statistical measure will be crude, but perhaps we can say that by the 1920s roughly one-fifth of city-dwellers and well under one-tenth of the entire population belonged to the salaried middle class described by Sakai and Morichika.[2] In addition, the sociocultural divide between those in this prewar middle class and the wage laborers of the working class was great. By the 1960s, much had changed. Membership in the middle class was shifting from a minority to a majority experience (although it certainly remained a heterogeneous category). Also, the distinction between middle- and working-class lives had diminished considerably; the number and social prominence of "despised" lower-class groups, such as longshoremen, had shrunk dramatically.

The middle class in Japan, as elsewhere, has been a shifting cultural construct as well as a shifting set of social behaviors. The most important cultural change, which both reflected and anticipated—or outran—the social change just noted, has been a revolution in the self-perception of Japanese people. Only a minority identified themselves as participants in middle-class life in prewar Japan. Then, beginning in the 1950s, in a major transformation from the prewar era, a vast majority came to label themselves part of a "mainstream" middle-class society. At the same time, one notable continuity marked the discourse surrounding middle-class life: ongoing tension between celebratory and anxiety-ridden visions of the present and future. In discussions of middle-class life, themes of the "brightness" and "newness" of an emerging middle-class life have coexisted with those of fragility and fear of failure.

## Meiji and Taishō Prototypes: Organization Men and "Western Clothes Paupers"

Sakai and Morichika divide what they literally call "middle-level" society into "independent enterprisers" and those who live on salaries. The former category refers to people such as shopkeepers, wholesalers, and small-scale manufacturers, as well as doctors, lawyers, and perhaps professors. The latter include wage- or salary-earning office workers of various sorts: government bureaucrats and low-ranked clerks, managers in private corporations and financial institutions, and lower-level corporate functionaries or technicians. Sakai and Morichika identify this latter group as the wave of the future. By the end of the 1920s, the wave had arrived as part of a much broader political, social, and cultural convergence that came to define the interwar middle class.

From the early years of the Meiji era (1868 to 1912), and indeed before that, such salaried officials were often described by observers as impoverished and insecure. Around 1872, soon after the Restoration of 1868, the expression "kyūryō tori" (literally, "salary-earners") came into use to describe run-of-the-mill officials in the new government bureaucracy and state employees such as teachers and policemen. Given their social status, education and political power, and hereditary claims on income from the 1600s through the early 1870s, it is no surprise that former samurai warrior-officials occupied a disproportionate number of such positions in the Meiji government. It is rather noteworthy, however, that even former samurai could not rest on their laurels. Literary works of the 1880s such as Futabatei Shimei's *Floating Clouds* made fun of the desperate strivings of former samurai seeking to regain their social status by somehow staking a claim to such positions, and other sources from the 1880s stressed how poorly paid and impoverished such men and their families were.[3] It was already well articulated that one's native cleverness and ambition were keys to one's future.

As noted by the historian Louise Young in an argument that also draws on literature (Natsume Soseki's *And Then*), the inherited social capital of former samurai continued to offer some advantaged access to middle-class occupations such as businessman, bureaucrat, or teacher into the twentieth century.[4] But even as genealogical privilege remained significant in shaping life courses, the importance of education was growing. Sakai and Morichika wrote of an education-based "race for salary" in 1907. The institutional framework of such a race had been put in place as early as the late 1880s. In the years around 1890, major corporations such as Mitsui and Mitsubishi systematically began to recruit future managers from universities.[5] Simultaneously, at least some graduates of the top private and public schools began to view private-sector employment as an attractive alternative to positions in the government bureaucracy. The year 1894 also witnessed perhaps the first case of a major corporation hiring young women for clerical positions. The manager of the Osaka branch of the Mitsui bank, inspired by a visit to the Wanamaker department store in Philadelphia, hired several teenage girls who had recently graduated from higher elementary school to work in the accounting section. Thereafter, the practice of hiring young women to work in offices and retail sales in department stores gradually spread.[6]

The first two decades of the twentieth century have been identified by some as the time of the "birth of the salaryman class." Occupational surveys show a large increase in the proportion of office staff ("shokuin") positions in major cities (in Tokyo, from 6 percent in 1908 to 21 percent in 1920).[7] The number of vocational middle schools increased substantially, and a multi-tiered system of recruitment began to link these institutions, as well as higher schools and universities, to corporate and government employers. Those competing for these jobs reportedly came to include not only the children of former samurai but also the offspring of the old middle class of urban shopkeepers and manufacturers and middling farmers in the countryside.[8] These two decades were also a time when the Tokugawa-period retailers of dry goods remade themselves into modern department stores. These stores, led by Mitsui's pioneering Mitsukoshi store (formerly Echigoya), played an important role in creating the norms and behaviors of the modern middle class. Young describes how they systematically promoted and celebrated a new way to enjoy the fruits of one's labor in salaried middle-class jobs.[9]

One important sign of the fledgling social and cultural status of a modern middle class in Japan during these two decades was the lack of any single label for the new middle class that commanded widespread or majority use. In an important article on the history of the concept of the salary-man, Takeuchi Yō identifies an Edo-era (1600 to 1868) expression, "koshi-ben," as one of the earliest appellations to single out a portion of the emerging middle class of the modern era. The term literally refers to the lunch box ("bentō") that Edo samurai would attach to their clothes at the waist ("koshi"). Takeuchi turns, with others, to Futabatei Shimei's novel of 1887 for a literary depiction of the emerging middle class, in this case a modern office worker in Western clothes making his way to work with his lunch box attached, after the fashion of the Edo samurai. At the time, the expression "koshi-ben" was used to refer only to those in the lower levels of the official class who had a middle school education or less. Those with more education and strong family backgrounds could enter the civil service on the fast track and quickly move into top positions. By the turn of the century, according to Takeuchi, even those with higher education faced more systematic and slower-moving career trajectories, and they too came to be considered part of the lunch-box class.[10] The term "sarariiman" (salary-man) made its first appearance somewhat later, in cartoons of the 1910s that lampooned "Salary-man heaven" and "Salary-man hell." [11] But for about a decade the term coexisted with numerous other expressions, such as "hōkyū seikat-susha" (people living on salaries), "chishiki kaikyū" (intellectual class), "shinchūkan kaikyū" (new middle class), and more collo-quially, "zunō rōdōsha" (brain workers) as well as the familiar "koshi-ben kaikyū" (lunch-box class).[12]

By the late 1920s, the jumble of terms to describe those who held or aspired to middle-class status had been winnowed out somewhat. "Sarariiman" had become the most common appellation.[13] It was now widely understood to refer to a city-dwelling man of the middle class, with middling to high education, who worked for the government or a private company and owed his job to these credentials. This more standardized terminology was part of a broader convergence of trends. By the end of the 1920s, department stores had likewise become more standardized, and they had collectively come to symbolize a widely shared dream of a new, middle-class, consuming life.[14] A variety of other political and social developments also became part of an inter-war Japanese configuration of "modern times," one that was full of tensions as well as promise: political rule by party cabinets; the spread of liberal and Marxian ideas; increased opportunities for women as office workers; the conceit of the "modern girl" and "mod-ern boy" as social types; the great popularity of movies and jazz; and the spread of cafés and café waitressing as a modern alternative to the brothel quarters that reached back to the Edo era.[15] These trends were defining features of the world of the middle-class salaryman, his wife, and their children.

A certain exuberance, a dream of a glittering new modern life marked as "rational," "scientific," and "cultured," and the unre-strained pursuit of this life defined part of the middle-class experience of prewar Japan. But choruses of celebration were matched by those of anxious concern. Practices later identified to be at the heart of the social economy of the middle class—"permanent employment," or long-term job security, for regular male employees of large bureaucra-tic or corporate organizations—simply did not exist. Office workers were laid off en masse during periodic economic slumps. A foothold in the middle class was by no means secure; the boundary between the middle and lower classes was permeable. Such a state of affairs led Hara Kei, Japan's first commoner prime minister (1918) and him-self a great symbol of the very high end of middle-class success, to record the following lament in his diary in 1910: "To stop the spread of [socialism] we should draft social legislation. If people like teachers and policemen take even one false step, they might become socialists, so there is need to pay most attention to their treatment, and need for basic policies to prevent its spread."[16]

During the economic boom sparked by World War I, Japan's European competitors temporarily disappeared, leaving Japanese producers as the only suppliers for many domestic and Asian markets. One might have expected an exuberant spirit to prevail, but inflation surged alongside industrial production, and a sense of insecurity and struggle powerfully marked the emerging discourse of the modern middle class. Newspapers published the laments of those whose salaries did not keep up with inflation, such as this one, which appeared in the *Asahi* in February 1918, from an elementary school teacher supporting a family of five. After listing monthly expenses that totaled 20.75 yen, the author asserts that

> my monthly income after deductions [also enumerated] is 18 yen and change. Even 20 yen are not enough. How can we live on 18? There's no choice but to cut our rice costs a little by mixing in barley, more than 50 percent, and once a day making a meal of barley-rice gruel. Because charcoal is expensive, no one in the family has taken a bath for over a month, and we can hardly afford a cup of sake, or a few pieces of meat, or even a single potato. To buy a new kimono is out of the question. Is there anything so pitiful as the life of an elementary school teacher who cannot afford to dress his child in a New Year kimono or even eat "mochi"?[17]

This notion of an impoverished middle class was perhaps most powerfully encapsulated at the time in the apparent oxymoron of "a Western clothes pauper" ("yōfuku saimin"). "Saimin" (literally, a thin person) is a term for paupers found in the Chinese classics. It appears in Japanese government documents as early as A.D 862.[18] From the Meiji Restoration through the early twentieth century, those who wore Western clothes ("yōfuku") were typically seen as the relatively secure and best-educated upper stratum of the new Japan, living in a world far removed from the slums of the urban paupers. The dramatic yoking together of these two terms signaled that even those with credentials to join the upper ranks of middle-class society now faced lives of uncertain struggle and insufficient earnings.[19]

Fearful that impoverished, desperate middle-class men and women might become one with an angry proletariat, government officials such as Hara Kei, quoted earlier, tried to gain a handle on the scope of the problem posed by the Western clothes paupers. From the time of

World War I and into the 1920s, they carried out surveys of middle-class economic and social conditions, conducting research parallel to that aimed at factory laborers and the poor. One such study, undertaken by the Tokyo prefectural government in 1922, was explicitly described as part of an effort to "make the middle class ["chūtō kaikyū"] the standard and gradually raise the lower class to that level, and seek the fusion of lower and middle classes."[20] Provoking this concern was the fact that some salarymen were indeed moving toward a very different sort of "fusion": at the height of the inflation of World War I, schoolteachers and even some employees at major trading houses took cues from miners and factory laborers to form impromptu struggle groups demanding wage increases. In Tokyo, such groups had merged by 1919 into the Tokyo Council of Federations of People Who Live on Salaries ("Tokyo hōkyū seikatsusha dōmei kyōgikai"). Some female office workers took similar steps. In March 1920, fifty-two typists working in companies in Tokyo and Yokohama formed Japan's first union of female office workers and demanded higher pay and status on a par with that of regular male employees.[21]

I have translated the name of this Tokyo union of salarymen in a literal and clumsy fashion because the original does not read very smoothly either. The organizers made a considered choice to call themselves by the neologism "hōkyū seikatsusha" (people who live on salary) rather than adopt a much more straightforward term such as "hōkyū rōdōsha" (salaried worker). Statistical data suggest that the men in the lower end of middle-class occupations actually earned little more, and sometimes less, than skilled male laborers in shipyards and machine shops, and that female typists were paid not much more than textile workers. Data on clerical or white-collar wages are hard to come by for the interwar era; one anecdotal source from 1928 identifies the lower range of the class of "salary-earning Western clothes paupers" as taking home 20 to 30 yen per month. By contrast, the average wage of a skilled male machinist in 1927 was 2.6 yen per day, and that of a female textile worker stood at roughly 1.0 yen per day.[22] By opting not to label themselves "workers," these salaryman unionists made clear that, although they might draw on the organizing tactics of factory labor and they might not earn any more, they placed themselves in a different social category: middle-class "salaried persons." This was a distinction of cultural style or social identity and background—especially educational background—as much or more than it was a distinction grounded in wage levels. Organized factory laborers, for their part, reciprocated this view; they understood themselves to be part of a very different social group to the extent that the

Japan General Federation of Labor Unions (Nihon Rōdō Sōdōmei) in 1924 summarily rejected a request for affiliation from the Japan Salaryman Union.[23]

In the 1920s, the lifestyle of this salaried middle class was far from a majority experience. Nonetheless, a minority prototype of the mass middle class of the postwar decades had come into existence. The middle class of the early twentieth century and the interwar era deserved to be known as "new" in at least two ways. It was new in that education more than inherited status was the key credential that opened the door to middle-class occupations. It was also new in the exciting array of consumer goods and activities that came to define a middle-class lifestyle. As the members of this group looked at their society, the line between themselves and those they considered their inferiors was clear.

The mutual antagonism exemplified in the treatment of the Salaryman Union's affiliation request would diminish greatly in later decades. But even as the norms and experience of a middle-class life changed from a minority to a mass phenomenon, one characteristic linked, rather than distinguished, the prewar and postwar middle class: the Western clothes pauper's dreams for a bright new life sat uneasily alongside the fearful anxiety of struggling in the race for education and salary.

## Trends Across the War: The Minority Middle Class Persists

A life marked by office employment—for men as a career, for women as a rite of youthful passage—and access to the glittering promise of department store show-windows remained a minority experience not only through World War II but into the first postwar decade. The impact of the war on "middle-class-ness" as both social experience and self-understanding bears closer examination than I can undertake in this chapter. It appears that the experience of war and defeat had a powerful homogenizing or standardizing effect in the immediate postwar period in both regards. For example, in the wartime drive to mobilize the labor of women and youths of both sexes, the practice of recruiting directly from schools to private-sector employers was extended and regularized for people at a wide range of social levels. Also, although injunctions to practice frugality and the harsh facts of scarcity greatly dampened the enthusiastic consumerism of the middle-class minority of the interwar years, it has been plausibly argued that political and economic controls, economic hardships, and finally the physical devastation of Japanese cities by firebombing had combined to extend a realm of shared experience (or perceived shared experience) to most Japanese people by the end of the war.

As "everyone" became desperate together in war and defeat, the ground was prepared for the masses to "return" to a normality that for the first time was defined as a middle-class life for everyone. Yet not until well after World War II—that is, not until the late 1950s and 1960s—did "middle-class life" as both a mass experience and the self-identified status of the vast majority of people come to characterize Japanese society. Reference to the majority of the population in the early postwar years spoke instead of "the masses" (taishū), a term with a vaguely Marxian, proletarian resonance, or the more clearly political "working masses" (kinrō taishū), or "the nation's people" (kokumin). They were striving to achieve a "bright life" (akarui seikatsu) or a "new life" (shin seikatsu), terms that roughly evoked the relatively privileged minority status of the prewar middle class.

In spatial terms, the ascendance of the middle class in Japan is associated with the spread of urban or suburban living and the extension of metropolitan lifestyles to the countryside. These trends began with the spread of commuter rail lines and construction of suburban outposts in the early twentieth century, but not until the late 1950s did migration from country to city, and the outward growth of city into former countryside, combine to begin to make a metropolitan middle-class lifestyle the majority and defining experience of the "modern" Japanese adult. Even though millions moved to the cities in the 1950s, the sharp overall increase in population of these years allowed the rural population to remain high as well. Japan's agricultural population at the end of World War II accounted for roughly 50 percent of the populace, or 36 million people. A decade later, in 1955, this absolute number of people stood unchanged, and the proportion of the population in rural areas had fallen just slightly.

In addition, self-employment or family employment remained through the 1950s a more common experience than paid employment outside the family. For all the impressive growth of Japanese industry from the 1880s through the 1930s, the majority of the nation's labor force through the first postwar decade consisted of family members working on a family farm or fishing boat or in a small, family-owned retail, wholesale, or manufacturing shop in a village or city. The husband would be counted as the "business owner." The wife, on a farm or in a vegetable market, a sandal "factory," or a barber shop, would work alongside him and was counted as "family labor." Government statisticians did not classify these women as "employees," and typically they received no wages. From the 1930s through the 1950s, well over two-thirds of women workers were so-called family workers.

The structure of daily life and the life cycles of most Japanese people also retained well into the 1950s qualities that resist classification as part of a salaried "new middle class." We can see this in small facts with large implications. For example, a social survey of "laboring households" in the Keihin (Tokyo region) industrial belt in 1950 revealed that 139 minutes of a woman's average day—every day—were devoted to sewing.[24] This is a richly suggestive datum that merits brief discussion. Sewing machines entered Japan in the late nineteenth century as both an industrial technology for producing military uniforms in arsenals and an instrument of the upper-class, Westernized, elite woman's lifestyle. By the 1910s, the sewing machine was found in virtually every upper-class ("jōryū") household in the nation. But the sewing machine, like middle-class status itself, remained a minority possession in the early postwar era. Women in "laborer families" who spent long hours sewing would be doing much work by hand, and perhaps some by machine. The extensive time devoted to home sewing suggests that a commercialized consumer society, which had first emerged in urban Japan as far back as the late 1600s and had been so flamboyantly celebrated in the modern emporiums of the cities since the early years of the century, still coexisted with a significant realm of home-based, noncommercial, (re)productive activity. Ready-to-wear was still a novelty and a luxury.

The material conditions of Japanese life were little changed in the first postwar decade in many respects. A simple way to make the point is to note that photographs of daily life in the 1950s resemble those of the 1930s more than the 1970s. People in the countryside wore sandals and kimono-style everyday clothing. Houses still had thatched roofs, roads were unpaved, and oxen plowed fields. The consumer "necessities" of life in the 1970s were still either great luxuries or entirely out of reach: motorcycles, cars, electric fans, refrigerators, and televisions.

In other ways as well, individuals were not yet wholly integrated into or overtaken by the world of mass, bureaucratized, profit-seeking institutions that served as defining sites of middle-class life. Cultural and leisure activity through the 1950s, as before the war, remained tied to local community events, such as the shrine or temple festival, or holiday visits to nearby sites or ancestral villages; group tours to distant places, organized by travel agencies, had not yet become commonplace. Most people in Japan until the late 1950s were born at home, not in hospitals, and they were attended by midwives, not doctors. Most people died at home as well. Funerals and weddings took place at home (especially in the countryside) or at temples and shrines rather than at commercial establishments dedicated to providing these services.[25] The great milestones of individual and family life—birth, marriage, death—continued to be marked in relatively intimate settings.

## High Growth Trends: The Mass Middle Class Arrives

Social patterns began to change dramatically in the late 1950s. First, the countryside was shrinking. Both the number and proportion of full-time farmers began a sharp and steady decline, from 2.1 million full-time farm households in 1955 to well under half that number (830,000) in 1970. The proportion of the labor force employed in agriculture fell below 20 percent in 1970 and would continue falling, to less than 10 percent in 1985. This demographic shift created some empty ghost villages, but the countryside was not so utterly evacuated as these numbers suggest, because in many ways the city and new forms of employment and ways of life moved out to the countryside in what is, after all, a small chain of islands. (No place in Japan is more than eighty miles from the seacoast.) With better roads and the income to afford motorcycles and cars, postwar Japanese found it increasingly easy to live in the village and commute to work in the city or suburb.

Japanese education also began a dramatic transformation around 1960. Already in the late 1940s and early 1950s, increased numbers of youths began advancing to high school, but the proportion did not pass 50 percent until 1955. Then, from the end of the 1950s and into the 1960s, attendance rates soared, reaching 82 percent in 1970 and 94 percent by 1980. Large proportions also entered two- or four-year colleges. By 1975, 35 percent of high school graduates entered college each year, a rate exceeding that of most European societies and approaching the American rate.

In this context, the function and role of higher education in Japan as a socioeconomic sorting mechanism changed in important ways. Since Meiji times, the upper reaches of the university system had served as the port of entry into a small ruling elite of men and their relatively well-educated wives. Lesser universities and prestigious vocational high schools had screened a fairly privileged minority of middle-level and middle-class functionaries in government and corporate offices, as well as technical supervisors in factories. As colleges and universities opened their doors wider than ever and nearly everyone went to high school, these upper levels of the school system became a sorting machine for the middle-class masses.

The Ministry of Education and the leaders of corporate Japan observed this transformation and managed it with care. Advisory committees of businessmen in the early 1960s joined education bureaucrats to call for exam-focused public schooling that would impart basic skills to an expanded pool of new blue- and white-collar workers who would thus be able to adapt to rapidly changing production and office technologies. They wanted such schooling to award a hierarchy of credentials, from high school to junior college to college degrees, to help slot young men and women into appropriate levels and roles in the workplace. The expansion of Japan's notorious "examination hell" must be seen in this light. Against the wishes of many teachers who wanted to emphasize other modes of learning, the examination-centered school curriculum was designed to both sort young people and discipline them. It prepared them, boys especially, for a demanding, competitive working routine by offering vast experience at repetitive cramming for dull exams.

One important feature of mass higher education in the first decade of rapid growth sharply distinguishes this era from both the prewar era and the period from the 1970s through the 1990s: access was remarkably egalitarian. Students from the most economically privileged families who entered public universities—which were (and are) the most prestigious ports of entry to elite positions—in the 1960s were only slightly overrepresented, and the children of the poorest families were represented almost precisely in proportion to their numbers in the overall population. Of students in national universities in 1961, 19.7 percent came from the poorest 20 percent of families, and 20.2 percent were from the next quintile (roughly speaking, the lower-middle class).[26] This remarkably egalitarian profile of student backgrounds was testimony to the standardized quality of public schools across the nation as the economic miracle began. Equality then eroded gradually in the 1960s, and more quickly after 1970, as attendance at expensive, private, after-school examination-prep schools became a virtual prerequisite to pass university entrance exams.

Japanese workplaces also took on new postwar social characteristics as the middle-class way of life became ascendant in the 1960s. The proportion of family workers in the labor force dropped steadily, from two-thirds of all workers in the late 1950s to under half by the end of the 1960s. As high school education came to be the norm, it lost value as a job credential. In the 1940s and 1950s, an education-based hierarchy, with roots in the prewar era, dominated the workplace. Male and female middle-school graduates worked as blue-collar operatives with relatively limited future prospects. High school boys could take on skilled production or clerical jobs with a reasonable expectation of rising at least to foreman (in some cases beyond), while girls with high school degrees could move into secretarial office jobs in relatively prestigious companies. University graduates entered the elite managerial positions in corporate and bureaucratic offices. Then, as almost everyone went on to high school in the 1960s and 1970s, the high school diploma came to define a floor rather than a privileged middle point of entry. A better-educated and better-disciplined workforce was one result. Another was a significant closing of the gap between white- and blue-collar work, at least among men. When technicians and managers with college degrees had supervised production workers with a middle-school education, the differences in experience and expectations were great. By the 1970s, when virtually all employees had gone to school through age eighteen and college education itself imparted relatively little new knowledge or skills, the gap between the skills brought to the job by blue-collar high school recruits and white-collar college graduates was much smaller than in earlier decades.

A related characteristic of the postwar social condition of the high-growth era was the emergence of the nuclear family as the norm, both in practice and even more important in the reigning cultural image of typical and desirable family life. In fact, nuclear families, as defined in official statistics, had already accounted for 54 percent of all families in the 1920s, but the significance and definition of this concept must be further explored. Some of these so-called nuclear families were most likely extended families in transition, that is, grandparents had passed away before grandchildren were born. More significant than a modest further increase in the proportion of nuclear families from the 1950s onward was an increase in single-member households from 3 percent in 1955 to 14 percent in 1975, and the sharp fall over these same twenty years in the proportion of those families defined as extended, from one-third of all to just one-fifth. Many single-member households were young, unmarried wage-earners living in company dorms or apartments. The rise of one-person households and the decline in extended ones gave the slightly increased numbers of nuclear families greater prominence as the normative state of family life.

When Western commentators in the late 1950s began to speak of Japan's "new middle class," taking their cue from Ezra Vogel's landmark study, they were referring to nuclear families.[27] The adjective "new" marks a contrast to the families of the urban middle class of the prewar, wartime, and early postwar eras—the shopkeepers, small traders, and small manufacturers who had been the dominant presence in the neighborhoods of Japanese cities from early in the century (and before) until the 1950s. What was truly new about this "new middle class" was its expanded reach, not its existence in and of itself. Just as village life was transformed but not destroyed in the high-growth era, these older urban families did not disappear. Indeed, they remain numerous and a source of the vitality of city life in Japan to this day.[28] The social phenomenon of middle-class "salaryman" families did not obliterate old social forms. It coexisted with the old forms in social practice but overwhelmed them in social discourse, eventually provoking a reaction of nostalgia and yearning for the "authentic" social roots of Japanese city and country life.

The expanded new middle class took up residence in the growing suburbs of Tokyo, Yokohama, Nagoya, Osaka, and other cities. In the booming decades of the 1960s through the 1980s, huge apartment blocks sprouted in what had been rice or vegetable fields, and newly built single-family homes sprawled in all directions out of these cities. In the typical nuclear families of these years, the husband commuted by train to a demanding full-time job in an office or factory, and the wife devoted herself to the care of their children, rarely more than two in number, perhaps taking on a part-time job.

Japan's bureaucratic, political, and corporate leaders did not observe these trends passively. A variety of programs did not simply sustain the nuclear family but supported a particular version of it. Japan's postwar social security system was put into place from the 1950s through the 1970s, and reinforced thereafter, on the premise of the "standard" nuclear family with a strictly gendered division of labor.[29] Built into tax policy was a strong disincentive to women to work more than part-time: a spouse's income under approximately $10,000 was untaxed, but income over that amount was taxed at the primary earner's much higher rate. And the officially sponsored "New Life Movement" took on a new dimension in the mid-1950s when major companies started extensive programs to teach the wives of employees to be "professional" household managers.[30]

The postwar society of high-growth Japan was marked by a range of cultural changes related to these shifts in rural life, education, the workplace, and family structure. A spread and increase in the power of the mass media was a new departure of the late 1950s that reflected the takeoff in the number of households that owned televisions. Prodded by television and print advertising to acquire the new products flooding from Japanese factories, a heightened fever of consumerism permeated society. The consumeristic commercial culture that had emerged in the early twentieth century, especially among middle-class city-dwellers, engulfed the vast majority of Japanese people in these years. From being a society in which the majority of inhabitants worked most of the time to satisfy their relatively basic food, clothing, and shelter needs, Japan shifted to one whose members were "liberated" to pursue their wants and desires as shaped and manipulated by mass advertising.

New forms of desire emerged not only for things but for other people. One aspect of the postwar remaking of family life concerned how families came to be in the first place. In upper-class and middle-class Japan of the early twentieth century, marriages were typically arranged, although a somewhat subversive ideal of love as the basis of marriage had appeared among a minority. Through the 1950s, the arranged marriage was still quite common in the new middle class of white-collar salaried workers: the partners would be formally introduced by relatives or a professional marriage arranger and meet several times for a brief "look-see" (omiai).[31] But the ideal of the "love marriage," no longer considered subversive, was winning the day. The custom of dating became popular among college youths and young workers in the 1950s, and the word for "date" (deeto) was imported from English. Gradually but steadily, the proportion of Japanese marriages defined by the couples as "love matches" rose.

Japan of the postwar era also became for the first time a society in which large-scale, bureaucratic, and commercial institutions were omnipresent in the lives of most people. Hospitals became the almost universal sites for birth and death: in 1955, 82 percent of childbirths had taken place at home; in 1975 the proportion was a mere 1.2 percent![32] Weddings were transformed into lavish and costly spectacles, aggressively marketed and expertly performed in thousands of hotels and wedding halls nationwide.[33] Funerals and the various anniversary memorial services of Buddhist observance were also increasingly provided by such institutions. As bullet trains, automobiles, and jet travel came within reach of the middle class, mass tourism at home and, increasingly, abroad surged from the 1960s through the 1990s.

Finally, new ideas about what it meant to be Japanese began to spread widely. One constant in the identity of being Japanese is the popular conviction, dating back at least to the late Tokugawa era, that such an identity exists or ought to exist.[34] As the shared experiences of people changed and expanded in scope, the defining experiences and attitudes of this imagined community of "the Japanese" changed. From the late 1950s onward, Japanese people came to be knit together by new images of what it meant to be Japanese, broadcast by newly powerful and standardized media organs. When Crown Prince Akihito (Emperor Hirohito's son) broke tradition in 1959 and married the daughter of a wealthy industrialist, nonetheless a commoner, their union symbolized the modern postwar ideal of the love marriage and the nuclear family. Only a fraction of the population saw the parade, but a desire to watch the event reportedly sparked a huge boom in television sales. (Any direct cause-and-effect relationship might be spurious, since the wedding occurred just as the industry was taking off in any case.) But undeniably, the mass media provided the means to share this experience, and its producers and announcers defined its meaning for viewers. Five years later, Japan hosted the 1964 Olympics in Tokyo, signaling the nation's reentry into international society. Again, of course, only a small minority could actually attend the games. But everyone could share the experience by watching the games on television, this time in color.

In cultural terms, both the everyday and ceremonial experiences of middle-class, educated, urban Japanese families came to define a new image of contemporary "Japanese-ness" in the 1960s. This image was reflected in the eyes of TV cameras and beamed into homes proudly adorned with Sanyos or Sonys. The substance of home dramas and cartoons such as the hugely popular *Sazae-san* (a kinder and gentler precursor to *Kurayon Shin-chan* or, across the Pacific, to *The Simpsons*) showed viewers a narrow range of the shared middle-class lives and dilemmas of "we Japanese."

In various ways, then, patterns of social thought and behavior that have come to define the Japanese middle class (both in Japan and abroad) came together in the high-growth era of the late 1950s through the 1970s. All of these patterns were more or less related. We can understand this by considering briefly the new experience of being a mother in Japan of these years. Married women had fewer children in the 1960s than before. They did much less sewing. They relied increasingly on purchased, finished goods. The automation of housework freed up some of their time; the commercialization of various services, such as food preparation, did the same. But interestingly, these changes did not motivate women to seek work outside the home. Tax incentives and employer prejudice conspired to limit the number of women working full-time in long-term careers, although from the mid-1960s on, many married women, even those with children, chose to work part-time. But large numbers also committed themselves to remain full-time homemakers. This home-based role was defined as much by what mothers did for their children's education as by housework or support for their husbands. The very possibility of the so-called education mother of postwar and contemporary Japan was premised on a host of other changes: increased affluence that enables families to afford consumer goods and household appliances; living in nuclear families so that caring for in-laws was not a major task (at least while they were healthy); and raising fewer children in the first place. Justifying the decision of women in middle-class families to play this role in the long run was the promise that success in school would lead young boys to the good jobs that would guarantee them a secure mainstream life, and lead young girls to make suitable wives for these workers.

## Conclusion

According to reports such as that from the *Asahi* quoted at the outset, the three decades from the early 1960s through the early 1990s were the golden age, the short happy life—with apologies to Hemingway—of Japan's middle class.[35] The *Asahi* reporter made the case that "the foundations of a way of life in which everybody believed themselves part of the 'mainstream' is crumbling." The postwar middle classes were surely better off and more secure than the Western clothes paupers of earlier decades. But even during these years when the middle-class way of life was ascendant and often celebrated, an ongoing discourse of insecurity, centered on the struggle to enter and maintain a place in the middle class, has been remarkably persistent. The examination competition was "hell." The corporate treadmill might have offered considerable job security, but all salarymen knew they had to compete fiercely to reach section and division chief status ahead of their buddies and capture the holy grail of executive board membership. This last achievement would allow a man to stay on the job past the retirement age of fifty-five and avoid shifting to a lower-paid job in a subsidiary. Women, for their part, had to worry about their children's grades and exam scores if they were to win the esteem of neighbors and in-laws. In a 1977 essay, the noted social critic Murakami Yasusuke nicely evoked the underside of the anxiety of the mass middle class when he echoed the spirit of the Sakai-Morichika manifesto of 1907 and Hara Kei's fearful appraisal of 1910. In retrospect, his opinion seems overwrought, but he appears to have been serious when he wrote that if the government failed to develop policies to stabilize its livelihood, "the new middle class might turn itself into a mob of the betrayed."[36]

At century's end, the sense of crisis among the ranks of Japan's middle class, as conveyed throughout the media, including the *Asahi* article cited here, is profound. Probably the objective economic insecurity of the vast majority of Japanese people who count themselves members of the middle class is indeed greater than it has been in the past. In 1997, Nikkeiren, Japan's major business federation concerned with labor issues, described shifting employment patterns in a way that seemed to justify a perception of unprecedented crisis. It predicted the shrinking of the proportion of "employees who accumulate and use abilities over the long term [at a single employer]" and an increase in the number of "workers with specialized high-level skills" hired for short-term jobs on a contract basis. The head of Nikkeiren's labor law division bluntly and ominously claimed that "the transformation Japan must make in its industrial structure requires the flexibilization of people [hito ga ryūdōka]."

The *Asahi* article began with a bang, with its suggestion that the middle class was about to disappear, and Mr. A. in particular on the verge of losing job, home, and even domestic bliss. It ended with a whimper: "Of course, corporations in the future will require lifetime-type employees to carry on the core business of the enterprise. But it is expected that the proportion of such employees will decline from 80 percent [of the workforce of major corporations] to 70 percent over the next several years." Similarly, the corporate restructuring and downsizing behind the many loud announcements of 1999 ("Company X to cut five thousand jobs," and so on) has in fact been less drastic than it seems, and certainly less drastic than such practices typically have been in the United States.[37] These reductions are typically spread over two to five years and rely heavily on normal attrition, hiring freezes, and early retirement buyouts.

The threatening opening to the 1997 *Asahi* article and the sensational announcements of job cutbacks in 1999 appear somewhat hysterical when compared with the modest concluding prediction that the ranks of long-term workers might decline by 10 percent over several years, or in view of the relatively moderate programs of corporate restructuring. But the tone of despair is not unfamiliar. The middle-class experience—an urban or suburban, homeowning, modestly affluent nuclear family in which the parents are educated at least through high school and the children aspire to more, with a full-time salaried father and perhaps a part-time working mother—has reigned as "a way of life of which everybody believed themselves part" for only thirty years. But from well before this time people hoping to enjoy the happy life of the middle class have been intensely anxious about losing access to it, as have state officials and intellectuals who observed their situation.

But the postwar discourse of crisis differs from that of the prewar years in one important regard. People no longer talk of a crisis in which middle-class Japanese will find themselves threatened by a challenge from below. It has hardly seemed possible since the 1960s to identify a separate lower status (the working class) into which Murakami's "mob of the betrayed" might fall. The postwar and contemporary middle-class crisis is perceived and discussed as the crisis of all

Japanese. This is surely a major reason why even modest signs of insecurity receive immodest attention, or why a 10 percent decline in the ranks of the long-term career employee is seen as a crisis. Those concerned with matters of policy and politics must respond to both the gradual impoverishment of those who are subject to voluntary retirements and the like and the more intense rhetoric of a vanishing middle-class dream.

## Notes

Japanese names appear with last names first, even in English-language publications.

1. Quoted in Matsunari Yoshie et al., *Nihon no sarariiman* [*The Japanese Salaryman*] (Tokyo: Aoki shoten, 1957), 34. The term that I have translated as "middle-class society" is "chūtō shakai," which might literally be rendered "middle-level society." At this early stage in the discourse of social classes, a wide variety of terms for "middle class" were in use.

2. Takeuchi Yō draws on a 1920 government survey to suggest that 5.5 percent of the employed population nationwide were "salarymen"; see Takeuchi Yō, "Sarariiman to iu shakaiteki hyōshō," in *Nihon bunka no shakaigaku: Gendai shakaigaku*, edited by Inoue Jun, et al. ["The Social Symbol of the 'Salaryman,'" in *Sociology of Japanese Culture: Contemporary Sociology*.] (Tokyo: Iwanami shoten, 1996). Matsunari and his colleagues compare what would appear to be the Tokyo portion of the same survey (neither work offers a precise citation) to one of 1908 to note that in urban Tokyo those defined as "shokuin" (white-collar or clerical and technical staff) had increased from 5.6 percent of the employed population in 1908 to 21.4 percent in 1920; see Matsunari et al., *Nihon no sarariiman*, 31.

3. Matsunari and his colleagues cite a passage from *Japan's First Modern Novel: Ukigumo of Futabatei Shimei*, translated by Marleigh Grayer Ryan (New York: Columbia University Press, 1967), that describes such a troubled former samurai: "Alas, the changes in political climate had left him like a fish out of water. A man's arm may be strengthened by the practice of kendō, yet he cannot necessarily use a spade; when his mouth is weighted down with the solemn language of the feudal order, it is no easy matter for him to say 'yes, sir' like a shop clerk. Then peddling he felt would soil the good name of the family. He scurried about until, with great difficulty, he secured a post in the Shizuoka han administration. Although it was only a petty job [literally, 'barely a "koshiben" job'—see discussion later in the chapter], and he could not better himself, he was happy for he was able to give his only child, Bunzō, an education by generously lavishing on it a goodly portion of his meager income" (203); see Matsunari et al., *Nihon no sarariiman*, 17.

4. Louise Young, "Marketing the Modern: Department Stores, Consumer Culture, and the New Middle Class in Interwar Japan," *International Labor and Working-class History* 55(Spring 1999): 53.

5. For a discussion of this trend in the United States, see Olivier Zunz, *Why the American Century?* (Chicago: University of Chicago Press, 1998).

6. Matsunari et al., *Nihon no sarariiman*, 27–31.
7. Ibid., 31.
8. Ibid., 35.
9. Young, "Marketing the Modern," 56.
10. Takeuchi, "Sarariiman," 128–29.
11. Ibid., 127.
12. Ariyoshi Hiroyuki and Hamaguchi Haruhiko, eds., *Nihon no shin chūkansō* [*Japan's New Middle Class*] (Tokyo: Waseda University Press, 1982), 1.
13. For a lively discussion of the history of terms for "salary" and "salaryman" in the West, China, and Japan, see Nii Kaku, "Sarariiman-ron"[*On Salaryman*], *Chūō kōron* [*Central Review*] 43(December 1928): 39–40.
14. Young, "Marketing the Modern," 61.
15. Miriam Silverberg, *Japanese Modern Times* (Berkeley: University of California Press, in press); on prostitution and café waitresses, see Sheldon Garon, *Molding Japanese Minds: The State in Everyday Life* (Princeton: Princeton University Press, 1997), ch. 3.
16. *Hara Kei nikki* [*The Diary of Hara Kei*], June 13, 1910, cited in Ariyoshi and Hamaguchi, *Nihon no shin chūkansō*, 4.
17. *Tokyo Asahi Shinbun*, February 17, 1918, cited in Matsunari et al., *Nihon no sarariiman*, 44–45. "Mochi" are the sticky rice cakes traditionally prepared for the New Year holiday.
18. Nihon Daijiten Kankō iinkai, ed., *Nihon kokugo daijiten* [*Dictionary of the Japanese Language*], vol. 8 (Tokyo: Shōgakukan, 1974), 602.
19. Takeuchi, "Sarariiman," 131; Tanuma Hajime, *Gendai no chūkan kaikyū* [*The Contemporary Middle Class*] (Tokyo: Otsuki shoten, 1958), 6.
20. Ariyoshi and Hamaguchi (*Nihon no shin chūkansō*, 4) cite Tokyo-fu, *Tokyoshi oyobi kinsetsu chōson chūtōkaikyū seikei chōsa* [*A Survey of Living Conditions of the New Middle Class in Tokyo and Surrounding Towns and Villages*] (Tokyo: 1922).
21. On male and female organizing efforts, see Matsunari et al., *Nihon no sarariiman*, 46–57.
22. Takeuchi, "Sarariiman," cites Maeda Hajime, *Sarariiman monogatari* [*The Story of the Salaryman*] (Tokyo: Tōyō keizai shuppan, 1928), for the wages of Western clothes paupers (1–2). For the wages of factory workers, see Naikaku Tōkeikyoku, *Senkanki rōdō tōkei jitchi chōsa hōkoku* [*Interwar Labor Statistic Field Survey Reports*], vol. 4 (1927; reprint, Tokyo: Toyō Shorin, 1990).
23. Matsunari et al., *Nihon no sarariiman*, 60.
24. For one such survey, see Kawasaki City, ed., *Kawasaki rōdō shi* [*Kawasaki Labor History*] (Kawasaki 1987): women averaged 139 minutes a day for sewing, 179 minutes for cooking, just 58 minutes for shopping, and 57 minutes "spent with children" (200).
25. On births, weddings, deaths, funerals, and other rituals, see Irokawa Daikichi, *Shōwa shi: Sesō hen* [*History of Showa: Daily Life*] (Tokyo: Shogakkan, 1990), 25–32.
26. Thomas P. Rohlen, "Is Japanese Education Becoming Less Egalitarian? Notes on High School Stratification and Reform," *Journal of Japanese Studies* 3(Winter 1977): 41.
27. Ezra Vogel, *Japan's New Middle Class: The Salary Man and His Family in a Tokyo Suburb* (Berkeley: University of California Press, 1963).

28. Classic and recent studies of urban Japan include Ronald Dore, *City Life in Japan: A Study of a Tokyo Ward* (Berkeley: University of California Press, 1958); Theodore C. Bestor, *Neighborhood Tokyo* (Stanford: Stanford University Press, 1989); Jennifer Robertson, *Native and Newcomer* (Berkeley: University of California Press, 1991).

29. See Osawa (this volume).

30. See Andrew Gordon, "Managing the Japanese Household: The New Life Movement in Postwar Japan," *Social Politics* 4(Summer 1997): 245–83.

31. Vogel, *Japan's New Middle Class*, 175–78.

32. Irokawa, *Shōwa shi: Sesō hen*, 25–32.

33. Walter Edwards, *Modern Japan Through Its Weddings: Gender, Person, and Society in Ritual Portrayal* (Stanford: Stanford University Press, 1989).

34. Aizawa Yasushi was a pioneer in putting forth the idea of a unique Japanese identity. In his *New Theses*, he argued that the common people were insufficiently indoctrinated with awareness of their special heritage as descendants of the Sun Goddess. He called for rulers to teach "stupid commoners" to revere the "essence of the national body" (kokutai). See Bob T. Wakabayashi, *Anti-Foreignism and Western Learning in Early-Modern Japan: The New Theses of 1825* (Cambridge, Mass.: Harvard Council on East Asian Studies Monographs, 1986).

35. Ernest Hemingway, "The Short Happy Life of Francis Macomber."

36. Murakami Yasusuke, "Shin chūkansō no genjitsusei," *Asahi shimbun*, May 20, 1977, cited in Ariyoshi and Hamaguchi, *Nihon no shin chūkansō*, 4.

37. For interesting data showing that, in response to the same drop in GNP, U.S. corporations on average cut four times as many jobs from their payrolls as do Japanese corporations, see Arthur J. Alexander, *Structural Change and Economic Mobility in Japan*, Report 44A (Washington, D.C.: Japan Economic Institute, November 20, 1998), 6.

# 6

## Inflation: "The Permanent Dilemma" of the American Middle Classes

### Meg Jacobs

Since the country's earliest days, the American belief in a permeable class system, allowing for and encouraging an ethos of social mobility, has constituted the guiding national myth. For decades after the Revolution, that myth was grounded in the reality of a large property-owning class. Late-nineteenth-century industrialization, rather than obliterating the middle classes, resulted in the rapid growth of a new middle class, redefined as white-collar salaried workers. In the middle of the twentieth century, blue-collar wage-earners saw an increase in income that provided them with access to living standards comparable to those of white-collar workers. By the end of the century, three-quarters of all Americans, regardless of occupational differences, defined themselves as middle-class. Indeed, the United States stands alone among modern industrial nations in having no language of rigid class hierarchies.[1]

And yet middle-class expansion in the twentieth century generated its own class tensions, resulting from a bifurcated process of middle-class formation. One route to middle-class status sprang from the white-collar opportunities available in the new corporations and government bureaucracies that emerged at the turn of the twentieth century. A system of mass education combined with the needs of corporate and bureaucratic America enabled the sons and daughters of immigrants and farmers to join this rapidly expanding new middle class. Thus, between 1880 and 1930 the number of salaried employees increased eightfold, and by the 1950s clerks, salesmen, managers, and professionals accounted for 37 percent of the workforce. This new white-collar world provided job security and comfortable lifestyles. Though they worked for large routinized organizations, these employees retained an individualist ethos. Even if they belonged to professional associations or cultivated identities as company men, they remained largely unorganized. Their middle-class status derived from and was an integral part of the expanding apparatus of modern corporate capitalism.[2]

The second route to middle-class formation stemmed from the New Deal social contract, one that largely targeted blue-collar workers. Here the effort to transform the working classes into middle classes was public and explicit. With the support of the state, industrial workers organized in large numbers; in the fifteen years after 1932, union membership grew from 3 million to 15 million. Once organized and legitimized, workers carried out successful wage campaigns and thus came to enjoy material benefits and middle-class lifestyles, precisely because of an absence of rigid social hierarchies. In a celebratory spirit, *Fortune* editors hailed the arrival of "America's booming new middle-income class."[3]

These two routes, one private and predicated on unorganized individual relationships, the other public and based on organized negotiations, came into conflict. Although this dual-track process of middle-class formation is perhaps endemic to all modern economies, there are two factors peculiar to the United States. First, precisely because the United States lacks clear class boundaries, the question of membership in one vast amorphous middle class is hard to define and therefore subject to constant debate. Thus, the very myth of class inclusiveness, with its permeability and accessibility, has in fact exploded well-defined identities and led to a seemingly endless social process of measuring, comparing, and ranking. The absence of overt class struggles does not mean there are no social tensions. Intellectuals such as David Potter, Vance Packard, and C. Wright Mills have all famously noted that rapid advances could exact a psychological cost, and thus they talk about the white-collar middle classes as insecure and status-anxious. In the twentieth century, not only were white-collar workers plagued by status concerns, but their social positions were increasingly challenged by blue-collar workers who earned comparable incomes.[4]

The second significant factor is the absence in the United States of the kind of clear working-class voice that in many European countries has been expressed politically and programmatically through a labor or social-democratic party. Though an American labor party has perhaps been precluded by American economics, culture, and politics, its absence is nevertheless significant. When the new unionism emerged, its demands on the state and political culture were always mediated by the Democratic Party, which itself was divided by a multitude of interests and factions. Ira Katznelson is correct to point out the tensions in the New Deal coalition between southern whites and northern liberals. But the New Deal Democratic Party was also divided by economic interests in the North. At best, middle- and working-class voters forged an uneasy and always tenuous alliance within the Democratic Party.[5]

In postwar America, the politics of the bargaining table came into direct conflict with the politics of class inclusion. This was precisely the moment when organized labor, at the peak of its power, most rapidly challenged class lines. In just one generation after 1940, blue-collar income doubled.[6] As industrial workers and capital became more organized, the orientation of the white-collar middle class came into question. This middle class, because of its ill-defined and porous quality, alternately felt attracted to and under siege by organized labor. Likewise, the middle-class attitude toward big business fluctuated between fear and adulation. In general, as an unorganized mass, the middle class perceived a loss of economic and political power. At the same time, it was widely derided, at least by some intellectuals, as conformist and devoid of cultural autonomy.[7] Those factors heightened tensions between the unorganized white-collar middle classes and organized blue-collar wage-earners. Although perhaps not leading to pitched battles, these tensions did breed insecurity, anxiety, and ultimately partisan rivalry.

Those pressures played out particularly around the issue of inflation. Throughout the postwar era, Americans consistently lamented the continuous, albeit relatively small, increases in the consumer price index (CPI) that characterized the period. In public opinion polls, the high cost of living ranked as the number-one domestic problem in twenty of the thirty years from 1945 to 1975. In the 1950s, when annual inflation averaged less than 3 percent, Americans considered inflation the most important domestic problem in eight of the ten years they were surveyed.[8] This is not to claim that inflation was the only issue that unsettled the middle classes, but it was perhaps the least likely source of unease. In general, liberal economists regard mild inflation as a necessary and even beneficial by-product of economic growth and full employment. In this scenario, low levels of inflation serve as what the historian Charles Maier labels a "social lubricant," forestalling distributional conflict.[9] But while Keynesians and liberal intellectuals may have accepted the coupling of growth with mild inflation in the 1950s, the public did not.

This concern over inflation poses an empirical and theoretical puzzle. For economists, like Robert Schiller, who believe that low levels of inflation exact little or no economic cost, the public opinion data come as a surprise. For political scientists and political historians who assume that the middle class is indifferent to the mild inflation that accompanies the economic growth from which they benefit, the historical evidence is also puzzling.[10] In other words, the middle classes should not have minded the mild inflation of the 1950s. But they did.

We can best understand the concern over inflation as a symbolic issue through which battles of class formation played out. In an uncertain world marked by the multiple threats of nuclear annihilation and Communist subversion, the simultaneous blurring of class boundaries and an increasing sense of powerlessness heightened middle-class insecurities. Neither wage compression nor the unionization of labor that had made it possible received broad public support; instead, many Americans resented the inflation that those forces brought. In the popular mind, labor became increasingly associated with communism, corruption, and disruptive strikes. Just as important, union gains in securing wage increases made labor susceptible to charges of acting as a "special interest" and causing what many perceived as "ruinous inflation." Indeed, organized labor in key industries succeeded through wage-push inflation in seizing income not from big business but rather from the salaried middle class, retired people, savers, and government employees. The middle classes, including many highly skilled blue-collar workers who suffered from wage compression, came to see union power as illegitimate. In that context, Republicans used resentment over the "high cost of living" to their electoral and policy advantage. Even low levels of inflation became a political wedge between the organized working classes and the new middle classes. This chapter first explores the historical alliances and tensions between white-collar and blue-collar workers, then examines how inflation became a contentious issue. I conclude by describing how conservatives turned resentment over inflation into blame and won the battle over public perceptions of the costs and causes of inflation.

## The Middle Classes in the Early Twentieth Century

Clashes between organized and unorganized segments of the workforce began early in the twentieth century. As corporations and organized labor came to play a more central role in the nation's economy, politics, and culture, the old middle-class professionals and elites felt increasingly marginal. The historian Richard Hofstadter captured it best: "They were less important, and they knew it." And even the new middle classes perceived a lack of leverage and control. Amid a general upward price trend that began in 1896 and lasted through World War I, "the average middle-class citizen" felt aggrieved. With "trusts mushrooming almost every day" and "the working class organizing to protect itself," the salaried worker "saw himself as a member of a vast but unorganized and therefore helpless consuming public." The muckraking journalist Ray Stannard Baker grasped this sense of victimization:

> The unorganized public, where will it come in? The professional man, the lecturer, the writer, the artist, the farmer, the salaried government employee, and all the host of men who are not engaged in actual production or delivery of necessary material things, how will they fare? . . . Is there any doubt that the income of organized labor and the profits of organized capital have gone up enormously, while the man-on-a-salary and most of the great middle class, paying much more for the necessaries of life, have had no adequate increase in earnings?

As Hofstadter explained, this was "the complaint of the unorganized against the consequences of organization."[11]

These tensions, though real, remained largely latent, especially amid the flush times of the 1920s. A decade marked by economic growth and an explosion in consumer products, the 1920s witnessed an increase in the number of salaried workers and their standards of living. At the same time, organized labor experienced a setback and union ranks dwindled. In addition, tighter immigration laws restricted the number of newcomers searching for industrial jobs.[12]

The 1930s, of course, saw a dramatic surge in union membership. But with an unemployment rate of 25 percent, shared hard times had the effect of delaying class tensions. In fact, for an important moment, the middle classes forged an alliance with industrial workers under the mantle of the New Deal. Though many at first pointed to a lack of business confidence and overproduction as the main causes of economic decline, in the depths of the Great Depression the belief that prices were too high and beyond the consuming capacity of most Americans pervaded popular thought. That view received legitimacy from underconsumption theorists who held that a maldistribution of income and monopolistic control of prices had undermined the public interest. In the context of the Great Depression, arguments for redistribution put the interests of the middle classes in tandem with those of labor. The result was broad support for a new configuration of state power and governmental authority that endorsed a high-wage, low-price political economy and mobilized workers and consumers to that end. Labor-liberals argued with success that the organization of workers under the National Labor Relations Act (1935) was a key institutional remedy to the alleged underconsumption because it gave workers the right to organize and engage in collective bargaining for higher wages. Throughout the New Deal and World War II, this policy community continued to maintain that mass purchasing power guaranteed through higher wages provided the key to economic growth and general prosperity.[13]

But this cross-class alliance would not last. The fissures became clear in the first postwar strike wave. At the end of the war, unions represented one-third of nonagricultural workers, and they stood poised to extend their wartime wage gains. In the winter of 1946, the United Auto Workers (UAW) used "Purchasing Power for Prosperity" as its slogan in a strike against General Motors. Taking their cue from Office of Price Administration (OPA) economists, these workers argued that only their formula of high wages and low prices would prevent depression and sustain postwar prosperity. Without adequate consumer purchasing power, they maintained, the oversupplied channels of commerce would cause it to choke on its own product. UAW leader Walter Reuther explained, "We fight to make progress with the community and not at the expense of the community." He insisted, "We will not be a party to sand-bagging the American consumer."[14]

For a time, labor received popular and political support. In late 1946, the Congress of Industrial Organizations (CIO) released the widely praised Nathan Report, a technically sophisticated justification of the purchasing power thesis. Robert Nathan, formerly a liberal planner on the War Production Board, argued that corporations, flush with wartime profits, could afford to increase pay by 38 percent with no price increases. And indeed, many Americans—including white-collar, middle-class Americans—accepted this claim as true. For months the larger community supported the UAW's assertion that GM could afford to increase wages by as much as 30 percent without price increases. Nearly a year after the end of the war, 73 percent of the public favored the retention of price controls under the OPA.[15] Throughout the postwar strike wave of 1945 and 1946, the Truman administration, especially the newly created Council of Economic Advisers, gave official sanction to labor's rationale for its repeated strike campaigns.[16]

But inflation—or rather, the inability to control inflation—emerged as the Achilles' heel of postwar labor-liberalism. After the political defeat of OPA by its conservative enemies, consumer prices shot up by an annual rate of 16 percent within a year. The continuation and acceleration of immediate postwar inflation made it increasingly unpopular to push for wage advances that could only drive up prices further. Without price controls, manufacturers used wage increases as justification for raising the prices they charged consumers. The business community absolved itself of any responsibility for the inflationary specter by blaming labor. As the National Association of Manufacturers (NAM) explained, "The Nathan report is an attempt to fool the public into choosing higher wages which means higher prices. That obviously cannot be in the public interest."[17] General Electric president Charles E. Wilson criticized both labor and the administration. "Higher Prices are the legitimate result of the national wage-increase pattern which the present Administration has tolerated, if not actively abetted."[18] In nationwide newspaper advertisements, NAM blamed "labor monopoly" and industrywide bargaining for "rais[ing] the prices of the things you need." A full-page ad declared, "The price of MONOPOLY comes out of your pocket." Another insisted, "Industry-wide bargaining is no bargain for you." "How about some Pro-Public legislation?" another asked.[19] With no small hint of defensiveness, Walter Reuther explained, "Labor has no way to bargain collectively for price reductions."[20]

Business efforts to hold labor accountable for the high cost of living crystallized with the passage of the Taft-Hartley Act of 1947. Its conservative advocates argued that the public suffered from an excess of labor power. The law sought to contain the strength and influence of organized labor by banning foremen from joining unions, outlawing secondary boycotts, and allowing states to pass "right-to-work" laws that prohibited the union shop. To congressional Republicans under the leadership of Senator Robert Taft of Ohio, the dramatic wage-push inflation immediately following the war symbolized labor's strength. From this point on, even during the recession of 1949, they warned about the evils of inflation and explained it as the product of the wage-price spiral forced on the nation by what was then labeled "monopoly unionism." That phrase was a linguistic inversion of an earlier left-wing attack on monopoly capitalism. This anti-inflation campaign now added an economic argument to traditional American fears of organized power. It appealed to and reflected both the real and ideological concerns of small producers who, unlike General Motors and General Electric, could not protect themselves from the costs of inflation by passing them on. By conflating inflation with labor's power, conservatives in Congress and industry leaders aimed to undermine their opponents' strength and drive a wedge through the New Deal alliance of middle-class consumers and working-class laborers.[21]

The outbreak of the Korean War escalated the concern over inflation. Very quickly it became clear that Americans would have to devote 20 percent of their national production to the defense effort. In this circumstance, inflation posed an even larger threat than it had at the beginning of World War II because there was relatively little slack in the economy to absorb the increased defense production.[22] The consumer price index rose 10 percent in sixteen months.[23] From 1950 through 1953, concern about the high cost of living rivaled the concern about the ongoing war. After the Chinese entered the war in January 1951, the administration once again imposed wage and price controls.[24] Despite their uneven application, controls were effective because they worked in tandem with monetary restraint to keep inflation at 2.6 percent a year.[25] But those Americans who were innocent of economics believed that controls should have worked better. Their alarmist feelings became intensified as it became clear that the price index was continuing upward. *Life* magazine reported Director of Mobilization Charles Wilson's warning that "the country is about to go to hell in an overpriced basket."[26]

## "The Permanent Dilemma"

Not everyone regarded such low levels of inflation as a problem. Regardless of the effect on the fixed-income middle classes, Keynesians believed in the necessity of a trade-off between growth and some upward price instability. Liberal economists, including the leading business economist and Harvard professor, Sumner Slichter, began to support modest inflation because it facilitated both full employment and increased government spending. *Business Week* told its readers that high prices would not disappear anytime soon. "If you want full employment you have to have a continuously rising price level." As Slichter argued in a widely discussed article, "How Bad Is Inflation?" "A slowly rising price level is actually preferable to a stable price level. . . . The maintenance of a stable price level would conflict with other important interests of the country." Increasingly, Fair Deal economists came to accept the healthiness of an annual "slow inflation" of 1 to 2 percent, which allowed expansion that in turn generated higher living standards.[27]

But fears of inflation were never far below the surface in the recently affluent society. In May 1952, *Business Week* dubbed inflation "the permanent dilemma" and explained: "A prosperous country can have its own brand of discontentment. . . . The complaint isn't that things are bad, but the price of keeping them good is so high."[28] With large wage settlements, a commitment to cold war spending, and a full employment policy, the postwar economy came under continuous inflationary pressures. And though many firms and industries experienced increases in productivity, those gains were not evenly distributed. Left behind, for instance, were the service and construction industries, growing sectors that, faced with heavy demand, continued to raise their prices. In addition, the steel industry sought larger profits to support necessary modernization. Those forces combined to put stresses on any labor-management peace while passing on higher costs to the consumer. Thus, the specter of inflation remained throughout the 1950s as "the problem of prosperity." *U.S. News & World Report* concluded: "It's a good life, despite war, taxes, inflation."[29]

Though Americans had an overall sense of increasing living standards, the "Age of Inflation" fostered insecurity and anxiety. In part, these insecurities grew from the new experience of a continuous, though unpredictable, upward price trend. The regular reporting of historically high costs suggested a deviation from an earlier romanticized period of price stability. More important, the experience of inflation confounded the hopes of a secure and abundant postwar life that the nation's World War II propaganda had promised. In his 1944 State of the Union address, President Roosevelt announced his Second Bill of Economic Rights, which declared that all Americans had the right to a job and a secure and high standard of living: "The one supreme objective for the future . . . can be summed up in one word: Security." Congress passed the Employment Act of 1946, which asserted the country's commitment to "maximum production, maximum employment, and maximum purchasing power." Through the GI Veterans Bill that guaranteed education and home loans, millions of Americans moved to the suburbs, purchased a home, and obtained a college degree. America's success in making abundance more accessible stimulated inflation. The historian James Patterson explains that Americans soon came to feel entitled to abundance and demanded more. Thus, even amid anxieties about higher costs, public opinion polls consistently revealed that the desired Christmas gift was a new car or a new house.[30]

Indeed, the 1950s were a time when individuals felt growing pressure to demonstrate their social standing through material possessions.[31] That phenomenon became manifest as large sectors of the new middle classes sought to assimilate and assert their place in a new social stratum. The popular social critic Vance Packard captured that sense of striving nicely in his 1959 best-selling book *The Status Seekers*, subtitled "An Exploration of Class Behavior in America and the Hidden Barriers That Affect You, Your Community, Your Future."

Packard suggested that, though class lines had softened because of dramatic economic gains, social stresses had in fact become exaggerated. "Many people are badly distressed, and scared, by the anxieties, inferiority feelings, and straining generated by this unending process of rating and status striving. The status seekers, as I use the term, are people who are continually straining to surround themselves with visible evidence of the superior rank they are claiming."[32] The concept of status anxiety, first delineated by Richard Hofstadter and Seymour Martin Lipset, while much debated, was a reality and reflected real anxiety among the new middle classes. As the historian David Potter put it, "Everything would seem to lead to the conclusion that abundance has exacted a heavy psychological penalty for the physical gains which it has conferred."[33] In this context, small increases in the price of new items could generate stress disproportionate to their significance in one's overall budget or lifestyle.[34]

Blue-collar workers, also feeling this sense of striving and entitlement, found themselves with the union strength to assert their demands. The National Labor Relations Act had intended to institutionalize higher wages through collective bargaining. The postwar gains by organized labor demonstrated the success of that policy. Before the war, nearly 80 percent of a steelworker's income went toward a very basic standard of living. He could afford a new pair of shoes only every two years, and a new coat every six. In 1942, 30 percent of steelworkers lived in homes without indoor bathrooms. But in the fifteen years after the war, steelworkers' living conditions changed dramatically. The same steelworkers came to expect paid vacations, holidays, pensions, and health insurance as part of their earned benefits. And not just skilled workers saw wage gains, but semi-skilled assembly-line workers in unionized industries as well. The editors of *Fortune* understood the American union as the worker's "tool for gaining and keeping as an individual the status and security of a full citizen in capitalist society. That the union has made the worker to an amazing degree a middle-class member of a middle-class society— in the plant, in the local community, in the economy—is the real measure of its success." Three-fifths of all families now had some discretionary income.[35]

But those gains did not occur automatically. They came about because productivity increased, because other industrial economies had been bombed during the war and could not compete, and because workers continuously went on strike. In the postwar years, annual work stoppages reached all-time highs. In 1955 nearly four hundred strikes involved one thousand workers or more. The *Fortune* editors correctly claimed that "the American union is a militant union—

more militant, perhaps, than its European counterparts." Inflationary expectations encouraged unions to push in advance for higher wage gains. Indeed, the UAW had already accepted a private solution to the squeeze of such expectations. In its 1948 agreement with General Motors, the automaker offered cost-of-living adjustments (COLAs) that, in effect, institutionalized the notion of the "wage-price spiral," thereby providing workers with protection at the consumer's expense—and at the expense of the salaried worker. In 1950 auto workers signed the first five-year union contract predicated on COLAs. The *Fortune* writer Daniel Bell explained the historic nature of this "Treaty of Detroit," a contract that "unmistakably accepts the existing distribution of income between wages and profits as 'normal,' if not as 'fair.' . . . It is the first major union contract that explicitly accepts objective economic facts—cost of living and productivity—as determining wages, thus throwing overboard all theories of wages as determined by political power, and of profits as 'surplus value.'" But Bell's description reflected an ideal more than a reality. Strikes continued throughout the decade. The idea of a labor-management accord, much in evidence in historical and labor relations literature, represented but a wishful fable at best.[36]

Although the emerging Keynesian consensus on the left maintained that mild inflation would alleviate distributional conflict, the "creeping inflation" of the 1950s fueled tensions between social groups and thus led to the very conflict this technocratic elite had sought to avoid.[37] In his 1951 classic work *The Future of American Politics*, the journalist Samuel Lubell predicted that inflation would remain an insurmountable problem for the labor Left. Lubell correctly pointed to the New Deal Democratic coalition as the formative bloc in American politics. And yet he also underscored tensions within this alliance. Inflation was one of the divisive issues. Above all, the new Democratic coalition consisted of those who were fighting to get into the middle classes. And these new middle classes—the product of "the march of the masses"—rose in tandem with the growth of the government. This New Deal state, with its political rhetoric of mass abundance and promises of more, then generated heightened expectations for the favored sectors. "Our class struggle arises not from the impoverishment of the masses but from their progress. It is evidence not of the failure of the American dream but of its success." And yet inflation threatened to undermine this progress and tear apart the Democratic alliance because, as Lubell explained, inflation made it harder to give to one group without taking away from another. Thus, Lubell concluded, "inflation has clearly become the breaking point of the Roosevelt coalition." "No new economic gains can be promised any group of Democrats today without threatening the gains of other Democrats."[38]

A ready audience for these arguments emerged among those who suffered from lack of organization or adequate representation, the "unorganized workers and those living on pensions who have no channels through which to make themselves heard."[39] As Charles Maier correctly notes, creeping inflation typically reflects a successful alliance of corporations and unions against middle-class proprietors, pensioners, and savers.[40] The demographic fact that more and more workers were obtaining employment in professional and service-sector jobs during this period did create a real split between blue-collar workers and their white-collar middle-class counterparts. By all accounts, the group that fared worst from the wage-price spiral were those on fixed incomes: teachers, public servants, white-collar workers, pensioners. These Americans—6.3 million government employees, 4 million Social Security pensioners, and another 4 million retired Americans—constituted roughly one-third of the workforce. Salaried workers also feared losing their savings under inflation. Price increases became problematic because families had more and more of their savings invested in insurance policies. Such investments eroded in value, because of their fixed nature, and hence provided less security, not more. Inflation also raised interest rates and discouraged entrepreneurship. Even the well-off began to complain about the "Great Squeeze." *Nation's Business* reported the hardships of John R. Statistic, a fictionalized composite of a businessman and his family who had to make do on an annual salary of $12,000 (about $80,000 today): "He has understandable regret over . . . the dreams of affluence which have failed to materialize."[41]

In this inflationary environment, both unions and monopolies came under increased criticism as "vested interests" that had the power to generate the wage-price spiral, thereby undermining the general welfare. As the economist Walter Morton explained, "Laying the blame for economic evils in trade-unions and monopolies has a wide appeal. It is easy to succumb to this temptation because it is not likely to receive severe scrutiny. On the contrary, an attack upon such unpopular groups as unions and monopolists is quite welcome and therefore likely to meet with uncritical acceptance." Critics of the new Keynesian economics pointed out that compensatory thinking simply fueled these groups' demands because they were confident that the government would support them. As the conservative economist Henry Hazlitt explained, "The pressure on the politicians to continue a policy of inflation is enormous. For the fetish of today is 'full employment.'" Keynesians themselves also attacked "special interests," and indeed, the leading Keynesian, Alvin Hansen, had already begun to decry the lack of "restraint" exhibited by labor unions and called for them to demonstrate "social responsibility."[42]

## "Inflation Is the Great Thief"

Republicans embraced the fight against inflation as a key electoral issue in 1952. On June 15, the Bureau of Labor Statistics released a report placing the cost of living at an all-time high. According to the consumer price index, the American dollar now bought less than half the goods and services it had in 1939. Even though most Americans had come to expect a higher standard of living, including a car, a radio, a paid vacation, and a five-day workweek, most of them were unable to save as much as in the past and also found themselves in debt. A *U.S. News* report summed it up: "Most people are on a treadmill, or losing ground." The inflation since the start of the Korean War wiped out the gains in real purchasing power accrued since 1939.[43]

Above all, Republicans seized on inflation as symptomatic of New Deal–Fair Deal irresponsibility. Of the forty-two freshmen Republican candidates running for Congress, nearly all of them mentioned inflation in their campaigns. In fact, they discussed inflation and waste more than any other issue, including taxes, "creeping socialism," and the Korean War.[44] The Republican platform condemned the high cost of living and blamed Democratic policies: "The wanton extravagance and inflationary policies of the Administration in power have cut the value of the dollar in half. . . . If this Administration is left in power, it will further cheapen the dollar, rob the wage earner, impoverish the farmer and reduce the true value of the savings, pensions, insurance and investment of millions of our people."[45]

Throughout his campaign, Republican presidential candidate Dwight Eisenhower stressed the high cost of living. The personable general took great advantage of television to heighten the drama surrounding inflation. The year 1952, when approximately three-quarters of American households owned televisions, heralded the beginning of political TV spots.[46] These commercials did not determine the election, but they revealed the salient issues of the day. In one, a middle-aged woman holding her groceries declares, "I paid twenty-four dollars for these groceries—look, for this little." Eisenhower responds, "A few years ago, those same groceries cost you ten dollars, now twenty-four, next year thirty—that's what will happen unless we have a change." Another elderly woman laments, "You know what things cost today. High prices are just driving me crazy." Eisenhower soothes, "Yes, my Mamie gets after me about the high cost of living.

It's another reason why I say it's time for a change. Time to get back to an honest dollar and an honest dollar's work." In another, when a man asks which party will lick inflation, Eisenhower replies, "Well, instead of asking which party will bring prices down, why not ask which party has put prices up?" In many spots, the general breaks a pre-sawed piece of wood in half to demonstrate the decrease in the nation's purchasing power since the end of World War II.[47]

After winning the election, Eisenhower saw combating this inflation evil as his main domestic priority. As a fiscal conservative, the new president was staunchly committed to balanced budgets, a sound dollar, and fighting inflation. When Democrats regained control of Congress in 1954, their unwillingness to cut expenditures led the administration to rely on a more active use of restrictionist monetary policy. Federal Reserve Chairman William Martin shared Eisenhower's disdain for inflation and soon moved to restrict the money supply.[48]

Even when this policy achieved success by producing more price stability, inflationary fears were never far from people's minds. Martin's tighter credit coincided with the end of the Korean War and cuts in the federal budget. There ensued a thirteen-month recession in 1953 and 1954 during which unemployment reached a peak of 5.8 percent.[49] After the recession, prices held steady throughout 1955. But from 1953 to 1956, the press constantly reported that the consumer price index was at an "all-time high." The baseline for prices throughout this period was 1939, and according to reports, by 1956 the dollar's value had declined to fifty-two cents.[50] Senator Lyndon Johnson of Texas exclaimed in 1953, "The facts cited in the last report of the Bureau of Labor Statistics on the consumer price index [are] shocking. . . . The knowledge that the overall index has reached an all-time high is deeply disturbing."[51]

In 1956 the CPI increased at a rate of 3.5 percent, seemingly confirming the claims of all major Eisenhower officials that inflation posed the greatest threat to the economy. At a time when most people held bonds, not equity, in pension accounts, Secretary of the Treasury George Humphrey warned, "Inflation is the great thief. The young, the old, the sick, the small saver, all those least able to protect themselves are the helpless prey of wicked inflation. It must be held in check."[52] The White House aide Gabriel Haugue warned about the "Problems of Prosperity" and challenged the "depression-born thinking that the difficulty with our economy is oversaving and underconsumption." He rejected the idea that "creeping inflation is a tolerable price to pay for avoiding unemployment. . . . If we retain our depression psychosis about the tendency of the economy to run down, we become resigned to perpetual pumping up of our prosperity—hardly the way to keep it healthy."[53] To these officials, the cure came through balanced budgets, restrictive monetary policy, and government pressure to restrain wage increases.

By now, the idea of "wage-price inflation" was cemented in the public imagination. Both the public and the popular press translated abstract economic phenomena into concrete numbers. Business reports in the summer of 1956 explained that if United Steel Workers President David McDonald succeeded in winning his demand of a sixty-cent hourly increase, then the cost of a refrigerator would increase by fifteen dollars.[54] It weakened labor's case that by the late 1950s over half of all union contracts included cost-of-living adjustments that protected labor from price increases while loading the burden on non-unionized sectors and making workers vulnerable to political attack. The 1955 merger between the American Federation of Labor and the Congress of Industrial Organizations (AFL-CIO) further secured the idea of big labor as a monolithic force capable of subverting the economic well-being of the nation.[55]

Amid continued popular concern over the high cost of living, pro-stability forces stepped up their condemnation of organized labor. U.S. Steel lambasted labor and the institution of industrywide bargaining for driving up prices. "The abuse of labor monopoly privilege and the monetary policy that transfers to the public in higher prices the penalty of that abuse appear to be the main elements of institutionalized inflation." This, the company warned, amounted to a "permanent and alarming peacetime trend." U.S. Steel President Roger Blough had his own solution to beating "Old Man Inflation": tax cuts, wage cuts, and higher prices. From his point of view, higher wage demands led to "phantom profits"—profits not large enough to modernize and expand steel's capacity. "As a result of postwar inflation, it is possible for a company to earn what appears to be a most substantial profit, and still wither away." In the end, he appealed to the public to support higher steel prices as a necessary investment for the nation's interest in economic growth and national defense.[56]

This campaign against wage-push inflation reinforced a renewed legislative assault on organized labor. In the spring of 1956, NAM released its latest attack on labor. Denouncing the "purchasing power fallacy," the trade association asserted that "the wage-price spiral gets no one anywhere." It presented the wage-price spiral as an endless cycle: labor demands higher wages, which raise production costs, which in turn lead to higher prices. This attack was part of a renewed political campaign to encourage right-to-work laws, state-level legislation aimed at undermining industrywide bargaining. Again, manufacturers blamed the return of inflation in 1956 on wage increases forced on the nation by the labor monopoly. "The obvious remedy in this situation is to curtail the power of industrywide unions to engage in monopolistic practices and restore bargaining to a local level."[57] An Ohio steel-using parts manufacturer, the Timken Roller Bearing Company, took out anti-labor ads warning, "As STEEL goes . . . so goes inflation!" Beneath this warning the ad recited the current anti-labor rhetoric invoked by Ohio Senator John Bricker: "The right to work shall not be abridged nor made impotent." Business leaders and a reinvigorated conservative movement launched a major effort to na-tionalize right-to-work restrictions that had thus far been confined to the South and the Mountain West.[58] Even within companies, man-agers engaged in extensive public relations efforts to persuade union members of their faulty policies. NAM pamphlets routinely warned workers of the disastrous consequences of their wage demands.[59]

Although labor successfully flexed its political muscles in the 1958 and 1960 elections, leading to substantial Democratic gains, the unions reaped no political dividends. It did not help organized labor that two-thirds of union workers were concentrated in ten states. Un-der the direction of Senator John McClellan of Arkansas, the Senate held well-publicized hearings in 1958 that further discredited labor's claim to being anything other than a corrupt and self-serving interest. Though these hearings focused on the corruption in the Teamsters Union, the public did not make such distinctions. For many Ameri-cans, Marlon Brando's experience with corrupt labor bosses in the 1954 film *On the Waterfront* best captured their sentiments on unions. The passage of the Landrum-Griffin Act in 1959 allowed for more government regulation of union affairs and further restriction of union secondary boycotts and picketing.[60] Those challenges to labor's power led to a downward cycle. Even as labor waxed in numerical strength, its political defeat constricted its vision and helped trans-form it into something approaching a special interest. In the popular imagination (as well as in reality), the wage-price spiral was the real culprit of inflation and symbolized labor's corruption. John Kenneth Galbraith, the former deputy administrator for OPA in 1942 and ar-chitect of the price freeze, explained that in the competition to assign blame, "The public will always attribute the whole of the price in-creases at such a time to the presumed rapacity of the unions."[61]

## Conclusion

In some ways, it is easy to mischaracterize the 1950s simply as a period of emerging conformity and increasing prosperity. When David

Potter published his classic work *People of Plenty* in 1954, many Americans felt that they had entered the golden age of American capitalism. By 1956, more Americans were employed in white-collar work than in manual labor. By 1960, 80 percent of American families owned at least one car, and 90 percent owned a television set.[62] "If few can cite the figures," Potter wrote, "everyone knows that we have, per capita, more automobiles, more telephones, more radios, more vacuum cleaners, more electric lights, more bathtubs, more supermarkets and movie palaces and hospitals, than any other nation."[63]

But even in those supposed halcyon days of robust growth, the American people of plenty were engaged in a combative politics of plenty. The story of a booming economy absent economic struggle, contention, and blame is a myth. And the statistics of this "golden age" and the consensus history they have spawned are misleading. Far from achieving consensus, Americans engaged in highly contentious debates in mid-century, especially on the issue of inflation.

The debate over "creeping inflation" reflected historical tensions between the unorganized and the organized. Since the beginning of the twentieth century, the white-collar middle class was both ascendant and uncertain in its social standing. At times its members perceived themselves as agents of the new modern economy, but at other times they felt caught between the powers of large organized forces beyond their control. As generations of social historians have demonstrated, class is always a subjective constructed category, particularly when the markers of class distinctions are blurred. In the postwar period, the "problem of inflation" became a key battleground between the corporations and unions that sought to capture the loyalty of the middle classes in hopes of influencing public policy. Throughout the 1950s, conservative and even moderate politicians and businessmen correctly saw substantial wage gains as signifying union power and in turn succeeded in using them as a way to delegitimize organized labor. This brief history of the American middle classes in the twentieth century suggests that even low levels of inflation can become politically contentious, that growth in and of itself does not inherently end distributional conflict, and that upward economic mobility and the expansion of the middle classes do not automatically ease class tensions.

---

I would like to thank Rawi Abdelal, Howard Brick, Nelson Lichtenstein, Stephen Schuker, and the editors of the volume.

# Notes

1. For a discussion of middle-class expansion, see Olivier Zunz, "Class," in *Encyclopedia of the United States in the Twentieth Century*, vol. 1, edited by Stanley I. Kutler (New York: Scribner's, 1996), 195–220; Olivier Zunz, *Why the American Century?* (Chicago: University of Chicago Press, 1998), chs. 4 and 5; Michael French, *U.S. Economic History Since 1945* (Manchester: Manchester University Press, 1997); Robert M. Collins, *More: The Politics of Economic Growth in Postwar America* (New York: Oxford University Press, 2000); Claudia Goldin and Robert A. Margo, "The Great Compression: The Wage Structure in the United States at Mid-century," *Quarterly Journal of Economics* 107(February 1992): 1–34; Carole Shammas, "A New Look at Long-term Trends in Wealth Inequality in the United States," *American Historical Review* 98(April 1993): 412–31.

2. Olivier Zunz, *Making America Corporate, 1870–1920* (Chicago: University of Chicago Press, 1990); Susan Porter Benson, *Counter Cultures: Saleswomen, Managers, and Customers in American Department Stores, 1890–1940* (Urbana: University of Illinois Press, 1986); Seymour Martin Lipset and Reinhard Bendix, *Social Mobility in Industrial Society* (Berkeley: University of California Press, 1959), 48–56; Stephan Thernstrom, *The Other Bostonians: Poverty and Progress in the American Metropolis, 1880–1970* (Cambridge, Mass.: Harvard University Press, 1973).

3. Quoted in Daniel Horowitz, *Vance Packard and American Social Criticism* (Chapel Hill: University of North Carolina Press, 1994), 111. On the New Deal and labor, see Christopher Tomlins, *The State and the Unions: Labor Relations, Law, and the Organized Labor Movement in America, 1880–1960* (New York: Cambridge University Press, 1985); Steve Fraser, *Labor Will Rule: Sidney Hillman and the Rise of American Labor* (New York: Free Press, 1991); Colin Gordon, *New Deals: Business, Labor, and Politics in America, 1920–1935* (Cambridge: Cambridge University Press, 1994).

4. David M. Potter, *People of Plenty: Economic Abundance and the American Character* (Chicago: University of Chicago Press, 1954); Vance Packard, *The Status Seekers*, with an introduction by Daniel Horowitz (Boston: Bedford, 1995); C. Wright Mills, *White Collar: The American Middle Classes* (New York: Oxford University Press, 1951). See also Barbara Ehrenreich, *Fear of Falling: The Inner Life of the Middle Class* (New York: HarperCollins, 1989).

5. Theda Skocpol, *Protecting Soldiers and Mothers: The Political Origins of Social Policy in the United States* (Cambridge, Mass.: Harvard University Press), 47–54; Richard Oestreicher, "Urban Working-class Political Behavior and Theories of American Electoral Politics," *Journal of American History* 74(March 1988): 1257–86; Ira Katznelson, *City Trenches: Urban Politics and the Patterning of Class in the United States* (Chicago: University of Chicago Press, 1981); see also Katznelson (this volume).

6. For useful interpretations of postwar labor, see Nelson Lichtenstein, *The Most Dangerous Man in Detroit: Walter Reuther and the Fate of American Labor* (New York: Basic, 1995); Kevin Boyle, *The UAW and the Hey-*

*day of American Liberalism, 1945–1968* (Ithaca: Cornell University Press, 1995); Robert H. Zieger, *American Workers, American Unions, 1920–1985* (Baltimore: Johns Hopkins University Press, 1986).

7. David Riesman, *The Lonely Crowd: A Study of the Changing American Character* (New Haven: Yale University Press, 1950); William H. Whyte, *The Organizational Man* (New York: Simon & Schuster, 1956).

8. For public opinion data, see George H. Gallup, *The Gallup Poll: Public Opinion 1935–1971*, 3 vols. (Princeton: American Institute of Public Opinion, 1972); Louis Harris, *The Harris Survey Yearbook of Public Opinion, 1970–1973*, 4 vols. (New York: Louis Harris and Associates, 1971–74).

9. Charles S. Maier, "The Politics of Inflation in the Twentieth Century," in *The Political Economy of Inflation*, edited by Fred Hirsch and John H. Goldthorpe (Cambridge, Mass.: Harvard University Press, 1978), 70–71. See also Charles Maier, "The Politics of Productivity: Foundations of American International Economic Policy After World War II," in *Between Power and Plenty: Foreign Economic Policies of Advanced Industrial States*, edited by Peter J. Katzenstein (Madison: University of Wisconsin Press, 1978), 23–49; Alan Wolfe, *America's Impasse: The Rise and Fall of the Politics of Growth* (New York: Pantheon, 1981); Walter W. Rostow, *The Process of Economic Growth* (New York: Norton, 1952).

10. Robert J. Schiller, "Why Do People Dislike Inflation?" Working Paper 5539 (Cambridge, Mass.: National Bureau of Economic Research, 1996).

11. Richard Hofstadter, *The Age of Reform: From Bryan to FDR* (New York: Knopf, 1955), 137, 170; Ray Stannard Baker, "Capital and Labor Hunt Together," *McClure's* 21(September 1908): 463, as quoted in Hofstadter, *Age of Reform*, 214. It is interesting to note that Hofstadter was writing in the early 1950s, when tensions between unorganized and organized workers were pronounced.

12. On the 1920s, see Roland Marchand, *Advertising the American Dream: Making Way for Modernity, 1920–1940* (Berkeley: University of California Press, 1985). On the decline in unions, see David Montgomery, *The Fall of the House of Labor: The Workplace, the State, and American Labor Activism, 1865–1925* (Cambridge: Cambridge University Press, 1987).

13. I elaborate on these ideas in Jacobs, "'Democracy's Third Estate': New Deal Politics and the Construction of a 'Consuming Public,'" *International Labor and Working-class History* 55(Spring 1999): 27–51. See also Thomas Ferguson, "From Normalcy to New Deal: Industrial Structure, Party Competition, and American Public Policy in the Great Depression," *International Organization* 38(Winter 1981): 41–95; Thomas Ferguson, "Industrial Conflict and the Coming of the New Deal: The Triumph of Multinational Liberalism in America," in *The Rise and Fall of the New Deal Order, 1930–1980*, edited by Steve Fraser and Gary Gerstle (Princeton: Princeton University Press, 1989), 3–31; Peter A. Gourevitch, "Keynesian Politics: The Political Sources of Economic Policy Choices," in *The Political Power of Economic Ideas: Keynesianism Across Nations*, edited by Peter A. Hall (Princeton: Princeton University Press, 1989), 887–1106.

14. Walter Reuther, "GM Versus the Rest of Us," *The New Republic*, January 14, 1946, 42; George Soule, "Wages, Prices, and Employment," *The*

*New Republic,* November 5, 1945, 592–94; Lichtenstein, *The Most Dangerous Man in Detroit,* 231–34. Gallup polls reported that in the middle of the GM strike, 60 percent supported the UAW demands for higher wages. As late as May 1946, 68 percent favored the retention of price controls. Hugh Rockoff, *Drastic Measures: A History of Wage and Price Controls in America* (New York: Cambridge University Press, 1984), 101–2.

15. Rockoff, *Drastic Measures,* 85–127; Meg Jacobs, "'How About Some Meat?': The Office of Price Administration, Consumption Politics, and State Building from the Bottom Up, 1941–1946," *Journal of American History* 84(December 1997): 934–35; Craufurd D. Goodwin and R. Stanley Herren, "The Truman Administration: Problems and Policies Unfold," in *Exhortations and Controls*: *The Search for a Wage-Price Policy, 1945–1971,* edited by Craufurd D. Goodwin (Washington, D.C.: Brookings Institution, 1975), 12, 22–23.

16. Council of Economic Advisers, *First Annual Report of the President* (Washington: U.S. Government Printing Office, 1946); Robert Collins, "The Emergence of Economic Growthmanship in the United States: Federal Policy and Economic Knowledge in the Truman Years," in *The State and Economic Knowledge,* edited by Mary Furner and Barry Supple (New York: Cambridge University Press, 1990), 149.

17. Ralph Robey, "The Facts Versus the Nathan Report" (pamphlet), National Association of Manufacturers, December 30, 1946, Hagley Museum, Wilmington, Delaware.

18. "Why Prices Will Stay Above '39," *U.S. News,* May 9, 1947, 43–46; "Will Industry Generally Be Able to Absorb Wage Increases Now Being Made Without Raising Prices?" *U.S. News,* May 9, 1947, 36–37; "Laying the Blame," *Time,* May 12, 1947, 87.

19. All ads found in NAM pamphlets, Hagley Museum.

20. "Twelve Times No: The Welder, the Painter, the Press Operator . . . Auto Workers Prefer Cheaper Bread and Meat to Higher Pay," *Newsweek,* February 3, 1947, 22–23.

21. "Taft Says Truman Is Man to Blame for Higher Prices," *New York Times,* June 7, 1947, 1, 18. On the virulent anti-unionism of American managers, see Howell John Harris, *The Right to Manage: Industrial Relations Policies of American Business in the 1940s* (Madison: University of Wisconsin Press, 1982); David Plotke, *Building a Democratic Political Order: Reshaping American Liberalism in the 1930s and 1940s* (New York: Cambridge University Press, 1996); Sanford N. Jacoby, *Modern Manors: Welfare Capitalism Since the New Deal* (Princeton: Princeton University Press, 1997). These debates over inflation persisted through 1947 and became a central election issue in 1948. See "President's Statement on Taft and Prices," *New York Times,* June 6, 1947, 1, 18; "Truman Calls Special Session November 17 on High Prices and Relief in Europe," *New York Times,* October 24, 1947, 1, 2; "High Prices: Should We Restore Price Control?" *The New Republic,* October 20, 1947, 19–26; "High Prices: They Will Be One of Congress' Biggest Headaches as It Meets November 17," *Life,* November 10, 1947, 31–35; Kathleen Hall Jamieson, *Packaging the Presidency: A History and Criticism of Presidential Campaign Advertising* (New York: Oxford University Press, 1984), 34; Alonzo Hamby, *Beyond the New Deal: Harry S*

*Truman and American Liberalism* (New York: Columbia University Press, 1973), 247–65; Lichtenstein, *The Most Dangerous Man in Detroit*, 304–6.

22. Peter F. Drucker, "Why Don't We Stop This Inflation," *Saturday Evening Post*, May 5, 1951, 34.

23. John W. Sloan, *Eisenhower and the Management of Prosperity* (Lawrence: University Press of Kansas, 1991), 115.

24. Louis J. Walinsky, "Price Control: A Critical Review," *The New Republic*, May 28, 1951, 11–16; Harry S Truman, "Economic Controls," *Vital Speeches*, vol. xvii, no. 20, July 1, 1951, 550; James B. Carey, "The Racketeers of Inflation," *Vital Speeches*, July 1, 1951, 552–54. See also "Price Control—A Key to Mobilization," *CIO Economic Outlook* (April 1951): 25–31.

25. Herbert Stein, *The Fiscal Revolution in America*, rev. ed. (Washington, D.C.: American Enterprise Institute Press, 1990), 241–81.

26. "Inflation Is the Devil," *Life*, July 23, 1951, 30.

27. "Inflation: The Permanent Dilemma," *Business Week*, May 24, 1952, 32–33; Sumner H. Slichter, "How Bad Is Inflation?" *Harper's* (August 1952): 53–57; "Sumner Slichter Bets Americans Will Choose Inflation," *Business Week*, October 25, 1952, 100–2; "Steel and Living Costs," *The New Republic*, September 1, 1952, 7. For the idea of a trade-off between low levels of unemployment and inflation, see A. W. Phillips, "The Relation Between Unemployment and the Rate of Change in the Money Wage Rates in the United Kingdom, 1861–1957," *Economica* 25(November 1958): 283–99.

28. "Inflation: The Permanent Dilemma," *Business Week*, May 24, 1952, 32–33.

29. Henry Hazlitt, "The Great Swindle," *Newsweek*, June 25, 1956, 85; "Life in 1951 Is Best Ever," *U.S. News*, June 15, 1951, 36–37; George M. Humphrey, "True Prosperity in America," *Vital Speeches*, January 1, 1957, 185; E. A. Goldenweiser, "Must We Pay More for Everything?" *Harper's* (April 1951): 97–104.

30. FDR 1944 State of the Union Address quoted in *New York Times*, January 12, 1944, 12; John Blum, *V Was for Victory: Politics and American Culture During World War II* (New York: Harcourt, Brace, 1976), 16–21. As the political economist Fred Hirsch argues, "Economic liberalism is . . . a victim of its own propaganda: offered to all, it has evoked demands and pressures that cannot be contained." Fred Hirsch, *The Social Limits to Growth* (Cambridge, Mass.: Harvard University Press, 1976), 11; James T. Patterson, *Grand Expectations: The United States, 1945–1974* (New York: Oxford University Press, 1996).

31. During times of social flux and increased mobility, material goods often assume heightened importance as signifiers of status. See Milivoje Panic, "The Origins of Increasing Inflationary Tendencies in Contemporary Societies," in Hirsch and Goldthorpe, *The Political Economy of Inflation*, 137–60. See also Shelley Nickles, "Object Lessons: Industrial Design, Household Appliances, and the American Middle Class in a Mass Consumer Society, 1920–1960" (Ph.D. diss., University of Virginia, 1999), especially ch. 5.

32. Packard, *The Status Seekers*, 33. *Status Seekers* held the number-one slot on the best-seller list for four months and was on the list for over a year. Horowitz, *Vance Packard*, 133.

33. Richard H. Pells, *The Liberal Mind in a Conservative Age: American Intellectuals in the 1940s and 1950s* (Middletown: Wesleyan University Press, 1985), 333–34; Potter, *People of Plenty*, 108.

34. Eric F. Goldman, *The Crucial Decade and After: America, 1945–1960* (New York: Knopf, 1973), 25–26, 46–47; William H. Whyte Jr., "The Cadillac Phenomenon," *Fortune* (February 1955): 108–9; William H. Whyte Jr., "Budgetism: Opiate of the Middle Class," *Fortune* (May 1956): 156.

35. Editors of *Fortune*, in collaboration with Russell Davenport, *U.S.A.: The Permanent Revolution* (New York: Prentice-Hall, 1951), 91; Judith Stein, *Running America, Running Steel: Race, Economic Policy, and the Decline of Liberalism* (Chapel Hill: University of North Carolina Press, 1998), 8–9.

36. Editors of *Fortune* and Davenport, *U.S.A.*, 90; "Treaty of Detroit," *Fortune* (July 1950): 53; Lichtenstein, *The Most Dangerous Man in Detroit*, 280–81. See also Nelson Lichtenstein, *Solidarity and Citizenship: A Century of American Labor* (Princeton: Princeton University Press, 2002).

37. Fred Hirsch, "The Ideological Underlay of Inflation," in Hirsch and Goldthorpe, *The Political Economy of Inflation*, 263–84; John Goldthorpe, "The Current Inflation: Toward a Sociological Account," in Hirsch and Goldthorpe, *The Political Economy of Inflation*, 212, 215; Robert J. Gordon, "The Demand for and Supply of Inflation," *Journal of Law and Economics* 18(1975): 807–36. John Fleming points out that among heterogeneous groups, the distinction between relative price increases and an increase in the general price level might be blurred, a fact that results in different groups experiencing inflation differently. Also, high prices on key symbolic items like meat garner disproportionate attention. John Fleming, "The Economic Explanation of Inflation," in Hirsch and Goldthorpe, *The Political Economy of Inflation*, 13–36.

38. Samuel Lubell, *The Future of American Politics* (New York: Harper, 1952), 75, 218–19.

39. Harry S Truman, "Economic Controls," *Vital Speeches*, July 1, 1951, 550; "Invitation to Disaster," *The New Republic*, July 2, 1951, 6.

40. Maier, "The Politics of Inflation in the Twentieth Century," 37–72.

41. "Inflation Woes," *Commonweal*, September 28, 1951, 588; "Who Gets Hurt by 53-Cent Dollar," *U.S. News*, September 28, 1951, 11–13; Henry F. Pringle, "Middle-class Squeeze," *Nation's Business* (November 1951): 42–43, 60–61.

42. Walter A. Morton, "Keynesianism and Inflation," *Journal of Political Economy* 59(June 1951): 258–65; Henry Hazlitt, "We Have Asked for Inflation," *Newsweek*, May 7, 1951, 72. See also the following articles by Henry Hazlitt: "Inflation Is Government Made," *Newsweek*, March 12, 1951, 74; "Controls Create Inflation," *Newsweek*, April 16, 1951, 84; "An Anti-inflation Program," *Newsweek*, June 25, 1951, 71; "Price Fixing as Red Herring," *Newsweek*, July 16, 1951, 72; "Inflation for Beginners—I," *Newsweek*, September 3, 1951, 60; "Inflation for Beginners—II," *Newsweek*, September 10, 1951, 84; "Inflation for Beginners—III," *Newsweek*, September 17, 1951, 76; "Inflation for Beginners—IV," *Newsweek*, September 24, 1951, 75; "Price Control Follies of 1952," *Newsweek*, February 25, 1952, 84.

43. "Another Round," *Commonweal*, August 15, 1952, 451–52; "Are You

Better Off Than Before Korea?" *U.S. News,* August 22, 1952, 11–13; "Prices: Word from the Women," *Newsweek,* September 22, 1952, 84.

44. Gary R. Reichard, *The Reaffirmation of Republicanism: Eisenhower and the Eighty-third Congress* (Knoxville: University of Tennessee Press, 1975), 13, 16–17, 24.

45. *National Party Platforms,* vol. 1, compiled by Kirk Porter and Donald Bruce Johnson (Urbana: University of Illinois Press, 1978), 480–81, 500–1.

46. Edwin Diamond and Stephen Bates, *The Spot: The Rise of Political Advertising on Television* (Cambridge, Mass.: MIT Press, 1992), 38, 41; Patterson, *Grand Expectations,* 348.

47. Diamond and Bates, *The Spot,* 56–57; Paul F. Boller Jr., *Presidential Campaigns* (New York: Oxford University Press, 1996), 282; Sloan, *Eisenhower,* 14. See also Jamieson, *Packaging the Presidency,* 38–89; Patterson, *Grand Expectations,* 258–59.

48. Sloan, *Eisenhower,* 108.

49. Ibid., 134.

50. "Wage-Price Inflation Ahead?" *U.S. News,* May 11, 1956, 25–28; H. Scott Gordon, "The Eisenhower Administration: The Doctrine of Shared Responsibility," in Goodwin, *Exhortations and Controls,* 95–134.

51. Gordon, "The Eisenhower Administration," 100.

52. George M. Humphrey, "True Prosperity in America," *Vital Speeches,* January 1, 1957, 184–88.

53. Sloan, *Eisenhower,* 116.

54. "Steel—Why the Inflation Threat," *Newsweek,* June 4, 1956, 72; "Inching Inflation," *Fortune* (August 1956): 40; "Inflation Race—Who's Ahead, Who's Behind," *U.S. News,* August 3, 1956, 95–97; "Why Our Dollars Won't Go as Far," *Newsweek,* August 6, 1956, 19–20; "It Now Costs More Than Ever to Live," *U.S. News,* August 31, 1956, 44–45; "This Inflation Is Serious," *America,* September 8, 1956, 520; "Why Prices Are Rising," *U.S. News,* September 28, 1956, 27–29; "Beefsteak: $1.49 a Pound and Still Going Up," *U.S. News,* September 28, 1956, 30; "Cost of Living: What's Happening to It," *Business Week,* October 27, 1956, 169; "Why Inflation Is Threatening," *U.S. News,* May 18, 1956, 118–22; "Inflation Checked?" *The New Republic,* September 10, 1956, 6; "Inflation or Deflation?: Burns Says Both Must Be Avoided," *U.S. News,* June 1, 1956, 126–29.

55. "Who's Making the Big Money," *U.S. News,* August 31, 1956, 111–12; "Latest Argument for Pay Raises," *U.S. News,* August 31, 1956, 112–13; Benjamin L. Masse, "Joe Smith's Fifty-cent Dollar," *America,* November 24, 1956, 227–29.

56. Henry Hazlitt, "Built-in Inflation," *Newsweek,* May 28, 1956, 86; Roger M. Blough, annual address to U.S. Steel stockholders, May 7, 1956, as reprinted in "A Picture of the Wage-Spiral at Work," *U.S. News,* May 18, 1956, 64–66; "Steel—Why the Inflation Threat," *Newsweek,* June 4, 1956, 71.

57. National Association of Manufacturers, "Purchasing Power: Fact Versus Fallacy" (April 1956) and "A New Force for Inflation" (May 1956), NAM pamphlets, Hagley Museum.

58. Advertisement, *U.S. News,* May 18, 1956, 121. For the larger role that the Timken Roller Bearing Company played in undermining the legit-

imacy of unions and spearheading the right-to-work campaign, see Elizabeth Fones-Wolfe, *Selling Free Enterprise: The Business Assault on Labor and Liberalism, 1945–1960* (Urbana: University of Illinois Press, 1994).

59. National Association of Manufacturers, "The American Triangle of Plenty: Joe the Umbrella Maker" (September 1951), NAM pamphlets, Hagley Museum. More generally, see Fones-Wolfe, *Selling Free Enterprise*, 272–74.

60. Stein, *Running America*, 17, 22–25.

61. John Kenneth Galbraith, "Are Living Costs Out of Control?" *Atlantic Monthly* (February 1957): 37–41. Sloan (*Eisenhower*, 125–30) also notes that, by this time, combating inflation had become more difficult because of a negative balance of payments.

62. Patterson, *Grand Expectations*, 316, 323, 348; Kenneth T. Jackson, *Crabgrass Frontier: The Suburbanization of the United States* (New York: Oxford University Press, 1985), 7, 205.

63. Potter, *People of Plenty*, 84.

# Part II

## CONSTITUENCIES IN CONFLICT

# 7

## Public Policy and the Middle-class Racial Divide After the Second World War

*Ira Katznelson*

The same year the psychologist Kenneth Clark opened his searing analytical study of Harlem by averring that the country's "dark ghettos are social, political, educational, and—above all—economic colonies," and that "their inhabitants are subject peoples," President Lyndon Johnson addressed the June 1965 graduating class at Howard University.[1] Calling for a "move beyond opportunity to achievement," he chronicled "a widening gulf" between black and white Americans and assayed "the facts of this American failure":

> Thirty-five years ago the rate of unemployment for Negroes and whites was about the same. Today, the Negro rate is twice as high. In 1948 the 8 percent unemployment rate for Negro teenage boys was actually less than that of whites. By last year the rate had grown to 23 percent, as against 13 percent for whites. Between 1949 and 1959, the income of Negro men relative to white men declined in every section of this country. From 1952 to 1963 the median income of Negro families compared to white actually dropped from 57 percent to 53 percent. . . . Since 1947, the number of white families living in poverty has decreased 27 percent, while the number of poor nonwhite families decreased only 3 percent. . . . Moreover, the isolation of Negro from white communities is increasing, rather than decreasing, as Negroes crowd into central cities and become a city within a city.[2]

These developments pose a considerable puzzle. Despite a massive migration to the centers of job growth in the North, why had African

Americans experienced growing economic and class disparities with white America and deepening structural poverty during the post–New Deal golden era of economic expansion and white middle-class formation? Why had an unparalleled possibility been missed to include the most downtrodden in the full embrace of postwar prosperity and advance their membership in the country's growing middle class?

## Missed Opportunity

During the Depression of the 1930s, African Americans had experienced sharp downward mobility. They lost hold of the grab-handles they had secured by virtue of the movement northward during the First World War and the explosion in black cultural creativity and political activity during the 1920s, outside the clutches of Jim Crow. The principle of "last hired, first fired" placed many African Americans who had recently joined the North's labor force at a special disadvantage. Capitalism's collapse after 1929 also deepened the poverty of the vast majority of the South's black agricultural and domestic workers, the region's two largest occupational categories. Not only were they condemned to compete for ever-scarcer jobs, but the exit option that had opened up as a result of the robust demand for labor in the North during the periods of wartime mobilization and postwar prosperity had disappeared. Further, the small and already fragile black middle classes on both sides of the Mason-Dixon line came to be much more tenuously attached to occupational positions marked by a regular wage income, a nontrivial degree of employment stability, cultural respectability, and chances for mobility, the hallmarks of middle-class status. In all, the period from 1929 to December 1941, when American participation in the Second World War began, was almost uniformly bleak with respect to African American employment.

There was one exception to this outlook: the programs of public works and employment created by the "alphabet agencies" of the New Deal, including the CCC (Civilian Conservation Corps) and the WPA (Works Progress Administration). Although often restrictive and racist in their administration, these agencies produced jobs where there otherwise would have been none, and some were skilled and supervisory jobs. On balance, blacks were treated more poorly than white participants in these New Deal programs, but the advances they offered, together with other forms of cash relief, persuaded most African American voters (where they could vote—mainly outside the South) to shift their allegiance from the Republican Party, the party of Lincoln and Reconstruction, to Franklin Roosevelt's Democratic

Party, despite the presence of a southern segregationist wing at its core.

By the time the Second World War started, African Americans had become strong Democrats and New Dealers. During the war, their economic opportunities changed dramatically for the better in five key respects. First, as it did for other Americans, unemployment disappeared. Second, black migration to the North resumed, spurred by jobs, many of which were unionized and stable, in the war production industries; this renewed migration put pressure on southern as well as northern labor markets. Third, unionization advanced in both the Congress of Industrial Organizations (CIO) and American Federation of Labor (AFL) by leaps and bounds. By the end of the Second World War, more than 20 percent of the private workforce in the South belonged to unions, many multiracial; that proportion is nearly twice what it is for the United States as a whole today. Fourth, though the military was segregated until after President Truman's desegregation order of 1948, the armed forces did offer blacks occupational and literacy training, decent salaries, some mobility, and the "republican" asset of becoming soldier-citizens.[3] Fifth, the cultural and political terms of the Second World War as a war against fascism made the most outrageous expressions of racism increasingly suspect. In short, the period of war transformed the prospects of African Americans, absolutely and relatively, for achieving middle-class status more than any other large-scale development since Reconstruction, when the South had been occupied by northern troops.

The vibrant period of capitalist growth that followed the war in what was by far the globe's most dominant and effective economy gave lie to fears of a return to a pre-war low-employment equilibrium. Conjoined to the post–New Deal legitimacy of government intervention to stabilize the economy on broadly Keynesian terms, to build at least a rudimentary welfare state, and to begin to secure black civil and political rights, this moment might have become a period of black catch-up in economic terms, a moment when a new, nonsegregated, African American middle class made a robust appearance.

It did not. Notwithstanding these promising conditions, the golden age of general postwar prosperity proved to have disappointing payoffs for most blacks. Despite the sharp upward trends of the period toward better living standards, urbanization, economic growth, and remarkable intergenerational mobility, the racial divide did not close but in fact widened. At just the moment when the occupational (and cultural) order in the United States developed a big middle-class bulge, and when white Americans, especially the Catholic and Jewish children of the late-nineteenth- and early-twentieth-century immigrants from southern and eastern Europe who came before the gate closed in 1924, became predominantly middle-class, African Americans remained stuck in non-middle-class, economically marginal conditions. When President Johnson announced, five weeks after the assassination of his predecessor, a "Great Society" effort to eradicate poverty and complete the New Deal, it was widely understood to be an effort directed at black poverty and the exclusion of African Americans from the middle class. A full prior generation of prosperity had not erased the racial divide.

This chapter examines the puzzle posed by the missed opportunity of the postwar years. The many extant explanations, some more plausible than others, include the erosion of insulated, segregated, black middle-class niches under the impact of the civil rights movement, especially as a result of migration northward and the beginnings of desegregation in education; lags in skills training and access to higher education; a mismatch between skills acquisition and the characteristics of new jobs; persistent private discrimination by employers, banks, landlords, and other purveyors of economic opportunity; and a culture of poverty, including dysfunctional family structures. At Howard, under the heading "The Causes of Inequality," President Johnson cited deficits in medical care and housing as well as a lack of occupational and skills training. He also spoke movingly of the constitutive character of "ancient brutality, past injustice, and present prejudice."[4] As a remedy, he pledged a new round of comprehensive social policy innovation, but such policies never came to pass.

Johnson's account, like the vast majority of the literature on the economic standing of African Americans in the postwar years, considered public policy a principal corrective tool. Later, critics of the Great Society and of governmental social programs more generally attributed black poverty to the programs geared to alleviate it.[5] But both the advocates and critics of a robust social role for the federal government overlooked an important fact: the hallmark social policy innovations of the New Deal and Fair Deal themselves had operated more as brakes than as accelerators with respect to the incorporation of African Americans into the country's rapidly expanding postwar middle class. With the exception of a small body of scholarship that has examined the status of race in Democratic Party social policy from Roosevelt to Johnson,[6] both advocates and critics have considered the influence of black inclusion in these programs. Yet their central effect on the country's racial divide was produced by a *previous* pattern of differential exclusion. That is, the manner in which race had become a constitutive part of putatively universalistic programs in the 1930s and 1940s effectively produced a kind of affirmative action for white Americans that offered them a publicly organized and funded helping hand into middle-class status while denying the same assistance to African Americans. By revisiting the policymaking of the New Deal and Fair Deal era, we can see that the outcomes of public policy in the period spanning the New Deal to the start of the Great Society actually *reinforced* rather than counteracted both the proximate causes of poverty and the long-term, deeply inscribed racial legacies of American history that President Johnson addressed.

My causal argument about the sources of such differential treatment of black and white Americans pivots on the character of the period's governing political party. The cross-regional party alliance that fashioned and superintended the New Deal was more than an association of different interests or a corroboration of the truism that American political parties embrace unusually broad catchments. The Democratic Party conjoined two different political systems: one had undergone a transition to democracy as it incorporated new groups and voters who had arrived from overseas or migrated from the South; the other, through legislation and policing, had ensured racial separation, protected an exclusionary franchise, and secured an authoritarian polity so efficiently that the "southern way of life" had come to seem ordinary, hence normal. Racism, to be sure, was not confined to the South. Irrespective of where they lived, most white Americans before the civil rights era were indifferent to Jim Crow. Yet only in and around the former Confederacy did the formal political system utilize race to exclude adults from citizenship and full access to civil society. Private terror combined with public law and enforcement to make this political system authentically totalitarian. Competitive party politics did not exist. Electoral contests were enacted inside the one dominant party. The consortium of North and South represented by the Democratic Party thus brought together two radically different political systems under one federal umbrella.

Once in Washington as elected representatives in the House and Senate, the credentials of southern members were sanitized.[7] The ordinary rules of the liberal polity transmuted these representatives, despite their provenance, into delegates of the people just like any other. In the Congress, all legislators were equal: one representative, one constituency, one vote. Selected by a limited, exclusionary electorate denied the choices offered to voters in other regions, southern members allied together in Washington as "solid South" Democrats. In turn, they affiliated with other Democrats to compose House and Senate majorities during most of the New Deal period. Before 1932 the majority of the Democratic Party in Congress was southern.[8] Even after the massive nonsouthern realignment in partisanship in

1932 and 1936 that rendered southern representatives a numerical minority, the core of the party's senior members and its leading edge of continuity and legislative sway remained southern.

As the great agent of social policy change in the New Deal and postwar periods, this Democratic Party partnership of "strange bedfellows" produced a series of "strange deals" that together constituted a program of affirmative action for whites granted privileged access to state-sponsored economic mobility.[9] The South, where human inequality and exclusion from citizenship on the basis of color were inscribed in law and enforced by the coercive apparatus of the state, and which at the time represented the deepest negation of liberalism inside any Western liberal regime, succeeded in utilizing the main institutions of American representative democracy to transfer its racialized priorities to Washington and impose them, with little resistance, on the details of New Deal public policy. This intrusion of southern racial values, moreover, had especially important consequences for labor markets, and hence on the prospect that African Americans could join the movement to form a massive middle class.

## A Southern Veto

From the presidency of Woodrow Wilson until the landslide victory of Franklin Roosevelt, the Democratic Party in Congress was dominated by the South. It perhaps is thus not surprising that the social policies of the First World War and its immediate aftermath—including war risk insurance, dependency draft deferments, family allowances, vocational rehabilitation, and agricultural training—were designed and implemented in ways that did not challenge, but rather advanced, the racial disparities inherent in America's Jim Crow version of apartheid.[10] After the 1932, 1934, and 1936 elections, the South was reduced to a minority of some 40 percent inside the cohort of Democratic Party representatives in Congress. Notwithstanding this relative decline, southern senators and congressmen possessed a series of remarkable institutional advantages that exaggerated the capacity of their control of just over one-fourth of the seats in the Senate and the House. Their seniority was exaggerated by not having to compete in a two-party system. They thus secured a disproportionate number of committee chairmanships, giving them special gatekeeping powers. Further, supermajority provisions like the filibuster in the Senate served to advance southern power. These features of southern representation combined to make the preferences and sufferance of the South central to all the key features of the New Deal.[11] In effect, the South maintained a legislative veto throughout this formative period.

Put more abstractly, the core institutions of America's liberal regime—its pattern of congressional representation, the polity's most Lockean institution, and its party system, the country's most important extraconstitutional innovation—placed the South's tyrannical practices at the center of Washington's politics and policymaking.

Within the South, conflicts between Democrats and Republicans were virtually unknown because the Republican Party barely existed. Struggles among individuals and factions were resolved almost exclusively within the ambit of Democratic Party primaries. As a consequence, representation in Washington was the near-exclusive province of only one of the two great national parties. Further, this electoral arrangement was an integral part of a coherent racial civilization, with a distinctive heritage, economy, social geography, and culture. Within this unitary party framework there was in fact a great deal of heterogeneity, as in the contrasting political behavior and styles of upland whites and black belt whites.

Once southern politics moved outside the region, however, to the site of representation in Congress, these differences became much harder to discern. Now the South appeared as "solid." Virtually all southern members of the House and Senate acted, when they thought it to be necessary, to preserve the basic contours of their region's racial regime. This was the premise of southern representation. "Two party competition," V. O. Key observed in his classic study, "would have meant the destruction of southern solidarity in national politics. . . . Unity on the national scene was essential in order that the largest possible bloc could be mobilized to resist any national move toward interference with southern authority to deal with the race question as was desired locally."[12]

The racial civilization of the South, with its one-party regime based on a limited and exclusionary franchise and unitary national representation with regard to questions of race, was inserted into the national Democratic Party in a privileged manner. After the economic and political upheavals and electoral realignment of the last decade of the nineteenth century, the Democratic Party in Congress consisted mainly of representatives from southern and border states. From the debacle of 1896 to the election of Roosevelt in 1932, Democrats outside the South were able to secure only 40 percent of the popular vote. By contrast, within the South, at no time did the Democratic totals in congressional and presidential elections fall below 86 percent. As a result, during the first three decades of the twentieth century, the South not only controlled the party in Congress but was nearly coextensive with it, as some two in three Democratic members were southern. Equally important, during this period of southern control, representatives from the region amassed the seniority that would position them to control the committee structure of the Congress for nearly the next half-century.[13] Even at the height of the New Deal, the Democratic Party required southern acquiescence to the national program. Rising to oppose a 1940 anti-lynching bill, Congressman John Rankin of Mississippi cautioned northern Democrats to

> remember that southern Democrats now have the balance of power in both Houses of Congress. By your conduct you may make it impossible for us to support many of you for important committee assignments, and other positions to which you aspire. . . . You Democrats who are pushing this vicious measure are destroying your usefulness here. . . . The Republicans would be delighted to see you cut President Roosevelt's throat politically, and are therefore voting with you on this vicious measure. . . . They know that if he signs it, it will ruin him in the Southern states; and that if he vetoes it, they can get the benefit of the Negro votes this vicious measure would inflict in the North.[14]

The advantageous position of the South forced a policy strategy: new ways to structure the relationship between the state and the marketplace could be passed into law *provided* that the integrity of the South's racial civilization in all its basic aspects remained unquestioned as a matter of "local" option. The policy preferences of these Democrats, better characterized as progressive rather than conservative, were very different from those of the period's Republicans. But this progressivism, tightly bound up with the security of the white South, was different. Industrialists, planters, small farmers, and the white working class found a broadly common center of gravity after the institutionalization of a low-franchise, single-party polity in an "amalgam of Bourbon and Populist approaches" that permitted southern representatives to guard the traditional South while promoting economic modernization and sectional economic interests against a rapacious, capitalist, and industrial North.[15] Although progressives from the South and the West differed on the issues of states' rights and women's suffrage, together they provided the votes for the reform coalition in Congress and the bedrock support for Wilson's New Freedom. This reform impulse had a decided agrarian tilt and lacked any will to pass social-democratic social welfare legislation, provide assistance to the immigrant working class of the North in their factories and slums, or overcome its indifference to the bashing of labor unions and political organizations on the left after the First World War. But a reform impetus it was nonetheless; its proponents were keenly interested in the use of the state to redress imbalances between rich and poor regions and to organize and rein in the development of industrial and finance capital. Even during the period of Republican ascendancy in the 1920s, southerners displayed a strong affinity for statist reform and proved much more willing to vote for interventionist and regulatory economic measures than even the most liberal Republicans from the Middle Atlantic and New England states. Southern representatives, of course, were not cut from a single cloth. Some were sympathetic to the region's radical and populist legacies; others, the majority, were better characterized as pragmatic broker politicians. All of the South's representatives, however, coalesced on a regional platform with two main elements: preserving the intraregional racial order and redressing gross interregional inequalities. The white as well as the black South was poor. Residents of the region thus shared an interest in utilizing government policies to reduce local deprivation.[16]

Southern congressional voting before the Depression and the New Deal era nestled within sets of assumptions, institutions, and practices that soon were to expire. The largely agrarian, quasi-progressive reform impulses of southern members in the 1920s took aim at the hegemony of northern capital and the Republican Party in circumstances marked by national economic prosperity, a postwar disengagement from world affairs, the Democratic Party's minority status, the absence of civil rights from the national political agenda, a marginalized and very weak labor movement, repression of the organized Left, and a federal system that relegated issues of property rights and the organization of the economy to the states while limiting federal policies mainly to matters of infrastructure and the terms of commerce, such as internal improvements, subsidies (principally shipping), tariffs, the disposal of public lands, patents, and the currency.[17] During the Depression and the Second World War, these circumstances altered, and the South was confronted with difficult choices about policy and politics. Perhaps for the first time since the demise of the Knights of Labor, an agrarian-urban industrial alliance that could effectively challenge the prerogatives of capital became a possibility, but not without immense risks for the mores and social organization of the South. Southerners in Congress were forced to undertake a great balancing act. Now a minority of a majority party, but in control of many key congressional committees and institutional positions, they were reassured by the apparent resemblance between the New Deal and Wilson's New Freedom and by a dramatic increase in the much-needed largesse that federal public spending could provide. They maintained deep reservations, however, for they distrusted an enhanced central state that might under some circumstances become an instrument for a new Reconstruction and whose bureaucracies inevitably would be in the hands of administrators from other regions who would possess a great deal of discretion.

## Race and the Crisis of Policy

The U.S. social contract after the Second World War was grounded in the social policy initiatives of the New Deal, including the introduction of social insurance for the aged and the unemployed in the Social Security Act of 1935, the creation of a regulated framework for unions and collective bargaining in the National Labor Relations Act (NLRA) of 1935, and the establishment of rules for labor markets, including minimum wages and maximum hours, in the Fair Labor Standards Act (FLSA) of 1938. The postwar social contract was strongly identified with the massive veterans' benefits advanced by the Servicemen's Readjustment Act (the GI Bill of Rights) of 1944, the commitment to use governmental fiscal and monetary tools to advance the high levels of employment codified by the Employment Act of 1946, and the continuing augmentation of trade union membership despite the impediments to collective action introduced by the Taft-Hartley Act in 1947.

This constellation of policies put into place during the administrations of Presidents Roosevelt and Truman fueled the powerful economic engine driving postwar economic growth and the massive expansion of America's stable and increasingly prosperous middle class. The United States dominated the international economy at the end of the Second World War, controlling two-thirds of the globe's industrial production (having suffered no wartime damage, the U.S. economy had grown by nearly 70 percent during the war years). In the subsequent quarter-century, the country matched the growth rates of its earlier and most dynamic periods of economic development, thus contributing to even more robust rates of economic growth elsewhere in the developed world. Under the umbrella of U.S. power and international economic institutions, the American model based on New Deal policies became the template for postwar non-Communist Europe and Japan. In turn, prosperity elsewhere further propelled the formation of an American middle class of unprecedented inclusiveness. Following hard on the heels of a global depression of uncommon depth and the widespread decomposition of liberal constitutional regimes, the New Deal provided a successful alternative to bolshevism and fascism and transformed the life chances, work experiences, and economic security of the great majority of American citizens.

Not surprisingly, the New Deal is recalled and celebrated across the contemporary political spectrum for the course it charted, especially for the universalism of the Social Security Act and the GI Bill,[18] against which more targeted programs, such as Aid to Families with Dependent Children (AFDC, the now-defunct part of Social Security that became "welfare" in American parlance) and race-based affirmative action initiatives, have been measured and, more often than not, found wanting. "The plans for postwar demobilization," Theda Skocpol has observed, ". . . sought to address the needs of veterans in the context of building a stronger welfare state for all Americans."[19]

Not quite, we discover, if we revisit the period's domestic policies, including the GI Bill, which she views as the very embodiment of a "sense of national solidarity."[20] The universalism of these policies was merely putative. Their exclusionary features deepened, rather than mitigated, the postwar racial divide.

Utilizing the region's political assets, southern members of Congress defined the outer limits and composition of New Deal legislation in three key respects. First, and most familiarly, their structural veto made civil rights programs, even broadly popular initiatives like federal legislation to curb the horror of lynching, impossible to achieve. A certain symbolic politics of civil rights obtained in which the House of Representatives would pass anti-lynching bills that then died in the Senate, where the rules permitted an intense minority to prevail.

The only civil rights bills to come to the floor before the Second World War (in 1935 in the Senate and in 1937 in both houses) concerned lynching. Given the lack of overt support by the president, who feared southern defections, a ritual quality of interest on the part of most nonsouthern representatives of both parties, and the guarantee of the Senate filibuster, these debates were mainly symbolic opportunities for nonsoutherners to put their consternation about lynching on record and then move on. The motion to adjourn the 1935 Senate debate on an anti-lynching bill was supported by fourteen of thirty nonsouthern Democrats who wanted to return to mainstream New Deal business, as well as by seventeen of nineteen southern Democrats (the two who voted nay were from the Tennessee and Kentucky hill country). This pattern prevailed as Democrats continued to be unwilling to jeopardize desired legislation in the name of civil rights. Thus, in 1937, when Hugo Black sought to table an amendment to the Fair Labor Standards Act that would have added anti-lynching provisions to the legislation, he was supported not only by all twenty-two southern Democrats but by twenty-two of the forty-five nonsoutherners (all fifteen Republicans voted nay). By contrast, when nothing of substance was at stake—that is, when the House votes on anti-lynching were purely symbolic, as they were when the Senate could be counted on to kill the legislation—non-southern Democrats lined up in near unanimity to vote with the Republicans in favor of such legislation against a near-unanimous southern contingent, as was the case in April 1937 when the House passed an anti-lynching bill by the large margin of 277 to 120, with southerners responsible for 101 of the negative votes. Although southern members well understood that the proffered legislation posed no actual threat, many deeply resented the cynicism they detected in their northern colleagues. In the various debates, many southerners, as well as northern Republicans, observed that big-city Democrats had been sublimely uninterested in lynching and other civil rights matters before the movement of considerable numbers of blacks to the North.

Second, the region protected its racial order, and especially its low-wage, segregated labor market, by intruding key racialized exclusions based on occupational categories into every major piece of New Deal legislation, including the National Industrial Recovery Act (NIRA), the Wagner Act, the Social Security Act, and the Fair Labor Standards Act. A tremendous proportion of black workers in this period, more than half nationally and over 60 percent in the South, were quasi-serfs working as agricultural laborers or domestic servants. These were the two occupational categories excluded from each of these landmark pieces of legislation. Writing about the Social Security Act, "the most important and dramatic moment of expansion of national power in social welfare policy," Robert Lieberman notes that "providing social insurance coverage for these workers [would have] challenged local traditions of racial segregation and dependence in the political economy." These exclusions, which "imprinted on the emerging national welfare state the racial division that was a feature of the national labor market," were not limited to old-age insurance in the act but extended to unemployment insurance, thus "providing the benefits of stable employment and income support to white workers while denying them to African-Americans."[21]

Third, each key legislative initiative of the New Deal–Fair Deal era was implemented and administered in a decentralized manner designed to safeguard the southern racial order. The public assistance provisions of the Social Security Act, for example, relied on state and local public administration, leaving room both for wide disparities across the states in the provision of benefits and for racial discrimination within individual states. A 1943 study found that across the South, black children were qualifying in lower numbers than white children for public assistance and that in each southern state, with the sole exception of Tennessee, per capita benefits paid to support black children were lower than those paid to whites on "the general belief in the South . . . that Negroes can get along with less than whites."[22] Local administrators often deterred eligible blacks from applying, enforced "suitable home" provisions to reduce eligibility, and imposed work requirements differentially by race.

These characteristics of New Deal social policy entwined with the operation of labor markets to impose barriers to black entry into middle-class opportunity and mobility. Just as in the Social Security Act, public administration was decentralized and domestic and farmworkers were excluded from the National Recovery Administration's efforts to revise the relationship between government and markets by imposing sector-by-sector negotiations between labor and capital, with the national state acting as an arbiter, the Wagner Act's creation of a framework for successful labor union organization of the unorganized, and the Fair Labor Standards Act's establishment of minimum-wage and maximum-hours regulations. The manner in which the South imposed its will in these regards is particularly clear in the case of the FLSA, whose legislative record is both visible and complete.

Apart from civil rights bills, the only major legislation before the Second World War to provoke a significant sectional split within the Democratic Party concerned this regulation of wages and hours. In December 1937, the House of Representatives voted to recommit a bill that proposed a Fair Labor Standards Board with powers to set a minimum wage and maximum hours of work for the entire country irrespective of existing regional differences. In voting on this early version of the bill, a nearly unanimous Republican Party was joined by eight of ten southern Democrats to turn back the bill (216 to 198) against a nearly united nonsouthern Democratic Party. What was most striking about this debate was that the Democratic Party's coalition came apart on a labor matter that directly affected the viability of the southern political economy and its race relations by extending national standards that threatened to undermine the South's system of low-paid labor and, with it, its comparative advantage in securing northern capital for economic development.

Just six months after the rejection of the president's proposal in the House, the Fair Labor Standards Act was passed into law with the support of a small majority of southern members. What had happened to restore the coalition? Although a number of factors were at work, including a primary victory in Florida during the course of the spring 1938 debate by Claude Pepper who had campaigned on behalf of the bill, the most significant reasons concerned the dilution and revision of the legislation to make it conform to the pattern of previous major pieces of New Deal legislation. The act exempted domestic and agricultural labor. Further, it took regional wage differences into account by providing for the establishment of advisory wage boards in interstate occupations that were mandated to take into account "competitive conditions as affected by transportation, living, and production costs." Further, the revised legislation lowered the starting minimum wage to twenty-five cents per hour for the first year and thirty cents for the second (as compared to forty cents in the original bill) and permitted many firms to stay at this level for an additional five years before being required to pay a wage of forty cents an hour.

If the Fair Labor Standards Act was the most significant piece of labor market–oriented legislation before the war, the individual and family benefits made available by the GI Bill to the country's 16 million World War II veterans had an enormous effect on their employment prospects and economic mobility once they came home. Geared to assist men at a moment when the women who had been mobilized to work in their absence would be leaving the labor force, this landmark legislation provided for educational benefits in support of vocational and postsecondary education, employment counseling and placement by the U.S. Employment Service (USES), loans to buy farms and establish new businesses, and mortgages to purchase homes at a time of high demand. Conceptualized as recompense for the disruption of young lives by the war, the GI Bill in fact did far more. In all, nearly 8 million former soldiers and their families took advantage of the provisions of what was arguably the country's most significant and democratic piece of social legislation. About one in five postwar mortgages were underwritten by the Veterans Administration (VA), and well over 2 million veterans had their college or university education fully funded. As Theda Skocpol has observed:

> The vets proved to be unusually serious and successful students, and their huge influx in the late 1940s permanently transformed the American university system. Only about 9 of 100 young people attended college in 1939, but that rate almost doubled (to 16 out of 100) by 1947. American higher education expanded into an avenue for mass mobility rather than gentlemanly certification.[23]

Alas, the impact of the bill on black veterans, the mainly male group best poised within the African American community to secure middle-class status, was quite different with respect to each of the four key benefits conferred by the legislation.[24] These included: the right to use the placement and job counseling services offered by USES centers to find jobs commensurate with a veteran's skills; as an aid to reincorporation into the labor market, just over $1,000 in unemployment insurance, paid over the course of a year; guaranteed business and farm loans as well as housing mortgages; and up to four years of educational grants to subsidize vocational training or post-secondary education.[25]

Black soldiers had made enormous strides during the Second World War in acquiring skills that would potentially mesh with high-wage, skilled employment after the war. But the administration of the GI Bill placed barriers in their way. Like other New Deal legislation, this act was implemented in a decentralized fashion at the insistence of the South. When blacks who returned to that region sought to gain access to the provisions administered by the Veterans Administration or the USES, they had to do so at the local level. Thus, when eligible African Americans applied for job assistance, their applications were processed by employment centers whose job counselors, especially in the South, were almost exclusively white. In the South, where the large majority of black veterans still lived, virtually none were given access to skilled employment by the USES despite the experience of three in four with such work in the military. The agency reinforced an already racialized division of labor. In October 1946 in Mississippi, for example, of the 6,500 former soldiers placed in jobs, 86 percent of the skilled and semiskilled positions were filled by whites, and 92 percent of the unskilled jobs went to blacks. Because unemployment insurance was made available only to those who could demonstrate a willingness to take a suitable job, and because suitability was defined by the USES, many blacks were forced to take jobs far beneath their skill levels. Carpenters became janitors, and truck drivers had to work as dishwashers. Applications for self-employment business assistance were routinely denied to blacks on casuistic grounds. Sharecroppers, for example, were told they were ineligible for small-business loans because, having to share their profits with their landlords, they were not self-employed by definition.

The federal government did not make loans of this or any other kind directly. Rather, the Veterans Administration guaranteed loans. In consequence, it was private lenders who decided whether to lend to African Americans, and the vast majority would not, either because they lacked sufficient capital of their own or because, for nakedly racist reasons, they treated blacks as high-risk candidates. In Mississippi in 1947, the VA made just over three thousand loans; two went to blacks.

What of the education and training provisions of the GI Bill, either through funded apprenticeships or advanced schooling? An applicant for assistance with on-the-job training had to find an employer deemed "suitable" who was willing to take him on and then apply for a grant. For African Americans, this requirement proved an almost impassable barrier. In Georgia, blacks participated in only 6 of the state's approved 246 programs. When they did get in, they frequently were treated as cheap labor and offered little or no training. In some egregious instances, black workers were charged a fee by their bosses for the privilege of being trained. In such circumstances, completion rates were low, as were subsequent job placement rates.

When black veterans tried to use their schooling benefits, most found they could not. Universities required a high school diploma or an equivalency degree, and blacks disproportionately lacked this certification. Moreover, in the South higher education was rigidly segregated, and black colleges were ill prepared for the number of applicants who wanted to get in. In the academic year 1946–47, half of white college students were supported by the Veterans Administration; for blacks the figure was under one-third. By 1947 some twenty thousand black veterans had been turned down by historically black colleges and universities even though they qualified for admission.

Given the average fifth-grade education of black veterans, most sought to enroll in GI Bill vocational programs. These too required admission procedures in the face of scarcity. The Act allowed each state to determine the number of public vocational schools. Where blacks were most concentrated—again, especially in the South—the number of such schools was deliberately kept low, thus limiting black access; the institutions to which blacks did gain admission were largely geared to sending them on to "black jobs." By contrast, private schools, which charged the top tuition rates allowed by law, often were flimsy operations that provided little or no actual training.

In short, the period's most important public policy boosts to middle-class status for whites worked poorly, if at all, for African Americans. By 1950 virtually half of the black soldiers who had served in the Second World War had migrated away from the region of their birth. Though some caught up with veterans' benefits, most never did, often because they were trapped by the demands of their transitional status as newcomers. In all, only 5 percent of all black veterans benefited from the educational provisions of the GI Bill. Affirmative action, it thus might be observed, has had ironic precursors. Universalism, it is useful to remember, is not always what it seems.

## Conclusion

This brief chronicle is not an exhaustive account of the ways in which public policy was entwined with race and region to limit African American opportunities and advance those of whites. The South acted successfully to limit the labor movement to a narrow, non-southern, regional base. During the 1930s, the region went along with New Deal labor policy, especially the National Labor Relations Act, because southern representatives believed that their racialized way of life would be protected by the law's decentralized administration and exclusion of agricultural and domestic workers. A certain panic set in, however, when unions began to penetrate the South substantially during the tight labor market period of the Second World War, often on a multiracial basis. Quickly, southerners began to join Republicans in Congress to impose more restrictions on labor organizing. This effort culminated in the 1947 Taft-Hartley Act, which made it vastly more difficult both for the AFL and the CIO to succeed in their ambitious goals to unionize the South. In this way, the South imposed high barriers to the development of national corporatism. Instead of securing its goal of being recognized as a fundamental political class, labor now was regarded as one interest group among many participating in American politics. Moreover, it was seen as an interest group that mainly pursued private goals in industries and occupations, especially in the crafts, which either made entry especially difficult for African Americans or barred them altogether.

With the labor movement checked as a national political force, the South aligned with nonsouthern Democrats to promote expansive fiscal and monetary policies, and it avidly pursued a regional economic development strategy that combined a preference for open trade with robust military spending and infrastructural planning. Thus, as a result of what might be thought of as the switchboard of southern representation, the United States developed a Janus-like state. Inside the country's domestic political economy, and with respect to how the country's plurality of interests should be represented in Washington, the South compelled New Dealers to set aside the instruments of hands-on economic steering, development, planning, and corporatism. These economic instruments, which had become central to the country's national security state, were oriented to solving the crisis of liberalism by transmuting those aspects of intervention central to both communism and fascism into a democratic frame. Instead, the South forced a choice to manage the economy by utilizing more hands-off regulations as well as fiscal and monetary macroeconomic tools, thus leaving prerogatives of ownership and management relatively untouched. In addition, the region shaped a liberalism in which the interests of citizens would be represented not by business and labor acting as national corporatist bargaining agents, but by a more fluid and heterogeneous array of interest groups. This package of orientations and policies, Alan Brinkley has noted, was geared "to compensate for capitalism's inevitable flaws and omissions without interfering with its internal workings."[26] Such "internal workings" in the United States at the time included the instantiation of race at the heart of the country's labor markets.

Southern-defined or -affirmed developments in the 1930s and 1940s thus had a profound effect on the chances to ameliorate the racial divide and prospects for a nascent black middle class in the 1950s and 1960s. A national labor class, corporatist representation, and national labor markets were ruled out. The unions, the private institutions most inclined, for all their flaws and uneven attention to racial equality, to cross the racial divide and incorporate African Americans fairly, were confined to the North and Midwest (with pockets in the far West). Moreover, these unions contracted their policy horizons to focus on the conditions needed to underwrite settlements with employers that resulted in high wages and fringe benefits for their workers. With markets, including labor markets, left to operate largely on their own within capacious monetary and fiscal frameworks unencumbered by a more intrusive developmental state activity, existing racial inequalities remained securely entrenched. Employers largely were left alone before the Civil Rights Act of 1964 to pursue their private preferences with regard to race. Because the emergent black civil rights movement, especially in the South, lacked a labor partner, the movement focused almost exclusively on juridical issues of citizenship rather than on issues of economic opportunity and mobility. Thus, despite the late 1940s integration of the armed forces, the first modern civil rights bills in Congress, the initial stirrings of a mass civil rights movement, and a host of important Supreme Court rulings, beginning with outlawing the white primary in 1944, New Deal liberalism effectively reinforced Jim Crow and racial inequality. Only in the longer run would the New Deal's promotion of the modernization of the South undermine both conditions.

The United States experienced a transition to democracy in the 1930s and 1940s, even though the country underwent no major formal transformations to its broadly liberal governing norms and institutions and its formal constitutional design remained unaltered. The New Deal era was deeply marked by the reconstitution and broadening of partisanship as a result of the first full political inclusion of the mass of immigrants who had come from eastern and southern Europe before immigration restrictions were legislated and by the contested emergence and incorporation of a participant working class and organized labor as central political actors and counterweights to business power. This also was the period when African Americans began their movement from political peonage to political agency. This aspect of democratization, however, was only at a preliminary and much re-sisted stage when the Democratic Party, during the presidencies of Roosevelt and Truman, legislated the framework that would support the country's broadly successful experience of middle-class forma-tion. President Johnson's 1965 litany of racial sorrow might well have been a chronicle of accomplishment if African Americans had been included on full and equal terms in the New Deal and Fair Deal. More than a half-century after his commencement speech at Howard, we still are grappling with the failure to have done so.

## Notes

1. Kenneth B. Clark, *Dark Ghetto: Dilemmas of Social Power* (New York: Harper & Row, 1965), 11.
2. Lyndon B. Johnson, "To Fulfill These Rights," speech at Howard Univer-sity, June 4, 1965, reprinted in *The Moynihan Report and the Politics of Controversy*, edited by Lee Rainwater and William L. Yancey (Cam-bridge, Mass.: MIT Press, 1967), 127–28. The speech was drafted by Richard Goodwin and Daniel Patrick Moynihan.
3. When manpower needs grew most acute during the Second World War, General Dwight Eisenhower did integrate some units.
4. Johnson, "To Fulfill These Rights," 128–29.
5. Influential examples include Martin Anderson, *Welfare: The Political Economy of Welfare Reform in the United States* (Stanford: Hoover Press, 1978); Charles Murray, *Losing Ground: American Social Policy, 1950–1980* (New York: Basic), 1984.
6. For example, see Robert C. Lieberman, *Shifting the Color Line: Race and the American Welfare State* (Cambridge, Mass.: Harvard University Press, 1998); Jill Quadagno, *The Color of Welfare: How Racism Under-mined the War on Poverty* (New York: Oxford University Press, 1994).
7. V. O. Key Jr., *Southern Politics in State and Nation* (New York: Knopf, 1949), chs. 16 and 17.
8. David Sarashohn, *The Party of Reform: Democrats in the Progressive Era* (Jackson: University Press of Mississippi, 1989); David Burner, *The Politics of Provincialism: The Democratic Party in Transition, 1918–1932* (Cambridge, Mass.: Harvard University Press, 1986).
9. Writing in the 1950s, Denis Brogan, the famous Scottish historian of the United States, wrote: "Here the Liberal conscience is most deeply touched and his political behaviour seems (to the unfriendly outsider) most schizophrenic. The representative Liberal is a Democrat, or an ally of the Democrats, but in the ranks of 'the Democracy' are most of the most violent enemies of the integration of the Negro into the American community. This is no doubt accidental; it arises from the localization of the most acute form of the colour problem in the region where the Democratic party is traditionally strongest. The necessity of holding the national party together makes for strange bedfellows and strange deals." Denis W. Brogan, "American Liberalism Today," in *British Essays in*

*American History,* edited by H. C. Allen and C. P. Hill (New York: St. Martin's Press, 1957), 326.

10. For a fine treatment, see K. Walter Hickel, "Entitling Citizens: World War I and the Origins of the American Welfare State" (Ph.D. diss., Columbia University, 1999).

11. Even when the Democratic Party controlled Congress with unprecedented majorities, as it did after the landslides of 1932, 1934, and 1936, and thus when southern Democrats outnumbered Republicans, non-southern Democrats never composed a majority of the House or Senate.

12. Key, *Southern Politics,* 8–9.

13. For a discussion and relevant data on the role of southern Democrats in Congress, see David Brady, *Critical Elections and Congressional Policy Making* (Stanford: Stanford University Press, 1988), and Barbara Sinclair, *Congressional Realignment, 1925–1978* (Austin: University of Texas Press, 1982), especially the useful table on regional composition on page 19. See also the useful discussion of the advantages that accrued to the South over the long term in Richard L. Watson Jr., "From Populism Through the New Deal: Southern Political History," in *Interpreting Southern History: Historiographical Essays in Honor of Sanford W. Higginbotham,* edited by John B. Boles and Evelyn Thomas (Baton Rouge: Louisiana State University Press, 1987), 308–89.

14. *Congressional Record,* 76th Cong., 3rd sess., January 10, 1940, 248.

15. Watson, "From Populism Through the New Deal," 331.

16. A thoughtful discussion can be found in Erik N. Olssen, "Southern Senators and Reform Issues in the 1920s: A Paradox Unraveled," in *The South Is Another Land: Essays on the Twentieth-Century South,* edited by Bruce Clayton and John A. Salmond (New York: Greenwood Press, 1987), 49–65. See also Burner, *The Politics of Provincialism,* especially ch. 6. Burner reminds us that the prevailingly southern congressional Democrats of the 1920s were mostly holdovers from the Wilson years, and that even though they were in the minority, they held a balance-of-power position in disputes between western progressives and eastern conservatives in the Republican Party. Especially in the first half of the decade, the southern Democrats found common cause with the western progressives to frustrate many of the policy initiatives of Presidents Harding and Coolidge. Only after the disastrous 1924 election did the Democrats in Congress, fearing too close an identification with radicalism, become more acquiescent to presidential requests.

The unsurpassed overview of the economic situation of the South in comparison with other regions of the country is the classic text by Howard W. Odum, *Southern Regions of the United States* (Chapel Hill: University of North Carolina Press, 1936); a fine analytical overview is provided by William N. Parker, "The South in the National Economy, 1865–1970," *Southern Economic Journal* 46(April 1980): 1019–48.

17. The pre–New Deal state is nicely summarized in Theodore J. Lowi, "The Roosevelt Revolution and the New American State," in *Comparative Theory and Political Experience: Mario Einaudi and the Liberal Tradition,* edited by Peter J. Katzenstein, Theodore Lowi, and Sidney Tarrow (Ithaca: Cornell University Press, 1990), 192–95.

18. In "The GI Bill and U.S. Social Policy, Past and Future," *Social Philosophy and Policy* 14(Summer 1997), Theda Skocpol notes that the New Deal "encompassed both more- and less-privileged Americans" (115).

19. Theda Skocpol, "Delivering for Young Families: The Resonance of the GI Bill," *The American Prospect* 28(September–October 1996): 68.
20. Ibid., 71.
21. Lieberman, *Shifting the Color Line*, 24–25, 47–48, 26.
22. Richard Sterner, *The Negro's Share: A Study of Income, Consumption, Housing, and Public Assistance* (New York: Harper & Brothers, 1943), 285, 277.
23. Skocpol, "Delivering for Young Families," 67.
24. As the Second World War drew to a close, expectations for postwar mobility for black soldiers were high. Gunnar Myrdal, for one, predicted that "there is bound to be a redefinition of the Negro's status in America as a result of this War." Gunnar Myrdal, *An American Dilemma: The Negro Problem and Modern Democracy* (New York: Harper & Row, 1944), 997.
25. The relevant literature is scarce. I am especially indebted to the excellent paper by David Onkst, "'First a Negro . . . Incidentally a Veteran': Black World War II Veterans and the GI Bill of Rights in the Deep South, 1944–1948," *Journal of Social History* 31(Spring 1998): 527–44. I draw on his study for the data reported in the following paragraphs.
26. Alan Brinkley, "The New Deal and the Idea of the State," in *The Rise and Fall of the New Deal Order, 1930–1980,* edited by Steve Fraser and Gary Gerstle (Princeton: Princeton University Press, 1989), 112.

# 8

## The American Middle Class and the Politics of Education

### Margaret Weir

In the fall of 1994, just weeks after the first Republican Congress in a generation was elected, President Bill Clinton floated the idea of a "Middle-class Bill of Rights." The initiative proposed tax deductions for college tuition payments and other postsecondary educational training. For Clinton, who had failed in his high-risk bid to enact comprehensive health reform, the turn to education and the middle class signaled a retreat to safer ground. His move reflected what every American politician knows: when the battleground is the middle class, education represents the higher ground.

Long distinguished by its tradition of universal public schooling, the United States renewed its commitment to education after World War II with massive investments. Newly formed suburbs built thousands of new schools to accommodate the baby boom generation, and states transformed a desultory array of state colleges and institutes into coherent and well-funded systems of higher education. The federal government pitched in as well. Starting with the educational grants for veterans provided by the 1944 GI Bill of Rights, Washington provided financial assistance that both supported the actions of state and local governments and prodded them to take further action. This burst of investment in education offered occupational mobility to millions of Americans and supplied credentials for people in a range of occupations as they sought to upgrade their professional status. In the process, education helped to blur the lines that had once separated the working classes from the middle classes. In contrast to European nations, where postwar social welfare entitlements and institutions fostered security and solidarity across class lines, the vast expansion of education in the United States promised opportunities that would make the very notion of class obsolete and the need for social welfare minimal.[1] The high levels of support for education that were routinely registered in opinion polls indicated broad public approval for this distinctively American approach to smoothing class divisions.

The middle class and education thus appeared intertwined in a virtuous political relationship: expanded education created a broad middle class, and that middle class in turn provided political support for education. However, this simple equation, a staple of postwar American politics, falls short in two respects. First, it fails to recognize the inherent tensions in the relationship between education and the broad middle class. Expanded education, even as it opens new avenues for upward mobility, sorts the population into more- and less-educated categories. The significance of these categories for the middle class is not fixed: it can be understood only in a specific historical context. Second, the portrayal of the middle class as the backbone of support for education ignores the ambiguity of the middle class both as an object of political contention and as an actor. The terms on which the middle class participates in politics—the issues it engages, the identities it assumes, indeed, the very boundaries of the group itself—are all profoundly shaped by the institutional context in which politicians confront it and in which its own interests are formed.

This chapter examines the relationship between the American middle class and education from the immediate postwar era to the present. In the decades after World War II, historically contingent economic and political developments fostered a mutually reinforcing relationship between education and the broad middle class. Distinctive features of the postwar economy dampened the sorting functions of education, permitting its mobility and class-blurring characteristics to predominate. At the same time, developments in state and local political arenas—where education is primarily funded and provided— were unusually favorable to linking broad middle-class interests with educational expansion. These favorable political and economic conditions masked education's role in defining the external boundaries and internal divisions of the postwar middle class. When the economic and political ground shifted in the 1970s and 1980s, the divisive effects of education on a broad middle class appeared in sharp relief. The economy now amplified the sorting functions of education, and developments in state and local political institutions intensified the conflicts over education. Since 1980, presidential contenders across the political spectrum have showcased their strong support for education, but their consensual rhetoric belies the sharp divisions over the financing and organization of education. Even as education became more critical for achieving middle-class status, the political consensus that once supported the postwar expansion broke down.

## Public Education and the Golden Age of the White Middle Class

*Education, the Economy, and the Postwar Middle Class*

One of the staples of postwar accounts of the middle class is the central role of education in creating it. On the fiftieth anniversary of the GI Bill in 1994, magazines featured interviews with working-class veterans who never would have gone to college and entered white-collar occupations without the assistance of the GI Bill. The GI Bill opened the possibility of middle-class lives to millions of soldiers with working-class backgrounds. An estimated 2.2 million of 14 million eligible veterans took advantage of the tuition, stipends, and other assistance provided by the act.[2]

The GI Bill was only the beginning of the federal government's effort to expand access to higher education in postwar America. In 1948 the President's Commission on Higher Education (the Truman Commission) declared that higher education should not be "confined to an intellectual elite, much less a small elite drawn largely from families in the higher income brackets."[3] Two decades later, ongoing federal assistance and massive state support had indeed opened the doors of higher education far wider than they had been. The increase in total attendance was dramatic: in 1947, 2.3 million students (14 percent of all eighteen- to twenty-four-year-olds) were enrolled in higher educational institutions; by 1980 the figure was 12.1 million (40 percent of all eighteen- to twenty-four-year-olds).[4] Likewise, the percentage of high school graduates enrolling in college had grown from 45 percent in 1960 to 67 percent by 1997.[5]

The expansion of higher education helped to blur class lines in several ways. By promoting occupational mobility, higher education made the life chances of children from different backgrounds more similar. Access to higher education meant that fewer children followed in their parents' occupational footsteps.[6] As one study of American occupational mobility concluded, "A college degree cancels the effect of [social] origins on [occupational] destinations."[7] This outcome was possible because of the particular characteristics of the public education system in the United States. The structure of primary and secondary education facilitated access to higher education because it did not slot students irrevocably into future educational and vocational tracks, as was common in European countries. The relatively open structure of education created second and even third chances, contributing to the American sense of openness and opportunity. The expansion of higher education also helped to blur the lines of the occupational prestige hierarchy. Many occupations instituted new credentials that required attendance at institutions of higher education. As Heidenheimer notes, although the German and American occupational prestige hierarchies were similar, in the United States occupations used higher education credentialing "to improve themselves."[8] The range of semiprofessional occupational categories thus created softened the lines of occupational stratification and contributed to the notion of one big middle class.

Not surprisingly, education was central to the beliefs that the middle class held about itself and about American society as a whole. Yet the notion that education created the broad postwar middle class in the United States by promoting upward mobility is misleading. In the first place, the number of students who completed four years of college was much smaller than the number who enrolled in some form of higher education. In the key years in which the expanded middle class took shape, only a small percentage of Americans completed college. In 1940, 4.6 percent of the population age twenty-five or older had completed four years of college; by 1970 the number had risen to 11 percent, and by 1996 to 24 percent.[9] Second, and most important, higher education was not necessary for entry into the postwar middle class. Distinctive demographic patterns and economic forces in the decades after the war created a wage structure in which the income differences between workers with a college education and those without one were not so great.

Studies of postwar wage structures have identified a "great wage compression" between the 1940s and the late 1970s.[10] During the 1940s, the spread of wages narrowed as education and skill premiums and regional differences in earnings declined. The sharply increased demand for unskilled labor during the war and the wage control policies of the National War Labor Board helped set off the change. But after the war, this wage profile persisted. Ironically, the great expansion of postwar higher education contributed to holding down the wages of college graduates as the supply of college-educated workers grew sharply. At the same time, the relatively small cohort of unskilled workers was in high demand and able to command high wages. In addition to these factors of supply and demand, this compressed wage structure was reinforced by the political power of organized workers after the war. At the height of its membership and influence, organized labor was able to keep the minimum wage high and to press for wage increases well above the minimum for its own membership.

The enhanced availability of higher education after World War II, then, helped create a broad middle class primarily by enhancing occupational mobility. Occupation became a matter of individual choice and effort more than it had ever been. Nonetheless, access to middle-class lifestyles in the 1950s and 1960s did not depend on workers' educational achievements. Although manufacturers calibrated consumption goods according to the tastes and incomes of different class segments, the relatively narrow differentials in wages meant that the gulf separating these groups was not substantial.[11] Suburban lifestyles and enjoyment of the consumer goods that became the markers of a middle-class lifestyle were not restricted to those with higher education.

### The Politics of Educational Expansion

One of the most striking postwar developments was the broad consensus supporting the expansion of education. As the United States became a middle-class society, spending on education at all levels exploded and new channels of access opened up. Between 1950 and 1970, total spending on public education grew by 370 percent; spending on primary and secondary education grew by 318 percent, and spending on higher education by 580 percent. Spending far outstripped the growth in the school-age population: in the same decades, the primary and secondary school population increased by 71 percent, and the college-age population by 54 percent.[12] Much as the middle class supported this expansion, the growth of education was not simply a product of middle-class demands. It rested on distinctive features of federalism and localism that shaped the middle class both as an object of political competition and as an actor. Chief among these were the reemergence of states after their two-decade eclipse by the federal government and the flourishing of education in socially and economically homogenous postwar suburbs.

Armed with federal guarantees to pay for their college expenses, veterans placed extraordinary new demands on institutions of higher education: in 1946, the year after the war ended, veterans accounted for 48 percent of college students in the country.[13] Yet the success of federal initiatives in higher education depended on whether state governments could meet veterans' demands for higher education. Public higher education remained overwhelmingly a state responsibility. State systems of higher education varied widely. In the West, many states established university systems soon after statehood. In the East and Midwest, political opposition from private colleges had limited the public role in higher education primarily to teachers' colleges and technical institutes.

The surge in postwar demand for higher education sparked the creation and expansion of state systems of education across the country. Nationwide, just under half (46 percent) of the students who enrolled in higher education in 1940 attended public institutions; by 1970, after the expansion of higher education, that figure had jumped to 75 percent. The increase reflects the priority that many states placed on creating new institutions of higher education in the postwar decades by pouring resources into their systems of higher education. California, already boasting a strong public university system, was in the forefront. The state's 1960 master plan for coping with the coming surge in enrollments announced a social contract with the state's residents: California would guarantee access to higher education to all state residents who could benefit from it. Although the states varied in their effort to build systems of higher education, differences did not run along partisan lines. The greatest expansion in public higher education took place in New York State under the aegis of Republican Governor Nelson Rockefeller. In little more than a decade, Rockefeller transformed a small, underfunded state university system (the last to be established in the country) into the largest in the country.[14]

But it was not only ambitious governors who supported higher education; state legislatures, tightfisted on most social policy issues, also backed it. In many states, higher education became a beneficiary of pork barrel politics, with some sort of institution established in every state senate district.[15] State legislatures acted in a context of strong but diffuse public support for higher education. In one study of higher education conducted in the late 1960s, state legislators noted that they felt little public pressure on issues of higher education, with the exception of campus unrest. The most active political forces were university presidents and members of boards of regents.[16] This supportive but relatively insulated policy environment greatly facilitated expansion.

Distinctive political circumstances lay behind this favorable context for state activism. Since the 1930s, the states had been eclipsed by the federal government. As the federal government expanded its social role during the decade and a half of depression and war, states became backwaters of American political life. Reformers who had concentrated their energies at the state level during the Progressive era turned their focus to the much more promising arena of federal politics after the 1930s. Malapportioned state legislatures remained dominated by rural interests into the 1960s; governors were weak, state constitutions restrictive, and state revenue systems sharply limited. All of this began to change in the 1960s. Legislatures were reapportioned and began to meet annually in most states, rather than the previous norm of once every two years. States instituted new taxes, and ambitious governors sought new programs with which to build their reputations. Education, formally a state responsibility, provided a natural focus for these efforts.

Higher education was especially well situated to benefit from the efforts of states to reassert their place in the federal system. In the 1960s, higher education had few competitors in other policy domains. Although state spending on social welfare had increased under the pressure of federal social programs that required state contributions, such as Aid to Families with Dependent Children (AFDC, enacted in 1935) and medical assistance for the indigent (Medicaid, enacted in 1965), states were well able to control such expenditures. Legal rulings and expanded federal requirements that would require state social spending and reduce state discretion lay in the future. The growth of an educational lobby with few competitors allowed higher education to expand relatively unimpeded by divisive conflict or competition from other policy domains. By the 1960s, the pattern of state resources, institutional development, and organized constituencies had all placed higher education in an unusually favorable political light.

Political circumstances were also favorable for primary and secondary education during the postwar decades. Central among them was the new social and political geography that organized the educational demands of the expanding middle class. The growth of postwar suburbs, whose identities were uniquely bound up with their schools, fragmented the metropolitan public sphere into relatively homogeneous slices. Although suburbanization drew the white urban working class into a lifestyle that had only recently been the preserve of the middle class, it did not promote much mixing among income levels. The narrow price range of housing in postwar suburban developments ensured that there would not be much income diversity among the residents. For example, of the three Levittowns—the quintessential postwar suburb—built in these decades, the New Jersey development offered the greatest choice in housing: the three types of houses available for sale ranged in price from $11,500 to 14,500.[17] Moreover, in many of these new suburbs, young families who prized education above all other public services predominated. The remarkably homogenous age structure of postwar suburbs reflected the pent-up demand for housing and the effects of decades of depression and war on age and family structure. The growing opportunities and incentives for parents to leave undesirable school districts by buying houses in better districts propelled public education from the realm of politics into the realm of markets.[18] Families bought into communities that provided good schools, willingly paying the price.

Because primary and secondary schooling was traditionally funded by local governments through the property tax, the homogeneous social and political geography of the new suburbs carried important implications for public education. One implication was that there were few fundamental disagreements over the provision of public schooling as it expanded to educate the postwar baby boom. Ethnographic accounts of suburban life in the first decades after the war indicate that class-based conflicts occasionally erupted over curricula or spending issues.[19] The fast-growing suburbs inundated many school districts with a huge influx of children and confronted their parents with proposals for higher taxes. It was not uncommon for new homeowners, already financially stretched to the limits, to oppose such tax increases. But most striking in these accounts of postwar school politics in the suburbs is how swiftly such controversies were resolved. Schools remained insulated from deep and ongoing political conflict, and in most suburbs the nonpartisan conduct of school affairs allowed professional educators to maintain firm control over the schools. The dominance of families with children in these suburbs and the fencing out of the kind of controversies that would have been likely to arise with more diverse student bodies ensured broad general support for education.

Primary and secondary education also benefited from favorable political developments at the state level. The same activism that had spurred the expansion of higher education prompted many state governments to take on greater financial responsibility for primary and secondary schools as well. States stepped in to supplement the expenditures of localities so that by 1980, states shouldered at least half the cost of local schools. Some states greatly increased their contribution to education: in New York, one of the leaders, state expenditures on elementary and secondary education rose nearly 400 percent between 1960 and 1972.[20]

During the 1950s and well into the 1960s, the politics of primary and secondary education in the states remained a relatively closed arena. The central actors were professional associations of educators and politicians. The growth of teachers' unions added force to the expansion of state spending. In 1961 teachers launched their first major strike for collective bargaining rights. As state after state began to recognize teachers' unions, their demands for better pay and working conditions translated into higher spending on education. Between 1960 and 1970, the annual salary of instructional staff grew by 36 percent; spending per pupil in primary and secondary schools grew by 17 percent over the same period.[21] In state politics, where only a limited number of organized interests had lobbied before the 1980s, teachers' unions rapidly became a powerful political force. Even as the state political field grew more crowded in the 1980s and state politicians became more reliant on campaign contributions, teachers' unions held their own. Today they are one of the most powerful lobbies in state politics.[22]

The largely consensual expansion of spending on education at all levels and the increased access to higher education that characterized the postwar decades thus rested on distinctive characteristics of federalism and localism. State officials and organized actors, such as administrators and teachers, took the lead in pressing for expansion, and educational politics remained a remarkably insulated arena of policymaking in these decades. The middle class was a supportive but passive proponent of the great postwar expansion in American education.

*Managing Expansion: Middle-class Exclusion and Sorting*

Even as educational expansion helped shape the self-understanding and aspirations of the blended middle class, it not only created exclusions that set class boundaries but generated new internal class divisions. The most strikingly dissonant chord in the postwar story of middle-class growth was the exclusion of most black Americans. Finding the terms on which black Americans would be included constituted a central drama of educational politics after civil rights reached the national agenda in the 1960s. Less visible were the sorting arrangements built into the institutions that undergirded educational expansion. In both higher education and primary and secondary schools, expansion was accompanied by new divisions that marked lines of differentiation within the middle class. These exclusions and sorting mechanisms were integral to the middle class and to postwar educational arrangements; challenges to them faced stiff resistance.

Although the Supreme Court struck down "separate but equal" educational systems in 1954, its ruling in *Brown vs. Board of Education* had little impact for the next ten years, and even then its impact on opening the doors of the middle class to African Americans remained limited. Because of their deep disadvantages, black Americans also did not immediately benefit from the opening of higher education. Black veterans were eligible for the benefits of the GI Bill, but their low levels of high school completion prior to the war limited their college enrollment, especially in the South, where blacks on average had completed only five years of schooling.[23] In his chapter in this volume, Ira Katznelson emphasizes the South's role in shaping federal legislation that excluded blacks. Yet the South was not the only bar to black admission into the middle class and into its educational institutions. In addition to the South's role in national politics, the pattern of postwar metropolitan development created new divisions that excluded blacks in the North as well as in the South. Impoverished black migrants who came to the North in search of better jobs during World War II continued arriving in large numbers throughout the 1950s as southern agriculture was mechanized. They left the Jim Crow South only to find new forms of exclusion that would effectively bar them from the new middle class.

The central social feature of postwar suburbs was their exclusion of racial minorities. In recent years, historians have documented the many mechanisms that prevented African Americans from joining the exodus to the suburbs.[24] They have underscored the role that federal policies played, ranging from overtly discriminatory appraisal criteria for federally insured mortgages to poorly enforced antidiscrimination laws. States reinforced the pattern of exclusion by failing to use their authority over land use policy to check the proliferation of separate political jurisdictions in the growing suburbs. At times states actively promoted measures that facilitated suburban separatism by race and class. The courts emerged as the greatest defender of the localism that underlay the segmented social geography of postwar America.[25] Addressing a barrage of legal challenges from the 1960s on, the courts resolutely upheld the rights of localities to use zoning and other regulations that stopped short of outright racial discrimination to shape the character of local communities. In 1974 the Supreme Court issued the death knell for efforts to bridge the urban-suburban racial divide in education when it ruled in *Milliken vs. Bradley* that racial desegregation could not be mandated across local political boundaries.

The fragmented character of postwar suburban development made public education for the white middle class a politically insulated arena in which social and economic homogeneity generally translated into support for public schools. Although states and the courts entered educational politics in unprecedented ways in the 1960s, they did little to undermine the fragmented pattern that defined the public arena in education. The states' growing activism in school politics remained circumscribed by the character of local political divisions. By the 1960s, those divisions in many states were geographic and racial: the urban-suburban division had become a racial divide. For example, in New York during the 1960s, more than 90 percent of black and Latino students in the state attended school in the state's six large urban school systems.[26] For the most part, the suburban white middle class remained untouched by the social costs and tumult over racial integration that shook urban school districts in the 1960s and 1970s. In primary and secondary education, the exclusions that helped define the middle class as white thus withstood decades of challenge.

The white middle class that emerged from this system of education, however, was far from homogenous. Even as postwar suburbanization created a new middle class, it laid down lines of differentiation within it. Income differences between suburban jurisdictions translated into different levels of support for public schools. These differences did not attenuate over time. In fact, quantitative studies of suburbanization in the first decades after World War II indicate that in most metropolitan areas the suburban communities tended to become more, not less, differentiated by income. This tendency was especially pronounced in those regions (the Northeast and Midwest) where political fragmentation allowed communities to use zoning laws to shape the course of local development.[27]

The extension of state assistance to local districts did little to temper such divisions. Even the most generous states did not alter the distribution of students into districts of varying fiscal capacity and need, nor did they gear their financial support to equalizing spending across these districts. If anything, state aid formulas tended to discriminate against cities.[28] The domination of state governments by rural interests was a long-standing problem for urban areas, but when suburban power in state legislatures grew in the 1960s, the position of the cities did not improve. Despite persistent efforts, these school districts were unable to persuade rural and suburban legislators to increase aid to their needy students. Legal challenges to these arrangements brought before the Supreme Court failed. In 1973 the Court refused to make differences in spending across school districts a constitutional issue, declaring that education was not a fundamental right. As desirable as more equal spending across districts might be, it could not trump the value of local control inherent in the use of property taxes to fund the schools.[29]

Thus, key features of primary and secondary education continued to rest heavily on local prerogatives despite decades of unprecedented legal action and increased state involvement with education. Local control made the politics of education relatively uncontentious, but it also reinforced racial exclusion and sorting along income lines. When local control faced challenges, white Americans across the class spectrum fought to maintain the arrangements that had created an exclusive and internally stratified middle class.

In higher education, the politics of sorting and exclusion was conducted in more insulated arenas, guided by professional recommendations rather than public demands. This insulation allowed for the creation of extensive sorting mechanisms that initially attracted little public disapproval. It also facilitated the creation of mechanisms—notably affirmative action—that promoted a limited degree of racial inclusion.

In fact, even in the most generous and activist states, the postwar social contract to provide higher education remained conditional. The equalizing impact of the tremendous expansion of higher education was tempered by the diffusion of mechanisms for differentiating and sorting this newly enlarged group of students. Community colleges, the two-year institutions formerly known as junior colleges, played a central role in this sorting process. California's 1960 master plan provided an influential model for other state systems of higher education. Seeking to preserve the high ranking of the state university system, the plan looked to the expansion of community colleges as "the first line of defense for the University of California as an institution of international academic renown."[30] California's three-tiered system of higher education further buffered the university with a middle layer of state colleges offering four-year degrees. No other state followed such a strict hierarchy in its public system, but state politicians everywhere saw community colleges as a way to meet the new demands for higher education and at the same time to limit spending.[31]

Originally middle-class institutions, community colleges became disproportionately populated by students from lower-middle-class and working-class backgrounds in the 1950s and 1960s. The majority of those entering community colleges planned to use them as gateways to gain a bachelor's degree rather than as terminal vocational programs. But the impact of attending community colleges for these students was double-edged: studies showed that community colleges drew more lower-income students into higher education but also channeled these students away from four-year colleges.[32]

By 1970 the growth of public four-year colleges and public universities had made enrollment in some form of higher education a reliable expectation for a growing middle class. The differentiation within the system of higher education, the continuing low levels of enrollment among the poor and especially minorities, and lopsided federal and state spending on more elite schools underscored the limits of the egalitarian impulse behind the expansion of higher education.[33] Yet there was little public challenge to these new arrangements. As expansion increased the availability of new educational opportunities, much of the concern about this differentiation was deflected. Moreover, sorting was hard to challenge because it was justified by the extensive use of testing, whose postwar history Nicholas Lemann chronicles so well in *The Big Test*.[34] Lemann notes the growing public misgivings about testing as the central sorting device as early as the 1970s. However, little came of such doubts: testing experts and their allies in higher education bureaucracies had constructed an insulated domain clothed in elaborate scientific justification. Politicians, who may have preferred more open systems, did little to challenge sorting arrangements, which educators defended as essential to the health of the state systems of higher education.

The political insulation of the admissions process allowed universities to develop affirmative action as a mechanism for racial inclusion. In both private colleges and public systems of higher education, affirmative action became the means to facilitate enrollment of underrepresented minority students whose test scores alone would not qualify them for admission. The widespread practice of affirmative action in university admissions was a critical element in the creation of the black middle class. Long barred by racial discrimination from many high-wage blue-collar trade unions and often relegated to inferior jobs when they were admitted into unions, black workers without a college education were far less likely to enjoy the high incomes that helped to blur the class lines between blue- and white-collar whites.[35] Together with the public-sector jobs that opened up after the civil rights movement, access to higher education became the main route for black Americans seeking entry to the middle class.[36] Yet affirmative action fit uneasily within the sorting mechanisms that had been developed since the war. As Lemann puts it, the inherent contradiction between the meritocratic system of testing and affirmative action was a "national conflict waiting to happen." [37]

Thus, the institutional contexts in which educational decisions were made crucially shaped the way education intersected with the broad middle class. The localism of primary and secondary education ensured racial exclusion and income stratification in middle-class education. But the homogeneity within suburban school districts also limited conflict over school spending. Educational lobbies, especially teachers' unions, mobilized to persuade states to supplement local spending, although not to correct fiscal inequities. The combination of expansion and insulation in higher education created enhanced opportunity that was combined with sorting and a measure of racial inclusion. Played out against an economic backdrop in which the advantages conferred by education were limited, these arrangements provided a formula for producing a distinctively American middle class: mostly white, expansive but internally stratified, and dependent for its continued existence on the limited wage differentials between college and non-college-educated workers.

## The Erosion of the Middle Class and the Politics of Education in the Post–Civil Rights Era

The economic and political conditions that produced the postwar middle class shifted in the 1980s. New economic conditions highlighted the sorting functions of education as a college diploma came to define the line between a prosperous upper-middle class and an array of much less secure groups below it. The political context favorable to the education boom in the postwar era likewise eroded: developments in federalism dislodged education from its preeminent position in state politics, and a more diverse age profile weakened support for schooling in the suburbs. At the same time, ongoing challenges to racial exclusion and income sorting created a more contentious politics of education.

### The Growing Educational Divide

In his famous 1949 lecture on "Citizenship and Social Class," the British sociologist T. H. Marshall described the expansion of education in postwar Britain as part of a project to create social rights that would shrink the entire edifice of social inequality.[38] Yet Marshall recognized that education was double-edged: although it might sweep away older patterns of class privilege, education would create new inequalities as it sorted students according to ability. Marshall hoped that these inequalities too could be tamed by an array of new social rights that were now the badge of common citizenship in the British welfare state. In the postwar United States, the inequalities caused by education were tamed, not by the common benefits of the welfare state, but by a market economy that put middle-class lifestyles within reach of less-skilled as well as college-educated workers. As these market conditions collapsed in the 1980s, the broad middle class began to pull apart, and education's relationship to the middle class became much more complex.

The economic conditions that created the broad middle class began to unravel in the 1970s when average wage growth first slowed; it remained stagnant for the next three decades. During the 1970s, when the differences between white- and blue-collar wages were smaller, a college degree offered no guaranteed escape from the economic doldrums. The Harvard economist Richard Freeman provided statistical evidence in his 1976 book *The Overeducated American* to complement widespread anecdotes about college graduates driving taxis.[39] But in the 1980s, the wage structure widened, and education began to play a much greater role in determining earnings than it had in the immediate postwar decades. For male workers, the income differential between a high school and a college education was now substantial. The 45 percent of the workforce with no education beyond high school no longer shared the same future prospects as those who had attended college.[40] In the place of the broad postwar middle class that combined high school and college graduates, a class structure fractured along educational lines began to emerge.

The "college premium"—the average amount a college graduate earns over a non-college-educated worker—was 31 percent in 1979 before rapid wage dispersal began. By 1993 the college premium had grown to 53 percent. This difference was driven primarily by the decline in wages of less-educated workers. Technological change, increased international trade, and the decline of unions all played a role in reducing the wages of less-educated workers.[41] Between 1979 and 1994, college graduates saw their real weekly earnings rise by 5 percent; by contrast, the real weekly earnings of high school graduates declined by 20 percent.[42] Moreover, this divide grew even as the percentage of the labor force with a college degree increased from 22 percent in 1979 to 29 percent in 1994. The economist Frank Levy aptly describes the contemporary United States as "a country where an opportunity society and a class society coexist within the same borders."[43]

## The Contentious Politics of Education

As the economic stakes involved in getting a college degree rose, education became even more important for reaching middle-class status. Yet the political conditions that had fostered the postwar expansion of education were substantially altered by the 1980s. Developments in both federalism and localism attenuated support for spending on education at all levels. The combination of weaker political backing and the increased salience of education threatened the tenuous postwar recipe of access, sorting, and affirmative action in higher education. In primary and secondary schooling, political weakness and ongoing efforts to reduce exclusion and sorting threatened to bring down the entire structure of postwar schooling.

The growing social and economic divergence between educated and less-educated workers could have been tempered by the assurance that higher education was widely available. Yet throughout the 1980s and 1990s, increases in college costs and restrictions on financial assistance made college less, not more, accessible to lower-income Americans. In the 1980s, the Reagan administration tightened the terms of federal loan and grant assistance and reduced federal lending. Nor did states pick up the slack: in the 1980s and 1990s, states were reluctant to pour resources into education, as they had done thirty years earlier. Total public spending on higher education since 1976 has just kept pace with inflation, but the cost per student has risen by 40 percent.[44] The result has been higher tuition and fees. On average, tuition and fees doubled between 1976 and 1995. In some states, increases were steeper. By the late 1990s, tuition at California's public colleges and universities was four times higher than it had been twenty years earlier.[45] Although private giving to higher education has doubled in the same time period, it has not made up the difference. Private giving still accounts for the same proportion (8 percent) of overall spending on higher education as it did twenty years ago. Private charitable giving, moreover, disproportionately goes to private, relatively elite institutions.[46]

To understand why education has languished, even though it was once a broadly popular public program from which state leaders reaped substantial political benefits, we must examine the development of federalism, particularly the political consequences of the decentralization that began in the 1970s. As states took on more responsibilities and faced new claims on their resources, education lost its preeminent position in state capitals. In contrast to the 1960s, when advocates of education spending faced little competition, demands on state budgets multiplied in the 1980s. In Washington, the standoff between a Republican president and a Democratic Congress throughout the decade increased mandated state responsibilities. Unable to boost federal social spending to their satisfaction, congressional Democrats enacted regulations that required states to expand their spending on federal-state social programs, such as Medicaid. State budgets reflected the new pressure: average state spending on education peaked at 40 percent of general expenditures in 1970; the nearest competitor, public welfare, amounted to 16 percent of state spending in that year. By 1996 education had fallen to 33 percent of state spending, and public welfare had risen to 23 percent.[47]

In addition to the expansion of claims on state resources, state spending on education suffered from the tax revolt that began with California's Proposition 13 in 1978. State political leaders across the country took the anti-tax message to heart. The political success of the anti-tax movement underscored changes in the economic conditions that confronted the middle class in the 1970s. Since the 1950s, being middle-class in the United States meant owning a home. Yet homeowners faced acute economic strains in the 1970s; escalating property taxes in a context of inflation and slow growth provided the immediate impetus for the passage of Proposition 13.[48] Since then, education has vied with tax cuts—and has often lost—as the policy most likely to win middle-class votes. Throughout the economic boom of the late 1990s, state politicians continued to cut taxes even in the absence of vocal anti-tax movements.

The appearance of new claimants for state funds exacerbated these trends. Policies that promised to appeal to those already in the middle class were the strongest contenders: most prominent among these was spending related to crime and prisons. Rising crime rates coupled with increasingly strict sentencing practices made corrections the fastest-rising component of state spending in many states during the 1990s. In some states, including California, once the leader in access to higher education, expenditures for prisons began to rival those for higher education.[49]

The new pressures on spending have forced even the most generous states to reconsider their promise to provide access to all state residents who can benefit from higher education. Tuition and fee increases created new barriers to students from low-income families. As resources have become more constrained, state university systems must increasingly confront the tension between providing high-quality education and promoting broad access. Many states have continued to support their most prestigious flagship universities at the expense of other parts of the state university system. Less hierarchical public systems, such as the State University of New York, now face a choice between "access and quality education."[50] Although New York State legislators resisted efforts to move to an explicitly more stratified system, tuition and fee hikes effectively limited access.

The interaction between reduced access to higher education and a sharper income divide based on education presents a potent threat to mobility, one of the central underpinnings of the postwar middle class. It also intensifies the competition for access to higher education. One of the casualties of intensified competition is affirmative action in college admissions: once insulated from public scrutiny, admissions criteria in public universities across the country have faced challenge. Eliminated by public referendum in California in 1996 and restricted by judicial decisions in several other states, affirmative action has seen a reduction in its ability to open the doors of the upper-middle class to underrepresented minorities, although it has not been completely abandoned.[51] The reduction of affirmative action raises questions for the continued vitality of the black middle class, a significant sector of which has only a precarious hold on middle-class status.[52] The challenge of preserving access to higher education and the mobility it creates is made all the more acute by the large wave of new enrollments with which systems of public higher education will be confronted in the next decade. In many states, including the largest state systems (California, Texas, and New York), a significant portion of the new students seeking enrollment are the children of immigrants from Latin America and Asia who came to the United States in large numbers during the 1980s and 1990s. The intersection of low income, ethnic distinctions, and reduced access to higher education will present policymakers with a challenge that, if left unaddressed, could re-create the enduring economic and social divisions that postwar America had prided itself on subduing.

In primary and secondary education, challenges to the features of localism that predominated during the postwar decades promise to alter the relationship between education and the middle class, but the direction of change and the ultimate impact on the middle class are far from clear. The fiscal inequities created by local school finance have been an ongoing target of reform. Although the Supreme Court declined to address this issue, it has been the focus of the lawsuits brought in thirty states to obtain more equal spending across districts. In the sixteen states where these suits were successful, the stratification of spending characteristic of American education has been tempered, although not eliminated.[53] The long battles over such measures, their limited implementation, and their modest success testify to the endurance of the local system of primary and secondary education finance. The imperviousness of most white suburban political jurisdictions to racial integration further underscores the political strength of the exclusionary and stratifying arrangements that govern primary and secondary education.[54] Support for these arrangements is reflected in the stable rates of public school attendance—hovering around 89 percent for the past four decades.[55] The continuing division of suburban jurisdictions along income and racial lines will facilitate the emerging pattern of stratification in which an upper-middle class with superior education pulls apart the broad middle class.

Changes in the social geography of suburbs, however, suggest that localism may no longer provide the same support for educational spending that it once did. Most significant is the changing age profile of the suburbs—and of the voting population more broadly. Analysis of state spending on education over time demonstrates that the percentage of the population over sixty-five exercises a significant negative effect on state and local spending.[56] Such effects are strongest when the racial composition of the school-age population differs from that of the elderly voters. This is a particularly ominous trend for the large, economically vibrant states where the proportion of immigrants in the school-age population has grown in recent decades. In California, for example, non-Latino whites are a declining percentage of the school population, dropping from 53.7 percent in 1986 to 39.5 percent in 1996.[57] Analyses of support for school bonds reveal similarly negative effects of an aging population on local spending on education. Support for school bonds was at its highest in the early 1960s, when 72 percent of school bonds passed; since the early 1970s, support has hovered at around 50 percent.[58]

The greatest threat to the existing system of public education comes from those who experienced its worst features. African Americans, who were largely relegated to inferior urban schools, have lent limited but strategically essential support to the project of dismantling the entire system of public education. The abysmal minority experience with the segmented system of public education has made some inner-city African Americans receptive to replacing the current district-based system of educational provision with school vouchers. Such a system would provide each child with a voucher to attend the school of his or her choice, rather than being assigned to a particular school. Moreover, voucher plans allow students to use public money to attend privately run schools, thus ending the state monopoly on the provision of public education. Alliances of conservative Republicans and liberal African Americans were critical in enacting the only three publicly funded voucher programs existing in 2000, in Milwaukee, Cleveland, and Florida.[59] African American political support was critical to the political success of these initiatives: states and cities attempting to enact vouchers without such support have failed. African American proponents of vouchers maintain that such radical change is the only way to challenge the poor education that has kept one-third of the black population in poverty.

Among the key barriers to the spread of vouchers are the teachers' unions. Still one of the strongest lobbies in state politics, teachers' unions have blocked voucher proposals across the country. But their political position is not as strong as it once was. When the national educational agenda shifted to emphasize the quality of schools in 1983, teachers' unions became a favorite target of reformers.[60] The voucher movement threatens to divide African Americans and teachers' unions, two constituencies that have traditionally joined to provide strong support for public education. On their own, teachers' unions are much more politically vulnerable to being portrayed as special interests working against the broad interest of American children, much as unions were blamed for inflation in the 1950s (see Jacobs, this volume).[61]

The impact of vouchers on the exclusions and stratifications of the postwar era depends entirely on how such programs are structured. At their best, they may raise new ladders into the middle class for excluded minorities, who under the present system are relegated to schools that offer few such opportunities. At their worst, they may reduce political support for spending on schools as the main constituencies that have supported such spending—in particular teachers' unions—are weakened. Depending on their design, educational voucher programs may also exacerbate the emerging divisions within the middle class by allowing an upper-middle class to use public funds to subsidize its further retreat from institutions that promote some income mixing. Voucher programs remain extremely limited, and their legal future is still in doubt. Yet their growing political popularity reflects a major challenge to the political alliances and institutional arrangements that have shaped primary and secondary education for the last half-century.

## Conclusion

With its links to culturally approved ideals of reward for individual effort, public education in the United States expanded much earlier and at higher levels than in European countries, where social welfare provision played a much greater role in the lives of most citizens. In the decades after World War II, federal, state, and local governments all reaffirmed the national emphasis on education and extended it to higher education. As prosperity expanded the middle class, broader access to higher education affirmed its openness. The legacy of the racial caste system in the South and the racially exclusionary pattern of postwar suburbanization in the North made entry into this expanded middle class through education much more accessible to whites than to blacks. After decades of failing to pry open the doors to the middle-class life using antidiscrimination measures alone, African Americans achieved a measure of entry by the 1970s through affirmative action. A significant segment of black America, however, by then trapped in northern cities as well as in the rural South, found no toeholds on the ladders leading to the middle class. Neither the market nor the educational system provided them with the rudiments of middle-class life.

Reaffirming the social contract with middle-class Americans is much more complex today than in the postwar decades. The impact of the market and education on the middle class has been transformed. Because the market widens the gulf between educated and less-educated workers, education now plays a much more double-edged role than it once did. Education sorts even as it promotes mobility; today such sorting jeopardizes the expanded middle class as lines of internal class stratification threaten to become markers of new class boundaries.

What vision of education could stem the erosion of the middle class and address both enduring and emerging exclusions? Any effort to forge a new social contract with a large and open middle class must contain at least three core features. First, the American promise of providing second and third chances through education must be reinforced by making lifelong learning a realistic possibility. Not only should credible training systems be supported, but living stipends for workers who engage in retraining should be offered. Second, public policy must acknowledge the connection between the quality of local school districts and access to higher education. The potent combination of racism and localism made this issue taboo throughout the postwar era. Some states, notably Texas, have begun to experiment with new university admissions criteria that guarantee access to students from all districts. Such new approaches, supplemented with infusions of resources to low-income school districts, are only first steps in tackling this most intractable problem of American education. Finally, education needs to be seen as only one among several key elements of a new social contract. Americans are easily tempted to believe that education can solve all social and economic problems. But as we have seen, education played an important but limited role in creating the postwar middle class, and distinctive labor market conditions reduced the economic significance of education. Today, as the market moves educated and less-educated workers further apart, government has a much more important role to play in ensuring basic security to all workers, including health care, income security, and access to opportunity.

---

I would like to thank Ben Bowyer for research assistance and the Institute for Governmental Studies at the University of California at Berkeley for research support. Andrew Barlow, Charles Feigenoff, Hiroshi Ishida, Meg Jacobs, William Kelly, Leonard Schoppa, Herman Schwartz, and Olivier Zunz all provided helpful comments on earlier drafts of this chapter.

## Notes

1. On the American propensity to treat education as a central component of welfare, see Arnold J. Heidenheimer, "Education and Social Security Entitlements in Europe and America," in *The Development of Welfare States in Europe and America*, edited by Peter Flora and Arnold J. Heidenheimer (New Brunswick: Transaction Books, 1987), 269–304; Morris Janowitz, *Social Control of the Welfare State* (New York: Elsevier, 1976).

2. Edward Kiester Jr., "The GI Bill May Be the Best Deal Ever Made by Uncle Sam," *Smithsonian* 25(November 1994): 128–37.

3. Cited in Steven Brint and Jerome Karabel, *The Diverted Dream: Community Colleges and the Promise of Educational Opportunity in America, 1900–1985* (New York: Oxford University Press, 1989), 69.

4. Enrollment data from U.S. Department of Education, National Center for Education Statistics, *Digest of Education Statistics, 1998* (Washington: U.S. Government Printing Office, 1998), 196, table 172; enrollment data include full-time and part-time enrollment. Cohort data from U.S. Bureau of the Census, *Statistical Abstract of the United States: 1999* (Washington: U.S. Government Printing Office, 1999), 15, table 14; *Statistical Abstract of the United States: 1985* (Washington: U.S. Government Printing Office, 1985), 26, table 27; and *Historical Statistics of the United States: Colonial Times to 1970*, series A29–42 (Washington: U.S. Government Printing Office, 1975), 10. The higher education cohort is based on the population between ages eighteen and twenty-four.

5. National Center for Education Statistics, *Digest of Education Statistics, 1998*, 208, table 183.

6. Michael Hout, "More Universalism, Less Structural Mobility: The American Occupational Structure in the 1980s," *American Journal of Sociology* 93(May 1988): 1358–1400.

7. Ibid., 1391.

8. Heidenheimer, "Education and Social Security Entitlements in Europe and America," 289.

9. U.S. Department of Education, National Center for Education Statistics, *Digest of Education Statistics, 1997* (Washington: U.S. Government Printing Office, 1998), 105, table 8.

10. Claudia Goldin and Robert A. Margo, "The Great Compression: The Wage Structure in the United States at Mid-century," *Quarterly Journal of Economics* 107(February 1992): 1–34; see also the discussion in Claude S. Fischer et al., *Inequality by Design: Cracking the Bell Curve Myth* (Princeton: Princeton University Press, 1996), 152–55.

11. On postwar consumption and the middle class, see Olivier Zunz, *Why the American Century?* (Chicago: University of Chicago Press, 1998), chs. 4 and 5.

12. Education spending data are from U.S. Department of Education, National Center for Education Statistics, *Digest of Education Statistics, 1999* (Washington: U.S. Government Printing Office, 2000), 35, table 32. The population data are from U.S. Bureau of the Census, *Statistical Abstract of the United States: 1999*, 15, table 14; *Statistical Abstract of the United States: 1985*, 26, table 27; and *Historical Statistics of the United States: Colonial Times to 1970*, 10. The primary and secondary popula-

tion is based on the number of five- to seventeen-year-olds; the higher education cohort is based on the population between ages eighteen and twenty-four.

13. Keith Olson, *The GI Bill, the Veterans, and the Colleges* (Lexington: University Press of Kentucky, 1974), 35.

14. Donald Axelrod, "Higher Education," in *Governing New York State: The Rockefeller Years*, edited by Robert H. Connery and Gerald Benjamin (New York: Academy of Political Science, 1974), 131–45; Henry J. Steck, "How Good and How Large a State University?: Dilemmas of Higher Education Policy in New York State," in *Governing New York State*, edited by Jeffrey M. Stonecash, John Kenneth White, and Peter W. Colby (Albany: State University of New York Press, 1994), 277.

15. This is what University of California President Clark Kerr's Master Plan sought to head off. See Nicholas Lemann, *The Big Test: The Secret History of the Meritocracy* (New York: Farrar, Straus & Giroux, 1999), 130–36.

16. Heinz Eulau, *State Officials and Higher Education: A Survey of the Opinions and Expectations of Policymakers in Nine States* (New York: McGraw-Hill, 1970), 49–50.

17. See Herbert J. Gans, *The Levittowners: Ways of Life and Politics in a New Suburban Community* (New York: Pantheon, 1967), 6–7.

18. Ira Katznelson and Margaret Weir, *Schooling for All: Class, Race, and the Decline of the Democratic Ideal* (New York: Basic, 1985), ch. 8.

19. See Gans, *The Levittowners*, ch. 5; Katherine S. Newman, *Declining Fortunes: The Withering of the American Dream* (New York: Basic, 1993), ch. 3; Louis H. Masotti, *Education and Politics in Suburbia: The New Trier Experience* (Cleveland: Press of Western Reserve University, 1967).

20. See Kenneth K. Wong, *Funding Public Schools: Politics and Policies* (Lawrence: University Press of Kansas, 1999), 52; Michael D. Usdan, "Elementary and Secondary Education," in Connery and Benjamin, *Governing New York State*, 225.

21. National Center for Education Statistics, *Digest of Education Statistics, 1999*, 50, table 39.

22. See, for example, Dante Chinni, "Teacher's Pets," *Washington Monthly* 29(January–February 1997): 22–25.

23. David H. Onkst, "'First a Negro . . . Incidentally a Veteran': Black World War II Veterans and the GI Bill of Rights in the Deep South, 1944–1948," *Journal of Social History* 31(Spring 1998): 517–44.

24. See, for example, Kenneth T. Jackson, *Crabgrass Frontier* (New York: Oxford University Press, 1985), chs. 11 and 12.

25. See Richard Briffault, "Our Localism, Part I: The Structure of Local Government Law," *Columbia Law Review* 90(January 1990): 72–85.

26. Usdan, "Elementary and Secondary Education," 228.

27. John R. Logan and Mark Schneider, "The Stratification of Metropolitan Suburbs, 1960–1970," *American Sociological Review* 46(April 1981): 175–86.

28. See Philip Meranto, *School Politics in the Metropolis* (Columbus, Ohio: Charles E. Merrill, 1970), ch. 5.

29. *San Antonio vs. Rodriguez*, 411 U.S. 1 (1973).

30. Cited in Brint and Karabel, *The Diverted Dream*, 87.

31. Kevin J. Dougherty, *The Contradictory College: The Conflicting Origins, Impacts, and Futures of the Community College* (Albany: State University of New York Press, 1994), 167–68.

32. See the evaluation of the evidence on the impact of community college attendance in Dougherty, *The Contradictory College*, 49–61; Brint and Karabel, *The Diverted Dream*, 90–92.

33. William H. Sewell, "Inequality of Opportunity for Higher Education," *American Sociological Review* 36(October 1971): 793–809; W. Lee Hansen and Burton Weisbrod, "The Distribution of Costs and Direct Benefits of Public Higher Education: The Case of California," *Journal of Human Resources* 4(Spring 1969): 176–91; Christopher Jencks et al., *Inequality: A Reassessment of the Effect of Family and Schooling in America* (New York: Harper & Row, 1972).

34. Lemann, *The Big Test*.

35. On exclusion and the job markets that black workers faced, see Jill Quadagno, *The Color of Welfare: How Racism Undermined the War on Poverty* (New York: Oxford University Press, 1994), ch. 10; Thomas J. Sugrue, *The Origins of the Urban Crisis* (Princeton: Princeton University Press, 1996), ch. 4.

36. Michael K. Brown and Steven P. Erie, "Blacks and the Legacy of the Great Society: The Economic and Political Impact of Federal Social Policy," *Public Policy* 29(Summer 1981): 299–330.

37. Lemann, *The Big Test*, 164.

38. T. H. Marshall, "Social Class and Citizenship," in *Class, Citizenship, and Social Development* (New York: Doubleday, 1964), 96–97.

39. Richard B. Freeman, *The Overeducated American* (New York: Academic Press, 1976).

40. See Frank Levy, *The New Dollars and Dreams: American Incomes and Economic Change* (New York: Russell Sage Foundation, 1998), especially 190–91.

41. For a review of arguments about the causes of growing inequality, see Peter Gottschalk and Timothy M. Smeeding, "Cross-national Comparisons of Earnings and Income Inequality," *Journal of Economic Literature* 35(June 1997): 646–51.

42. Peter Gottschalk, "Inequality, Income Growth, and Mobility: The Basic Facts," *Journal of Economic Perspectives* 11(Spring 1997): 30.

43. Levy, *The New Dollars and Dreams*, 190–91. The picture is complicated further by the fact that inequality within groups has also increased: among groups with similar levels of education, inequality rose between 1979 and 1994.

44. Roger Benjamin and Stephen J. Carroll, *Breaking the Social Contract: The Fiscal Crisis in Higher Education* (Santa Monica: Council for Aid to Education, an independent subsidiary of RAND, 1998).

45. Roger Benjamin and Stephen J. Carroll, *Breaking the Social Contract: The Fiscal Crisis in California Higher Education* (Santa Monica: Council for Aid to Education, an independent subsidiary of RAND, 1998), 17.

46. Benjamin and Carroll, *Breaking the Social Contract: The Fiscal Crisis in Higher Education*. http://www.rand.org/publications/CAE/CAE100/index.html, accessed July 3, 2000.

47. On state spending, see Richard F. Winters, "The Politics of Taxing and Spending," in *Politics in the American States*, 7th ed., edited by Virginia Gray, Russell L. Hanson, and Herbert Jacob (Washington, D.C.: Congressional Quarterly Press, 1999), 323.

48. Peter Schrag, *Paradise Lost: California's Experience, America's Future* (Berkeley: University of California Press, 1998), 133–39.

49. In 1998 California spent 8.5 percent of its general fund on corrections and 12.9 percent on higher education; in 1970, 4 percent of the general fund had gone to corrections, and 14 percent to higher education. See Schrag, *Paradise Lost* 95.

50. Stephens Report, quoted in Steck, "How Good and How Large a State University?," 287.

51. On affirmative action, see Lemann, *The Big Test;* Lydia Chavez, *The Color Bind: California's Battle to End Affirmative Action* (Berkeley: University of California Press, 1998); William G. Bowen and Derek C. Bok, *The Shape of the River: Long-term Consequences of Considering Race in College and University Admissions* (Princeton: Princeton University Press, 1998).

52. See Mary Pattillo-McCoy, *Black Picket Fences: Privilege and Peril Among the Black Middle Class* (Chicago: University of Chicago Press, 1999).

53. For an overview of contemporary state school financing and equity issues, see Wong, *Funding Public Schools,* 57–58, 71–90. For descriptions and analyses of these state activities, see William N. Evans, Sheila E. Murray, and Robert Schwab, "Schoolhouses, Courthouses, and Statehouses After *Serrano*," *Journal of Policy Analysis and Management* 16(Winter 1997): 10–31; Douglas S. Reed, "Twenty-five Years After *Rodriguez:* School Finance Litigation and the Impact of the New Judicial Federalism," *Law and Society Review* 32(1, 1998): 175–220. There is evidence that where the courts have ordered radical equalization that infringes on local spending prerogatives, one consequence is lower spending and flight to private education. See Caroline M. Hoxby, "All School Finance Equalizations Are Not Created Equal" (unpublished paper, Department of Economics, Harvard University); available at *www.economics.harvard.edu/faculty/hoxby/papers.html* (accessed June 1, 2000).

54. There are exceptions: a handful of racially changing suburbs experienced sharp conflicts over school desegregation in the 1980s and 1990s. See Jennifer Hochschild and Michael N. Daniels, "Can We Desegregate Public Schools and Subsidized Housing?: Lessons from the Sorry History of Yonkers, New York," in *Changing Urban Education,* edited by Clarence N. Stone (Lawrence: University Press of Kansas, 1998), 23–44.

55. National Center for Education Statistics, *Digest of Education Statistics, 1999,* table 3.

56. James Poterba, "Demographic Structure and the Political Economy of Public Education," *Journal of Policy Analysis and Management* 16(Winter 1997): 49–57.

57. National Center for Education Statistics, *Digest of Education Statistics, 1998,* 60, table 45.

58. Maris A. Vinovskis, *Education, Society, and Economic Opportunity* (New Haven: Yale University Press, 1995), 198–99.

59. Felicia Wong, "The Good Fight: Race, Politics, and Contemporary Urban School Reform" (Ph.D. diss., Department of Political Science, University of California, Berkeley, March 2000). A 1998 poll found that 54 percent of African American parents thought vouchers were a good or excellent idea, compared with 36 percent of white parents. See the data reported by Public Agenda at *www.publicagenda.org/issues/nation—divided. cfm!issue—type = education* (accessed June 1, 2000).

60. U.S. National Commission on Excellence in Education, *A Nation at Risk: The Imperative for Educational Reform* (Washington: U.S. Government Printing Office, 1983).
61. See Kate Rousmaniere, "Teacher Unions in Popular Culture: Individualism and the Absence of Collectivity," *Working USA* 3(September–October 1999): 38–47.

# 9

## Changing Gender and Family Models: Their Impact on the Social Contract in European Welfare States

### *Chiara Saraceno*

In the industrialized countries of Europe, the family is increasingly the subject of social policy debates that focus on two critical issues. First, changes in family and individual behavior are modifying the way societies reproduce themselves. Second, welfare restructuring in many countries involves a redrawing of the line between state and family responsibilities and redefining expectations, particularly family obligations.[1] Thus, the "family question" is at the center of the policy decisions and theoretical debates that underlie the restructuring of the welfare state that was created as part of the postwar social contract.

According to Colin Crouch, this social contract included a balance among the following four features: an industrial rather than agricultural, occupational, and economic structure; a primarily capitalist framework; a sociologically liberal institutional structure in relation to traditional community institutions; and the idea that nearly every adult living in the state possessed certain rights of citizenship.[2] Although the effort to balance these four features identified the industrialized European countries as having a common heritage and outlook, the variations in how this balance was struck produced diversity among them. Moreover, these balances were not attained without internal tensions, conflicts, and contradictions. The ways in which societies tackled these tensions and conflicts further differentiated them from each other, while opening unique avenues for change.

## Assumptions About Gender and the Family in Postwar European Welfare States

Within the postwar social contract, societies managed the potential tensions between private loyalties and market requirements by separating the spheres and rules belonging to family relationships and those belonging to the workplace. The gender division of labor within the family has been a crucial means for effecting this separation, both symbolically and practically. Welfare state arrangements are a second means by which societies have addressed these tensions. These two means of managing potential conflict between the public and private spheres—family arrangements and welfare state arrangements—overlap and interact. Families, both households and kin networks, have been the locus of income redistribution and the link to welfare state benefits for those who have no direct access to them owing to their age or gender. At the same time, the models of gender and intergenerational behavior and patterns of solidarity and obligations that families embody have been central to welfare arrangements and helped to differentiate welfare regimes.[3]

Welfare state provisions have also affected the gender and intergenerational arrangements within families by institutionalizing family dependencies. This was so well established by the 1960s as to appear natural, although to varying degrees in different countries.

Indeed, most European nations at the turn of the twentieth century had introduced social legislation along three lines. First, the labor market participation of women and children was regulated. Second, insurance measures against loss of work income (due to unemployment, old age, or sickness) were introduced. Third, some family dependencies were acknowledged, as in the case of family allowances, the extension of the coverage of health services to family dependents, and the introduction of survivor's pensions.

In regulating labor relations and conditions and defining which needs might be socially acknowledged and supported, societies have implicitly used social legislation and then social policies to regulate family and household formation. This occurred in two ways: by redefining the relationships of dependence and interdependence between genders and generations, and by modifying the conditions and costs of reproduction, in effect rewarding or discouraging particular family patterns. The effects of this system can be seen in the introduction of old-age pensions at the beginning of the century. Having a pension, in fact, allowed the elderly not only to look with a degree of security to their future after work but to avoid depending too exclusively on their kin. Restrictions on the labor of children and women combined with the introduction of compulsory schooling constituted a de facto means of regulating gender and intergenerational relations in workers' households by distinguishing household members as either "workers" or "family dependents."

The first items of social legislation, so-called protective legislation, were generally addressed not to the core workers (skilled male workers), who were the later target of social insurance, but to the "weak" and marginal workers.[4] In effect, protective legislation institutionalized two categories of "weak" and marginal workers on the basis of age and gender. This determination was in turn taken as an indicator of family status: women workers were all seen as potential wives and mothers, and children as mainly their parents' dependents. In making these determinations, this kind of legislation for a long time excluded these same "weak" categories of workers from eligibility for the benefits available to core workers. They could not have access to the positions that entitled them directly to social insurance protection and could gain access to such insurance only as children and wives. The progressive extension—since the interwar years—to wives and children of some of the protection accorded to workers (mainly health care) and the introduction of the survivor's pension (to benefit wives and children) may be read as a reaction to that initial exclusion.[5]

With the spread of industrialization, there was an increase in the proportion of the male population working full-time in a salaried status, which gave them access to welfare state provisions, a sharp decrease in the proportion of the female (particularly married) population in paid work, and a decrease in the proportion of children of both genders in the workforce.[6] This was especially clear in the countries that were industrialized the earliest and the most intensively. At the same time, there was an increase in household and family unpaid work. This process culminated in mid-century, when Western industrialized countries had the highest proportion ever of full-time housewives among the adult female population.

The ideal household model behind this process was premised on the presence of a male breadwinner responsible for providing income and mediating social protection for women and children.[7] It also assumed the presence of a wife and mother responsible both for occasionally providing needed income and for systematically providing care, particularly for young children and the frail elderly. We might thus argue that as social rights based on labor market attachment developed in industrialized societies, there was a gradual and parallel extension of those rights based on family attachment and family dependence. The "familization" of social rights for women and children, as well as for the frail elderly, was thus parallel to and intertwined with the individualization of social rights for adult, able-bodied working men.

We might suggest that this strengthening of the male breadwinner model was a consequence of the progressive extension in the postwar years of the middle-class household and family model to the lower class, among whom the working mother was increasingly perceived as an indicator of family instability and less than adequate respectability. A respectable working-class family ideally comprised a man able to provide for wife and children and a woman fully devoted to homemaking. Fulfilling this ideal, however, required some support. Thus, social policies addressed to the male breadwinner as such may be interpreted as an element of that family wage that would allow wage workers to replicate the middle-class family model. Over the years, these policies covered a wider range of social classes, including the middle classes—following the spread of dependent (salaried) labor relations at all levels—but also extending, to a varying degree, to the self-employed, particularly in the postwar years.[8]

Yet the various social actors could not agree on what exactly was meant by family wage—what it should comprise, how it should be packaged, and who should receive it. That disagreement led to conflict between the labor movement and entrepreneurs, between trade unions and feminist groups, and in some countries (France, for example) between entrepreneurs and the state. The way in which the different options were articulated, the alternatives negotiated, and the conflicts decided has deeply marked social policies in each country. These resolutions have in turn affected how the issue of family dependencies and interdependencies is thematized even today.[9] Although the male breadwinner model did prevail in all welfare states at the beginning, the extent to which it prevailed in each state depended on how the issue of the family wage was put forth and negotiated. How the family wage was treated depended in turn on power relations, on the prevalent value and cultural models concerning family organization, and on the explicit and implicit targets of the various measures approved or proposed. An important role was played by Catholicism and by Catholic parties in continental Europe, insofar as they supported both the gender division of labor and the autonomous, solidaristic role of the family as a crucial locus of redistribution. Yet, although in all countries with a strong Catholic culture and important Catholic parties the role allocated to families for redistributive purposes was more significant than in others, the specific policies developed for this purpose were quite different. They ranged from strong income support for either marriage (as in Germany) or parenthood (as in France and Belgium) to very weak support for families (as in the

Mediterranean welfare states). In the Mediterranean countries, the role of (extended) family solidarity and the gender division of labor within it were enforced more through absence of policy than through the specific shape or content of policies themselves.

Looking at how the family wage was conceptualized in demands and constituted in practice offers a different perspective on the historical and comparative analysis of welfare state development. Instead of focusing mainly on the details of social security schemes, such an approach focuses on boundaries and reciprocal obligations between individuals and the state, between individuals and the family, between the family and the state, within the family, and between the market and the state, as they are suggested and shaped by social policies.

Thus, in the United Kingdom at the beginning of the century, demands for benefits for dependent family members, particularly for children, revolved around the relationships between men and women and their respective responsibilities. When the Beveridge Plan introduced child benefits to the United Kingdom, the male breadwinner model, based mainly on marriage, was well established in both social security policy and individual behavior. In France, pronatalist concerns about the cost of children prepared the way for a family policy designed to support children rather than marriage per se. This system developed alongside, and even predated, the standard social security provisions. Family allowances, first introduced by employers as a means both to avoid the impoverishment of their workers due to family size and to keep basic wages low, in time came to represent a universal entitlement and a substantial portion of wages. In Sweden, pronatalist concerns combined with an emphasis on individual freedom to motivate the state to expand reproductive choices and to focus on services and redistribution in kind rather than in money. Although the main or sole breadwinner in the 1930s and 1940s in Sweden was usually a man, the family wage was a mixture of income and services rather than a pure breadwinner wage, as in the United Kingdom, or a wage-plus-family-allowance, as in France and later in Germany, and to a lesser degree in Italy.

These different ways of packaging the family wage institutionalized boundaries between the responsibilities of men and women, and between those of the family and the state. They also created different definitions of what was needed to support children and more generally what was best for families: income transfers rather than in-kind services, full-time homemaker mothers rather than dual-earner parents, and so forth. Family wage practices also shaped the assumptions that could be applied to national welfare states. Thus, measures developed for pronatalist reasons in France over time could be reframed as mother-friendly measures, or at least as largely neutral with regard to a mother's work status, or even her civil status. On the contrary, in the United Kingdom the emphasis on protecting the role and respectability of the male breadwinner for a long time delayed support for working mothers and even reduced social protection for working women, who were seen as dependent wives. At the same time, it legitimized single mothers' dependence on social assistance well beyond their children's early years. The focus in Sweden on in-kind redistribution and on choice, together with such labor market developments as the expansion of the tertiary sector, particularly public administration (owing also to the expansion of social services), allowed the growing number of working mothers and single mothers to be more easily accommodated. It is important to note, however, that such accommodation by no means included fully equal status for women in the labor force and for men in caring responsibilities.

In Italy, as in other Mediterranean countries, the focus on extended kin solidarity, mixed with a male breadwinner model, made for ambivalent family policies.[10] Core workers, rather than working fathers as such, were highly protected. Social services remained largely undeveloped, while a system of fragmentary redistributive measures granted some kind of minimum income to various categories, in the expectation that both income and care would be pooled and shared across not only households but kin networks.

Without totally sharing a path-dependent perspective either on welfare state development or on family arrangements, we cannot ignore the institutional weight and cultural expectations embedded in these different ways of conceptualizing and packaging family wages and family obligations. Those expectations resonate in present-day attempts to grapple with demographic, economic, and social changes, particularly those that touch on the gender and intergenerational arrangements that sustained the social balances and contracts of the postwar years.

## The Changing Basis of Family Arrangements in the Postwar Era

Existing institutional arrangements are called into question by the aging of the population, with its accompanying increase in the demand for care, by women's increasing participation in the labor market and declining fertility (two phenomena that shrink the theoretically available pool of caregivers), and by the increasing instability of marriage, with its risk of weakening ties between fathers and children. All these phenomena, in fact, together with a decline in male full-time employment and in the industrial share of occupations, have undermined the basis of the male breadwinner model across Europe. New forms of access to social rights and ways of providing care are being called for.

### Increasing Women's Labor Force Participation

Women's lives have changed quite dramatically in the industrialized countries since the postwar years, especially over the past one or two generations. In all OECD countries, women's activity rate (labor force participation rate) has increased substantially since the late 1970s, and the women's share of employment grew at a faster rate than that for men.[11] At the same time, women born most recently tend to remain in the labor force throughout their adult life, even when they have children. In the 1990s, half of all mothers with children under age ten in Europe were employed outside the home.[12] Table 9.1 synthesizes the degree of change from the 1960s.

Important intercountry differences remain in activity rate, in the relevance of the informal sector, in the share of part-time work, and in the gender gap in earnings. Nonetheless, since the late 1980s, mothers with young children in most developed countries have on the whole increased their labor force participation.[13] The number of families in which both parents hold a regular part-time or full-time job has been steadily growing. This phenomenon, which reverses a trend visible in the 1950s and 1960s when young mothers were the most numerous group of women outside the labor force, has a number of causes. First, young women are on average better educated than older ones. Having grown up in the expectation of gender equality, they aspire to better, more attractive jobs. Second, the social experience of growing male unemployment and thus the increasing fragility of the male breadwinner model has made the dual-worker family a normal and self-protecting strategy. Finally, the growing rates of divorce encourage young mothers to enter and remain in the labor force. Holding a job, from this point of view, is insurance for a woman and her children against the uncertainty of marriage.

Thus, two of the main preconditions for social legislation based on the male breadwinner model have been substantially weakened: the reciprocal insulation of paid work and family life and the availability of free (female) care within the family and kin. This occurs first and foremost in those very social classes that in the first half of the twentieth century had most fully developed the family model of the male

**Table 9.1   Nondependent Populations of Eighteen Countries in Paid Employment, 1960 and 1995**

| Countries | 1960 | | | 1995 | | |
|---|---|---|---|---|---|---|
| | All | Male | Female | All | Male | Female |
| Austria | 73% | 92% | 57% | 65% | 78% | 52% |
| Belgium | 52 | 79 | 27 | 55 | 65 | 46 |
| Switzerland | 63 | 90 | 37 | 68 | 78 | 58 |
| Germany[a] | 65 | 89 | 44 | 60 | 71 | 47 |
| Denmark | 66 | 95 | 40 | 70 | 81 | 60 |
| Spain | 48 | 92 | 18 | 42 | 61 | 24 |
| France | 58 | 80 | 37 | 56 | 62 | 50 |
| Greece | 59 | 84 | 36 | 48 | 69 | 34 |
| Italy | 53 | 80 | 27 | 48 | 65 | 33 |
| Ireland | 59 | 85 | 32 | 53 | 64 | 42 |
| Japan | 70 | 90 | 52 | 71 | 84 | 58 |
| Norway | 55 | 86 | 25 | 73 | 79 | 66 |
| Netherlands | 55 | 87 | 23 | 62 | 74 | 50 |
| Portugal | 53 | 91 | 17 | 56 | 63 | 50 |
| Sweden | 60 | 85 | 35 | 65 | 67 | 63 |
| Finland | 67 | 86 | 50 | 60 | 65 | 56 |
| United Kingdom | 61 | 87 | 38 | 61 | 69 | 53 |
| United States | 59 | 83 | 36 | 72 | 80 | 64 |

*Source*: Adapted from Colin Crouch, *Social Change in Western Europe* (New York: Oxford University Press, 1999), 58.
[a]The former West Germany.

breadwinner and full-time homemaker: the middle classes. Labor force participation in fact is now higher among well-educated women. At the same time, women's labor force participation may reproduce and even strengthen social inequalities, insofar as a working couple's social homogamy may redouble such inequalities in access to labor market and social resources.

*Marriage Instability and the Weakening of Father-Child Ties*

Although separation and divorce affect only a minority of all children even in countries with high divorce rates,[14] marriage instability has led to a growing proportion of children who for a period live with only one parent and of women who are solely responsible for their care and maintenance. As may be expected, there are substantial national variations. Children in Great Britain, Denmark, and Sweden are much more likely to be affected than children in France and Germany, and especially in Italy, Portugal, and Spain.[15] Nonetheless, the trends are very similar everywhere in the industrialized world, including Central and Eastern Europe. Moreover, since the average duration of marriages that end in divorce has been declining, the age of the children involved tends to be lower now as well, although the chance of children being involved in a marriage breakup has diminished, since a larger share of marriages ending in divorce are childless.[16]

If separation and divorce are the main factors in the increase in the proportion of one-parent families in recent years, the growth of the proportion of children born outside marriage is another. With the exception of the Mediterranean countries, the number of children born to unmarried mothers has increased substantially in recent decades. For example, in the United Kingdom, one-third of all births are to unmarried mothers; in Ireland the figure is one in six. The proportion is also high in Scandinavia, although in those countries a substantial quota of these children are born to cohabitant parents.[17]

The burden of raising the children has settled on women. Over 90 percent of non-widow, one-parent families are headed by a mother. One-parent families are therefore in effect single-mother families.[18] In all countries, one-parent, and particularly single-mother, families tend to be poorer than two-parent families, even though the proportion of single mothers who hold a job is higher than the proportion of married women with a job in dual-parent households.[19]

The higher risk of poverty incurred by single-mother families rests largely on the gender division of labor and responsibilities within marriage as well as in the labor market. Single mothers have to face the dual responsibility of being the main breadwinner and the main caregiver in a labor market in which breadwinners are usually perceived as free from caring responsibilities. Single mothers also deal with social organizations that take for granted the flexibility and availability of a mother's time (in school schedules, in the availability of child care services, in the hours that shops, public offices, and so forth are open for business). For these reasons, one-parent families have a lower risk of falling into poverty in countries where the employment of mothers is both more widespread and accommodated by social services, such as the Scandinavian countries and France.

Marriage instability and the growth of single-mother families undermine the male breadwinner model behind social policies on two grounds: they add breadwinning to the caring responsibilities of mothers, while increasingly divesting fathers of any breadwinning responsibilities at all. Fathers who do not live with the mother of their children often contribute only a fraction of the cost of children, irrespective of their own income level, and often do not even acknowl-

edge their financial obligations toward their children after their relationship with the mother has ended.[20]

*Reduced Fertility*

In most developed countries, the fertility rate is well below the substitution level; in some of the countries where it is lowest—Italy,
Spain, Portugal, Japan—it continues to decrease; in other countries
that were the first to fall below the substitution level in recent
years—France and Sweden in particular—a reversal is apparent. Up to
the 1970s, fertility rates and the fertility decline were strictly and
inversely associated with both the rate of labor force participation by
women and their level of education. In the last twenty years, the association has been almost reversed, at least in intercountry comparisons: the fertility rate is now lowest in the countries where women's
labor force participation is lowest, and countries with a high level of
women's labor force participation—such as Sweden—have the highest fertility.[21] This reversal suggests that where society accommodates
working mothers, at the cultural as well as the organizational level,
and at the same time acknowledges the economic and time costs of
raising children,[22] women experience fewer constraints in reconciling
their caring and working responsibilities. On the contrary, where
such accommodation is lacking and raising children is still perceived
as solely the private responsibility of parents, and particularly
mothers, women are more likely to deal with the conflicting demands
on their time and income by reducing the number of children they
bear. Thus, somewhat paradoxically, the persistence of a breadwinner
model—particularly when, as in the Mediterranean countries, it is
extended to include wider kinship ties and obligations—has a negative impact on fertility and thus undermines its own demographic
basis. With fewer children being born, the pool of future workers
making social security contributions to the pension system is reduced, as is the number of future caregivers for the frail elderly. At
the same time, as studies have indicated, the persistence of the male
breadwinner model also renders more rigid the core (male) labor force,
on whom the welfare of entire households and sometime other kin
depends, leaving less room both for a rebalancing of the welfare state
in favor of the younger generations and for the introduction of greater
flexibility into the labor market.[23]

Notwithstanding these differences, reduced fertility and greater life
expectancies have changed not only the age balance within the population of all countries but also the experience of childhood and grow-

ing up, on the one hand, and the form of kin relationships and inter-generational ties, on the other. There are more grandparents than grandchildren in all of these countries. And children—particularly in countries where fertility is lowest—are more likely to have two or three generations of adults in their kin network and fewer siblings and cousins.

This phenomenon is usually debated and analyzed from the point of view of either its consequences for intergenerational solidarity and redistribution (its impact, for instance, on the pension system or on health services and expenses) or the desirability of policies aimed at supporting or encouraging fertility so as to avoid too great an inter-generational imbalance. It is rarely discussed in terms of children's experience of growing up. Because children now are likely to have very few peers in their household and kin network, there may be a new role for child care services and schools in general as the primary arenas for developing peer relationships and horizontal socialization.

## The Aging of the Population

In addition to the imbalance in the intergenerational accounts, and particularly in the financing of the pension system, another conse-quence of lower fertility is that the elderly are less likely to have daughters and daughters-in-law in the kin network who are available to take care of them, not only because more women are in the labor force, but because there are fewer women to begin with. This imbal-ance is all the greater since the number of the elderly is increasing not only in relative but in absolute terms, owing to the lengthening of life. A longer average life span has a great impact on intrafamily and kin circumstances and expectations as well as on social expecta-tions concerning family obligations, particularly with regard to gen-der and intergenerational expectations.

Dependency is typically the condition of only a fraction of the pe-riod we call old age, and it affects only a small proportion of the el-derly at any one time. When dependency develops, however, it is very costly not only in terms of health care and services but in terms of demands on relationships. Notwithstanding great inter- and intra-country differences, in all countries there is an expectation that chil-dren have an obligation to care for their needy elderly parents, even if they are not on good terms,[24] and even if this obligation is enforced legally only in a few countries. The combination of longer life spans, reduced fertility, and increased labor force participation by women throughout their adult life is adding to the imbalance between the demand for care and the availability of care within the kin network.

Recent data on Italy point to the dramatic changes underlying this phenomenon: while the generation of women who were in their forties in 1980 might have expected to have one or more elderly persons in their kin network for about twelve years, women in their forties in 2000 could expect to have the same experience for eighteen years. Moreover, the kin network of the older cohort included on average one grandmother and ten grandchildren; the younger cohort includes three grandparents and six grandchildren.[25] As a matter of fact, the same data indicate that the former cohort of women, while in their forties, were mostly in a caregiving position with regard to the elderly in their kin network, but that members of the latter cohort, given their higher activity rate and the better health of the elderly, more frequently receive care. But we may wonder what will happen when today's many healthy caregiving elders need care themselves and find themselves having to rely on a reduced pool of daughters and daughters-in-law, who will be involved in the labor market.

This imbalance may be further deepened by marital instability, insofar as the end of a marriage may sever or loosen the intergenerational ties that were supported during the marriage by the relationships between women across kin: that is, between daughters-in-law and parents-in-law.

## Diversities and Tensions in the Definition of Family Dependencies in the 1990s

National differences in the ways these phenomena present themselves, as well as in the ways policies address them, are accounted for not only by differences in national labor markets and economies but by differences in the prevailing religious, political, and family cultures. Particularly relevant, from this point of view, are the models of gender relationships and of intergenerational solidarity incorporated into social arrangements and national welfare regimes. Thus, even if broad changes in family arrangements are to a large degree common to all Western developed countries, and particularly to those of Western Europe, they have somewhat different starting points and draw on different institutional and cultural resources. They also reflect different conceptions of the responsibilities of the state (including local government), the community, households, and kin: using the European Union jargon, we might say that they reflect different conceptions of the principle of subsidiarity.[26]

In fact, in the case of state-family relations, subsidiarity might mean that the state does not intervene except in the extreme cases in which families are not able to solve problems on their own—that is, when they are for some reason inadequate or unfit. Subsidiarity might also mean that the state has an obligation to support families in fulfilling their "normal" obligations. Considered in this light, subsidiarity can motivate different policies: those that enable women to stay home with their children, those that enable women to reconcile family and work responsibilities, or those that enable parents to share child care responsibilities. Underlying these policies are ideas about the "normal family" and the "normal parent" that in turn may be more or less class biased.

Two distinct phenomena have further complicated the situation in recent years. The first is the increasing use of market regulations within public social services, particularly for the elderly, together with a growing tendency to contract out these services to nonstate bodies.[27] The second is the widespread introduction of some payment for care.[28] Both these phenomena affect the delivery of all social services, but they are particularly visible in services and activities for the frail elderly and the handicapped.

There are many reasons behind the increasing recourse to delegating social and caring services to nonstate bodies: from widening the range of choice available to users to cutting public expenditure. Reasons and contexts differ among countries, as do outcomes. In some countries in particular, as Mary Daly and Jane Lewis observe, there has been a substantial change in the way services are provided, but the nature of the reforms has been characterized more by continuity than by change; in other countries, by contrast, such changes have dramatically affected the quality and sometimes even the quantity of the care provided.[29] Moreover, contracting out may have quite different meanings, as well as outcomes, depending on the strength of the third sector in a given country (as well as within it), on its internal composition, and on its relative importance vis-à-vis both the market and the state in providing services. It is well known that the different European countries have quite distinct traditions with regard not only to the relative importance of markets but also to the relative importance of the third sector (an item not adequately accounted for in most welfare state typologies, including Esping-Andersen's). These distinctive traditions, in turn, give a distinctive content to the concept and practice of subsidiarity in each country. In the Nordic countries, little space is given to either the market or the third sector; in the Netherlands, Belgium, and Germany, the third sector has been historically institutionalized as a partner of the welfare state. France has a much less institutionalized third sector than Italy, where the growing trend toward explicitly creating partnerships with the (often confessional) third sector in social services provision is based on its long history of having been an implicit, and even subsidized, partner. In the United Kingdom, the third sector—more specifically, the voluntary organizations—has a long-established history, although its partnership with the British welfare state is institutionally much weaker than in the Netherlands, and it is less linked to ethnic or religious institutions than in Germany or Italy.[30]

In addition, the reasons behind the introduction of payments for care vary substantially. The intention may be to substitute for more expensive services, as with the payments made to family caregivers in the United Kingdom and in certain Italian regions. In other cases, these payments may be designed to enlarge the options available to care recipients, as with the benefits paid to the invalid elderly in Germany, Austria, and France so that they can pay for care. The payments may also be designed to grant more rights to both caregivers and care recipients while promoting more family involvement. This is the case with the Swedish and Norwegian schemes, in which family caregivers for the elderly are not only paid but also receive contributions toward a pension and sick leave; this recruitment of family members fosters a generally good service provision. Moreover, the recent choice offered in the Scandinavian countries between obtaining a place in a child care service or receiving an allowance to be used in alternative ways (either to pay for a stay-at-home parent or to pay for a private caregiver) may also be perceived as an enlargement of available choices. Nonetheless, in all these schemes, although the boundaries between the family, the state, the market, and the third sector may be affected quite differently depending on the overall package to which they contribute, it is certainly clear that it is mostly women who are called upon, and more or less paid, to be caregivers. Therefore, this form of support might be seen to re-create or reproduce the traditional gender structure of family caring obligations precisely at a moment when there are fewer daughters available for this kind of work.

I address these issues with regard to two areas that have been particularly crucial for both family and kin arrangements and welfare state arrangements: the obligation to provide and care for children and the obligation to care for the elderly. As we shall see, mainstream as well as gender-oriented welfare state typologies are further complicated by the fact that the two sets of arrangements do not overlap.

## Defining Obligations to Provide for Children

In all countries, parents are defined as the primary responsible actors on behalf of their children. Nonetheless, the specific nature of these obligations varies quite widely, not only at the level of shared values but as described in legislation. There is also a great variation in the degree to which the state may enforce, or stand as surrogate for, parents' obligations.

Values and opinions may differ on how to interpret the presence or absence of a public responsibility toward children. Some believe that public child care services interfere with family autonomy and responsibility. Others interpret the absence of such services as an indicator of social irresponsibility toward children and their parents and neglect of the individual rights of children. These different evaluations, in turn, reflect different ideas and priorities about family and parental responsibilities. They also reflect different conceptions of the autonomous rights of children, as well as of the subsidiarity principle.[31]

Two issues are involved here: who should care for the children, and who should bear the costs of raising them.[32] Both issues are twofold. Each addresses the responsibilities within a household, primarily between the parents, but also the division of responsibilities between families and the community and between families and the state.

In all countries, parents' duties of guardianship and care generally cease when their children become eighteen or nineteen years old—the age when children become "adults"—and in some cases even before. In the Scandinavian countries and the United Kingdom, the end of these duties also involves the end of any legally enforced financial obligation, but in other countries the parents' legal financial obligations continue until the child is "self-supporting." In some countries, that obligation may continue indefinitely. In Germany, Italy, Spain, Austria, Belgium, and Luxembourg, for instance, children unable to support themselves, even if able-bodied, can claim support from their parents throughout their life if they are in need.[33] On the contrary, in Sweden, Denmark, and Finland, students are entitled to financial support from the state in their own right, and without any account taken of parental income, from age eighteen (or twenty)—just after their parents lose entitlement to a child allowance.

Whatever their duration, parents' financial obligations are not reinforced by the state equally in all countries. In the majority of EU countries, the state shoulders a portion of child support for all children up to a certain age, through child allowances or child benefit schemes. In others, such as Italy, Greece, Spain, and Portugal, only selected economically deprived groups receive support.[34]

Another indicator of the degree to which the state assumes direct financial responsibility for raising children is the regulation of child support when one parent, particularly the father, is absent. It is a crucial issue, given the increasing fragility of marriage. In recent years, policies have developed along two lines that are sometimes separate and sometimes integrated: the strengthening and enforcing of fathers' responsibilities, and the partial adoption by the state of fathers' responsibilities. Legislation, as well as juridical and social practice in many countries, tends not only to encourage but to enforce fathers' responsibilities toward their children irrespective of their relationship with the mothers. Thus, in the case of separation and divorce, joint custody is preferred or even enforced (as in France).[35] In the United Kingdom, concern about the plight of unwed mothers led to legislation that strongly enforces—albeit with no great success—fathers' obligation to support financially all their children, irrespective of their relationship with the mother.[36] The second approach does not on principle deny parents' (fathers') responsibility, but it tries to distinguish it from the personal relationship between the parents and focuses on the need for support rather than on the ideal supporter. In France and the Scandinavian countries, the state offers support in case a father does not or cannot provide support. The collection of support from a noncohabiting parent is always—and particularly in conflictual cases—the state's responsibility.

Despite these programs of state support for children, their main source of support is their parents' wages. The mid-century social contract granted a male breadwinner a wage that could also pay for a full-time mother. In the absence of a father, many countries provided a social assistance benefit to the mother while at the same time exempting her from the requirement to be available for work. It is interesting that two of the countries that had the most generous exemption until the late 1980s—the United Kingdom and the Netherlands— have quite radically changed their outlook in the 1990s. They now treat lone mothers mainly as breadwinners, expecting them to be available for work as soon as possible and to some degree ignoring their caring responsibilities and needs.[37]

One way to support the cost of children is to support the conciliation between family and paid work responsibilities for both sexes, but particularly for mothers. Maternity and parental leaves are the traditional means toward this end. Another is the provision of child care services.

If we take into account the kind and duration of maternity and parental leaves, the kind and degree of provision of child care services, and so forth,[38] we can group the countries into four categories that differ in part from the most popular typologies in welfare state analyses:

1. The Scandinavian countries, France, and Belgium have systems in which the state and local governments actively support mothers in combining paid work and family responsibilities through a flexible and generous (in terms of income replacement) leave policy and readily available child care services. Parental leave is also a possibility in all of these countries. In addition, in Sweden a portion of the leave must be taken only by fathers or it goes unused. In these countries, women's participation in the workforce is high, even among mothers. Compared with other countries, the incidence of part-time work in Sweden is high not only among women but also among men.

2. Germany, Austria, the Netherlands, and Luxembourg support a strong division of labor between fathers and mothers and at the same time encourage a "sequential" investment by women in family and paid work. Maternity leaves are comparatively long, and income replacement is generous, but child care services, particularly for children under age three, are scarce, and school hours are not convenient for families in which both parents are in a paid job. As a consequence, women's activity rate in these countries is lower than it is in the first group of countries, although increasing. Mothers of very young children tend to remain at home, then to work part-time when their children are older.

3. The United Kingdom is a category of its own, since conciliating family and paid work responsibilities is mostly considered a private affair. Maternity leaves and child care services are not readily available. Many working women do not work sufficient hours to be covered by social security guarantees and entitled to paid maternity leave, which in any case is less generous in the United Kingdom than in most EU countries. Women's activity rate is quite high, but it follows a sequential or alternating pattern:[39] 75 percent of women are in the labor market, but only 50 percent of mothers.

4. The southern European countries share a cultural emphasis on the gender division of labor within the family, a belief in the crucial role of mothers' presence and care in the early childhood years, and a high reliance on kin to support individual and household needs, including child care needs. Women's activity rate in these countries is the lowest in Europe. Women who do work do so mostly full-time, since part-time jobs covered by social security are scarce. Also, single mothers tend to be in the labor market to a higher degree than married mothers. A large number of women work in the informal labor market.[40]

These differences point to national variations in assumptions not only about gender and parental roles but also about the state's responsibilities toward regulating, or supporting, specific patterns of gender relations, parental obligations, and children's individual rights.

Even these patterns are shifting. The Scandinavian countries have well-established child care services but are now considering the provision of some kind of home care allowance or extended parental leave as an alternative to child care in centers. The thinking is that options for parents will be expanded and all children will be granted the same amount of resources, as is not the case when services are offered only to children of working parents. Since it is mostly women who take advantage of this opportunity, particularly within the least-skilled groups, concern has developed about the gender implications of such a measure. As often happens with proposed measures supporting mothers, this one can be read either as a measure that enables women to deal more flexibly with their work and family obligations or, on the contrary, as a measure that encourages women to remain home.[41]

Of course, a major means by which the state and the public share the burden of the cost of children is formal education. Education, however, is rarely included in welfare analyses and typologies. From the limited perspective of this chapter, I mention only two somewhat contradictory phenomena. First, research on social mobility indicates that the redistribution of chances and social capital through the school system does not offset the role of social origins, and particularly of the family, in determining mobility chances in terms of social class.[42] At the same time, the education gap between the sexes has been closing quite substantially, changing the balance of resources between daughters and sons. As more better-educated young women enter and stay in the labor force, it is not unforeseeable that the overall pattern of class reproduction through families will change as well.[43]

## Defining Obligations to Care for the Disabled and the Frail Elderly

The persistently gendered nature of caring is evident also in the provision of care for the handicapped and the frail elderly. Research has indicated that most kin-caregivers are daughters, daughters-in-law, granddaughters, nieces, and particularly wives.[44] Given the age differential between spouses, particularly in the older cohorts, and the longer life expectancy of women, family caregiving for a frail elderly person is usually performed by an elderly wife. Another implication is that "family care" through a spouse is more available to frail elderly men than to frail elderly women. In Italy, for instance, 58.6 percent of men over the age of eighty live with a spouse and 20.8 percent live alone, compared with 12 percent of women of this age who live with a spouse and 50.4 percent who live alone.[45] Policies that implicitly or explicitly expect families to be available for care often seem to ignore the responsibility and burden they are allocating to elderly women in the first place.

When a spouse is not available, caring is performed most often by other female kin. For a long time, the most common family structure in all European nations has been the nuclear family. Elderly couples and single persons often live by themselves. Therefore, if and when they become frail, caring by kin involves quite a number of changes, negotiations, and arrangements that also seem underestimated by policies that stress mainly family obligations. There are fewer adult daughters and daughters-in-law, a higher percentage of them are in the labor force, and their time is divided between their preexisting family and work obligations. In addition, they often live in a different household (and often in a different city) from that of the kin needing care. Research has indicated that in countries where family obligations are particularly binding and these relations are reinforced by policy, the kin network of the elderly is dense but their overall social network is reduced.[46] In other words, the elderly—and particularly the frail elderly—in these countries may not only count on kin more often but are also more exclusively dependent on them. If they have no kin available, they are left with few resources.

The level of public obligations differs quite substantially among countries and has a considerable impact on both the resources and rights of those needing care and the conditions for and constraints on women as family caregivers. Interestingly, with the exception of the Scandinavian countries, there is no clear overlap between countries that provide generous child care and those that provide generous frail elderly care.[47] For instance, the Netherlands, Norway, Germany, and the United Kingdom, which make little provision for children under three, offer substantial public support for the frail elderly. The reverse is true for Belgium and France. This contrast, again, points to differences in legal as well as cultural definitions of intergenerational obligations within families and kin networks.[48]

Only the Scandinavian countries acknowledge the individual rights of care recipients, irrespective of their family situation. The state is neutral with regard to both gender and family obligations to care for the elderly and support them financially. Other countries, such as Italy, Spain, and Portugal, either provide few services or base them on the unavailability of kin (often specifically the absence of female kin).

In still other instances, services are offered but the family-kin situation is considered in collecting contributions.

## Issues at Stake in the Redefinition of the Gender-Family Contract

The male breadwinner model is under stress in most European countries. It was already under tension in some Scandinavian countries in the 1960s, mainly owing to a long-standing tradition of female independence, a narrower and shorter definition of family obligations, and the earlier deinstitutionalization of marriage.[49] That model has become increasingly fragile in most other European countries as well because of demographic and cultural shifts, changing conditions for gender and generational roles and relationships, and the pluralization of family arrangements. Thus, the balance between the familization and defamilization of needs and rights, as constructed through the male breadwinner model in the postwar social contract, is no longer tenable.

Although the effectiveness of the model has diminished, some of the problems it tried to address are still with us, including: access to social rights by those who are not self-sufficient because of age or health; adequate protection of interpersonal relationships and obligations from market as well as bureaucratic rules and demands; the preservation of intergenerational relationships and solidarity; and the balance between the three dimensions involved in caring relationships—the need and right to be cared for, the need and right to care for, and the need and right not to be crushed by caring obligations. In a complex way, all of these problems hinge on the interdependence in which individual lives are embedded and receive their meanings as well as resources—that is, the balance between the individualization of rights and interests and their embeddedness in relationships. From this prospective, we may reassess the recent debate about defamilization versus refamilization trends in social policy.

Various authors have suggested that a useful indicator in constructing welfare state typologies might be the degree to which economic and social rights are granted to individuals of all ages and family conditions or are contingent on family circumstances.[50] From this perspective, defamilization would indicate "the extent to which they can uphold an acceptable standard of living independently of the (patriarchal) family."[51] Conversely, familization, or refamilization, would indicate both that entitlements are based on family membership and that a number of needs are (re-)allocated to families and kin. Recent country-specific and comparative research indicates that contemporary welfare state reforms seem to point in both directions at the same time. On the one hand, measures have been enacted to strengthen individual rather than family entitlements, as in the many pension reforms that have reduced the coverage of survivors' pensions or in the emerging expectation that mothers will participate in the labor market. On the other hand, the increasing role of means-tested benefits in many countries and the blurring of boundaries between social security and social assistance provisions strengthen the family base of entitlements, especially since means-testing is done on the basis of household income. As Diane Sainsbury argues, this in turn affects married or cohabitant women's entitlements more strongly than those of their partners.[52]

Yet the concepts of both familization and defamilization appear less univocal in meaning than at first glance. As we have seen earlier, family obligations may differ both in intensity and in the range of relationships involved. Thus, while the intensity of parents' obligations toward their children is about the same from the legal point of view in Germany and Italy, it is different for the range of institutionally defined kin obligations. This in turn implies that individuals living in countries where institutional and cultural obligations cover a wider range of relationships may, on the one hand, count on substantial and differentiated informal resources and, on the other hand, find themselves in competition with each other for family resources. Moreover, family-kin networks may suffer from a wider range of more intensely competing demands than in other countries.

Defamilization is even more complicated. First, defamilization may be the extreme consequence of lack of economic and social resources. In other words, it may be the more or less unintended consequence of changes in the economy, in the labor market, or in the rules concerning the rights of immigrants. To a less dramatic degree, this consequence is also apparent in the impact of work schedules on participation in family life. Usually this phenomenon is most visible when wives and mothers enter the labor market. It becomes immediately apparent that they have less (or no) time to "construct" family life, care for children, prepare meals, cater to their husbands, and care for relatives. But the defamilization of men[53] (as well as the familization of women and children) was the main principle on which the "traditional" family was constructed in modern times.

Thus, policies intended to refamilize or defamilize might have quite a different meaning for men and women, for different class and ethnic groups, and for countries in which these processes have a different history and have reached a different point. For instance, while payments for care in the form of substitution of income benefits for social services in the case of small children may de facto encourage the persistence of a strong gender division of labor within the family, particularly within the low-income strata, policies intended to encourage fathers to take a leave to care for their children may be read as an attempt to refamilize men in a more gender-equal framework.[54] And in general, the introduction of family-linked paid leaves of absence for men and women may be interpreted as a way of acknowledging family obligations in a context characterized by strong work attachments and participation. In essence, this approach acknowledges that the social rights of citizens should not be limited to their rights as (paid) workers. Finally, defamilization in the sense of allocating some of the traditional duties and responsibilities to actors other than the family may occur in different ways and directions: through allocation to the public sphere, but also to the third sector or to the market.

These are not neutral moves, but neither are they univocal in their meaning, depending as they do on national and local cultures and circumstances and the resources of specific social groups. It is clear that in order to rebalance family and state, as well as gender and intergenerational obligations, both defamilization and refamilization are needed, depending on actors and places as well as on life dimensions. In any case, these trends are shaping new and more or less contested balances between families, markets, states, and third sectors in the provision of services. At the same time, they constitute the new terrain on which discourses about needs, obligations, interdependence, and independence are being developed within gender and intergenerational relationships.

## Notes

1. Chiara Saraceno, "Family Change, Family Policies, and the Restructuring of Welfare," in *Family, Market, and Community: Equity and Efficiency in Social Policy*, Social Policy Studies 21 (Paris: Organization for Economic Cooperation and Development, 1997); Franz-Xaver Kauffman et al., eds., *Family Life and Family Policies in Europe*, vol. 1: *Structures and Trends of the 1980s* (Oxford: Clarendon, 1997).
2. Colin Crouch, *Social Change in Western Europe* (New York: Oxford University Press, 1999), 34–35.
3. See Gøsta Esping-Andersen, *The Three Worlds of Welfare Capitalism* (Princeton: Princeton University Press, 1990). See also the feminist scholarship: Jane Lewis, ed., *Women and Social Policies in Europe: Work, Family, and the State* (Cheltenham: Edward Elgar, 1993); Jane Lewis, "Gender and Welfare Regimes: Further Thoughts," *Social Politics* 4(Summer 1997): 160–77; Mary Langan and Ilona Ostner, "Gender and Welfare: Towards a Comparative Framework," in *Towards a European*

*Welfare State?* edited by Graham Room (Bristol: SAUS, 1991), 127–50; Diane Sainsbury, ed., *Gendering Welfare States* (London: Sage, 1994); Diane Sainsbury, *Gender, Equity, and Welfare States* (Cambridge: Cambridge University Press, 1996); Barbara Hobson, "No Exit No Voice: Women's Economic Dependency and the Welfare State," *Acta Sociologica* 33(1990): 235–50; Ann Orloff, "Gender and the Social Rights of Citizenship: State Policies and Gender Relations in Comparative Research," *American Sociological Review* 58(June 1993): 303–28; Julia S. O'Connor, Ann S. Orloff, and Sheila Shaver, *States, Markets, and Families* (Cambridge: Cambridge University Press, 1999); Arnlaug Leira, *Welfare States and Working Mothers: The Scandinavian Experience* (Cambridge: Cambridge University Press, 1992); Goran Therborn, "The Politics of Childhood: The Rights of Childhood in Modern Times," in *Families of Nations: Patterns of Public Policy in Western Democracies*, edited by Francis G. Castles (Aldershot: Avebury, 1993); Anne H. Gauthier, *The State and the Family: A Comparative Analysis of Family Policies in Industrial Countries* (Oxford: Clarendon, 1996).

4. Thus, in England the first Children's Act was approved in 1840, while unemployment, invalidity, and old-age insurance were not introduced until 1911. In France, women with children were covered by protective legislation later than their British counterparts, in 1892, but French old-age insurance was not passed until much later still, in 1910, and the social insurance law was authored only in 1930. In Italy, women were assimilated to children from the point of view of protective legislation in 1902; this law came after the introduction of work accident insurance (1898) but predated unemployment and old age insurance (1919).

5. In addition, the policies that were addressed to (or advocated for) women as mothers implied this crucial exclusion of women from the core labor market, thus casting a doubt on all "maternalist" interpretations of welfare state development. The thesis of a maternalist origin of the welfare state has been particularly developed in and with reference to the United States, starting with the seminal work by Theda Skocpol, *Protecting Soldiers and Mothers: The Political Origins of Social Policy in the United States* (Cambridge, Mass.: Harvard University Press, 1992), which has spurred both research and a rich critical debate. See, for instance, Seth Koven and Sonya Michel, eds., *Mothers of a New World: Maternalist Politics and the Origins of Welfare States* (New York: Routledge, 1993); and the conference panel in *Studies in American Political Development* 8(Spring 1994): 111–49.

6. Hans Peter Blossfeld and Catherine Hakim, eds., *Between Equalization and Marginalization: Women Working Part-time in Europe and the United States of America* (Oxford: Clarendon, 1997); Crouch, *Social Change in Western Europe.*

7. Feminist analysts have introduced the concept of the "male breadwinner" as an explicit critique of the interpretive shortcomings of the prevailing welfare state analyses and typologies, particularly Esping Andersen's (*Three Worlds of Welfare Capitalism*). See Jane Lewis, "Gender and the Development of Welfare Regimes," *Journal of European Social Policy* 2(Fall 1992): 159–73; Lewis, "Gender and Welfare Regimes: Further Thoughts"; Sainsbury, *Gendering Welfare States.*

8. For instance, old-age pensions, including survivors' ones, were extended

to the self-employed, as were paid maternity leave and health insurance covering dependent family members. However, we should note that in the countries with a high proportion of self-employed in the overall population—such as the Mediterranean European countries—the welfare state offers fewer benefits, and old-age pensions make up a higher percentage of overall social expenditure.

9. See also Susan Pedersen, *Family, Dependence, and the Origins of the Welfare State: Britain and France, 1914–1945* (Cambridge: Cambridge University Press, 1993).

10. Chiara Saraceno, "The Ambivalent Familism of the Italian Welfare State," *Social Politics* 1(Spring 1994): 32–59; Chiara Saraceno, *Mutamenti della famiglia e politiche sociali in Italia* (*Family Changes and Social Policies in Italy*) (Bologna: Il Mulino, 1998); Manuela Naldini, "Evolution of Social Policy and the Institutional Definition of Family Models: The Italian and Spanish Cases in Historical and Comparative Perspective" (Ph.D. diss., European University, Florence, 1999; London: Frank Cass, in press).

11. Commission of the European Communities, *Employment in Europe* (Luxembourg: Office for Official Publications of the CEC, 1993); Organization for Economic Cooperation and Development, *Employment Outlook* (Paris: OECD, 1995).

12. Jane Millar and Andrea Warman, *Defining Family Obligations in Europe: The Family, the State, and Social Policy* (London: Family Policy Studies Centre, 1996); Jonathan Bradshaw et al., *The Employment of Lone Parents: A Comparison of Policy in Twenty Countries* (London: Family Policy Studies Centre, 1996). In the mid-1990s, even in Italy—which, like Spain, is usually identified as a country with a persistent housewife model—the majority of mothers of preschool-age children were in the labor force.

13. Ruth Jallinoia, "Women Between Family and Employment," in *Changing Patterns of European Family Life: A Comparative Analysis of Fourteen European Countries*, edited by Katja Boh et al. (London: Routledge, 1989), 95–122. For a specific analysis of trends in the southern European countries, see María J. González, Teresa Jurado, and Manuela Naldini, eds., *Gender Inequalities in Southern Europe* (London: Frank Cass, 2000).

14. Greg J. Duncan and William Rodgers, "Lone-Parent Families and Their Economic Problems: Transitory or Persistent?" in *Lone Parents: The Economic Challenge* (Paris: Organization for Economic Cooperation and Development, 1990), 43–68; Kathleen Kiernan and Malcolm Wicks, *Family Change and Future Policy* (London: Family Policy Studies Centre, 1990).

15. By the mid-1980s, one-parent families were 17 percent of all families with children in Sweden, 14 percent in Denmark and the United Kingdom, approximately 13 percent in France and Germany, between 10 and 12 percent in Belgium, Luxembourg, and the Netherlands, between 5 and 10 percent in Ireland, Italy, Portugal, and Spain, and less than 5 percent in Greece. See Kiernan and Wicks, *Family Change and Future Policy*; see also Yin-Lin Irene Wong, Irwin Garfinkel, and Sara McLanahan, "Single-Mother Families in Eight Countries: Economic Status and Social Policy," Working Paper Series 76 (Luxembourg: Lux-

227

embourg Income Study, 1992); Sheila B. Kamerman and Alfred J. Kahn, "Single-Parent, Female-headed Families with Children in Western Europe: Social Change and Response," *International Social Security Review* 42(1989): 3–34; François Hopflinger, "Haushalts- und Familiensstrukturen in intereuropäischen Vergleich" (*Households and Family Structures in Inter-European Comparison*), in *Die Westeuropäischen Gesellschaften in Vergleich*, edited by Stefen Hradil and Stefen Immerfall (Opladen: Leske und Budrich, 1997), 97–138. This data must be read with caution, since different countries use different criteria both to define "a child's presence" in the family (on the basis of age) and to single out one-parent households. See, for instance, Linda Hantrais and Marie-Thérèse Letablier, *Familles, travail, et politiques familiales en Europe* (*Families, Employment, and Family Policies in Europe*) (Paris: Cahiers du Centre d'Études de l'Emploi, Presses Universitaires de France, 1996).

16. William Goode, *World Changes in Divorce Patterns* (New Haven: Yale University Press, 1993).

17. Louis Roussel, *La famille incertaine* (*The Uncertain Family*) (Paris: Éditions Odile Jacob, 1989).

18. See also Kauffman et al., *Structures and Trends in the 1980s*.

19. Widows and their children are usually better protected through social security than separated and divorced mothers, and the latter can usually count on their husband's support with regard to their children more than unmarried single mothers. See Irwin Garfinkel and Sara McLanahan, *Single Mothers and Their Children: A New American Dilemma* (Washington, D.C.: Urban Institute Press, 1986); Richard V. Burkhauser and Greg J. Duncan, "Economic Risks of Gender Roles: Income Loss and Life Events over the Life Course," *Social Science Quarterly* 70(March 1989): 3–23; Mavis MacLean, "Lone-Parent Families: Family Law and Income Transfers," in OECD, *Lone Parents*, 91–100; Judith A. Seltzer, "Legal Custody Arrangements and Children's Economic Welfare," *American Journal of Sociology* 96(January 1991): 895–929; Demie Kurz, *For Richer, for Poorer: Mothers Confront Divorce* (New York: Routledge, 1995); Jørgen E. Larsen, "Lone Mothers: How Do They Work and Care in Different Welfare State Regimes?" in *Gender, Welfare State, and the Market*, edited by Thomas P. Boje and Arnlaug Leira (London: Routledge, 2000), 206–25.

20. Paul Festy, "Après la séparation: Diversité et stabilité des comportments" (*After Separation, Diversity, and Stability in Behaviors*), *Population* 3(May–June 1988): 517–36; OECD, *Lone Parents*; An Magritt Jensen, "Gender Gaps in Relationships with Children: Closing or Widening?" in *Gender and Family Change in Industrialized Societies*, edited by Karen O. Mason and An-Magritt Jensen (Oxford: Clarendon, 1995); William Marsiglio, ed., *Fatherhood: Contemporary Theory, Research, and Social Policy* (Thousand Oaks: Sage Publications, 1995); Terry Arendell, *Fathers and Divorce* (Thousand Oaks: Sage Publications, 1995); Claude Martin, *L'après divorce: Lien familial et vulnérabilité* (*After the Divorce: Family Ties and Vulnerability*) (Rennes: Presses Universitaries Rennes, 1997); Marzio Barbagli and Chiara Saraceno, *Separarsi in Italia* (*Marital Instability in Italy*) (Bologna: il Mulino, 1998).

21. Eurostat, *Demographic Statistics* (Luxembourg: European Statistical Of-

fice, 1999); Gøsta Esping-Andersen, "Welfare States Without Work: The Impasse of Labor Shedding and Familialism in Continental European Social Policy," in *Welfare States in Transition: National Adaptations in Global Economics*, edited by Gøsta Esping-Andersen (London: Sage Publications, 1996), 66–87.

22. This has been done by societies that provide an adequate amount and quality of child care services, as well as generous maternity and parental leaves and child benefits. It should be added, moreover, that in the Scandinavian countries parents are financially responsible for their children only until they reach majority.

23. See, for example, Organization for Economic Cooperation and Development, *Employment Outlook* (Paris: OECD, 1998).

24. See François Leseman and Claude Martin, eds., *Les personnes âgées: Dépendence, soins, et solidarités familiales: Comparisons internationales* (*The Elderly: Dependence, Care, and Family Solidarity*) (Paris: Les Études de la Documentation française, 1993).

25. Istituto Nazionale Di Statistica (ISTAT), *Annual Report 1999* (Rome: ISTAT, 2000), 457–58.

26. Subsidiarity, a well-known concept in Catholic social doctrine, is an entrenched feature of some European welfare states—such as those of the Netherlands and Belgium, and of Austria and Germany in part—where deeply rooted religious and ethnic divisions have given rise to distinct social institutions that have become acknowledged partners in, or parts of, the national welfare state. The European Union jargon assumes that no higher body should perform what a lower body performs better.

27. Julian Le Grand and William Bartlett, *Quasi-Markets and Social Policy* (London: Macmillan, 1993); Organization for Economic Cooperation and Development, *Caring for Frail Elderly People*, Social Policy Studies 14 (Paris: OECD, 1994); Jane Lewis, ed., *Gender, Social Care, and Welfare State Restructuring in Europe* (London: Ashgate, 1998).

28. Adalbert Evers, M. Pijl, and Claire Ungerson, eds., *Payments for Care: A Comparative Overview* (Aldershot: Avebury, 1993); Claire Ungerson, "Social Politics and the Commodification of Care," *Social Politics* 4(Fall 1997): 362–82; Lewis, *Gender, Social Care, and Welfare State Restructuring in Europe*.

29. Mary Daly and Jane Lewis, "Introduction: Conceptualizing Social Care in the Context of Welfare State Restructuring," in Lewis, *Gender, Social Care, and Welfare State Restructuring in Europe*, 1–24.

30. See, for example, Ralph M. Kramer, "The Roles of Voluntary Social Service Organizations in Four European States: Policy Trends in England, the Netherlands, Italy, and Norway," in *Government and Voluntary Organizations*, edited by Stein Kuhnle and Per Selle (Brookfield, Vt.: Avebury, 1992), 34–52.

31. Therborn, "The Politics of Childhood."

32. Jane Jenson, "Who Cares?: Gender and Welfare Regimes," *Social Politics* 4(Spring 1997): 182–87.

33. In Italy, legally enforced financial obligations extend to adult children, parents, grandchildren, parents-in-law, siblings (including adult siblings), nephews, and nieces.

34. For an evaluation of the nation-specific packages available to families

with children in the OECD countries, see Jonathan Bradshaw et al., *Support for Children: A Comparison of Arrangements in Fifteen Countries* (London: Her Majesty's Stationery Office, 1993).

35. Some research in the United States (for example, Seltzer, "Legal Custody Arrangements") confirms this, indicating that joint legal custody encourages divorced fathers to invest in their children in ways similar to those of fathers in two-parent households. Yet some studies point to the risk of strengthening fathers' over mothers' power without substantially modifying the gender division of labor and of responsibilities. See Carol Smart and Selma Sevenhujsen, eds., *Child Custody and the Politics of Gender* (London: Routledge, 1989); Selma Sevenhujsen, "Justice, Moral Reasoning, and the Politics of Child Custody," in *Equality, Politics, and Gender*, edited by Elizabeth Meehan and Selma Sevenhujsen (London: Sage Publications, 1991).

36. See, for example, Kirsten Scheiwe, "Labor Market, Welfare State, and Family Institutions: The Links to Mothers' Poverty Risks," *Journal of European Social Policy* 4(August 1994): 201–34; Annemieke Van Dreuth, Trudie Knijn, and Jane Lewis, "Sources of Income for Lone-Mother Families: Policy Changes in Britain and the Netherlands and the Experiences of Divorced Women," *Journal of Social Policy* 28(October 1999): 619–41.

37. Sainsbury, *Gender, Equality, and Welfare States*; Van Dreuth, Knijn, and Lewis, "Sources of Income."

38. Ann Phillips and Peter Moss, *Who Cares for Europe's Children?* Report of the European Child Care Network (Brussels: Commission of the European Communities, 1988); Judith Gornick et al., "Supporting the Employment of Mothers: Policy Variation Across Fourteen Welfare States," *Journal of European Social Policy* 7(February 1997): 45–70; Linda Hantrais and Steen Mangen, eds., *Family Policy and the Welfare of Women* (Loughborough: Cross-national Research Papers, 1994); Hantrais and Letablier, *Familles, travail, et politiques familiales en Europe.*

39. That is, British women either first raise their children and then enter the labor market, or alternate periods of full-time child raising and periods of partial participation in the labor market.

40. Italy is unique among these countries. It has one of the longest maternity leave systems, with a generous income replacement, as well as a relatively long parental leave, which since March 2000 puts a premium on fathers taking a portion of it. Also, child care services for children between ages three and six is highly available, covering more than 80 percent of all children in this age bracket, while child care services are provided for fewer than 5 percent of children under three at the national level. See also Saraceno, *Mutamenti della famiglia.*

41. Jeanne Fagnani, "A Comparison of Family Policies for Working Mothers in France and West Germany," in Hantrais and Mangen, *Family Policy*, 26–34; Jeanne Fagnani and Evelyn Rassat, "Garde d'enfant et/ou femme à tout faire?: Les employées des familles bénéficiaires de l'AGED," in *Recherches et prévisions* [Allocations Familiales, CNAF] 49(September 1997): 51–58; Karin Waerness, "The Changing 'Welfare Mix' in Child Care and in Care for the Elderly," in Lewis, *Gender, Social Care, and Welfare State Restructuring in Europe*, 207–8; Arnlaug Leira, ed., *Family*

*Change, Practices, Policies, and Values* (Stamford: JAI Press, 1999), ix–xxii.

42. See, for example, Robert Erikson and John Goldthorpe, *The Constant Flux* (Oxford: Clarendon, 1992).

43. Crouch also suggests this, but from the point of view of the changing gender composition of occupational classes rather than from the point of view of class membership. Crouch, *Social Change in Western Europe*, 254.

44. Janet Finch and Dulcie Groves, eds., *A Labor of Love: Women, Work, and Caring* (London: Routledge & Kegan Paul, 1983); Janet Finch, *Family Obligations and Social Change* (London: Routledge & Kegan Paul, 1989); Claire Ungerson, ed., *Gender and Caring: Work and Welfare in Britain and Scandinavia* (London: Harvester Wheatsheaf, 1989); Franz Höllinger and Max Haller, "Kinship and Social Networks," *European Sociological Review* 6(May 1990): 103–24; Carla Facchini and Renzo Scortegagna, "Italy: Alternatives to Institutionalization and Women's Central Role," in Leseman and Martin, *Les personnes âgées*, 33–69; Julia Twigg, ed., *Informal Care in Europe* (York: University of York Social Policy Research Unit, 1993); OECD, *Caring for Frail Elderly People.*

45. Women over eighty who do not live alone or with a spouse, however, are more likely than men to live in a child's household.

46. Höllinger and Haller, "Kinship and Social Networks"; L. Lecchini, D. Marsiglia, and M. Bottai, "Anziani e reti di relazioni sociali," in *Continuità e discontinuità nei processi demografici: L'Italia nella transizione demografica* (Cosenza: Università degli Studi di Calabria, Società Italiana di Statistica, 1995), 575–88.

47. Anneli Anttonen and Jorma Sipila, "European Social Care Services: Is It Possible to Identify Models?" *Journal of European Social Policy* 5(Summer 1996): 87–100.

48. Millar and Warman, *Defining Family Obligations in Europe.*

49. See, for example, L. B. Knudsen, *La position des femmes sur le marché de travail au Danemark: Evolution entre 1983 et 1989* (Women's Position in the Labor Market in Denmark: 1983–1989 Trends) (Brussels: Equal Opportunity Unit of the European Commission, 1991). Note that in the Scandinavian countries the welfare state is defined as "the people's home" (*folkshemmet*).

50. Hobson, "No Exit No Voice"; Hobson, "Solo Mothers"; Orloff, "Gender and the Social Rights of Citizenship"; O'Connor, Orloff, and Shaver, *States, Markets, and Families*; Eithne McLaughlin and Caroline Glendinning, "Paying for Care in Europe: Is There a Feminist Approach?" in Hantrais and Mangen, *Family Policy*, 52–69.

51. McLaughlin and Glendinning, "Paying for Care," 65.

52. Sainsbury, *Gender, Equality, and Welfare States.*

53. Meaning both the "removal" of men from the domestic sphere for most of their time and the individualization of their social rights.

54. See Sainsbury, *Gender, Equality, and Welfare States.*

# 10

## At the Limits of New Middle-class Japan: Beyond "Mainstream Consciousness"

### William W. Kelly

It was one paradox of class in Japan through the second half of the twentieth century that class consciousness was high among academic social scientists but seemingly low among officials and the public. In this regard, class talk in Japan has the same standing as in the United States, the other advanced industrial society that is equally unwilling to formulate structured social inequality in the idiom of socio-economic class. In both countries, social scientists share a central and sophisticated concern with class analysis, but public officials and ordinary people are disinclined to talk about themselves and others in terms of class position.

### Middle Class or Mainstream? Class Structure Without Class Talk

As observed by many analysts, from Tocqueville through Veblen to present-day commentators, the "American Way" is to dissolve class into the vagaries of consumption tastes and lifestyles.[1] Americans commonly use the term "middle class" to talk about such matters as individual identity, community type, lifestyle, and voting patterns, but we also use the term much more frequently to indicate our consumption orientation or position ourselves morally than to specify economic location. Since the 1930s Depression, upward of eight out of ten Americans have located themselves within the middle class when asked in many different kinds of polls to choose between lower, middle, and upper locations. Poll self-identification has remained invariant in spite of widening income and asset inequalities since the late 1970s.

A similar pattern, although a different dynamic, holds true for Japan. Class has been a prominent topic of social science research for the last fifty years, and it is still deployed by intellectuals and what remains of the organized labor movement. In the first postwar decade, scholars like Tsurumi Shunsuke debated about how independent "popular culture" was from "mass culture."[2] By the late 1950s, scholars had divided sharply on how to interpret the first Social Stratification and Mobility (SSM) survey, which was undertaken in 1955 by the Japan Sociological Society and whose design was greatly influenced by survey programs in American sociology. One of the contested findings of the first SSM survey was a growing new middle class.[3] Social scientists continued to dispute the survey findings through the 1960s; for example, Odaka Kunio and Yasuda Saburō argued over the mobility and class identification issues that arose from the second SSM study.[4] In the following decade, both scholars and journalists took up the question of whether the annual Prime Minister's Office poll demonstrated a broad middle "class"-ness or middle "mass"-ness.[5] Then, as a speculative "bubble economy" overheated in the 1980s, controversy centered on whether the expansive postwar middle, however defined, was now fragmenting into widening differentials between what some warned were the "new rich" and "new poor."[6] The sustained recession of the 1990s at least reined in many of the new rich and defused the commentary about "kakusa," or a wealth gap. Academics have instead turned to other kinds of stratification debates, such as that between the sociologists Tominaga Ken'ichi and Imada Takatoshi, who propose modernist versus postmodernist interpretations of stratification and status perception.[7]

These debates about class and mass, and the research agendas behind them, have significantly influenced academic formulations of contemporary Japan. Despite their often sharp differences, they collectively demonstrate that socioeconomic inequalities have persisted, in one form and degree or another, and that class continues to be a salient analytical distinction. There is broad agreement, for instance, that from the mid-1950s to the mid-1970s, aggregate economic growth and state policies to enhance personal income and expand welfare significantly equalized income, assets, and educational attainment across the Japanese population. But since the mid-1970s, there has been an equally significant widening of income, asset, and education differentials. Ishida Hiroshi, in a rigorous test of several competing hypotheses about class structure and status hierarchies, found strong support for the importance of firm size in explaining differential benefits and status. Income and prestige were more closely correlated with the size of one's company than with one's occupation or education.[8]

However, the purpose of this chapter is not to join this sociological literature but rather to unpack a term of more popular than academic currency, one that has denoted social inclusiveness rather than categorical differentiation. This term is "chūryū." Its usual English gloss is "middle class," although we should understand it more accurately as "mainstream." Its most frequent compound, "chūryū ishiki," translates as "mainstream consciousness." The significance of this term and its compound, I argue, is in signaling the ways in which the Japanese population has generally assented to the post-1960s societal order.

This assent was neither predictable nor passive. The assertion of a social contract frequently emphasizes the efforts of political and economic leaders to incorporate and accommodate broad segments of a national population. The Japanese establishment in particular is often seen to have been particularly successful in co-opting people as citizens, workers, and consumers into a national compact. The initiative, however, may well have come from below, especially if we begin, with Kent Calder and others, from a premise of official equivocation and establishment uncertainty:

> Across the long decades of growth, an increasingly stable and affluent Japanese society confronted a fractious political system, the unsettling pluralistic heritage of occupation, and an economy with little tolerance for political instability, due to its ambitious, risky, and highly leveraged economic growth strategies.[9]

Identification with a societal mainstream took place in spite of, and not in terms of, objective differentials that sociologists and economists continued to recognize and register as those of social class. Chūryū has been a potent construct for organizing life and valuations of life in Japan over the last several decades, and any effort to understand the real differences in socioeconomic position and life chances that have existed and continue to exist in Japan must take this term seriously.

Significantly, chūryū does not feature prominently in sociological surveys such as the decennial SSM, but it has been the key term in the annual Survey on the People's Life-Style that the Prime Minister's Office has conducted since 1958. The poll asks respondents to place themselves in one of five positions relative to the wider population ("much above," "just above," "the same as," "just below," and "much below an average well-being"; see figure 10.1). Since at least

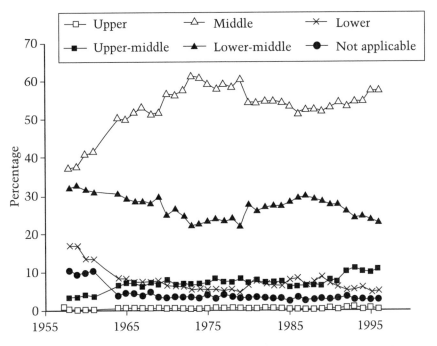

**Figure 10.1** Mainstream Consciousness in Japan, 1958 to 1996 *Source:* Prime Minister's Office, Survey on the People's Life-Style.

the late 1960s, about 90 percent of the respondents have placed themselves in the middle, upper-middle, or lower-middle stratum, leading government white papers and media commentary to interpret the results as demonstrating that contemporary Japan has a broad mainstream population. Japan as a "90 percent middle-class society" has been the consistent claim for three decades, although the real effect of this "mainstream" identification has been to "declass" and "massify" the debates about social stratification.

Mainstream consciousness became a popular phrase in the 1960s as the domestic economy was heating up, corporate managers were trying to defuse leftist labor unions, and the ruling Liberal Democratic Party tried to be more inclusive. For example, the media of the decade made much of what was termed "the mass mainstream of 100 million people" (ichiokunin sōchūryū), which resonated for most Japanese adults of the time in powerful and prideful contrast to the phrase that had been the national self-characterization just after World War II: ichiokunin sōkyodatsu ("100 million people in a state of trauma").[10] It is not hard to imagine how establishment interests were served by this rhetoric of mandarin planners and commentators.

A Japanese sense of exceptionalism became a cultural nationalism of homogeneity and hard work. Economically, such an image both promoted and responded to new patterns of saving as well as spending. Politically, it restated societal consensus at a time of student unrest, environmental protest, the "oil shocks," the "Nixon shocks," and other serious perturbations.

Yet an orientation toward the mainstream had also deeply conditioned everyday life by the 1960s. It is true that it was only in that decade that middle-class occupations (conceived expansively as not only managers and professionals but also white-collar employees and the old urban middle classes) increased rapidly, though they have never engaged a majority of the working population to this day. Nonetheless, it was in the 1960s that certain key elements of middle-class life and location became nationalized into a model of "mainstream" life that has since powerfully represented designs for living.

Like the term "middle class" in post–World War II America, then, the Japanese use of "mainstream" does not refer to a class category but to a category that works to transcend class. It is this notion of mainstream life or consciousness that is often said to have had hegemonic force over the last thirty years, at least symbolically from the Tokyo Olympic year of 1964 through the death of the Shōwa emperor in 1989 and into the 1990s. And it is this folk term, "mainstream consciousness," and not class structure per se that is the focus of my concern in this chapter.

My argument is that this orientation toward mainstream definitions of lifeways and life chances has had directive force not because it has been touted rhetorically by officials and the media, but more significantly because it has been embedded in a particular matrix of public discourse and institutional fields. It is this embeddedness that has given wider salience to certain social forms and cultural meanings of middle-class location. To demonstrate this argument, the next section outlines how societal development since World War II has been a process of restructuring and standardizing differences around new axes rather than homogenizing lifestyles and equalizing life chances.

If the postwar social contract has been shaped and sustained by the conditioned and conditioning participation of the population, this same population can effect systemic change. This is indeed the importance of several trends of the last decade that portend a serious weakening of the lineaments of this social contract. The final section identifies three such vectors of change that signal turbulence in the mainstream.

## "Mainstream Consciousness" and the Restructuring of Difference: The Social Formation of New Middle-class Japan

The force and meaning of mainstream identity must be understood as mutually conditioned by several other rubrics of public talk and by a particular institutional grid that was characteristic of post-1960s Japan. In my own writings, I have used the term "new middle class" social formation to characterize structurally and situate historically the Japan of the four decades from the early 1960s through the 1990s. There are of course other constructs for these decades—such as "managed society," "company-ism," "the educational credential society," and "information capitalism." Each has been valuable in permitting a line of analysis that is often more complementary than alternative to the others.[11]

For me, new middle-class (henceforth NMC) Japan is a distinctive "social formation" in the sense, for example, that Pierre Bourdieu and Jean-Claude Passeron use the concept to mean a two-dimensional "system of relations of power and relations of meaning between groups and classes."[12] More than class structure or society, the concept of social formation captures some of the fractious dynamism of autonomous but linked fields. It more clearly problematizes the degree and nature of integration, and the term itself is constructively ambiguous. ("Formation" connotes simultaneously "forming," "formed," and "formative".) A social formation is a concatenation of discourses and institutions through and by which lines of power are drawn and certain propositions and values are endowed with a naturalizing authority.

Analytically, then, NMC Japan has emerged in the decades since the early 1960s as a reticulation of certain thematics of public talk and several central social fields. In earlier papers, I have outlined at least six such loosely bounded sets of public talk and three such institutions, which collectively serve to both incorporate and differentiate the population, by discursive location and social position. Here I sketch them only cursorily.

The first thematic of public talk centers on *culture*. It is much remarked that, after Japan's defeat in World War II, official and mainstream versions of the national identity shifted from the explicitly Shintō religious foundations that had underwritten the prewar imperial doctrine of "kokutai" to more overtly ethnic bases of "Japaneseness." By this sanitized mono-ethnic nationalism, Japaneseness became a matter of psyche, not politics. A Japanese "culture" was imagined by the stereotypic extension of personal traits to unique national "character"; thus, "treatises on Japanese culture" (Nihon bunka-ron), "treatises on Japan" (Nihon-ron), and "treatises on the Japanese people" (Nihonjin-ron) have been virtual synonyms of the media and popular literature. This move had the clear advantage of personalizing and naturalizing membership in the national community for a state whose own political character has been accused of everything from aggression to ineptitude. At the same time, by further associating culture as character with culture as heritage, this public talk exacerbated the dichotomies of modernity and tradition as they were mapped onto genders, regions, and neighborhoods.[13]

Japanese cultural exceptionalism not only offered a broad channel for notions of a mainstream but also mitigated some of the frictions of another contemporary discourse, that of the *center and the regions*. The concentration of population, resources, and influence in metropolitan Tokyo is a long-term process, but it was greatly accelerated in the mid-1950s. Japan now has a unipolar geography akin to that of a number of European nations, and the ladders of success and opportunity in education, media, politics, and corporate employment all tip upward toward Tokyo. The subordination of much of the rest of Japan as "regional" has been ideologically offset by the grounding of much Japanese culture as "tradition," which is sentimentally felt to remain vibrant in the rural heartland. Regional Japan is valorized nostalgically as it is depleted economically.[14]

Modern Japan has had a special fascination for typologizing and stereotyping historical "generations" in a way that we might more precisely consider to be *cohort talk*. The focal point of commentary in the postwar decades has been the so-called Shōwa hitoketa, the "single-digit Shōwan" cohort born in the first nine years of the era (that is, 1926 to 1934). This cohort has been a point of departure and a measure for much of the subsequent generational talk, even more definitively than its rough U.S. equivalent, "the children of the Depression," defined postwar America age-grades.[15] The single-digit Shōwans are the cohort whose childhood and youth spanned the "dark valley" of the Depression and the war. It is the generation that was old enough to have suffered but young enough not to have inflicted suffering. It managed the psychological divide and social chaos in the war's aftermath, becoming the bedrock of postwar recovery and boom. In the early postwar decades, the single-digit Shōwans became, in the popular imagination, the "workaholic company men" and the "education mamas" whose selfless efforts on behalf of corporation and children ensured present and future prosperity. They are now poised as Japan's first mass senior-citizen cohort, the first wave of an aging society. Throughout their lives, then, they have stood at the peak of an age-graded moral cline, by which judgments of the postwar population are often cohort-stratified. For decades, commentators have wrung their hands anxiously over each succeeding youth cohort, among whom they always find dangerous portents of weakening social commitment and rising personal indulgence.

Finally, a focus on *life cycle,* or "life course," gained widespread currency in the 1970s, somewhat later than the other elements of public talk, although the rhetorical normalizing of life transitions had already been a part of public talk in modern Japan. (For instance, there were public conventions about an "appropriate age" for marriage ["tekireiki"].) From political, economic, and social motivations, however, a more comprehensive discourse was elaborated around the notion of the "eighty-year life span," which periodizes the life course according to institutional position (as student, worker, spouse, parent, and so on).[16]

Not surprisingly, the rhetoric of life cycles is strongly gendered; indeed, *gender* inflects each of these public discourses and has constituted its own discursive field.[17] In contemporary Japan, the discourse of gender has privileged an obligatory marital heterosexuality and a mutual social dependency at home, at work, *and* at play. The male and female life cycles have been structured in a way that emphasizes differential natural endowments and limitations that channel normal energies toward separate sets of complementary commitments in both public and domestic spheres.[18]

Thus, projections and claims of "mainstream consciousness" have only gained currency and definition in relation to these and other thematics of public talk.[19] Even this is not sufficient, however; mainstream consciousness has required social grounding as well as the mutual conditioning of these ideologically potent discourses. This social grounding has been found in the key institutional sectors of the NMC social formation. By this, I mean that the reorganization and wider reach of certain institutions have patterned lifeways in the last four decades, especially in the three key sectors of work, family, and education.

The twin images of *work* in the late Shōwa economy were those of a uniquely "Japanese company" model of lifetime commitment, bottom-up recruitment of school-leavers, promotion and pay primarily by years of service, and enterprise unions, on the one hand, and the "dual economy" of a modern, large-firm sector dominating a traditional, small-firm sector, on the other. However, it is more accurate to say that the workplaces of these decades have girded the double hierarchies of an industrial structure of large and small firms and regular and nonregular employment statuses. The former is actually a continuum from large corporations and government bureaucracies to subcontractors, entrepreneurs, independent artisans, and small retailers. The latter occupational hierarchy ranges from male white-collar managers (the "salarymen"), professionals, and skilled blue-collar workers down through female clericals and part-timers to seasonal and casual labor.

The hierarchies intersect at their higher ends with the privileged, permanent, and mostly male regular employees of the large firms and ministries. The Japanese company model originally suggested that a bedrock of traditional values upheld the organizational features of this core. Labor historians, however, have taught us that the elements of large corporate organization were forged during several contentious periods of struggle in the twentieth century. One result has been a considerable white-collarization of male blue-collar workers in large firms. At the same time, to protect this core and minimize corporate exposure to downturns, these companies remain flexible by externalizing their expansion and contraction with nonregular workers and chains of subsidiary affiliates.[20]

Legal reform (the postwar constitution and new civil code), demographic changes (rising longevity and declining fertility), and economic transformations (employment shifts, urban expansion, consumer marketing) combined in the postwar years to promote and valorize the Japanese *family* as a conjugal couple and nuclear household organized by the strict role complementarity of a rice-winner husband-father and a caregiver wife-mother. What is important to emphasize is that the family has not become a "haven in a heartless land," a refuge from social engineering. Rather, its roles and routines have been reorganized in ways that lend critical support to the more "public" institutions of schools and workplaces.[21]

For virtually every Japanese born after World War II, twelve years of formal *education* have become the link between home and work, childhood and adulthood. Postwar Japanese education has managed to combine the mass schooling of a literate citizenry with a rigorous culling for elite positions in society.[22] The rigor and quality of the broad, uniform curriculum and the equitable funding of the overwhelmingly public elementary and secondary school system have been rapturously described by journalists and academics alike. At the same time, the funnel of the school credential society narrows quickly. Late Shōwa Japan quickly became a rather strict meritocracy, largely measured by educational achievement. Educational prestige has come to be determined by school reputation, which is now indexed by entrance exam competitiveness. And increasingly, exam success has required extracurricular private study in the shadow sector of the infamous cram schools and prep academies.

What I am emphasizing here is that these dominant yet shifting constructs formed unifying frames for people's experience but also created new categories of distinction among the population. The institutional fields that came to reorganize lifeways in the decades after World War II standardized but did not homogenize patterns of life. What was produced was thus a structured differentiation of workplaces, family forms, and school outcomes. This is the sense in which "mainstream consciousness" could come to represent both a broadly inclusive and sharply stratified sense of social identity.

At the same time, it is imperative to understand that these ideologies and institutions, which frame much of everyday life and consciousness, are themselves structured over time. How did they come to take shape, how have they been reproduced, and what is the potential for their transformation into something else?[23] Ideologies and institutions, in distinct ways, have a powerfully directive ability to co-opt alternatives and make people complicit in structuring their lives. And even as they set limits and "normalize" lives, they depend precisely on those actors, who move within, through, and sometimes against these boundaries of the feasible and the desirable. Subject positions shape but are also reshaped by positioned subjects.

Much of the anthropological literature of postwar Japan can be read as ethnographic representations of the emergence and reproduction of this social formation.[24] Our many studies show that this sense of the differences-that-standardize lies at the core of folk notions of the contemporary "mainstream." And it is this discursive and institutional formation, not the broadening and contracting of a middle-income stratum in straightforward socioeconomic terms, that is essential to appreciating the postwar social contract in Japan.

Such a formulation of the sources and nature of public support for societal arrangements also suggests how such arrangements may be challenged. In the final section of this chapter, then, I turn to possible ways out of and beyond the NMC social formation. What are the kind of actions that are both intelligible within the logic of NMC but identifiable as reforming its patterns and loosening the hold of "mainstream consciousness"?

## Beyond "Mainstream Consciousness"

Events over the decade of the 1990s surprised most Japan analysts at every turn. We all witnessed—but few had foreseen—the decomposition of central elements of both the international system and the domestic arrangements that had sustained Shōwa Japan through its postwar decades. The breakup of the Soviet Union, the death of the Shōwa emperor, the collapse of the 1980s bubble economy into a prolonged recession, the continuing disarray of the post-1955 political system—these and other developments present us with a far more chastened and anxious object of contemplation than the confident Japan of the late 1980s.

Retrospectively, it is widely argued that postwar Japan was dependent on a special and now-defunct hothouse international political economy that included: an undervalued yen in a dollar-denominated world economy; a U.S. security umbrella in a bipolar superpower struggle; and an edge in high-value manufacturing technologies in an era of industrial capitalism. I find these observations undeniable and consequential, but I prefer to locate my own speculations within three other general claims about the present moment.

First, NMC Japan was ideologically marked by a historically unique generation (the single-digit Shōwans), and it was dependent on a particular demographic profile (a youthful age structure together with low but stable and sustainable fertility). For fifty years, Japan was a distinctive combination of a generation rooted in but not responsible for the prewar past and a society made youthful by the immediate postwar baby boom. As this generation begins to die off and the demographic profile ages, we can expect serious repercussions.

Second, in important respects the NMC arrangements and inducements that were consolidated by the mid-1960s have, ironically, proven too successful for their own good. They have produced what William Steslicke once called the "dilemmas of success."[25] The educational arms race (that is, the continuing escalation of parental investment and student effort to gain an edge in school admissions) and the hyper-concentration of resources and population in metropolitan Tokyo are two examples of the fatal attraction of certain values and standards in drawing more seekers of success in their terms than can be accommodated.

Finally, in part for this very reason, many argue that NMC Japan is quickly exhausting itself through its own contradictions and resentments. The population has had enough of "rich Japan, poor Japanese," and the decade of the 1990s produced much skepticism and cynicism about the official sloganeering: "raising the quality of life," "expanding leisure," "promoting privatization," "a dawning age of culture," and the "internationalization" of Japan.

Each of these three claims is a compelling predisposing condition for expecting an incipient punctuation of the existing social formation. Still, they do not specify the shifts in people's actions that foreshadow such a restructuring. What I would like to outline in this section are three tendencies of the present that seem to challenge seriously the social order of NMC Japan: the increasing tendency of the elderly population to live alone or only with a spouse; the rapidly rising percentage of women who are postponing marriage; and the growing percentage of entrants to elite public universities who have graduated from private and national schools with six-year middle and high school programs rather than from public high schools. These three diagnostics hardly exhaust the possible shifts that have the potential to restructure NMC Japan, but each poses alternatives and exposes contradictions that cannot be easily contained by present arrangements. They suggest the waning power of a "mainstream consciousness" to channel aspirations and effort.

### Old Age and Elder Care

We have heard so much about Japan as an "aging society" that the phrase itself is a bit long in the tooth. Still, preemptive crisis-talk has proven an effective technology of power in postwar Japan, and visions of an aging society may rank among the most effectively preemptive of all. Official talk about aging began in the early 1970s, when Japan still had the most youthful population profile in the Organization for Economic Cooperation and Development (OECD). Only in the 1990s did Japan's broad-base population pyramid become a tall, thin rectangle (see figure 10.2).

Geometric images are backed by a barrage of arithmetic. The number of youth age ten to nineteen declined 25 percent in the 1990s. The number of people over sixty has increased 35 percent. The year 1995 marked the first-ever decrease in the total labor population (that is, the number of workers age fifteen to sixty). By 2013, about one-quarter of the population will be older than sixty-five, making Japan the "oldest" nation in the world, and it is estimated that pensions, social insurance, and medical costs will require 23 percent of GNP. (Over half the elderly population at that point will be older than seventy-five.)[26] The birthrate in metropolitan Tokyo is projected to fall to 1.1, pushing the "dependency ratio" of workers to nonworkers to unsustainable heights.

Japan's aging society is envisioned as resting on the twin pillars of private care and public resources, and both are already showing signs of having reached the limits of personal and political tolerance. Now in their seventies, the single-digit cohort Shōwans are graying into Japan's first "mass longevity" elders. For the moment, the moral stat-

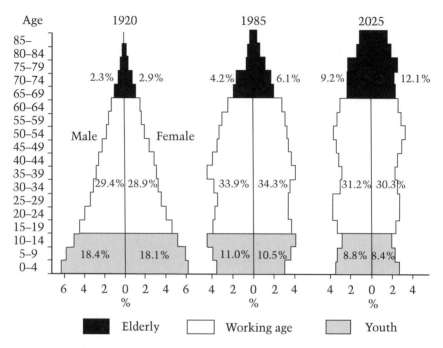

**Figure 10.2** Japan's Population Pyramid: 1920, 1985, 2025  *Source*: Author's compilation.

ure of this particular historical generation is extremely significant in mitigating resentment about the escalating costs of an aging society. As these "honorable elders" pass, however, it becomes much less likely that public entitlements and private caregiving will be extended adequately.[27]

Two features of the present Japanese situation are distinctive. The first is the relatively high rate of employment for Japanese men (and for women to a lesser extent) over sixty-five, some of whom want to work but others of whom must keep working after mandatory retirement to remain financially independent. The second is the government effort to promote three-generation families and privatize elder care. (In Japan, privatization refers to the family, not to the marketplace!) The fruits of this effort are borne out statistically. About 60 percent of Japanese over the age of sixty-five live with their children (and two-thirds of those households also include their grandchildren); one in four elderly live as a spouse couple, and only 15 percent live alone. Thus, Japanese elderly live with their children at four to five times the rate in the United States, and eight times the rate in Great Britain. Their roles include caring for grandchildren, cooking, housework, laundry, and home repairs.

These two features seem to be at cross purposes—high rates of working to remain financially independent and high rates of living with children. However, they are very possibly the distinct patterns of the young-old and the old-old; that is, the high rate of elderly employment reflects the need of the young-old to supplement limited pension income and their strong desire to remain financially and residentially independent of their children—for as long as they remain healthy. The high rate of living with children reflects the lack of public- and private-sector long-term care facilities and the legal and ideological presumptions of family responsibility.

Together, these characteristics of Japan's elders have kept the burden of responsibility on individual and family means, with public facilities and resources providing only backup. Yet neither independent living nor family care is accomplished easily, and both test the often subtle distinctions between preference and necessity, as well as the different perspectives of the younger and older generations.

The arguments that flare up around what David Plath called the "intimate politics of co-residence" are much more frequently concerned with social relations than financial abilities.[28] For that reason, I think an important diagnostic is the rising rate of elderly who live alone or with only their spouse. In 1980 these numbered only 6 percent of all households, but by 1992 the figure had risen steadily to 11 percent of all households (and fully 40 percent of the over-sixty-five population). I do not know what threshold would portend a fundamental challenge to the uneasy balance of public and private responsibilities, but it has already reached a level that threatens to open a chasm between the two.

### Women and Marriage: Crisis and Resistance

Two developments of the 1980s have been frequently assessed for their subsequent effects on marriage, family, and gender relations in the 1990s. First, for much of that decade, the growing labor shortages for a broad spectrum of blue-collar, clerical, and low-level technical positions opened up opportunities for women as companies sought to avoid hiring foreign guest workers. The heated controversies surrounding the 1986 Equal Employment Opportunity Law and the divided evaluations of it were significant, but the law had only an indirect impact on the majority of working women, who were choosing or constrained by *jobs*, not *careers*.

Second, it was much ballyhooed by the end of the decade that Japan's men faced a marriage crisis and that society at large faced a fertility collapse. Indeed, the numbers in the cohorts of marriageable men exceeded those of marriageable females (in both absolute numbers and regional distribution), and for that reason and others, the fertility rate, which had stabilized around the replacement rate for much of the previous three decades, fell steeply to 1.57 in 1990. In this year of what the media tagged the "1.57 shock," the title of Tanimura Shiho's best-selling novel, *Kekkon shinai ka mo shiranai shō-kōgun*, was appropriated to express a broad syndrome: the title can be translated as "Maybe I won't get married after all"![29]

This proved to be more than just media hype, as it became evident around that time that large numbers of women in the thirty- to thirty-five-year-old cohort were in fact remaining unmarried. By 1995 a stunning 48 percent of women and 67 percent of men age twenty-five to twenty-nine were unmarried, and in metropolitan Tokyo well over half of women were turning thirty without having married. Even those who married were delaying having children; in 1997, 40 percent of couples married for four years did not yet have children. In that year, the fertility rate dropped below 1.40.[30]

The postponement of marriage and the correlated sharp decline in the fertility rate have provoked some government response, such as the four-ministry "Angel Plan," which took flight in 1994 to great fanfare but with few funds. There has also been much chauvinistic hand-wringing by (male) bureaucrats about female obligations and maternal urges, but what was "crisis" for men was read as "resistance" by women. Countless talk shows, magazine columns, and books have been fueled by debates about the motivations of such resistance and whether it represents procrastination or refusal. Perhaps the most common interpretation is that more tertiary education and expanding employment opportunities for metropolitan women that have not only offered them goals and satisfactions that would be compromised by marriage responsibilities but provided them with the income to pursue these goals. Polling data continue to report a desire by women to marry eventually but a preference to wait for the right circumstances.[31]

However, I am dubious that the pull factors are so decisive. No doubt, metropolitan women have been delaying marriage because they have found the job front to be improving and the home front *not* improving, but I suspect that they are more frustrated by the latter than encouraged by the former. Their "resistance" may be less the pursuit of opportunity than escape from constraint. I find support for this notion in the extended depressed economy of the 1990s. It is women—and especially university-educated women—who have been the first to feel the job freeze and the workforce reductions. And yet these workplace frustrations have not driven them down the aisle into the arms of waiting husbands. Age at marriage has continued to climb, and fertility continues to fall. It is not so much an attitude of "I don't want to get married" as "I don't want to get married just yet," or, "I don't want to get married until I find the right guy."[32]

The larger point for me about female marriage resistance is that women who postpone marriage appear to have understood that the most effective way to beat the social logic of Japan's boom decades, by which the home was caught between work and school, is simply to avoid (re)entering one—that is, to "exit" the system, or else to linger outside the domestic door long enough to create panic within, before going back in.

I suspect too that a good part of the motivation is the aging population. Even more than in the United States, care for those elderly who cannot care for themselves is overwhelmingly treated in Japan as the responsibility of a female relative. Indeed, surveys frequently find that the major concern of women over forty in Japan is aging—not their own but that of their parents, their parents-in-law, and their husband. It is often said that a woman experiences three old ages: in her fifties, she must care for her parents (and sometimes her spouse's parents); in her sixties and seventies, she must care for her husband; and in her seventies and eighties, she must finally care for herself. Marriage, many fear, involves sole responsibility for managing a household with an absentee husband, for raising the children, and for elder care of parents and in-laws.

These responsibilities have never been easy, and they are only exacerbated by the factors discussed here: mass longevity, state efforts to keep primary care a family responsibility, more nuclear households, and rising female workforce participation (now well over 50 percent for all married women, and about 70 percent for women in their forties). These factors ensure that a substantial number of Japanese women will face the dilemma of Akiko, the middle-aged woman in Ariyoshi's immensely popular 1972 novel *Kōkotsu no hito*.[33] Akiko is pressured by her family to quit her legal secretary position to care for her father-in-law when he becomes senile. She accepts her caretaking duties with doleful resignation and, by the novel's end, expresses satisfaction with the nurturing role she has played in her father-in-law's last days. More than twenty years later, she remains a sympathetic figure—and the book continues to sell—but skepticism about such quiet resignation is strong among younger women.

In short, for Japan as a self-designated aging society, the increasingly public tensions between the genders are potentially even more significant than those between the generations. Women's organizations in Japan are far larger and more assertive than its national associations for older citizens. It is likely that future public policies and programs for older Japanese will have to accommodate the private choices that individual women are now making about marriage and children as much as they seek to address the needs of the burgeoning elderly population.

## School Competition and the Education Arms Race

The severe recession throughout the 1990s intersected with a shifting population profile to pose serious threats to tertiary education and the school-to-work transition. As any reader of the Japanese press knows, the entry-level hiring scale of major corporations shrank dramatically in that decade. The papers were full of anecdotes of elite graduates in "job shock" (jobbu shokku) accepting ever-lower entry positions to gain entrance to first-tier corporations, or resigning themselves to less prestigious company openings, with ripple effects down the educational ladder. At the same time, the number of eighteen-year-olds in the population was declining sharply, from 2.05 million in 1992 to 1.51 million in 2000, placing enormous pressures on the already shaky finances of lower-tier private universities and junior colleges.

Declining job opportunities and a shrinking college-age cohort have combined to exacerbate the competition for elite universities. The consequence may well be the collapse of the tense balance between public- and private-sector secondary education that has held for the last three decades. A complement to public high school education thought to be sufficient for elite university entrance was a heavy dose of after-school private cram academy, supplemented if necessary by a postsecondary year in a private exam prep school. Very quickly—that is, in the last five years or so—the more assured route has become an emerging tier of elite private high schools that offer six-year secondary programs. Symptomatically, in 1993 the percentage of applicants who were admitted to the various faculties of Tokyo University from private high schools reached 50 percent (1,984 of the 4,010 accepted). Of the top thirty placement high schools, twenty-one were private institutions, led as usual in recent years by 171 successful students from the elite Kaisei Academy.

After admitting their students by highly competitive exams at the end of their sixth-grade year (somewhat analogous to the fateful "eleven-plus" exams in Britain), these schools, in effect, combine the three years of junior high school and the three years of high school. They move their students through the Ministry of Education secondary curriculum in four and a half or five years, leaving the balance for specific preparation for university entrance exams.

The particular school-to-work transitions of contemporary Japan have depended on the tight calibrations of school and work prestige hierarchies.[34] For several decades, the widely discrepant outcomes of the individuals moving through school into workplaces have been accepted without widespread public outcry or collective resistance (though certainly with much private frustration and grievance and occasional personal tragedy). In large part, the successful have claimed legitimacy, and the failures have been mollified through the publicness of the process—the ostensibly equal funding of secondary facilities, the national curriculum, and the rigid entrance exam criterion. If private high schools continue to attract more and more of the top university-bound students, this talent drain will clearly threaten the rationale of the entire present school-to-work complex.

The sociologist Ishida Hiroshi has shown—conclusively, to my mind—that elite higher education did not have a statistically significant social mobility effect in the last thirty years.[35] Government policies, teachers' union agitation, public opinion, and private expectations notwithstanding, children of advantaged parents were consistently overrepresented in elite universities. Moreover, private secondary graduates have disproportionately filled the postwar entering classes at Tokyo University at least since the early 1970s, an effect of the 1967 Tokyo metropolitan educational reforms. Clearly, misrecognition of meritocracy has been pervasive, and it is possible, I suppose, that a thoroughgoing privatization of the upper tier of secondary education will neither fundamentally shake the institutional linkages nor challenge the legitimacy of school outcomes or workplace destinations. I doubt it, however. If indeed present tendencies become future trends, a very different public-private tension will develop, and the stage will be set for a whole new educational arms race on much more transparently unequal class and regional terms.

## Final Contentions

It is certainly not my contention that these changes in the status of the elderly, women, and students are the three most decisive statistical indicators of societal change in late-twentieth-century Japan. But I do believe that they are measures of the fundamental social restructuring now occurring in Japan. And their significance is dual—for both social structure and social action.

Structurally, it is ironic that generational cohorts, gender roles, and stratified educational outcomes are among the axes of difference that are helping to unbind Japan's postwar social contract here at the beginning of the new century. After all, the moral force of the single-digit Shōwans, the complementarity of gendered role dichotomies, and the fairness of educational outcomes were key ideological tenets of the "mainstream." These are now becoming structural fault lines that expose the tenuousness of the mainstream arrangements.

The other point is the formulation of social action that underlies my approach. Each of these three social diagnostics represents a point where private action rubs against and begins to unravel the delicate skein of ideologies and institutions. And there need not be organized activism to collectivize such individual decisions. Indeed, in all three dimensions, structural change is resulting from the cumulation of disparate, parallel, personal actions—those of middle-aged and elderly generations as they distance themselves from one another, those of women in delaying marriage, and those of youth and their parents as they move entirely to private-sector education.

This is not a claim premised on a rational choice voluntarism, which takes individual intentionality as the independent causal agent of structural outcomes and a universal rationality as the presumed basis of that intentional choice-making. I presume rather the recursive structuring of individual agency, cultural meaning, and institutional form, as well as the multilayered consciousness of actors, who act under varying constraints and with subtle degrees of reflective knowledge, discursive articulation, and tacit understandings—but who act effectively nonetheless.

High school students and their parents, the elderly and their children, and the metropolitan marriage resisters of the late 1980s and 1990s are positioned subjects who are maneuvering within and around that which they find meaningful, desirable, and/or necessary. They may act with only partial and contingent understanding of their own actions, and these actions may be private and pragmatic. However, those qualities make the effects of their actions no less consequential. Most public commentary, domestic and foreign, about Japan at the millennial turning point paints a dark portrait of a nation adrift, plagued with social malaise, political sclerosis, and economic stagnation. The trends on which this chapter has focused would seem to lend further support to such pessimism. However, authors who fire off national obituaries and revolutionary manifestos shoot themselves in the foot as often as they penetrate the intended target. One can safely conclude, however, that whatever the shape of the emerging social formation, it will be a transformation, not a reproduction, of the New Middle-class Japan of the last thirty years.

## Notes

Japanese names appear with last name first, even in English-language publications.

1. Recent examples include Benjamin DeMott, *The Imperial Middle: Why Americans Can't Think Straight About Class* (New York: Morrow, 1990), and Brackette F. Williams, "A Class Act: Anthropology and the Race to Nation Across Ethnic Terrain," *Annual Review of Anthropology* 18(1989): 401–44.

2. Tsurumi Shunsuke, *A Cultural History of Postwar Japan, 1945–1980* (London: Kegan Paul International, 1987).

3. Odaka Kunio, "Nihon no kaikyū kōzō wa dō kawatta ka: Chūkanso no ugoki o chūshin to shite" (How has Japanese class structure changed?: Focusing on movements in the middle class), *Jiyū* 7(June 1960): 131–54. An English version appeared as "The Middle Classes in Japan," in *Class, Status, and Power: Social Stratification in Comparative Perspective*, 2nd ed., edited by Reinhard Bendix and Seymour Martin Lipset (Glencoe: Free Press, 1996), 541–51.

4. Yasuda Saburō, *Shakai idō no kenkyū* (A study of social mobility) (Tokyo: Tokyo University Press, 1971).

5. A brief English-language summary of their differences can be found in Murakami Yasusuke, Kishimoto Shigenobu, and Tominaga Ken'ichi, "Debate on the New Middle Class," *Japan Interpreter* 12(Winter 1978): 1–15.

6. Hakuhodo Institute of Life and Living, *Bunshū no tanjo* (The birth of the micro classes) (Tokyo: Nihon Keizai Shimbun sha, 1985); Ozawa Masako, "Consumption in the Age of Stratification," *Japan Echo* 12(Autumn 1985): 47–53; Watanabe Kazuhiro, *Kinkonkan* (Tokyo: Shufu-no-tomo sha, 1984).

7. Compare, for instance, Tominaga Ken'ichi, "Hoshuka to posuto-modan no aida" (Between growing conservatism and the postmodern) *Sekai* 525(March 1989): 233–48, and Tominaga Ken'ichi, *Nihon kindaika to shakai hendō* (Japan's modernization and social change) (Tokyo: Kōdansha, 1990), with Imada Takatoshi, *Modan no datsu-kōchiku: Sangyō shakai no yukue* (Deconstruction of the modern) (Tokyo: Chūō kōron sha, 1987), and Imada Takatoshi, *Shakai kaisō to seiji* (Social stratification and politics) (Tokyo: Tokyo Daigaku shuppankai, 1989). A useful and judicious English-language overview of these postwar debates can be found in Kosaka Kenji, ed., *Social Stratification in Contemporary Japan* (London: Kegan Paul International, 1994).

8. Ishida Hiroshi, *Social Mobility in Contemporary Japan: Educational Credentials, Class, and the Labor Market in a Cross-national Perspective* (Stanford: Stanford University Press, 1993). On the early postwar trends toward equalization, see Margaret A. McKean, "Equality," in *Democracy in Japan*, edited by Ishida Takeshi and Ellis S. Krauss (Pittsburgh: University of Pittsburgh Press, 1989), 201–24. The diverging fortunes since the mid-1970s are analyzed in Kosaka Kenji, "Aspects of Social Inequality and Difference," in Kosaka, *Social Stratification in Contemporary Japan*, 34–53, and also in Tachibanaki Toshiaki, *Nihon no keizai kakusa: Shotoku to shisan o kangaeru* (Economic differentiation in Japan: Considering incomes and assets) (Tokyo: Iwanami, 1998).

9. Kent E. Calder, *Crisis and Compensation: Public Policy and Political Stability in Japan, 1949–1986* (Princeton: Princeton University Press, 1989), 442.

10. For a powerful evocation of that period, see John W. Dower, *Embracing Defeat: Japan in the Wake of World War II* (New York: New Press, 1999), especially ch. 2, "Kyodatsu: Exhaustion and Despair."

11. I use "new middle class" in, for example, "Finding a Place in Metropolitan Japan: Ideologies, Institutions, and Everyday Life," in *Postwar Japan as History*, edited by Andrew S. Gordon (Berkeley: University of California Press, 1993), 189–216. "Managed society" is a term given currency by Kurihara Akira, *Kanri shakai to minshū risei: Nichijō ishiki no seiji shakaigaku* (The managed society and popular reason: The political sociology of everyday consciousness) (Tokyo: Shin'yosha, 1982). Osawa Mari prefers "company-ism," which she has formulated in "Bye-bye, Corporate Warriors: The Formation of a Corporate-Centered Society and Gender-Biased Social Policies in Japan," *Annals of the Institute of Social Science* 35(1994): 157–94. See also Osawa (this volume). Takeuchi Yō has developed Japan as an educational credential society in 1995 in *Nihon no meritokurashii* (Japan's meritocracy) (Tokyo: Tokyo University Press, 1995). Tessa Morris-Suzuki wrote earlier of Japan's "informational capitalism" in *Beyond Computopia: Information, Automation, and Democracy in Japan* (London: Kegan Paul International, 1988).

12. Pierre Bourdieu and Jean-Claude Passeron, *Reproduction in Education, Society, and Culture* (London: Sage Publications, 1990), 5.

13. William Kelly, "Japanology Bashing," *American Ethnologist* 15(May 1988): 365–68; John Lie, "The Discourse of Japaneseness," in *Japan and Global Migration*, edited by Mike Douglass and Glenda Roberts (London: Routledge, 2000), 70–90.

14. See William Kelly, "Japanese Farmers," *Wilson Quarterly* 14(Autumn 1990): 34–41; William Kelly, "Regional Japan: The Price of Prosperity and the Benefits of Dependency," *Daedalus* 119(Summer 1990): 209–27.

15. Glen H. Elder Jr., *Children of the Great Depression: Social Change in Life Experience* (Chicago: University of Chicago Press, 1974).

16. David W. Plath, "The Eighty-Year System: Japan's Debate over Lifetime Employment in an Aging Society," *The World and I* 3(May 1988): 464–71; Inoue Shun et al., eds., *Raifu kōsu no shakaigaku: Gendai shakaigaku* (Sociology of the life course: Contemporary sociology), vol. 9 (Tokyo: Iwanami shoten, 1996).

17. Anne Allison, *Permitted and Prohibited Desires: Mothers, Comics, and Censorship in Japan* (Boulder: Westview Press, 1996); Osawa Mari, *Kigyō chūshin shakai o koete: Gendai Nihon no jendaa de yomu* (Overcoming the corporate-centered society) (Tokyo: Jiji tsūshin sha, 1993).

18. See, for example, Walter D. Edwards, *Modern Japan Through Its Weddings: Gender, Person, and Society in Ritual Portrayal* (Stanford: Stanford University Press, 1989).

19. Although I have been referring to these thematics as "discourses," to be more precise we must understand them both as discourses—the procedures for and substance of the situated talk that fashions social identities—and as ideologies—representations of knowledge and experience that articulate interests in a way by which compliance may be both secured and contested.

20. On this twentieth-century history, see Takeuchi Yō, "Sarariiman to iu shakai-teki hyōchō" (The social symbol of the salaryman), in *Nihon bunka no shakaigaku: Gendai Shakaigaku* (The sociology of Japanese culture: Contemporary sociology), vol. 23, edited by Inoue Shun et al. (Tokyo: Iwanami shoten, 1996), 125–42; Andrew Gordon, *The Evolution of Labor Relations in Japan: Heavy Industry, 1853–1955* (Cambridge, Mass.: Harvard University Press, 1985); Andrew Gordon, *The Wages of*

*Affluence: Labor and Management in Postwar Japan* (Cambridge, Mass.: Harvard University Press, 1998); Gordon (this volume).

21. Osawa Mari discusses this in detail in her contribution to this volume. See also Kathleen S. Uno, "The Death of 'Good Wife, Wise Mother'?" in Gordon, *Postwar Japan as History*, 293–322.

22. A recent useful characterization is Okano Kaori and Tsuchiya Motonori, *Education in Contemporary Japan: Inequality and Diversity* (Cambridge: Cambridge University Press, 1999).

23. It is important to note that however closely articulated these institutional arenas had become, their emergence was uncertain, fitful, and distinct. For instance, the rapid drop in fertility, from over four children per family to two per family, took place quickly in the first half of a single decade, the early 1950s, underwriting a family form that would persist for forty years. See Yamamura Kozo and Susan B. Hanley, "'Ichi Hime, ni Taro': Educational Aspirations and the Decline in Fertility in Postwar Japan," *Journal of Japanese Studies* 2(Winter 1975): 83–125. Subsequently, in the late 1950s and early 1960s, the concessions in self-determination that workers traded for more secure work conditions and wages eroded union autonomy but promoted mainstream allegiance among blue-collar workers (Gordon, *The Wages of Affluence*). Simon Partner has shown that the consumer revolution that embraced the electrical goods industry was not complete until the late 1960s, while the participation of youth in secondary and tertiary education did not reach high levels until the mid-1960s. See Simon Partner, *Assembled in Japan: Electrical Goods and the Making of the Japanese Consumer* (Berkeley: University of California Press, 1999); on education, see Thomas P. Rohlen, *Japan's High Schools* (Berkeley: University of California Press, 1983).

24. William Kelly "Directions in the Anthropology of Contemporary Japan," *Annual Review of Anthropology* 20(1991): 395–431.

25. William E. Steslicke, "The Japanese State of Health: A Political-Economic Perspective," in *Health, Illness, and Medical Care in Japan: Cultural and Social Dimensions*, edited by Edward Norbeck and Margaret Lock (Honolulu: University of Hawaii Press, 1987), 24–65.

26. The United Nations defines an aged population as one in which at least 7 percent of citizens are sixty-five or older. It took the United States seventy years for the percentage of elderly to climb from 7 percent to 14 percent; the same increase took forty-five years in Great Britain and Germany, eighty-five years in Sweden, but only twenty-five years in Japan. These and other statistics are drawn from Ministry of Public Welfare, ed., *Shōshi shakai o kangaeru* (Thinking about a society with few children), Ministry White Paper for Heisei 10 (Tokyo: Ministry of Public Welfare, 1998).

27. John Creighton Campbell, *How Policies Change: The Japanese Government and the Aging Society* (Princeton: Princeton University Press, 1992); Hashimoto Akiko, *The Gift of Generations: Japanese and American Perspectives on Aging and the Social Contract* (Cambridge: Cambridge University Press, 1996); Susan Orpett Long, ed., *Caring for the Elderly in Japan and the United States: Practices and Policies* (London: Routledge, 2000). John Campbell does, however, take an optimistic view of the potential of the new long-term care insurance program instituted in 2000. John Campbell, "Changing Meanings of Frail Old

People and the Japanese Welfare State," in Long, *Caring for the Elderly,* 82–97.

28. David Plath uses this phrase in "The Age of Silver: Aging in Modern Japan," *The World and I* 3(March 1988): 505–13.

29. Tanimura Shiho, *Kekkon shinai ka mo shiranai shōkōgun* (The I-might-not-get-married-after-all syndrome) (Tokyo: Shufu-no-tomo sha, 1990).

30. Ministry of Public Welfare, ed., *Shōshi shakai o kangaeru.* The 1999 rate dropped even further, to 1.34.

31. Ibid., 37, 59.

32. In a 1997 survey by the Prime Minister's Office, two-thirds of female respondents delaying marriage cited their increased economic resources through employment, and over half also cited the freedom of independent living. In another government survey that year, over half of unmarried female respondents age twenty-five to thirty-four cited not having yet met an appropriate potential spouse as their reason for remaining single; the second most common reason was an unwillingness to give up the freedom and pleasures they were currently enjoying. See ibid., 37. "Independence" is apparently more a measure of personal disposable income than a mark of independent living. Fully 80 percent of unmarried women in their twenties still live with their parents; even for those in their early thirties, the figure falls to only about 70 percent!

33. Ariyoshi's novel was translated into English by Mildred Tahara as *The Twilight Years* (Tokyo and New York: Kodansha International, 1984).

34. James E. Rosenbaum and Kariya Takehiko, "From High School to Work: Market and Institutional Mechanisms in Japan," *American Journal of Sociology* 94(May 1989): 1334–65.

35. Ishida, *Social Mobility in Contemporary Japan.*

# 11

## Twelve Million Full-time Housewives: The Gender Consequences of Japan's Postwar Social Contract

### Mari Osawa

On February 26, 1999, the Keizai Senryaku Kaigi, an advisory council on economic strategy chaired by Higuchi Hirotarō, submitted to Prime Minister Obuchi Keizō its report on strategies to revitalize the Japanese economy. The council demanded a transformation of the "Japanese-type system of society overvaluing equality and equity" into a "healthy and creative competitive society."[1] It is quite clear from this report that the members of the council assumed that Japanese society is not only egalitarian but in fact one where equality in income and asset distribution prevails. This view is endorsed by the nearly 90 percent of the population who perceive themselves as in the "middle" of society. Recently, however, these assumptions, the very basis of the council's proposals, have been seriously questioned.

A concise but profound book written by Tachibanaki Toshiaki, a professor of economics at Kyoto University, points out that the "income distribution of Japan is becoming unequal, and an international comparative study has shown that the myth of equal society [byōdō shinwa] can no longer be maintained."[2] Remarkably, this provocative book was awarded the 1998 Economist Prize.

According to Tachibanaki, income distribution in Japan since 1900 can be divided into three long-term phases: 1900 to 1945, a period of growing inequality; 1945 to 1973, a period of equalization; and 1973 to 1993, another period of increasing inequality.[3] This analysis focuses on interhousehold income distribution. Gaps in individual earnings are relatively small when compared by education level and occupation, but large compared by company size and particularly by gender. The latter two kinds of earnings gaps have been widening since the late 1970s.[4]

Thus, the myth of an equal society coincided with reality for individual earnings only during the period of high postwar economic growth. Nonetheless, the prime minister's highly prestigious advisory council is now laying out strategy and proposals for the new century based on the illusion of historical equality. To make strategy recommendations for the new century that are better attuned to social realities, the Japanese government needs to recognize the gender consequences of the approach it has taken to middle-class expansion and the postwar social contract.

As I argue in this chapter, the stay-at-home wife of the salaryman had emerged by the 1970s as an essential member of the ideal middle-class family. She took charge of her children's education, cared for her aging in-laws, and allowed her husband to concentrate on pursuing his corporate career. This ideal, moreover, shaped the very structure of Japan's social insurance programs. They were organized around the assumption that women would be available to provide care for needy family members and that women would be adequately served by social benefits for the family delivered directly to the primary breadwinner. This approach has always been an awkward fit with social reality, given the diversity of family circumstances in which Japanese women have lived. However, it is challenged today more than ever by the rising generations of women who are unwilling to accept the subservience and vulnerability that are their lot if they marry, have children, become stay-at-home mothers for a while, and then settle for part-time work thereafter.

## High Economic Growth and Family Change in Postwar Japan

### Labor Force Participation

During Japan's period of rapid economic growth from 1955 until the early 1970s, the average annual growth rate averaged 15 percent in nominal terms and 10 percent in real terms; other industrialized countries were growing annually at 6 to 9 percent in nominal terms. In 1969 Japan's gross national product became the second largest in the Western world, outstripping that of European countries. As a consequence of the high birthrate in the 1940s, 1.1 million to 1.4 million high school graduates entered the labor market each year during this high-growth period, providing employees for rapidly expanding industries.[5]

There was at the same time a mass migration of youth from rural to urban and industrial areas, while members of self-employed agricultural families left the land to become employees of companies.[6] Companies institutionalized the "nenkosei" (seniority wage system), for it minimized the cost of wages as long as the number of employees in the youngest age group increased. The prospect of long and stable employment until retirement age, which has often been called "shūshin koyō" (lifetime employment system), was enjoyed by blue-collar workers as well as white-collar employees thanks to the demands of in-house labor unions. So-called Japanese-type employment practices were thus formed through the joint efforts of management and labor under conditions of high economic growth.[7]

In the meantime, the number of women in the labor force increased, though it did not keep pace with the increase in the female working-age population. As a result, women's labor force participation rate declined until 1975. The decline in women's participation affected sectors differently. Most female family workers were in agriculture in the 1950s, when more than 40 percent of the employed were farmers. By 1975, however, the proportion of farmers in the labor force had declined to 14 percent. At the same time, the number of employees in manufacturing and service industries increased, and the proportion of women married to "salarymen" increased. This decline also affected age groups differently. The participation rate of women in their late twenties and early thirties declined significantly in the period of high economic growth (figure 11.1) and began to form the well-known M-shaped curve of female participation rate by age group that has remained constant to this day. A compulsory retirement system that forced women employees to stop working either upon marriage or at age twenty-five was openly applied in many companies and made it virtually impossible for women to work continuously throughout their lives.[8] Moreover, the relative inadequacy of public day care facilities in urban areas made it very difficult for women with children to be employed in anything except domestic work.

The growing emphasis on education for children also affected women's equality. The participation rate of youth in the economy, particularly those younger than twenty, fell to less than half in the same period (figure 11.1). The main cause was the dramatic rise in the number of young people remaining in school. The proportion of senior high school students, nearly 60 percent of the eligible population in the early 1960s, had stabilized at over 90 percent in the early 1970s. The number of junior high school graduates recruited by com-

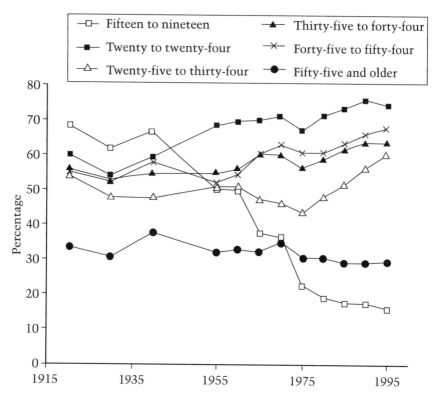

**Figure 11.1** Japanese Female Labor Force Participation, by Age Group, 1920 to 1995 *Source*: Sōmuchō (Management and Coordination Company), *Kokuseichōsa* (National census).

panies was surpassed by the number of senior high school graduates in 1965. Technological innovations required new workers with a relatively high level of learning.[9]

The increasing number of teenagers in school made entrance examinations more competitive. In the early 1960s, when the so-called "block (dankai) generation" born between 1945 and 1949 began taking the high school entrance exam, getting children into good high schools and colleges became the main preoccupation of families. The cliché "education mom" appeared in the press in the late 1960s for good reason: the mother came to have primary responsibility for the outcome of the competitive entrance exams.[10]

Similar factors led to an increase in the labor force participation rate for women in their late thirties or older (figure 11.1). A shortage of younger labor and rising starting salaries as early as the beginning of the 1960s led employers to try to mobilize middle-aged and older

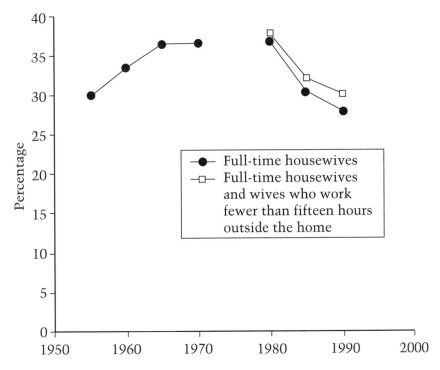

**Figure 11.2**  Percentage of Full-time Housewives of Salarymen Among Japanese Married Women, 1955 to 1990  *Source*: Sōmuchō (Management and Coordination Agency), *Kokuseichōsa* (National census) (1955 to 1970); Do., *Rōdōryokuchōsa Tokubetsuchōsa* (Labor Force Special Survey) (since 1980).

women. With the sharp decline in the birthrate in the early 1950s and the mass introduction into households of electric appliances such as washing machines, women became available for work. Their household workload was reduced, and their supplementary income was useful for meeting swelling household expenditures.[11]

Summing up, the number of full-time housewives of salarymen increased during the period of high economic growth and during the 1970s (figure 11.2). Their number increased from 5 million in 1955 to 11 million in 1980, but since the end of the 1970s, they have declined in number. After decreasing to 9 million in 1985, the number of full-time housewives stabilized around that figure. Simultaneously, the number of women working part-time has increased since the 1970s. Female part-time workers are overwhelmingly middle-aged married women, and since 1985 they have been regarded as dependents of their husbands in the basic pension system if their income is lower than 1.3 million yen a year and their husbands are employees. The

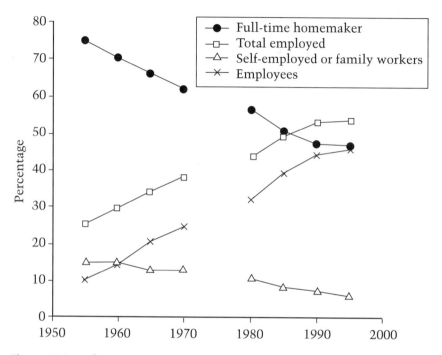

**Figure 11.3** Labor Force Status of the Wives of Japanese Salarymen, 1955 to 1995 *Source*: Sōmuchō (Management and Coordination Agency), *Kokusei-chōsa* (National census) (1955 to 1970); Do., *Rōdōryokuchōsa Tokubetsu-chōsa* (Labor Force Special Survey) (since 1980).

number of such dependent wives has reached 12 million. The proportion of full-time housewives among those married to salarymen has gone down steadily, from 75 percent in 1955 to 46.6 percent in 1995. Though the statistics are not continuous, it is safe to estimate that couples consisting of a salaryman and full-time housewife became a minority early in the mid-1980s (figure 11.3). The proportion of such couples among all married couples, moreover, has stayed at the 30 percent level it attained in 1955, reaching nearly 38 percent only during its peak in the late 1970s (figure 11.2). Despite these facts, the Japanese establishment still considers the nuclear family of a salaryman with a full-time housewife the "standard" Japanese household.

*Full-time Housewives and Salarymen*

We now turn to the question: Who are the full-time Japanese housewives and their husbands? And what kind of social consciousness do they have?

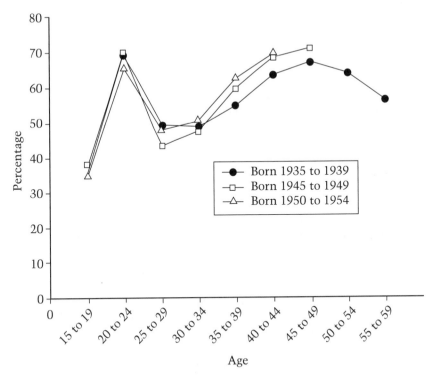

**Figure 11.4** Japanese Female Labor Force Participation Through Prime-Age Adulthood, by Age Cohort *Source*: Sōmuchō (Management and Coordination Agency), *Rōdōryoku chōsa* (Labor Force Survey).

Women's labor force participation rates, broken down by age cohort, show that the dankai generation of women born between 1945 and 1949 recorded the lowest figure at the bottom of the M-shape curve: 43.3 percent in 1974, when they were in their late twenties (figure 11.4). The number of women in this age group participating in the labor force was 3.5 million (70 percent) in the late 1960s, but only 2.2 million in 1974. In other words, 1.3 million women in this age group left the labor force during that five-year period.

It should be noted, however, that 1974 was an extraordinary year for employment. It was influenced by President Nixon's dollar shock in 1971 and the first oil crisis in the autumn of 1973. In the economic recession of 1974, the sharpest postwar downturn before the present recession, companies made concerted efforts to reduce personnel and rationalize their management, and their methods were not gender-neutral. From 1974 to 1975, the female labor force decreased by

600,000, while the male labor force actually increased by 570,000. In the same two years, the average labor force participation rate of women dropped by 2.5 percent to 45.7 percent—its lowest point in history—while that of men declined only slightly (by 0.7 percent to 81.4 percent).

The first oil crisis hit the employment of Japanese women significantly harder than that of Japanese men. This response was unique to Japan. According to the Organization for Economic Cooperation and Development (OECD), in no advanced country of the West did the rate of withdrawal of women workers from the labor force during the recession period of the mid-1970s exceed that of male workers.[12]

Broken down by age cohort, the female labor force participation rate showed the sharpest drop in the dankai generation of women, who were age twenty-five to twenty-nine in 1974. Around 80 percent of women in their late twenties were married then. It stands to reason that the great majority of women who left the labor force in the recession were married, and that they became full-time housewives. Until 1974, average real earnings by age for men born in the 1940s had been following the same upward path of the earnings of men born in the late 1930s (figure 11.5). Hence, dankai generation women quit their jobs presumably expecting that their husbands' earnings would rise as steeply as in the period of high growth.

Their expectation was not realized (figure 11.5). Dankai generation women who had quit jobs in their late twenties returned to the labor force in their late thirties; during their ten-year absence, there had been slow growth in their husbands' earnings. Still, according to a comparative study of the household income of employees in 1983 and 1984 conducted by Uzuhashi Takafumi, the proportion of household income from the wages and salary of the household head is significantly higher in Japan than elsewhere, despite women's return to work.

Uzuhashi shows that the proportion of household income from wages and salary was 94.9 percent in Japan, as compared with 85.9 percent in Korea, 81.2 percent for blue-collar workers in Germany, 83.1 percent for white-collar employees in Germany, 77.5 percent in the United States, 90.8 percent in the United Kingdom, 79.6 percent in Israel, 85.1 percent in Taiwan, and 86.7 percent in New Zealand. Of these, the average proportion of income from the wages and salary of the household head in total household income was 83 percent in Japan, as compared with 63 percent for blue-collar workers in Germany, 71 percent for white-collar employees in Germany, and 63 percent in Israel. The average proportion of household income derived from the wages and salary of wives of heads, on the other hand, was

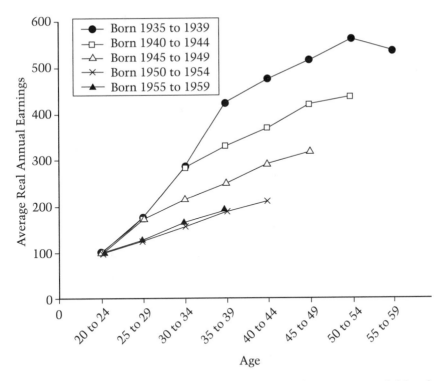

**Figure 11.5** Japanese Male Wage Progression Through Prime-Age Adulthood, by Age Cohort  *Source*: Rōdōshō (Ministry of Labor), *Chinginkōzōkihontōkei Chōsa* (Wage Census); Sōmuchō (Management and Coordination Agency), *Shōhisha Bukka Shisu* (Consumer Price Index).

*Note*: Average real earnings are indexed. Within each age cohort, 100 equals that cohort's earnings at age twenty to twenty-four.

only 7.9 percent in Japan, as compared with 11.9 percent for blue-collar workers in Germany, 8.8 percent for white-collar employees in Germany, and 14.4 percent in the United Kingdom.[13]

Uzuhashi concludes that the structure of Japanese employees' household income can be compared with that of other nations in three ways: as we have seen, the proportion of income from wages and salary, particularly of the household head, is high; the proportion of income from interest, dividends, and rents, as well as from social security benefits, is low; and income from wages and salary as well as income from interest, dividends, and rents and from social security benefits rise steeply by age. Hence, the economic health of the household depends on a "corporate job" for a long time, and the pressure on the male household head to earn such an income is intense. At the same time, the dependency of Japanese households on the state's social security system is very low compared with Germany, Israel, and the United Kingdom. Interhousehold assistance through gifts and remittances is thin compared with such practices in Korea and Taiwan.[14] Thus, the corporate-centered and gendered nature of Japanese society is clearly reflected in the structure of household incomes.[15]

A class analysis of SSM (Social Stratification and Mobility) survey data in 1985 done by Hashimoto Kenji shows that when their wives are not employed, men in the new middle class tend to be strongly aware of themselves as members of the middle class, to have lower consciousness of the working class, and to show higher support for the ruling Liberal Democratic Party. His definition of the new middle class is a class of men in professional, administrative, and clerical jobs and women in professional and administrative jobs. Hashimoto concludes that the households of the new middle-class men with full-time housewives form the core of corporate-centered society.[16]

On average, those men with full-time housewives are 44.6 years old, have 13.4 years of education, and earn 5.6 million yen a year. New middle-class men with working wives are 43.5 years old, have 13.2 years of education, and earn 4.9 million yen a year. The latter group is not so different from the former group in average age and years of education, but their average income is significantly lower than that of the men whose wives do not work. Also significant is that new middle-class men with full-time housewives are more likely to work for larger companies and to fill management positions, and less likely to be members of labor unions. Here we have the profile of "the new conservative" who maintains the corporate-centered society.[17]

## The "Japanese-style Welfare Society"

### Japan's Social Security and Welfare Services System

Social security in Japan today is the largest item in the national general budget, at 18 to 20 percent. On the expenditure side, there is no doubt that social security is at the center of the social policy system. The constitution of Japan has established citizens' right to live. The state's obligation to provide social security is found in section 25: "Every citizen has the right to live at least a healthy and cultural life," and, "The state should try to raise and promote social welfare, social security, and public health in every aspect of life." Japan's social security system comprises five areas: public assistance, social welfare, social insurance, public health, and support for war victims.

Four features were built into the system when it was designed during the period of high economic growth in the 1960s.

First, social security programs were implicitly designed to *supplement the family*, on the assumption that the family would extend help to any of its members in time of need. Hence, social security programs were quite ill equipped to help when families became increasingly unable to perform their function of rendering assistance to all members. This feature reflects the system's "subsidiarity," the concept that Gøsta Esping-Andersen uses in his typology of welfare state regimes.[18] I have called it *dependence on the family*. The principles of subsidiarity are revealed clearly in the Japanese practice of treating the household as a unit in administering public assistance and in the peripheral role of the children's allowance program. The principle of subsidiarity in public assistance dictates that a potential recipient's assets and capacity to work, his or her relatives' supportive capacity, and the various forms of assistance available under other laws should be fully evaluated before that person becomes eligible to receive public assistance (except in cases of urgent necessity). The range of in-law as well as blood relatives who must support each other is widely prescribed by the civil codes to include even the third degree of consanguinity—aunts and uncles are expected to support their nieces and nephews, and great-grandparents are similarly obligated to their great-grandchildren and vice versa. Subsidiarity in Japan's social security system is stronger than in the corporatist welfare states of Europe.

When the children's allowance program was finally established in 1971, it was touted as the completion of the Japanese social security system; Japan's system, it was claimed, had become just like those of the advanced Western European countries. In reality, however, the program provided only a tiny monthly allowance of several thousand yen for each child of a family beginning with the third child, until his or her graduation from junior high school, and on the condition that the family's annual income not exceed a certain ceiling. Moreover, the program was characterized not as an independent component of the social security system but merely as one of the children's welfare programs that constituted the social welfare system. When compared on the basis of International Labor Office (ILO) statistics, the ratio of Japan's outlay for family allowances to its total social security outlays was far smaller than in Western and Northern European countries, and even that ratio has been continuously on the decline.[19] The peripheral nature of the children's allowance program should be regarded as consistent with the principles underlying other Japanese social security programs, such as the principle of subsidiarity undergirding the public assistance program, the principle of treating a household as a unit in medical insurance, and the principle of treating a married couple as a unit in employee pensions.

The second feature of the social security system is that the image of the family and its functions upheld by the social security programs is based on a *stereotyped gender division of labor.* In this division of labor, the husband is the breadwinner, the wife takes care of domestic affairs, and she is thus implicitly dependent financially on her husband. As pointed out earlier, the proportion of this "standard" type of married couple stayed below the 40 percent level between 1955 and the mid-1980s. Thus, the social security system constructed in the period of high growth was designed on the questionable assumption that one-third of society defined the norm.

The gender bias is evident in the social insurance system's assumption that men are the standard insured. It recognizes as policy issues, and responds to, those "standard" risks that members of society are commonly thought to have. Conversely, we can identify those who are recognized as standard members of society from the risks covered by social insurance programs. Pension programs, for example, cover the risks of losing earning capacity at retirement in old age (superannuation) and of losing a breadwinning spouse or parent by death (survivor's pension). The employment insurance program defines "unemployed" as the condition of being unable to find a job while available for work, and it covers interrupted earning capacity. Treated as standard members of society are those individuals who engage in paid work throughout their productive years and maintain a spouse and children, then lose earning capacity only by mismatch in the labor market or at retirement. The bias of these laws is clear when we consider that a full-time housewife's loss of her husband through a no-fault divorce is equivalent to becoming unemployed. Yet under the social insurance system, losing a breadwinning spouse or parent through divorce is not recognized as unemployment, nor is the need to give up working to bear and raise children or to care for the elderly. Social insurance programs do not cover lost earnings in these cases.

Japan's social insurance system is diversified into a complex of component programs, each with its own financial requirements and specifications for contributions and benefits. The type of program an individual may participate in varies depending on a number of factors having to do with his or her occupational status, including whether the individual is employed, the industry in which the individual is employed, the size of the business entity for which the individual works, and the type of employment relationship. Needless to say, all these factors affecting occupational status are extremely gender-sensitive.[20] Women are normally assumed to be a dependent spouse of the insured in social insurance programs. The wife can share in the benefits that the programs guarantee her husband, but she can do so only incidentally and indirectly—she is not personally qualified to receive health insurance or pension benefits. This becomes immediately clear if we look at, for instance, the employees' pension system, which treats a couple as a single unit and regards the pension as payable only to the husband (the insured). Gender and occupational differences lie at the heart of Japanese labor policy and illustrate what I mean by the male-centered "gender bias" of the Japanese social security system.

The third basic feature of Japan's social security system is the license it gives to large corporations to operate programs of their own on terms that are very favorable to themselves and their own employees but inaccessible to outsiders. This reflects the system's *big company–centered nature.*

In the employees' health insurance system, the benefits available from a health insurance society, which is usually organized and managed by a large corporation with one thousand or more employees, are far greater than those provided by the government-administered employees' health insurance program, which covers employees of smaller companies. Because of their financially stronger conditions, the health insurance societies in the employees' system can also assess smaller contributions and pay better benefits than the government-run programs, and they often provide a wide range of fringe benefits and run various health and recreational facilities for the use of their own members and their families. In addition, the employees' pension fund programs operated by the larger private firms generously supplement their employees' old-age pensions with additional benefits.

The employees' pension fund system was established by the 1965 reform of the Employees' Pension Law, which contracted out the income-related portion of the state pension scheme. This law was applied mainly to larger firms, because an official permit to establish a fund required a membership of one thousand or more. These funds established by private firms to administer the contracted-out pension scheme proved beneficial to firms and their employees in a number of ways. Employees were able to draw lucrative pension benefits, which were 30 to 300 percent larger than those paid by the state pension scheme (the difference was called "plus alpha"). The companies, for their part, were allowed to operate their own employees' pension insurance systems as quasi-public programs with various tax incentives attached to them. These programs were also useful in nurturing a strong sense of affiliation and loyalty among employees.

The fourth basic feature of Japan's social security system is the exclusion of anyone who does not hold a *Japanese passport*. The system excludes foreigners in both principle and practice. Though the situation changed around 1980 after Japan signed the International Covenants on Human Rights and the Convention Relating to the Status of Refugees, support programs for war victims continue to exclude foreigners by nationality. Hence, Korean and Taiwanese war victims who were subjects of the Great Nippon Empire until 1945 are still denied any support or compensation.[21]

In sum, Japan's social security policies, along with the country's industrial and education policies, have contributed to the promotion of productivism and corporate interests, even if such contributions were somewhat limited during the period of high economic growth, when social security benefits were suppressed and the system counted heavily on the obligation of families to support their members. Moreover, in administering social security programs of such limited scope, the government has been extremely apprehensive that it might make some people lazy through indiscriminate public assistance. On the other hand, it has enabled regular employees of large corporations, a privileged minority among Japanese workers, to enjoy with their dependent family members far better security through occupational and state welfare programs. The great majority of employees of large corporations are male, while their female employees are young, unmarried women who usually quit after several years of service.[22] The big company–centered nature of the social security system significantly overlaps with its male-centered gender bias.

*Policies for a "Japanese-Style Welfare Society" in the 1980s*

It should not be overlooked that during the period of rapid economic growth the government was advocating, at least as a policy goal if not in practice, the need to make the Japanese "welfare state" comparable to those in Western Europe. And with the end of rapid economic growth at the beginning of the 1970s, the Japanese public began to want "not growth but welfare," and "not production but life." Under the administration of Prime Minister Tanaka Kakuei, legislation brought this desire to fruition in 1973, which is called "fukushi gannen" (the first year for welfare).

In the stagflation after the first oil crisis, however, the arguments for "not growth but welfare" faded away all too soon. "Overhauling welfare" became the catchphrase in the late 1970s. The government departed radically from its earlier policy goal and instead portrayed Western European welfare states not as models for Japan but rather as examples of the serious drawbacks of such systems that should be avoided by all means. A "Japanese-style welfare society"—with individual members of society, not the state, tapping Japanese "goodness and strength" to help one another—was loudly recommended at the end of the 1970s.[23] It was argued that welfare states were burdened with an overgrown public sector, and that under the pressure of the ongoing depression they were being pushed ever more deeply into fiscal crisis. Moreover, critics of the European model maintained that generous welfare programs made a country's economy and society inefficient and encouraged capital flight. The Ad Hoc Commission on Administrative Reform would base Japan's basic welfare policy on this idea.[24]

Before examining the reforms of the social policy system enacted in the 1980s, let us consider the aggregate expenditure of the Japanese welfare state in 1980 and its "type." First, social expenditure, defined by the OECD as social security plus education spending, amounted to 17.3 percent of GDP in Japan in 1981—the second-lowest figure among nineteen countries.[25]

Another way of looking at Japan's welfare system is to use the scale proposed by Esping-Andersen. Japan's welfare state regime conforms to the conservative corporatist model outlined by Bo Öhngren in this volume.[26] A more detailed look at Esping-Andersen's rating shows that Japan scores in the middle on his summary index of conservatism, high on liberalism, and low on socialism. Japan has a mid-level score for conservatism because its degree of statism, measured as expenditure on pensions to government employees as a percentage of GDP, is slightly over half of the mean for the eighteen countries surveyed, while its degree of corporatism, measured as the number of occupationally distinct public pension schemes, is rather high. Its score for liberalism is high because its degree of means-tested relief for the poor, measured as a percentage of total public social expenditure, is higher than the mean, and more important, because the degree of its market influence, measured as private-sector shares of total pension spending and total health spending, is high. Its score for socialism is low partly because its degree of universalism, measured as the average percentage of the population age sixteen to sixty-four eligible for sickness, unemployment, and pension benefits, is lower than the mean, and also because the degree of equality in the benefit structure of these programs is only half of the mean of eighteen countries.[27] In sum, the Japanese welfare state follows the conservative corporatist model with the stingiest benefits possible.

Yet another insight into the Japanese system comes from looking at it in light of the indices of female work desirability devised by Alan

Siaroff.[28] Female-to-male ratios of administrative and managerial workers as well as university and college students increased during the 1980s in Japan, though the gender ratio in wages not only did not improve but actually deteriorated. The index of female work desirability remained unchanged throughout the 1980s, while in other countries this index increased gradually. Thus, in the 1980s, even though the Japanese welfare state was close to "liberal" Anglo-Saxon countries in aspects of aggregate expenditure and degree of market influences, it was far from them in terms of female work desirability.

The reforms of the social policy system in the 1980s introduced under the slogans "overhauling welfare programs" and "establishing a Japanese-style welfare society" were meant to "reward" women for safeguarding the welfare of the family in their dual capacity of wife and mother. Such women were envisioned primarily as housewives who sometimes hold part-time jobs to supplement the family earnings. Accordingly, the reforms granted welfare benefits in the form of tax credits on earnings to the husband in order to maintain the gendered division of labor between husband and wife.

The reforms in the social insurance system were preceded by several reforms in the public assistance and social welfare programs. The latter shifted much of the responsibility for supporting a person in need from the welfare state to his or her family and relatives and lowered the upper income limit for eligibility. In other words, public assistance and social welfare programs became increasingly dependent on the family and increasingly selective in their application.

The series of changes in social welfare programs, beginning with a 1980 revision of the standard for charging fees to the elderly for accommodations in welfare institutions for the aged, fit this pattern. These changes included a shift of emphasis from institutional care to home care and a switch from free care to fee-based care, that is, the changes were part of a shift toward private-sector initiatives and away from public-sector initiatives. Changes in fees for accommodations were followed by two more initiatives in 1981: lowering of the maximum income for eligibility for the children's allowance and the "straightening-up" of public assistance. The benefits paid to "boshi setai" (female-headed households) were considered most in need of reform because a rising divorce rate had rapidly increased the number of such families since the beginning of the 1980s. Indeed, of the total number of persons receiving public assistance, members of female-headed families posted the most rapid increase. Local authorities therefore were repeatedly instructed to encourage mothers to press their former husbands more strongly to take responsibility for their children and to persuade these women to make a greater effort to work.

Another reform based on much the same philosophy was that of giving precedence to the neediest female-headed households in the allocation of the child-rearing allowance. The income ceiling making a needy family eligible to receive the allowance was lowered, and the amount of the allowance for poorer groups was raised slightly (by only three hundred yen a month) to give precedence to the neediest. Government offices such as the Management and Coordination Agency and the Board of Audit warned that both the marital status of mothers heading single-parent families and the incomes of their partners, if any, were not being accurately assessed, and therefore that such mothers sometimes continued to receive the allowance illegally after remarriage.

Efforts to reform public assistance programs and give precedence to the poorest strata of fatherless households in the allocation of child-rearing allowances were undertaken to strengthen a preconceived notion of the best kind of Japanese household, but they clearly did not improve the living standard of female-headed households. Indeed, the implication of these efforts was that the well-being of a woman who has abandoned the role of wife is not worthy of public support, even if the "base" of her home has grown extremely weak because she continues to fill the role of mother. The assumption of these policy measures was that a woman's most important role is that of wife, one who sustains a male corporate-warrior. The wholesale efforts to make the social security system ever more dependent on the family were in effect measures to beef up the system's male-centered orientation.

The basic structure of Japan's social insurance programs was not substantially changed. Regular employees of large corporations continued to be treated most favorably. For example, the ratio of supplementary health insurance benefits, paid typically by the health insurance societies organized at the larger corporations, to total benefits declined in 1982, but soon increased again to about 5 percent of the legally specified benefits. This increase can partly be ascribed to the 1984 reform that enabled the societies to provide new supplementary benefits. In addition, these societies have continued to spend more than twice the amount of supplementary benefits to operate health and recreational facilities to promote the health of the insured and their dependents. The discrepancies in expenditures made by companies of different sizes for health and recreation-related services are far greater than the differences in their expenditures for their employees' housing programs; these discrepancies have increased since the mid-1970s.

In another arena, private pension programs, including corporate pensions, have expanded their share of the old-age pension system. In April 1984, the Ministry of Health and Welfare approved the pension programs of two companies, Mitsubishi and Ajinomoto, that offered 300,000 yen a month in pension benefits. Large corporations prefer to increase their own corporate pensions rather than increase their contributions to the public pension system, which is accessible to outsiders. In retrospect, we might suspect that one of the main purposes of the cutbacks to the publicly administered old-age pension programs was to promote such corporate programs.

A recalculation of the pension budget carried out in 1980 revealed that the pension budget at the beginning of the twenty-first century would be far more costly than was projected in the 1970s. Concurrent with the recalculation, the Ministry of Health and Welfare commissioned a study of corporate pension programs. The report, compiled in July 1981, argued that public pension programs in Japan covered areas that in Western countries were usually covered by corporate pension programs. As a result, the report maintained, corporate pension programs in Japan had been restricted to less significant roles than their counterparts abroad.

The report offered no grounds for this argument. As mentioned earlier, the private-sector share of total pension spending was relatively high in Japan at 1980, actually the third-highest among the eighteen countries in Esping-Andersen's analysis. The government-sponsored report asserted, however (albeit in a roundabout manner), that the benefit levels of the public pension programs should be reduced, and that corporate pension programs should be expanded by every means possible.

Among the steps subsequently taken to make the employees' pension fund system more "flexible" were the granting in 1984 of greater freedom to corporations in the design of their supplementary pension fund benefits and the easing in 1989 of many restrictions on how these funds managed their assets, a measure that they had been eagerly seeking for many years. The supplementary benefits per employee provided by the employees' pension funds of larger corporations are far greater than those paid by smaller ones, and the discrepancies between companies of different sizes have widened since the mid-1970s.

At the same time, virtually all of the reforms undertaken during the 1980s failed to reverse, even minutely, the gendered division of labor. Only the introduction of the "basic pension," which takes the individual as the unit for pension calculation, partially offset the employee pension system's practice of treating a married couple as one unit.

This new system, however, treats the individual as a unit only halfheartedly. An employee's wife whose income is lower than 1.3 million yen a year is regarded as a dependent of her husband and classified as an "insured person of category 3" and thus exempted from paying the premium for herself. The number of women in category 3 has stayed at just 12 million. Once the annual income of an employee's wife exceeds the ceiling of 1.3 million yen, she must start paying her own premiums in the capacity of an insured person of category 2 (when employed) or category 1 (when operating her own business), but she also loses her qualification as a category 3 insured person when her husband leaves or loses his job. Also, the 50,000-yen-a-month housewife's pension benefit (in 1984 prices), which becomes available after forty years' participation in the program, is not likely to upset the gendered division of labor. On the contrary, the basic pension program, with its prescription for category 3, encourages a married woman to ensure that, even if she seeks employment, her income always remains under 1.3 million yen a year. In other words, she is encouraged to work on a part-time, not full-time, basis.

In the 1990s, the only major reform of the social security system was legislation covering long-term care insurance, which was implemented in April 2000 in a seriously anomalous way. It was a lost decade for social security reform. The increase in the percentage of women in the Japanese workforce since 1975—the so-called feminization of employment—seems to have had a far greater impact on the gendered nature of the system than any reforms to the system. In the 1980s, there was much talk of the "social advancement of women," and the decade was called the "era of women." The Equal Employment Opportunity Law was passed, and the female worker protection clauses of the Labor Standard Law were relaxed in 1985. Japan also ratified the United Nations Convention on the Elimination of All Forms of Discrimination Against Women.

Despite these ostensible gains, the overall wage gap between Japanese women and men, including part-time workers, has widened since the late 1970s. The percentage of women in each employees' social insurance program has either remained unchanged or increased only slightly during this period. The proportion of women among the insured has also decreased (see figure 11.6). In other words, the number of employed women not covered by any of the programs because of their status as "paato" (part-time workers) has increased significantly.

After the Equal Employment Opportunity Law (EEOL) was implemented in 1986, the number of female employees in non-agricultural sectors had increased by over 5.3 million by the end of 1997, but 3.9 million of them were part-timers working less than thirty-five hours a week. If those part-time employees working longer hours had been included, the growth of part-time employment in the period would have been even more rapid. The overall gender wage gap in Japan has

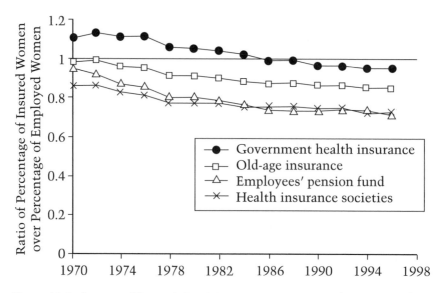

**Figure 11.6** Japanese Women's Participation in Various Employees' Social Insurance Programs, 1970 to 1996   *Source*: Sorifu Shakaihoshō Seido Shingikai Jimukyoku (Prime Minister's Office, Secretariat for the Advisory Council on Social Security); *Shakaihoshō Tokei Nenpou* (Yearbook of Social Security Statistics); Rōdōshō Fujinkyoku (Ministry of Labor Women's Bureau), *Hataraku josei no jitsujō* (Situation of working women).   *Note*: Figures are ratios of the percentage of women insured in each program over the percentage of total number of female employees.

widened because there has been such an increase in the number of women part-time workers at the same time that the wage gap between women full-time workers and part-time workers has widened.

How can we evaluate the policies relating to women in the 1980s? It is well known that Japan's original EEOL stipulated only that employers make efforts to treat women and men equally in recruitment, hiring, placement, and promotion and prohibited discrimination against women in education and training, occupational welfare, retirement, and discharge (without sanctions). It did not introduce any new provision on wage discrimination, which has been officially prohibited by the Labor Standard Law since 1947. In the Ministry of Labor's view, recruiting and hiring women only for part-time jobs or subsidiary jobs does not violate the EEOL.[29] According to its new interpretation, "women-only" jobs widen job opportunities for women and are consistent with the goals of the law, while "men-only" jobs are unlawful. In other words, the EEOL adopted the weakest policy possible, one that effectively encourages gender discrimination while, at least from an official point of view, obscuring it.

On the outcomes of the original EEOL, Hanami Tadashi, then chairman of the Central Labor Standards Council, saw that private companies were increasingly differentiating their workers into two distinctive groups to use them more effectively. One group consisted of a small number of efficient (male) core workers, and the other included a "large number of peripheral workers who can be readily replaced." "It is obvious," Hanami concluded, "that women and immigrant workers are expected to constitute the latter group. The gist of the problem is that laws such as the Equal Employment Opportunity Law fit in perfectly with this design."[30] In other words, the law in effect sanctioned the marginalization of female workers. Was that a by-product of its policy goal—or the goal itself?

When the reformed EEOL was implemented a decade later, in April 1999, the proportion of various "atypical" workers, including part-time female workers, had reached 45 percent. These workers continue to be unable to claim equal treatment with male regular workers under the EEOL, for their work conditions are inferior not because of gender but because of their employment category. Although the EEOL had been reformed and strengthened significantly, very little has changed for 12 million Japanese full-time housewives.

## Notes

Japanese names appear with last names first, even in English-language publications.

1. Keizai Senryaku Kaigi, *Nihon keizai saisei heno senryaku tōshin* (The report on the strategy to revitalize the Japanese economy) (Tokyo: Keizai Senryaku Kaigi, 1999), 1, 3, 17.
2. Tachibanaki Toshiaki, *Nihon no keizai kakusa* (Economic stratification in Japan) (Tokyo: Iwanami shinsho, 1998), 205.
3. Ibid., 67.
4. Ibid., 95–105.
5. Itō Masanao, "Seichō keizai, kigyō, to kokka" (Growing economy, corporations, and the state), in *Gendai Nihon shakai ron* (On contemporary Japanese society), edited by Watanabe Osamu (Tokyo: Rōdōjunpōsha, 1996), 218.
6. Kase Kazutoshi, *Shūdan shushoku no jidai* (The era of collective recruitment) (Tokyo: Aoki shoten, 1997).
7. Nomura Masami, *Shūshin koyō* (Lifetime employment) (Tokyo: Iwanami shoten, 1994).
8. Kumazawa Makoto, *Portraits of the Japanese Workplace, Labor Movements, Workers, and Managers,* edited by Andrew Gordon, translated by Andrew Gordon and Mikiso Han (Boulder: Westview Press, 1996), 164, 168.
9. Itō, "Seichō keizai," 216–18.
10. Nakanishi Shintarō, "Kodomo" (Children), in Watanabe, *Gendai Nihon shakai ron,* 420–22.

11. Oba Ayako and Ujihara Shojirō, eds., *Gendai fujin mondai kōza 2: Fujin rōdō* (Series on contemporary women's problems, vol. 2: Women's labor) (Tokyo: Akishobō, 1969), 355–56.

12. Organization for Economic Cooperation and Development, *The 1974–1975 Recession and the Employment of Women* (Paris: OECD, 1976).

13. Uzuhashi Takafumi, *Gendai fukushi kokka no kokusai hikaku: Nihon moderu no ichizuke to tenbō* (International comparison of contemporary welfare states: In search of the position of the Japanese model) (Tokyo: Nihonhyōronsha, 1997), 44–50.

14. Ibid., 67.

15. Osawa Mari, *Kigyō chūshin shakai o koete: Gendai Nihon no jendaa de yomu* (Transcending the corporate-centered society) (Tokyo: Jiji tsūshin sha, 1993); Osawa Mari, "Bye-bye, Corporate Warriors: The Formation of a Corporate-Centered Society and Gender-Biased Social Policies in Japan," *Annals of the Institute of Social* Science 35(1994): 157–94; Osawa Mari, "Will the Japanese Style System Change?: Employment, Gender, and the Welfare State," *Journal of Pacific Asia* 3(1996): 69–94.

16. Hashimoto Kenji, "'Kigyō shakai' Nihon no kaikyū/kaisō kōzō to josei rōdōsha" (Class formation of Japanese corporate-centered society and women workers), *Nihon Rōdō Shakai Gakkai Nenpō* (Annals of the Japan Association of Labor Sociology) 6(1995): 74–75.

17. Ibid., 75.

18. Gøsta Esping-Andersen, *The Three Worlds of Welfare Capitalism* (Princeton: Princeton University Press, 1990), 27.

19. International Labor Office, *The Cost of Social Security: Thirteenth International Inquiry, 1984–1986* (Geneva: ILO, 1992), tables 7 and 10.

20. Osawa Mari, "The Feminization of the Labor Market," in *The Political Economy of Japanese Society*, vol. 2: *Internationalization and Domestic Issues*, edited by Banno Junji (Oxford: Oxford University Press, 1998), 143–74.

21. Tanaka Hiroshi, "Nihon ni okeru gaikokujin rōdōsha mondai" (Guest workers' problems in Japan), *Shakai-seisaku akkai Nenpō* (Annals of the Society for the Study of Social Policy) 38(1994).

22. Mary Brinton, *Women and Economic Miracle: Gender and Work in Postwar Japan* (Berkeley: University of California Press, 1993), 51–52.

23. Tada Hidenori, *Gendai Nihon shakaihoshō ron* (On the contemporary Japanese social security system) (Tokyo: Koseikan, 1994); Osawa, "Bye-bye, Corporate Warriors."

24. Shinkawa Toshimitsu, *Nihon-gata fukushi no seijikeizaigaku* (The political economy of Japanese-style welfare) (Tokyo: San'ichishobou, 1993).

25. Mori Kenzō, *Igirisu fukushi kokka no kenkyū* (On the British welfare state) (Tokyo: Tokyodaigakushuppankai, 1990), 338–39.

26. According to Esping-Andersen, Japan's decommodification score is in the middle with Italy, France, Germany, Finland, and Switzerland. The indices of decommodification are the ratio of social insurance benefits (pension, unemployment insurance, sick insurance) to after-tax earnings (the replacement rate); the number of years of contributions required to qualify for a standard pension; and the individual's share of pension financing. Unfortunately, however, Esping-Andersen's scoring is not sufficiently consistent, especially for Japan and the United States. There are mistakes in either the decommodification scoring of old-age pensions,

sickness benefits, and unemployment insurance or the combined score. The decommodification score of Japan's three programs is only 22.3 in aggregate, while the combined score is 27.1. If 22.3 is valid, Japan scores in the low-decommodification group with typically "liberal" welfare states. Esping-Andersen, *The Three Worlds of Welfare Capitalism*, 50, 52, 54.

27. Ibid., 70–71, 74.
28. Alan Siaroff, "Work Welfare and Gender Equality: A New Typology," in *Gendering Welfare States*, edited by Diane Sainsbury (Thousand Oaks: Sage Publications, 1994). Siaroff's figures are for the 1980s.
29. Nakajima Michiko, Yamada Shozō, and Nakashita Yūko, *Danjo dōitsu chingin* (Equal pay for women and men) (Tokyo: Yūhikaku sensho, 1994), 259–63.
30. Hanami Tadashi, "Nihon-teki sabetsu no kōzō" (The structure of Japanese-style discrimination) *Jurisuto* 988(October 15, 1991): 17.

# *Part III*

---

# VANISHING BORDERS AND THE SOCIAL CONTRACT

# 12

## Disinflationary Adjustment: The Link between Economic Globalization and Challenges to Postwar Social Contracts

### Nobuhiro Hiwatari

The most significant change in the global economy since the first oil crisis of the mid-1970s has been the drastic increase in the movement of capital across national borders, a change that dwarfs the increase in trade. The expansion of both capital movement and trade in recent years has been concentrated among the advanced industrial states.[1] The era of mobile capital coincides with an unequivocal convergence toward lower inflation rates among all industrial democracies. Indeed, recent inflation and capital mobility trends are closely interrelated (see figure 12.1). The quadrupling of oil prices known as the first oil crisis triggered high inflation and induced the recycling of petrodollars, a development that in turn generated the increase in global capital mobility.[2] Since the mid-1970s, the flow of global capital has forced governments with inflation rates higher than those of their trading partners to carry out disinflationary policies, which usually lead to cuts in budget deficits and government expenditures, even at the cost of significant unemployment. Indeed, in the 1980s, as disinflationary policy became prevalent, most industrial states recorded unemployment rates not seen since the pre-war 1930s.

The inability of governments to guarantee employment and social protection, as they had prior to the oil crisis, has put the postwar social contract under stress and weakened the sense of security and entitlement among the middle classes. Noteworthy is the fact that

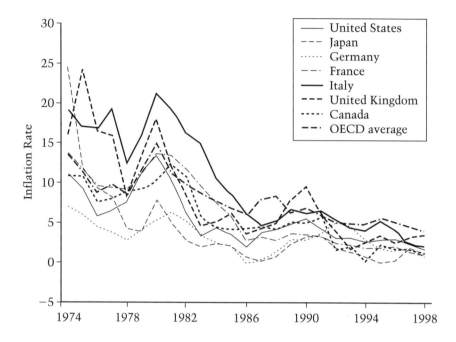

**Figure 12.1** Inflation in Seven Industrialized Countries, 1974 to 1998
*Source*: Author's compilation.

capital controls were regarded as vital in order to insulate the "embedded liberalism" of postwar societies—the common denominator of postwar social contracts in which states promoted economic growth and security (especially employment and social protection)—from the disruptions of the international economy.[3] No wonder globally mobile capital is a challenge to postwar social contracts. Indeed, many of the chapters in this volume depict the post–oil crisis years as a period in which the boundaries of the middle classes have been either changed or challenged. The disinflationary constraint is the link between the new global economy and the challenges to the postwar social contract.

This chapter hopes to explain how globally mobile capital has compelled governments, some more than others, to challenge existing social contracts (of employment and economic security) and to confront vested interests. More concretely, it first explains how capital mobility forces states to become disinflationary under the circumstances in which governments enact disinflationary policy and pursue institutional reforms even at the cost of an economic downturn and high unemployment. Contrary to society-centered liberal theory, which assumes that policy changes reflect the preference of dominant societal coalitions, I claim that governments enact disinflation policy in reaction to the dire economic consequences of high inflation, especially external imbalances and currency speculations. Under such circumstances, we see the government trying to mobilize the support of social groups, not social groups trying to influence the state. Second, this chapter focuses on the wage bargaining system as the institution that high-inflation countries are compelled to review and low-inflation countries have been able to reinforce. Third, I show that both high- and low-inflation countries have to face the issue of fiscal reconstruction (deficit reduction). Apart from increasing taxes, the major target for fiscal reconstruction has been social welfare expenditures.

Governments try to change (or maintain) the wage bargaining system and enact fiscal and social policy retrenchment in a coherent way. Some governments try to preserve existing social contracts by facilitating coordinated wage moderation and reaching a compromise among existing groupings, in pursuit of fiscal and social policy retrenchment; other governments try to renegotiate existing arrangements by confronting unions to change existing wage bargaining. In other words, we can expect to see distinctive government reactions to the global constraint of disinflation, and distinctive ways in which party governments challenge or reinforce existing social contrasts.

In this chapter, I explain why high inflation cannot be tolerated in a world of global mobile capital and construct three typical patterns of policy adjustment to the constraint of the new global economy. I then test my framework by examining the six largest industrial democracies—the United Kingdom, the United States, France, Italy, Germany, and Japan (which are also the countries discussed in this volume). Finally, I briefly recap the implications of this chapter's attempt to build a theory of democratic policy adjustments.

## The New Dilemma for Party Governments in a Disinflationary Global Economy

The drastic increase in global capital mobility, facilitated by financial liberalization, exerts a disinflationary constraint on all states.[4] As economies become more integrated in terms of flows in goods and capital, the differences in the interest rates among countries put pressure on the currency of those countries with a looser monetary policy. This happens because, with capital decontrol, capital flows toward the countries with a tight monetary policy (that is, higher interest rates), causing depreciation of the currency of countries with a looser monetary policy. The more integrated the economies, the less room there is for monetary policy divergence because interest rate differences generate severe exchange market pressure on the currencies. Thus, in a world of global capital mobility, the governments' ability to pursue autonomous monetary policy that diverges from that of the economically dominant low-inflation countries becomes restricted by exchange-rate disruptions and currency speculations. High inflation not only has the same effect as loose monetary policy but also appears in tandem with it because inflation rises when governments loosen their monetary policy to stimulate the economy. In short, governments are severely restrained in their ability to expand their economy unilaterally and are often forced to tighten their economy, even if doing so causes economic hardships. It might seem that the only exceptions to this constraint are countries that can expand their economies without igniting inflation above the inflation rates of their trade partners. However, even stable low-inflation states have had to prevent their anti-inflationary institutions from being eroded by increased global competition and by popular demands for government expenditure during economic downturns.

This systematic effect of global capital mobility has aggravated the fundamental dilemma in a democracy between a party government's need to enact disinflationary policies that are credible to the markets and its need to win democratic support for its unpopular policies if it is to stay in power. On the one hand, party governments that fail to enact disinflationary policies and maintain anti-inflationary commitments that are *credible* to the market become increasingly vulnerable to speculative attacks and more likely to lose control of the economy. Such a situation is sure to destroy the reputation of the government in power. On the other hand, the policies that such a government has to implement to assure the markets of its disinflationary commitment, such as tight monetary policy and expenditure cuts, are those that cause economic hardships and thus are unpopular with the electorate. In fact, speculation probably occurs when market actors suspect that an elected government cannot honor its anti-inflationary commitments because of their unpopularity.

An extensive survey by Barry Eichengreen, Andrew Rose, and Chares Wypolz of speculative attacks supports my contention that governments are compelled by global markets to enact disinflationary policies when their attempts to reflate the economy unilaterally cause high inflation that leads to an external economic crisis.[5] The symptoms of an external economic crisis are a rapidly deteriorating trade balance, currency speculation, and the depletion of foreign reserves as the government tries to stabilize the currency. Furthermore, governments must not only cope with temporary crises but also institutionalize anti-inflationary commitments, since the disinflationary constraint they face is permanent. According to Eichengreen and his colleagues, speculative attacks occur when economic fundamentals such as worsening current account deficits warrant currency devaluation but a government does not rein in its recent and sharp expansionary policy because of economic stagnation and high unemployment. In general, devaluations occur after periods of expansionary monetary policy because such policy leads to price and wage inflation, as well as weak external accounts and loss of reserves. Speculative crises are less predictable than devaluation because the market is betting against not only the deteriorating economic fundamentals but also the political resolve of elected officials to take painful and unpopular measures to restore economic stability. Facing such a crisis, governments try to convince the market of their disinflationary resolve by tightening monetary policy and starting to reform inflation-generating practices, in particular the wage bargaining system and government expenditures, even at the cost of a sharp economic downturn and a rise in unemployment, *until the inflation is subdued.* My case studies of disinflationary reform supplement the statistical evidence collected by Eichengreen and his colleagues by showing that currency crises have indeed compelled governments to start enacting disinflationary reforms and that this happened in the absence of any changes in the power of social groups.

The fact that capital mobility has imposed a *structural* constraint can be seen if we compare figures 12.1 and 12.2. On the one hand, the convergence among advanced industrial states toward lower inflation is clear. The steady trend implies that global forces have compelled governments to continue to adhere to disinflation. On the other hand, there is no discernible pattern with regard to unemployment except the fact that some countries have allowed it to rise to unprecedented highs. This means that countries are forced to control inflation at the cost of high unemployment. In other words, the decline of inflation cannot be explained by idiosyncratic characteristics or by technical or cyclical trends, but is the result of political choices within permanent constraints. The inability of elected governments to secure employment and their need to restrain expenditures in order to adjust to such constraints have forced them to review postwar social contracts.

## The Hypothesis: The Three Democratic Politics of Disinflationary Adjustment

The major argument of this chapter is that there are three typical patterns of democratic adjustment to the political dilemma imposed by the disinflationary global economy. Since the dilemma is between

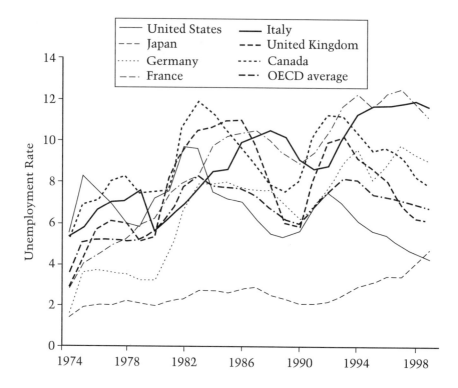

**Figure 12.2** Unemployment in Seven Industrialized Countries, 1974 to 1998
*Source*: Author's compilation.

credible policy commitment and democratic feasibility, the patterns derive from two factors: the extent to which unpopular reforms are necessary to lower inflation, and the way in which elected governments mobilize support to enact such unpopular policies.

With regard to the first point, the global economy distinguishes between two kinds of countries: *high-inflation* states that have to enact drastic reforms to lower inflation, and stable *low-inflation* countries that have to maintain anti-inflationary institutions. Under the disinflationary constraint of capital mobility, most countries have to change their wage bargaining practices and balance their budgets to lower inflation. Only major countries with constantly low inflation have to be concerned about preserving the anti-inflationary institutions of coordinated wage bargaining and fiscal discipline. Thus, global capital makes opposing demands on these two kinds of countries.

On the second point, countries should differ in how their governments mobilize democratic support for unpopular disinflation and retrenchment reforms. It has been widely accepted that among democracies there are two typical ways in which parties compete with each other to win popular support for their policies and control government to enact their policies: the *majoritarian* (Westminster) model of adversarial politics, and the *consensus* model of accommodative politics. To build a theory of policy adjustments in democracies, I extend the logic of the two democracies to the issue of how governing parties expect to mobilize support for and distribute the costs of establishing (or maintaining) credible institutions for disinflation.

The standard dichotomy of democratic politics has been best elaborated and empirically established by Arendt Lijphart.[6] According to Lijphart, the two types of democracies differ significantly in the number of parties that constitute the party system, the power concentrated by the executive branch, the electoral systems that shape the number of viable parties, and the way in which interest groups are organized in the policy process. The majoritarian type favors effective governing by the majority over responsive governing for the majority. Thus, the majoritarian democracies concentrate power in the representatives of the majority, and parties tend to be exclusive, competitive, and adversarial. Conversely, consensus democracies try to maximize the size of the majority by sharing, dispersing, and limiting the power of government, and party relations tend to be characterized by inclusiveness, bargaining, and compromise. The majoritarian democracies are characterized by two-party systems that are created by disproportional electoral systems (typically, single-member districts), which also help concentrate executive power in single-party majority cabinets that dominate the legislature. Furthermore, the governments in majoritarian democracies tend to avoid being captured by interest groups and prefer pluralistic competition between such groups. In contrast, the proportional election system of consensus democracies tends to create multiparty systems and coalition governments. As a result, the parties share power in government, in the legislature, and with corporatist interest groups in order to enhance policy accommodation and facilitate policy implementation. Lijphart's research on thirty-six democracies shows the empirical validity of the majoritarian-consensus dimension in classifying democracies.[7]

So far, I have explained the dilemma of party governments in realizing that disinflation can be captured by a framework that combines the extent of necessary reforms and the pattern of democratic politics in enacting such reforms. Furthermore, in making disinflationary adjustments, governments exert choices in three policy areas: monetary and exchange-rate policy, wage bargaining mechanisms, and fiscal and welfare retrenchment. With regard to monetary and exchange-rate policy, in a world of capital mobility a government can lower inflation (or keep inflation low) by raising domestic interest rates, at the cost of currency appreciation, or pegging its currency to that of a low-inflation country and allowing that country to set domestic interest rates.[8] In addition, governments wishing to counter inflation must change their wage bargaining practices, since it is well established that high wages are the major cause of inflation. To install wage moderation, governments can try to weaken and decentralize national union power based on the Calmfors-Driffill model (the centralization theme),[9] or it can promote export sector–led wages based on the Swenson model (the coordination theme).[10] The centralization theme claims that both decentralized and comprehensively organized centralized unions can restrain wages while intermediately organized unions cause inflation through competitive wage bidding. Decentralized unions are too weak to win large wage increases, whereas comprehensive unions can internalize the inflationary costs of their wage settlements and moderate wage increases to prevent high wages from increasing unemployment among their members. Intermediately strong unions, however, tend to bid up wages because they can force employers to accept high wage increases without internalizing the negative externalities of high inflation. Thus, the government can enfeeble inflationary wages by further decentralizing the unions. In contrast, the coordination theme, based on the specific factors model of international trade, argues that wage moderation happens when employers and unions in the export sector align to maintain international competitiveness and check domestic sectors from offering higher wages. According to this idea, a government can endorse coordinated wage bargaining to curb wage increases.

Finally, to make their disinflationary commitments credible, governments have to show fiscal responsibility and curb social expenditures because the accumulation of public debts (as a result of reflation during economic downturns) usually ignites inflation or signals the government's inability to make difficult choices. Governments can build fiscal credibility either by strengthening the power of the fiscal agency vis-à-vis spending agencies or by legislating a binding balanced-budget law to overcome the problems of fragmented decision-making.[11] In addition, governments can enact fiscal retrenchment and cut social programs by targeting programs that benefit specific groups, thereby alienating such groups, which have to bear the burden, or they can reform comprehensive programs and spread the burden.[12]

**Table 12.1   Patterns of Disinflationary Adjustment**

| State | Majoritarian Democracy | Consensus Democracy |
|---|---|---|
| High-inflation | | |
|    Monetary policy | Retains monetary autonomy | Fixes exchange rate |
|    Wage settlement | Confronts unions | Seeks union cooperation |
|    Fiscal adjustment | Caters to supporters and burdens opponents | Shares costs and benefits |
|    Welfare retrenchment | Specific programs | Comprehensive programs |
|    Applicable countries | United Kingdom<br>United States | France<br>Italy |
| Low-inflation | | |
|    Monetary policy | Retains monetary autonomy | Retains monetary autonomy |
|    Wage settlement | Preserves wage coordination | Preserves wage coordination |
|    Fiscal adjustment | Caters to supporters and burdens opponents | Shares costs and benefits |
|    Welfare retrenchment | Specific programs | Comprehensive programs |
|    Applicable countries | None | Germany<br>Japan |

*Source*: Author's compilation.

Now that I have clarified the alternatives that governments have, I now explain how they differ in each type of democratic adjustment. The results are summarized in table 12.1.

### High-inflation Majoritarian Democracies

Countries with majoritarian governments are characterized by centralized and strong executive powers, and the parties of such countries are institutionally compelled to mobilize support among exclusive groups and confront opponents. As a result, such governments can be expected to prefer to retain monetary autonomy in order to use their discretion in interest and exchange rates to mobilize support. Furthermore, to reform wage bargaining practices, majoritarian governments prefer to confront the unions and break "wage rigidity" by promoting union decentralization so that wages will be further set by the market.

Finally, to mobilize support for their disinflationary programs, the governments of majoritarian democracies can be expected to reward their constituents. Thus, it is in the interest of such governments to control a powerful fiscal agency. But since increase in expenditure is hard to come by, rewards are more likely to take the form of tax cuts and property rights. Moreover, when it is necessary to curb budget deficits, majoritarian governments prefer delegating power to the fiscal agency rather than passing a binding balanced-budget bill. To balance the budget, the tax system should shift the burden toward opponent groups, and expenditure cuts should target the programs that cater to them. Thus, tax reforms and proposals to cut spending programs are likely to target specific groups, be they the better-off or the poor. Conversely, comprehensive programs with a large middle-class constituency, like public pensions or health care, are likely to be protected. Although the radicalization of policies is constrained by the need to maintain a majority, disinflationary reforms in majoritarian democracies are likely to reproduce adversarial politics.

## High-inflation Consensus Democracies

Governments in consensus democracies have difficulty in building disinflationary credibility because they share and disperse executive power among several parties. Thus, these governments have a stronger incentive to establish binding disinflationary resolve by abandoning autonomy over interest rates and pegging their currency to an anti-inflationary international "anchor" currency. Furthermore, consensus democracies should be more likely to pursue wage moderation by promoting social partnership between employers and employees and coordinating wage moderation than by attacking and decentralizing the unions.

Finally, to gain consent to their fiscal and welfare retrenchment, consensus governments should try to distribute the costs of adjustment across the broadest range of groups. Thus, such governments are more likely to reform comprehensive programs with a large constituency, like public pensions or health care, than cut programs that cater to specific groups and offer side payments in exchange for retrenchment. Tax reforms and expenditure cuts that target specific groups are difficult because they contradict the need to forge a broad compromise among different groups, while employment programs are likely to be protected to win the cooperation of the unions in wage moderation. Also, consensus democracies are more likely to be compelled to show their fiscal resolve by passing a binding balanced-budget act. In short, governments in consensus democracies tend to depend on external discipline mechanisms, such as pegged exchange rates and balanced-budget legislation, to constrain themselves and credibly enforce disinflation while maintaining accommodative politics.

### Low-inflation Democracies

I assume that the distinction between adversarial and accommodative politics is less relevant in low-inflation countries because these governments are dependent on, and seek to preserve rather than change, existing anti-inflationary institutions. The task for low-inflation countries is to explain how they maintain monetary autonomy and wage coordination since those outcomes cannot be taken for granted. For instance, common wisdom expects global market integration to erode coordinated wage bargaining.[13] Low inflation tends to appreciate the currency, especially if wage coordination enhances export competitiveness that results in external surpluses and growth. Currency appreciation deepens the distributional conflict between the nontradable sector and international investors that prefer the ongoing trend and the tradable sector (both exporters and import-competitors) that prefers a lower exchange rate. This conflict threatens to undermine nationwide wage coordination since the export sector threatened by currency appreciation prefers wage moderation, while the domestic sectors can afford wage increases. More problematically, if the government loosens economic policy and lets the currency depreciate in the interests of the tradable sector, the economy may overheat, increasing inflationary pressure. The same danger appears if governments try to compensate wage moderation by increasing expenditure to promote employment. Thus, governments in low-inflation countries have to maintain fiscal policy discipline. In short, my framework predicts only that some external constraint related to trade surpluses will reinforce wage coordination and fiscal discipline and that the pattern of fiscal and welfare retrenchment will depend on the type of democracy.

## The Cases

Having laid out predictions on how each type of adjustment differs, I am ready to test the argument with concrete cases. I have selected the six largest industrial democracies—the United Kingdom, the United States, France, Italy, Germany, and Japan. I apply a focused comparison because detailed narratives are necessary to examine the different processes of disinflationary adjustment to establish causal links between the types of democracies and policy reforms. In the conclusion, however, I discuss briefly the applicability of this framework to other industrial democracies.

Looking back at figure 12.1, it is obvious that only Germany and Japan have had consistently low inflation rates. For most of the period under investigation, there has been a significant gap in inflation rates between Japan and Germany, on the one hand, and France, Italy, and the United Kingdom, on the other hand, with the United States recording intermediary numbers. Because high inflation in Japan and Germany has been exceptional and swiftly subdued, they are readily classified as low-inflation states. Japan's inflation shot up in 1974 to nearly twice the OECD average after the first oil crisis, but it had dropped to the OECD average by the following year; German inflation exceeded the European Union (EU) average only in 1992 and 1993 as a result of the reflationary policies needed to smooth German unification. Furthermore, neither Germany nor Japan was externally compelled to enact disinflation since both countries enjoyed a balance-of-payments surplus and currency appreciation (see figure 12.3). The inflation trends in figure 12.1 show that the United Kingdom, the United States, France, and Italy were forced to cope with inflationary tendencies in the late 1970s, early 1980s, and, to a lesser degree, early 1990s. The external balances depicted in figure 12.3 show that for the high-inflation countries, these periods coincide with external imbalances.

According to Lijphart's measurement, among our six cases, the United Kingdom is a typical majoritarian democracy, while Italy, Japan, and Germany are consensus democracies.[14] The presidential systems of the United States and France are hybrid systems. In Lijphart's overall index, France is in fact a majoritarian democracy, but that is solely the result of its highly unique and disproportionate electoral system. In all other indices, the French democracy is far less majoritarian than the United States and closer to Germany. If we rectify these problems, we can regard France as a (hybrid) consensus democracy. Incidentally, in Lijphart's index the United States appears much less majoritarian (or more of a hybrid) than usually thought solely because the uniquely American separation of powers nullifies the notion of executive dominance. In any case, however, the fact remains that the United States can be regarded as a majoritarian democracy.

As a result of these classifications, we conveniently have three pairs of countries—one pair for each type of adjustment politics. The United Kingdom and the United States are high-inflation majoritarian democracies, France and Italy are high-inflation consensus democracies, and Germany and Japan are low-inflation consensus democracies. The next section examines whether external imbalances trig-

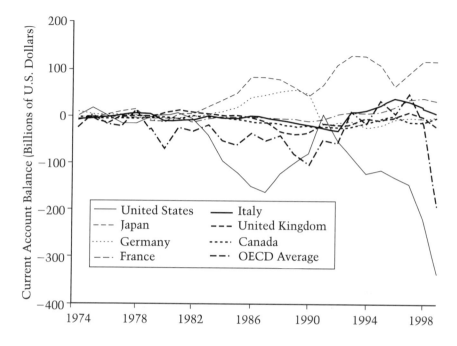

**Figure 12.3** Current Account Balances in Seven Industrialized Countries, 1974 to 1998 *Source*: Author's compilation.

ger disinflationary reforms and whether adjustment politics show the expected characteristics.

## The Evidence

*Disinflationary Reform by Adversary Mobilization: The United Kingdom and the United States*

The implementation of disinflation reforms in the United Kingdom and the United States after they suffered severe economic problems in the late 1970s shows the features expected from my hypothesis. Both governments embarked on disinflation in reaction to the inflation and balance-of-payments deficits of the late 1970s, and these measures led to institutional reforms in the early 1980s. The governments of both countries had built up their disinflationary credibility in the early 1980s by stubbornly adhering to extremely tight monetary policy until inflation was subdued, despite extraordinary rises in unemployment and exchange rates. To gain democratic support for such policies, the two governments mobilized pro-market forces by making them beneficiaries of tax cuts, privatization, and deregulation, while confronting the unions and targeting public assistance and employment programs to reduce the budget deficit. Both governments, however, were unable to realize their ambitious plans to overhaul universal programs such as public pensions and health care because of their broad popularity.

The United Kingdom and the United States also differed in a way somewhat expected from my hypothesis. Adversary mobilization was more straightforwardly seen in the United Kingdom—a typical majoritarian democracy characterized by intense partisan competition, strong party discipline, and cabinet dictatorship—than in the United States, where disinflationary reform had to accommodate its opponents because of divided government and weak party discipline in Congress. Interestingly, the desire to reward supporters during the boom of the mid-1980s weakened the British government's monetary discipline, overheated the economy, and aggravated inflation, and it eventually caused the market to attack the pound in 1992. The market bet against the government's commitment to protect the exchange-rate parity (which the United Kingdom joined in 1990) and continue tight monetary policy amid rising unemployment. Thus, the conflict between credible disinflation commitments and democratic politics resurfaced in the 1990s. The United States was able to ease that dilemma by reducing the detrimental effect of its disinflationary high interest (and high exchange) rate by forcing two of its trading partners, Germany and Japan, to appreciate their currencies.

In the late 1970s, inflation in the United Kingdom and the United States amid rising unemployment and external imbalances compelled these governments to enact disinflationary policies by adversary mobilization. In the United Kingdom, the Labour government, faced with high inflation and balance-of-payments and budget deficits in 1975 and 1976, announced large expenditure cuts despite high unemployment. By 1976, a sterling crisis had forced the government to ask for International Monetary Fund (IMF) aid and carry out sharp reductions in spending and public borrowing. The dramatic change in government policy led to the escalation of adversary mobilization. The "Social Contract Between Labour and the Trades Unions Congress (TUC)," in which Labour had promised to increase social expenditures in exchange for union cooperation with its incomes policy, collapsed. The TUC faced rank-and-file revolts over pay restraint, while the Labour government was weakened by backbench rebellions. The Labour-Left presented its "alternative strategy" of closed markets and radical socialism to guarantee employment after the 1976 expenditure cuts. Meanwhile, the Tory neoliberals condemned postwar governments for maintaining excessive money supplies and valuing full employment over inflation control.[15] The Labour government's request for continued pay restraint in 1979 triggered a wave of labor disputes that paralyzed public services and swept the Conservatives into power.[16]

In the United States, the rise of inflation and trade deficits after 1977, followed by stagnation and increased unemployment in 1979, compelled the Carter administration to compromise on tax cuts, deepen expenditure cuts, and delegate anti-inflationary autonomy to the Federal Reserve. The president's decision to cut back public works expenditures in the 1977 stimulus package and to drop the promised tax rebate out of concern for inflation strained his relations with congressional Democrats. The fear of inflation compelled the president to curb ballooning social policy expenditures, caused by cost-of-living adjustments, and overrule his advisers on an election-year corporate tax cut, while the Federal Reserve was given rein to pursue tight monetary policies. Meanwhile, the Republicans pushed for the drastic Kemp-Roth tax cut plan (a 30 percent income tax cut over three years), which Ronald Reagan adopted as the cornerstone of his economic recovery plan.[17]

Once in power, both the Thatcher and Reagan governments enacted reforms aimed at permanently reducing inflation. To reduce the budget and balance-of-payments deficits, the Thatcher government restrained money supply and applied high interest rates, allowing a rapid surge in the pound. Such a policy aggravated the recession and unemployment and caused the manufacturing shakeout of 1979 to 1981, which irreparably damaged the United Kingdom's endogenous export industries. The government curbed spending and increased the value-added tax (VAT) and national insurance premiums to reduce public debts. Fiscal austerity was maintained despite a harshly critical open letter from more than 360 economists, a large-scale cabinet revolt, and the eruption of riots in a number of cities in mid-1981. And as soon as the economy showed signs of recovery, easing budget restraints in 1983, the government started to cut income taxes but did not increase welfare spending until 1986.

The targets of fiscal retrenchment in the United Kingdom were employment and income support programs. Throughout the 1980s, the government incrementally tightened unemployment insurance eligibility, taxed unemployment and income support benefits, extended the contribution period for unemployment insurance, and linked welfare benefits with training programs. In comparison, ambitious ideas to reform universal programs such as public pensions and the National Health Service were mostly frustrated because of the popularity of these programs. The 1980 Social Security Act only went so far as to change the indexing formula and encourage private pensions, instead of abolishing the Supplementary Earnings Related Pension Schemes. Dismantling the National Health Service was never seriously contemplated, and health insurance reform consisted of increasing patient payments and encouraging the development of private health plans.

The prime minister mobilized the support of pro-market forces by expanding property ownership—council houses were sold, and public corporations privatized—and curbing the power of the trade unions in wage bargaining. The sale of public housing proceeded in several stages, with financial incentives, and the priority of privatization was to increase the number of individual shareholders and enhance government revenues rather than to encourage competition. To restrict the unions' strike activity in disputes, labor laws were changed frequently in the 1980s to make union leaders accountable to individual members by establishing regular secret ballots, protecting the individual against closed shops, and containing the scope of trade union immunities. Furthermore, the government prevailed in the confrontation with public-sector union militancy in the early 1980s that climaxed with the miners' strike of 1984 and 1985. As a result, the better-off unions and their members supported labor reform and embraced strike-free agreements, private health care, cooperation with management, and privatization (the "new unionism").[18]

In the United States, the Reagan administration advocated drastic tax and expenditure cuts, while the Federal Reserve continued a tight monetary policy. High interest rates to control inflation and fund the budget deficits were strictly adhered to even though they caused high unemployment, an unprecedented surge in the dollar, and significant damage to export industries. Compared to the Conservatives in the United Kingdom, however, the Reagan administration had to compromise on its reforms. The president's election pledge of lowering income and capital gains tax rates and installing accelerated depreciation on investment was enacted in 1981, with the help of conservative Democrats. However, Reagan's proposal to make drastic cuts in social welfare expenditures to fund the tax cuts did not materialize; spending cuts were made primarily in programs for specific groups. The 1981 Omnibus Budget Reconciliation Act tightened eligibility requirements and lowered benefit levels for means-tested assistance and reduced (or eliminated) employment and educational programs for the poor. In contrast, Social Security reform was limited to a bipartisan compromise to keep the program solvent, after it became a partisan issue that cost the Republicans the 1982 mid-term election. Ambitious health care reforms also did not materialize. Furthermore, after 1982 the budget deficit became a persistent problem, and a stalemate emerged in which the president insisted on tax cuts while the reunited House Democrats resisted domestic spending cuts, revived some of the social programs cut earlier, and passed some redistributive tax increases. This stalemate stalled fiscal reconstruction in the 1980s, and the tax reform was a revenue-neutral bipartisan compromise. Even the president had to compromise on his policy of limiting public assistance by agreeing to expand AFDC (Aid to Families with Dependent Children) and job training in the 1988 Family Support Act.[19]

Finally, both the United Kingdom and the United States used control over interest and exchange rates to cater to domestic demands. In the United Kingdom, retaining monetary autonomy destroyed disinflationary credibility in the early 1990s. Until 1984, the British government had tried to reduce money supply, and the prime minister had ruled out joining the ERM (exchange rate mechanism). Thereafter, between 1985 and 1988, when the economy showed strong signs of recovery with low inflation and a strong pound, Chancellor of the Exchequer Nigel Lawson did "shadow" the deutsche mark (that is, stabilize the pound's exchange rate with another currency). However, the purpose of this policy was not to counter inflation but to stimulate the economy by keeping interest rates low so as to cap currency appreciation. In other words, when faced in 1985 with the dilemma of defending the pound by raising interest rates and allowing the currency to depreciate, the chancellor chose growth over inflation reduction. When high wages and current account deficits provided obvious signs of an overheating economy, the prime minister did force the uncapping of sterling and the deutsche mark, but she refused to join the ERM, arguing that doing so would be tantamount to admitting that the government could not run its own anti-inflation policy. In reality, the Thatcher government was reluctant to employ the strong dose of necessary disinflation because the recession, with dropping house prices and a credit crunch, had hit the Thatcherite middle classes of southern England and was no longer confined to the blue-collar workers of the north and the midlands.[20]

When the United Kingdom did join the ERM in 1990, it did so in a way that weakened the disinflationary utility of fixed exchange rates and caused a political debacle that not only ended Thatcher's tenure but also set the path to a policy catastrophe that irreparably damaged the Tories. In exchange for joining the ERM, the prime minister insisted on and won an interest rate cut, which spoiled the purpose of joining to show anti-inflation resolve. Infighting within the Tory Party over European monetary integration eventually brought down her successor, John Major, as well. Blaming the ERM for the recession in the early 1990s, the Major government vacillated between spending cuts that risked deepening the recession and a relaxation of fiscal policy that would increase public borrowing. Since the United Kingdom refused to carry out a managed devaluation within the ERM or to raise interest rates to defend the ERM parity, investors began betting against the United Kingdom's publicly stated policy of remaining in the ERM, and this led to the pound's humiliating departure in 1992 amid speculation attacks. The Major government was severely discredited by its failure to remain in the ERM; that failure also left deep scars in the Tory Party and decisively reversed the popularity of the two major parties, opening the path to a Labour landslide in 1997.[21]

The U.S. government also used monetary policy to pursue its disinflationary goals. Unlike the United Kingdom, however, the United States could prod its trade partners to let their currency appreciate in order to ameliorate the domestic harm of high inflation rates and large trade deficits. Since the late 1970s, the United States, facing persistent trade deficits, has pressured trade-surplus countries like Germany and Japan (as well as Taiwan and Korea in the mid-1980s) to appreciate their currencies and enact fiscal stimulus packages to increase domestic consumption. During such episodes—initially in the late 1970s and again in the mid-1980s and early 1990s—the U.S. government coerced countries that ran large trade surpluses with the United States into appreciating their currencies, against the backdrop of emerging protectionism in Congress. In all of these incidents, once the dollar fell, the U.S. Treasury refused to intervene to support the dollar until the depreciation threatened to become inflationary, and then the Treasury made stimulation of the Japanese and German economies a quid pro quo for stabilizing the dollar. Thus, the uniqueness of the United States as the largest market and a key currency country enabled it to externalize part of the adjustment costs by threatening retaliation to pry open foreign markets, internationally funding its public debt, and forcing trade-surplus countries to coordinate exchange rates.[22]

To sum up, this brief description shows that disinflation in the United Kingdom and the United States basically fits our expectation. Both countries were compelled to undertake disinflation when attempts to reflate the economy in the late 1970s led to an external economic crisis. In carrying out reforms to institutionalize their disinflationary commitment, both governments sought to reward pro-market forces while they confronted the unions, targeted social programs catering to specific groups, and retained monetary policy autonomy. Furthermore, and also as expected, the British government fit our predictions of majoritarian disinflation better than the more hybrid majoritarian democracy of the United States.

## Disinflationary Reform by Accommodative Mobilization: France and Italy

As in the United Kingdom and the United States, it took an external economic crisis—currency depreciation and a worsening balance of payments—caused by high inflation for the governments of France and Italy to take countermeasures. Such problems hit France and Italy in the mid-1970s, in the mid-1980s, and in 1992 and 1993. However, in the mid-1970s the French and Italian governments, and the Italian government in the mid-1980s, were unable to muster enough democratic support to institutionalize credible disinflationary reforms. Attempts in the mid-1970s failed in both countries because the unpopularity of disinflationary programs led to a change of government or governing formula. As a result, the two countries by the mid-1980s had started to depend on external discipline to establish the credibility of their disinflationary commitment. External discipline took the form of abandoning monetary autonomy by tying their currencies to the deutsche mark and therefore synchronizing their interest rates with Germany's. Such externally imposed constraints helped the French and Italian governments to bind themselves, quell opposition, and spread the cost of disinflation by accommodating domestic groups. In both countries, the government sought cooperation from the unions to curb wages and tightened comprehensive programs to broadly distribute the costs of expenditure cuts. By depending on external discipline, the governments of France and Italy continued consensual reforms despite frequent changes in governments.

The difference between France and Italy also can be explained by the fact that France is more of a hybrid democracy, according to Lijphart, than Italy. France also differs from Italy in having decisively adopted disinflationary reforms after 1983. Ironically, because of its strong administrative state and the two-bloc competition, usually associated with majoritarian democracies, French governments made decisive policy changes in a more adversarial manner than did the more typically consensus democracy of Italy. Italy continued to backslide on disinflationary reforms as soon as external balances recovered, until 1992, when the markets questioned the credibility of Italy's commitment to making the reforms necessary to meet the tighter constraints imposed by the Maastricht Treaty. The accommodative politics of Italy undermined its disinflationary credibility until the EU issued a sine qua non that Italy had to meet if it wished to enter the European Monetary Union (EMU). When Italy faced another currency crisis in 1992, it totally rearranged its state institutions—including an electoral reform that made the system more majoritarian—to facilitate the effective implementation of disinflation.

France made a commitment to disinflationary reforms after the failure of a disinflationary attempt in the 1970s and another external economic crisis caused by the unilateral reflationary policies of the Mitterrand presidency. In the mid-1970s, shortly after the first oil crisis, Prime Minister Raymond Barre introduced policies to counter inflation after facing a large balance-of-payment deficit and high depreciation. Barre hoped to restore growth and competitiveness by lowering inflation instead of resorting to trade protection or public debt. Thus, Plan Barre consisted of monetary targeting, fiscal austerity, government credit restriction, control of the public sector and minimum wages, and the abolishment of control over industry. However, despite high interest rates, nominal wages continued to increase and unemployment soared. When widespread discontent with the Plan Barre enabled François Mitterrand to beat the incumbent in 1981, the new prime minister enacted ambitious policies to stimulate the economy in order to cope with unemployment.

Mitterrand's reflation policies caused double-digit inflation, capital flight, and a large trade deficit, despite three large negotiated devaluations between 1981 and 1983 within the ERM, during which Germany consented only after France promised to maintain a tight monetary and fiscal policy. After ruling out capital controls and coordinated reflation among EC countries (opposed by Germany and the United Kingdom), the French government sharply reversed its economic policy in 1983, steering it toward austerity ("rigueur") based on stabilization of the franc ("franc fort"). The new policy consisted of a public-sector wage freeze and a price freeze, and it continued despite a deeper recession and unprecedented unemployment. Thus, after 1983 France tenaciously pursued the policy of disciplining and strengthening the economy by synchronizing its monetary policy with Germany's. The policy was adhered to despite the franc crisis of 1992 and 1993 and changes in government—the "cohabitation" between 1986 and 1988 (in effect, a Gaullist government), the Socialist majority between 1988 and 1993, and a second "cohabitation" after 1993.[23]

Italy also took disinflationary measures when it was hit by external economic problems in the late 1970s and mid-1980s. However, Italy did not decisively enact disinflationary reforms until after the 1992 currency crisis, which had led to the collapse of the party system. Earlier reforms were stalled despite inflation remaining relatively high as the country improved its trade balance. In the mid-1970s, Italy devalued the lira and accepted measures dictated by the IMF when it faced labor militancy, wage inflation, budget deficits, and a balance-of-payments crisis. To achieve wage moderation and fiscal austerity, the government solicited the cooperation of the unions and the Communist Party (Partito Communista Italiano [PCI]) between 1976 and 1979. Although the unions cooperated, the Christian Democrat (Democrazia Cristiana [DC]) governments failed to deliver the reforms in agriculture, pensions, hospital pay, and law and order on which the PCI had insisted, and they rejected the party's formal entry into the government. By 1979 the PCI had lost a significant number of votes and was compelled to return to the opposition. Thus, a consensual political arrangement to enact disinflationary reforms collapsed.

The five-party coalition ("pentapartito") that succeeded the DC-PCI alliance was more assertive toward the wage increases of the early 1980s, when inflation worsened the balance of payments and caused successive devaluations within the ERM. The pentapartito, eager to weaken the PCI and the Communist-led union (the Confederazione Generale Italiana del Lavoro [CGIL]), reduced wage guarantees for discharged workers and unilaterally revised the "scala mobile" (wage indexation). However, such reforms did not extend to fiscal retrenchment because attempts to cap expenditures were undermined by the intense party competition between the DC and the Socialists within the pentapartito over the distribution of public resources. Meanwhile, the balance of payments recovered, the value of the lira stabilized, and the pentapartito parties continued the practice of using social welfare schemes to nurture partisan support, thereby aggravating the public debt and spreading corruption. Finally, however, the 1992 lira crisis showed Italy that it had no choice but to drastically reduce its public debts if it were to qualify for the Maastricht convergence criteria and remain in the EMU. The economic crisis triggered a political crisis that led to the reform of the electoral system, the collapse of the pentapartito parties, which were already crippled by the "tangentopoli" (Bribe City) scandal, and the emergence of new parties as well as the inclusion of the former Communist Party (Partito Democratico della Sinistra [PDS]). Thereafter, the so-called technocratic governments (as well as the Berlusconi government) tenaciously reduced inflation and enacted welfare reform to reduce the public debt (as explained later in the chapter), despite frequent changes of government coalitions composed of heterogeneous parties.[24]

When compelled to enact disinflationary reforms, the French and Italian governments tried to restrain wage growth and make retrenchments in welfare policy in accommodating ways that were unseen in the United Kingdom and the United States, although France was more adversarial than Italy. In neither country did the government openly attack the unions or target specific groups. For instance, in France, wage increases were controlled in the public sector by freezing wages in 1982 and thereafter by indexing wages to the official inflation forecast. In the private sector, the government had encouraged firm-level collective bargaining by empowering workers through the Auroux laws, which inadvertently facilitated firm-level incorporation at the cost of weakening union organizations. Furthermore, to accommodate employee interests, France expanded training programs, provided firms with hiring incentives, increased public-sector employment, and enacted early retirement programs. Instead of targeting employment programs, welfare retrenchment was achieved by tightening eligibility and increasing contributions to comprehensive programs, especially pensions and health care. The change in the pension indexation formula in 1984 became part of the 1994 pension reform, which also changed the prolonged reference earnings and extended the minimum contribution period. In health care, the 1983 reform imposed budget caps on hospital financing, and the 1986 reform increased copayments.[25]

The Italian governments also sought cooperation from the unions in wage moderation and targeted comprehensive programs to curb expenditure disinflationary reforms. After the disintegration of the old ruling parties in 1992, the national unions began to reunite and consult at the top levels on issues such as abolishing the scala mobile, cooperating on income policy, making labor regulations flexible, and seeking retrenchments on welfare. In this new strategy, the national unions, led by the metal industry, accommodated the earlier changes by incorporating firm-level employee organizations (which had expanded in the 1980s as the microfoundation of social partnership). In welfare reform, the government spread the cost of retrenchment by tightening eligibility and increasing the amount of contributions to comprehensive programs. For instance, in the 1992 pension reform, the government raised the retirement age, extended the pension reference period from the last five years of employment to the last ten, increased the minimum contribution period, and eliminated certain early retirement benefits for public employees. In 1995 the government planned to eliminate "seniority" pensions (which favored early retirement), replace earnings-related pensions with ones related to contributions, end occupational pension inequalities, fix the retirement age at fifty-seven, tighten the eligibility for disability pensions, and introduce tax measures to promote supplementary private pension schemes. The 1992 health care bill converted local health units into autonomous "public enterprises" that were independent of local party organs and made the regions cover spending beyond their annual budget allocations through either higher taxes or higher copayments. Also, the government launched plans to allow health care users to "contract out," either individually or collectively, with a corresponding reduction of compulsory contributions.[26]

In short, disinflation policies in France and Italy were triggered by the same kind of external economic problems caused by inflation as seen in the United Kingdom and the United States. Drastically different from the practices of the majoritarian democracies, however, were the ways in which these countries solved the conflict between making credible policy commitments and obtaining democratic support for unpopular policies. The governments of both France and Italy depended on external constraints to bind themselves and secure domestic cooperation with disinflationary reforms. More concretely, and in contrast to the United Kingdom and the United States, France and Italy sought union cooperation on wage restraint and targeted comprehensive programs for retrenchment instead of specifically targeted programs.

*Reinforcement of Disinflationary Institutions: Germany and Japan*

In contrast to the four countries already discussed, Japan and Germany had inflation-absorbent institutions—wage coordination and fiscal discipline—that enabled them to maintain low inflation and consistent balance-of-payment surpluses. The challenge for these countries was reinforcing these institutions. The evidence shows they did so through the combination of the policy demands imposed by the United States and government reaction to increased international competition, reflected in their balance-of-payments problems. To quell domestic protectionist demands, the U.S. government demanded that Germany and Japan appreciate their currencies and then reflate their economies by fiscal stimulus in the late 1970s and mid-1980s, and Japan again in the early 1990s. Indeed, the U.S. demands on Germany and Japan closely coincided with the rise of U.S. trade deficits (see figure 12.3). The U.S. demand that Germany and Japan reflate their economies was based on domestic criticism that these countries were exacerbating U.S. trade deficits by exporting their way out of economic slowdown.

In both countries, rapid currency appreciation reinforced the coordinated wage setting led by the export sector, in which the unions moderated wages in exchange for job security measures. Fiscal spending compensated troubled sectors and helped ease unemployment, despite budget deficits. In addition, the evidence indicates that U.S. pressure strengthened the power of their monetary and fiscal agencies, which resisted such pressure, warned against loose wage and fiscal policy, and started fiscal reconstruction as soon as the economy showed signs of inflation and worsening external balances. Indeed, in both Germany and Japan fiscal reconstruction followed periods of weak trade performance. In other words, elected leaders maintained the autonomy of monetary and fiscal authorities in order to prevent external pressure from dictating fiscal policy and undermining international competitiveness. Finally, Germany and Japan implemented accommodative fiscal and welfare retrenchment, as would be expected from the fact that both countries are consensus democracies.

Germany and Japan differed, however, in the fiscal discipline mechanisms they chose and the degree of conflict in their fiscal retrenchment. In Germany, the Bundesbank acted to curb government expenditures by raising interest rates as soon as wage settlements showed signs of being related to inflation and deteriorating trade balances. In Japan, the Ministry of Finance (MOF) was more interested in taking the long view—in anticipation that the Liberal Democratic Party (LDP) would still be in power and in trouble when public debts became an issue—and in balancing the interests of the party's export-oriented business interests and domestic interests. That the Japanese unions were more quiescent than their German counterparts, and that the Ministry of Finance was more accommodative to various social groups in fiscal and welfare retrenchment, are different ways of saying that Germany was more majoritarian than Japan. Thus, their respective degrees of consensus democracy would explain the difference between the two countries.

In Germany, wage moderation and demand for employment were seen in the 1970s and 1980s during periods of economic slowdowns caused by the rapid appreciation of the deutsche mark against the dollar, and also during the post-unification recession of the early 1990s. Indeed, the metalworkers' union (IG Metall) assumed wage leadership after the first oil crisis when the unions recognized that double-digit wage packages, as realized under the leadership of the public-sector union in 1974, came at the cost of massive layoffs. At the firm level, employees obtained job security in exchange for wage moderation. Thus, workers in electronics and automobiles pressed management to avoid layoffs by relying on transfers and retraining, while the works councils of the steel industry agreed to layoffs in exchange for generous early retirement plans. At the industry level, the unions demanded the expansion of codetermination, the reduction of the workweek, and the preservation of employment policies in exchange for wage moderation and working-hour flexibility. The Social-Liberal coalition enacted a compromise expansion of codetermination in 1976, while IG Metall traded new flexibility in working hours for a shorter workweek in the bargaining rounds of the latter half of the 1980s.

Social partnership not only survived the 1980s but also was transplanted to eastern Germany after unification, where firm-level codetermination and comprehensive collective bargaining established a solid presence in a short period despite economic troubles and social instability. Industry, government, and labor reached a set of understandings, the 1992–1993 Solidarity Pact, that shows the persistence of social partnership. The federal government, already committed to massive spending in the East for infrastructure development and to an active labor market policy, agreed to extend new investment incentives to eastern businesses, to prolong privatization, and to support wage convergence between East and West Germany, while the unions agreed to hold down wage demands. When the recession affected the west and the Bundesbank tightened monetary policy, unemployment and employer determination to cut costs in fact resulted in firm-level compromises. In 1993 the works councils of the large automobile firms traded off pay and benefit concessions for new investment and job guarantees. In the metal industry, the social partners reached a compromise, after considerable union militancy, in which the employers secured wage restraint in exchange for provisions in regional contracts ensuring employment security. As a result, wages were fixed below inflation even at thriving industries such as construction and banking.

Furthermore, all observers of Germany agree that the 1982 neoliberal pledge of the incoming Helmut Kohl government to reduce union influence turned out to be mere rhetoric. Instead, labor market arrangements remained mostly intact, since neither the unions nor the employer associations were eager to back Kohl. The revision of the Work Promotion Act, fiercely opposed by the Social Democratic Party (SPD) and the unions, hardly had the publicized effect of restricting the unions' ability to strike, and attempts to reduce the influence of unions on works councils failed owing to splits within the government. Furthermore, after 1984, the Kohl government depended on an active labor market policy.[27] Thus, the Kohl government, unlike the Thatcher government, protected social partnership and employment programs and was not eager to enact tax cuts and privatization to mobilize supporters.

In Japan, developments almost identical to those in Germany appeared in the labor market, except that the Japanese export-sector unions were more quiescent even than their German counterparts because they were more dependent on employers than on public policy for employment security. Wage moderation and demand for employment were seen during periods of economic slowdown caused by the rapid appreciation of the yen against the dollar in the late 1970s, the late 1980s, and the early 1990s. After a 30 percent wage increase in 1974 led by the public-sector unions, the export-industry unions, led by the steel industry union, called for wage moderation at the 1975 wage round and accepted wages below the guidelines set by the employers' association. The export (metal) industry unions reasoned that wage moderation was necessary for employment security. Thereafter, coordinated moderation at the annual wage rounds and employment security commitments continued to be exchanged amid recurring economic difficulties. As a result, by the end of the 1970s the export (metal) industry unions had seized the leadership of the national union movement from the more political, radical, and militant public-sector unions. Meanwhile, large firms utilized corporate ties in relocating workers, both between major firms in different industries and between the parent firm and its subsidiaries or subcontractors, while the government provided assistance to encourage training and hiring. Starting in 1974, employers were subsidized for retaining, retraining, redeploying, or hiring redundant workers, and a set of new laws passed in 1977–1978 linked employment policy with industrial adjustment measures. In exchange for their cooperative and negotiated exit from depressed industries, firms were supplied with low-interest and government-guaranteed loans and preferential tax measures, provided that they could reach an agreement with the unions and use government employment subsidies. This adjustment policy regime has been renewed and revised every five years (in 1983, 1988, and 1993) since its inauguration.[28]

Although both Germany and Japan conceded to U.S. pressure to reflate their economies after currency appreciation, the resistance of both countries strengthened the position of the agencies in control of monetary or fiscal policies. The Bundesbank and the Japanese Ministry of Finance warned of the negative effects of inflation and large public debts, while worsening external balances increased support for—and compelled the governments to focus on—fiscal reconstruction and debt reduction.

In Germany, the government's ability to reflate the economy, especially through employment and public investment programs, was constrained by the Bundesbank, which tightened monetary policy at the first signs of inflation and deteriorating trade balances. For instance, the 1975 Budget Structure Act instructed the government to tighten retraining and regional investment programs, which had been expanded at the outset of the recession of 1974 to 1975. Similarly, another stimulus package enacted because of pressure from the United States in 1978 and 1979 was offset by an increase in indirect taxes and compelled the Social-Liberal coalition to delay tax cuts and to cut employment programs despite an economic downturn starting in 1980. In each case, the Bundesbank countered the demands within the SPD government and unions for more reflation. Indeed, it was the issue of economic policy that led the "Free Democrats" of the Liberal Democratic Party (FDP)—the most ardent supporters of the Bundesbank, fiscal austerity, and the "freeing" of market forces—to switch coalition partners, although all three major parties agreed on the need to curtail social programs to balance the budget. Thus, despite pledging an economic turnaround ("Wende"), the Christian-Liberal coalition's main success lay not in deregulation and privatization but in balancing the budget. Indeed, the Budget Reform Acts of 1983 and 1984 increased the VAT and social security contributions, imposed a forced loan on the better-off, postponed the annual increases in pensions and income support programs, increased health care fees, and cut family allowances, educational grants, and unemployment benefits. Furthermore, the tax cuts enacted between 1986 and 1990 after budget consolidation were meager and paled in comparison with the Thatcher tax cuts. The Bundesbank raised interest rates as soon as the Kohl government's fiscal expenditures to facilitate unification showed signs of inflation. This monetary tightening led not only to the Solidarity Pact but also to a European currency crisis in 1992, as described earlier, when it became clear that other governments could not endure such high interest rates.

As expected, welfare retrenchment focused on comprehensive programs and embodied compromises. The 1988 health insurance reform cut benefits (counterbalanced by a new home care provision) while increasing prescription drug prices. The 1992 reform went further and enabled the legislature to cap health care fees; this measure was passed by a cross-party alliance over the objections of the health care organizations, the medical profession, and the pharmaceutical companies, all of whom had to share the costs of this reform. Finally, to provide additional funds to eastern Germany while cutting the public debt, the government reached a compromise with the states, the unions, and the opposition in the Solidarity Pact. The states agreed to raising the VAT and funding the eastern states in exchange for revising the financial equalization scheme. The SPD, in opposition, agreed to deficit reduction and a tax surcharge (in 1995) in exchange for no welfare cuts.

In all of these cases, it has been argued that the reforms in Germany were tepid because the government had to accommodate the opposition ("cooperative opposition"), the "landes" (states) ("cooperative federalism"), and the social partners ("corporatism"). In this light, what observers regard as the structural problems of the German system are in fact testimony to the prevalence of accommodative mobilization.[29]

Similarly, the Japanese government also took positive steps to reduce public debts immediately after it had enacted the fiscal stimulus packages demanded by the United States. For instance, by the end of the 1970s, less than two years after it took measures to stimulate the economy at the prodding of the United States, the Japanese government had announced plans to curb public pension and health care costs and to introduce a new consumption tax. During the first half of the 1980s, the government curbed expenditures and enacted drastic pension and health care reform to reduce the public debt accumulated by earlier reflation. Similarly, plans to revive the consumption tax were announced as early as 1986 (enacted in 1989), in anticipation of worsening budget deficits. Also, shortly after the fiscal stimulus of 1992, the government agreed to raise the consumption tax in 1993–1994, despite weak signs of economic recovery and government instability after the LDP lost exclusive control of the government. Finally, it took a financial-sector meltdown, the worst postwar recession, strongly worded demands by the G-7 (in the thick of the Asian financial crisis), and a cabinet change after an election upset for the Japanese government to enact a large fiscal stimulus after 1998.

In these instances of welfare retrenchment and fiscal restructuring, the government focused on comprehensive programs and engineered broad policy compromises. In the health care and pension reforms of the mid-1980s, the government designed packages that curbed future social security expenditure while distributing the costs of reform across large producers. Since the government accommodated conflicting interests, the ruling party (the LDP) was able to pass the reforms with the cooperation of moderate opposition parties. Similarly, in the tax reform of 1989, the Ministry of Finance combined a new sales tax with the income tax cuts favored especially by large export producers and their employees, whose tax burden had increased in the early 1980s. Thus, business associations dropped their earlier opposition to any tax increase, while political parties began supporting it because it reconciled tax cuts with the expenditures demanded by the small producers hit by the high yen of 1985 to 1987. As in earlier welfare reforms, the moderate parties aligned with the LDP after the government reduced the new sales tax rate from 5 percent to 3 percent, added income tax cuts and measures to ease the transition for small firms, and pledged to increase social services (the Gold Plan). Similarly, the consumption tax of 1994 was passed by an LDP-Socialist coalition. As with the 1989 tax reform, the Ministry of Finance combined a consumption tax rate hike from 3 percent to 7 percent with a 5-trillion-yen income tax cut. Furthermore, the tax rate hike was passed after the new tax rate was reduced to 5 percent from 7 percent, and additional tax cuts and further social services commitments were made. In the New Gold Plan, the government committed itself to new expenditures on social services for the ill and elderly.[30]

In short, policy pressure by the United States—which demanded currency appreciation and fiscal stimulus—and fear of losing competitiveness reinforced coordinated wage bargaining and made the government dependent on economic agencies. Monetary and fiscal agencies in both countries warned against accommodating the U.S. request to reflate the economy and took swift steps that compelled the government to lower the public debt as soon as the economy showed signs of inflation or a deterioration of the balance of payments. Thus, it was external concerns that preserved the anti-inflationary institutions of Germany and Japan. Furthermore, as expected, both countries were accommodative in the enactment of fiscal and welfare retrenchment.

## Conclusion: Toward a Theory of Democratic Disinflationary Policy Adjustment

In this chapter, I have argued that the disinflationary constraint of capital mobility no longer enables governments to honor the postwar social contracts that underwrote employment security and social protection. External economic crises caused by the structural constraint of globalized capital have compelled governments to undertake disinflationary policy. However, the degree to which governments have had to challenge existing arrangements and divide the middle classes has depended on the inflationary profile of the state and the type of its democratic government. Of the three possible types of democratic adjustment—high-inflation majoritarian, high-inflation consensual, and low-inflation—the governments of high-inflation states, such as the United Kingdom, the United States, France, and Italy, had to challenge existing arrangements, while the majoritarian democracies of the United Kingdom and the United States were more divisive in their reforms. Furthermore, the path to disinflationary reform was more divisive in the United Kingdom than in the United States and France than in Italy, because the United States had fewer majoritarian characteristics than the United Kingdom and France was less consensual than Italy. Similarly, the politics of maintaining anti-inflationary arrangements was more confrontational in Germany than in Japan. Hopefully, the conceptual map detailed in this chapter will complement the country papers of this volume, which depict challenges to the postwar social contract and the changing boundaries of the middle classes and explain the reasons for the variety in recent changes. Having said that, in the remainder of this chapter I briefly outline the theoretical implications of the democratic adjustment argument and suggest that it can be extended to cases other than the ones examined in this volume.

### Implications of This Study

The framework of democratic disinflationary adjustment questions two common theories: the society-centered perspective on policies of adjustment to economic globalization, and the state-centered perspective on anti-inflationary institutions. I have stressed that party governments react to external economic crises and enact disinflation policies in the absence of a change in the influence of powerful social groups. This perspective runs against the dominant society-centered theories of economic adjustment. The most sophisticated version, formulated by Andrew Moravcsik, explains foreign economic policy as a two-level game in which state leaders bargain with other state leaders, on the one hand, and with domestic interests, on the other hand. Thus, government negotiators do not have an interest of their own but thrive in cross-pressure.[31] In a similar vein, most accounts of exchange-rate policy explain differences among countries on common issues by the different configuration of domestic interests.[32] However, without exaggeration or injustice we can say that such accounts never establish whether such interests determine policy; they only show that there were domestic interests in support of certain policies. The problem with such accounts is the exclusion of party differences and the possible mobilization of social groups by the party in power. However, without the notion of adjustment led by party government, it is impossible to explain why governments decide to enact highly unpopular policies or confront powerful social groups. It is party governments with stable partisan preferences and vested clients, not neutral negotiators, that try to solve the conflict between showing policy competence and mobilizing democratic support for unpopular policies.

Second, this chapter also questions the literature on central bank independence.[33] The state-centered claim that an institutionally independent central bank is disinflationary can be challenged on two fronts. On the one hand, the literature does not incorporate the view that the effectiveness of state agency depends on certain societal institutions. Recent research on central bank independence has recognized the complementary relations between central bank independence and centralized or coordinated wage bargaining.[34] Peter Hall and Robert Franzese take the argument one step further and ascribe to an independent central bank the role of merely facilitating disinflation based on coordinated wage bargaining. In effect, they assimilate the literature of central bank independence into the neo-corporatist literature of the 1980s, which had always claimed the importance of organized cooperation between employers and unions in wage coordination.[35] The evidence in this chapter supports the claim that coordinated wage bargaining led by the export sector is of crucial importance in countering inflation and that this mechanism can enhance the mandate of an independent central bank. On the other hand, the literature on central bank independence does not take into account the importance of support or mandates by elected governments. The literature assumes that parties are inherently inclined to pursue loose monetary and fiscal policy when in power to cater to the interests of the voters. However, such an argument cannot explain the recent *converging* decline of inflation rates among industrial states, regardless of the degree of central bank independence, or the willingness of elected officials to impose harsh and unpopular economic policies. Indeed, despite the weakness of their central banks, the United Kingdom, France, and Italy have undertaken severe monetary policies, while Japan has maintained low inflation. Thus, it seems that the resolve of the elected government, responding to the constraints imposed by the international economy, matter more than formal central bank independence in reducing inflation. Problematic is the assertion that state institutions like an independent central bank can enact tough policies without the consent of the democratic government in power, which will be held responsible for the unpopular policies managed by state institutions. Thus, this chapter argues in favor of a more refined account of central bank independence that takes into account the supportive role of coordinated wage bargaining and the dilemmas faced by elected government in institutionalizing disinflation.

*Extending the Argument*

Finally, there is the problem of how sensitive this argument is to the cases examined. I claim that the governments of industrial democracies have faced the dilemma of credibly enacting the policies required by global markets and maintaining democratic support to remain in power. In fact, we would expect that the dilemma is more acute for states other than the ones examined here because they are likely to be smaller states that are more dependent on trade and thus more vulnerable to changes in global markets. Such countries have a stronger need to stabilize their currency against those of their major trading partners and eventually are forced to enact capital liberalization. A preliminary examination of most countries, classified according to inflation rates and type of democracy (using Lijphart's data) seems to fit our hypothesis. For instance, high-inflation majoritarian democracies are mostly Commonwealth states (such as Canada, New Zealand, and Australia), and they show a pattern of adversarial politics similar to the United Kingdom's in the enactment of disinflationary reforms. However, these countries are highly dependent on trade and their need to stabilize their currency gives them less room for an autonomous monetary policy. As a result, governments are often routed because they are unable to use monetary policy to mobilize support for disinflationary reforms. As expected, the high-inflation consensus democracies, such as the Benelux states, use external constraints to discipline inflation and distribute the costs of disinflationary reform across social groups. Finally, low-inflation countries tend to reinforce anti-inflationary arrangements, but some governments have delayed capital decontrol (as in Sweden) to maintain domestic arrangements until recent times and have been ambivalent toward the EMU. Admittedly, it is unclear to what extent low-inflation countries like Switzerland and Austria will fit our expectations; a systematic comparison must be left for further research. However, it can be said at this point that the argument presented here is not limited to the cases examined and can be extended to other countries.[36]

---

The author wishes to thank the conference participants; Miura Mari and Jon Marshall for their comments; and Kanae Kamishima and Kodate Naonori for their research assistance.

## Notes

Japanese names appear with last names first, even in English-language publications.

1. Beth A. Simmons, "The Internationalization of Capital," in *Continuity and Change in Contemporary Capitalism*, edited by Herbert Kitschelt et al. (Cambridge: Cambridge University Press, 1999), 36–69.

2. On the relation between petrodollars, the expansion of offshore markets, capital liberalization, and global capital mobility, see Eric Helleiner, *States and the Reemergence of Global Finance: From Bretton Woods to the 1990s* (Ithaca: Cornell University Press, 1994), chs. 1 and 6; Michael C. Webb, "International Economic Structures, Government Interests, and International Coordination of Macroeconomic Adjustment Policies," *International Organization* 45(Summer 1991): 309–42.

3. John Ruggie, "International Regimes, Transactions, and Change: Embedded Liberalism in the Postwar Economic Order," *International Organization* 31(Fall 1982): 379–415; John Ruggie, "Embedded Liberalism Revisited," in *Progress in Postwar International Relations*, edited by Emanuel Alder and Beverly Crawford (New York: Columbia University Press, 1991), 201–34.

4. David M. Andrews, "Capital Mobility and State Autonomy: Toward a Structural Theory of International Monetary Relations," *International Studies Quarterly* 38(Summer 1994): 193–218.

5. Barry J. Eichengreen, Andrew K. Rose, and Chares Wyposz, "Exchange Rate Mayhem: The Antecedents and Aftermath of Speculative Attacks," *Economic Policy* (October 1995): 251–312.

6. Arend Lijphart, *Patterns of Democracy: Government Forms and Performance in Thirty-six Countries* (New Haven: Yale University Press, 1999). See also John D. Huber and G. Bingham Powell Jr., "Congruence Between Citizens and Policymakers in Two Visions of Liberal Democracy," *World Politics* 46(April 1994): 291–326; S. E. Finer, "Adversary Politics and the Eighties," *Electoral Studies* 1(August 1982): 221–30.

7. On one dimension that is relevant for this study, Lijphart establishes the following results: (1) Democracies tend to be dichotomized into those with disproportional electoral systems and those with proportional electoral systems; (2) disproportional electoral systems limit the number of effective parties close to two, while proportional systems create multiparty systems; (3) the smaller the number of effective parties, the larger the proportion of powerful single-party governments; (4) single-party governments tend to dominate the legislature; and (5) single-party governments and fewer numbers of effective parties each correlate with a high degree of interest-group pluralism.

8. In other words, according to the well-known Mundell-Fleming theorem, a government cannot set interest rates independently and stabilize exchange rates at the same time. Andrews, "Capital Mobility and State Autonomy"; Jeffry A. Frieden, "Invested Interests," *International Organization* 45(Fall 1991): 425–54.

9. Lars Calmfors and John Driffill, "Bargaining Structure, Corporatism, and Macroeconomic Performance," *Economic Policy* (October 1988): 13–61. For applications of this framework, see also Geoffrey Garrett and Christopher Way, "The Sectoral Composition of Trade Unions, Corporatism, and Economic Performance," in *Monetary and Fiscal Policy in an Integrated Europe*, edited by Barry J. Eichengreen, Jeffry A. Frieden, and Jürgen von Hagen (New York: Springer, 1995), 38–61; Alex Cukierman and Francesco Lippi, "Central Bank Independence, Centralization of Wage Bargaining, Inflation, and Unemployment: Theory and Evidence," *European Economic Review* 43(Fall 1999): 1395–1434.

10. Peter Swenson, "Bringing Capital Back In, or Social Democracy Reconsidered: Employer Power, Cross-class Alliances, and Centralization of Industrial Relations in Denmark and Sweden," *World Politics* 43(July

1991): 513–44; Peter A. Hall and Robert J. Franzese Jr., "Mixed Signals: Central Bank Independence, Wage Bargaining, and the EMU," *International Organization* 52(Fall 1998): 505–36.

11. Jürgen von Hagen and Ian J. Harden, "National Budget Process and Fiscal Performance," *European Economy: Reports and Studies* 3(January 1994): 311–418; Alberto Alesina and Roberto Perotti, "The Political Economy of Budget Deficits," *IMF Staff Papers* 42(March 1995): 1–31; Jakob De Haan and Jan-Egbert Strum, "Political and Institutional Determinates of Fiscal Policy in the European Community," *Public Choice* 80(January 1994): 157–72; Sung Deuk Hahm, Mark S. Kamlet, and David C. Mowery, "The Political Economy of Deficit Spending in Nine Industrialized Parliamentary Democracies: The Role of Fiscal Institutions," *Comparative Political Studies* 29(February 1996): 52–77.

12. See Paul Pierson, *Dismantling the Welfare State?: Reagan, Thatcher, and the Politics of Retrenchment* (Cambridge: Cambridge University Press, 1994), pt. 1.

13. Toben Iversen, "Power, Flexibility, and the Breakdown of Centralized Wage Bargaining: Denmark and Sweden in Comparative Perspective," *Comparative Politics* 27(June 1996): 399–436, and the literature cited therein.

14. See Lijphart, *Patterns of Democracy*, 312–13, appendix A, especially Lijphart's first-dimension results for the years 1971 to 1996. The factors that constitute the first dimension are listed in note 7.

15. The terms "liberal" and, more often, "neoliberal" are increasingly used in Europe to describe policies that Americans label "conservative."

16. Martin Holmes, *The Labour Government, 1974–1979* (London: Macmillan, 1985); Andrew Taylor, *The Trade Unions and the Labour Party* (London: Croom Helm, 1987).

17. Erwin C. Hargrove, *Jimmy Carter as President* (Baton Rouge: Louisiana State University Press, 1988), 42–107; Henry C. Kenski, "The Politics of Economic Policymaking," in *Economic Decline and Political Change*, edited by Harold Clarke, Marianne C. Stewart, and Gary Zuk (Pittsburgh: University of Pittsburgh Press, 1989); Dennis S. Ippolito, *Uncertain Legacies: Federal Budget Policy from Roosevelt to Reagan* (Charlottesville: University Press of Virginia, 1990), 50–60.

18. Martin Holmes, *The First Thatcher Government 1979–1983* (Brighton: Wheatsheaf Books, 1985), 18–107; Tony Atkinson and John Micklewright, "Turning the Screw: Benefits for the Unemployed, 1979–1988," in *The Economics of Social Security*, edited by Andrew Dilnot and Ian Walker (Oxford: Oxford University Press, 1989), 19–51; Martin Holmes, *Thatcherism: Scope and Limits, 1983–1987* (London: Macmillan, 1989), 19–37; Norman Johnson, *The Welfare State: A Decade of Change 1980–1990* (Hartfordshire: Harvester Wheatsheaf, 1990), 40–78; Nicholas Deakin, *The Politics of Welfare* (London: Harvester Wheatsheaf, 1994), 100–71; Pierson, *Dismantling the Welfare State?*, 54–120.

19. Paul E. Peterson and Mark Rom, "Lower Taxes, More Spending, and Budget Deficits," in *The Reagan Legacy*, edited by Charles O. Jones (Chatham: Chatham House, 1988), 218–33; David Beam et al., "Solving the Riddle of Tax Reform: Party Competition and the Politics of Ideas," *Political Science Quarterly* 105(Summer 1990): 195–215; Edward D. Berkowitz, *America's Welfare State* (Baltimore: Johns Hopkins University Press, 1991), 73–184; Thomas R. Oliver, "Health Care Market Re-

form in Congress: The Uncertain Path from Proposal to Policy," *Political Science Quarterly* 106(Fall 1991): 453–74; Pierson, *Dismantling the Welfare State?*, 135–39.

20. Richard Brown, "British Monetary Policy in the Light of European Monetary Integration," in *Monetary Implications of the 1992 Process*, edited by Sherman Heidemarie et al. (London: Pinter, 1990), 99–123; Philip Stephens, *Politics and the Pound: The Conservatives' Struggle with Sterling* (London: Macmillan, 1996), chs. 3–5.

21. Christopher Johnson, "The United Kingdom and the Exchange Rate Mechanism," in *The Monetary Economics of Europe: Causes of the Crisis*, edited by Christopher Johnson and Stefan Collignon (London: Pinter, 1994), 84–102; Stephens, *Politics and the Pound*, chs. 6–11; Pippa Norris, "Anatomy of a Labour Landslide," in *Britain Votes 1997*, edited by Pippa Norris and Neil T. Gavin (Oxford: Oxford University Press, 1997), 1–23.

22. Helleiner, *States and the Reemergence of Global Finance*, 132–33; C. Randall Henning, *Currencies and Politics in the United States, Germany, and Japan* (Washington, D.C.: Institute for International Economics, 1994), ch. 4.

23. Diana Green and Philip G. Cerny, "Economic Policy and the Governing Coalition," in *French Politics and Public Policy*, edited by Philip G. Cerny and Martin A. Schain (New York: Methuen, 1980), 159–76; Peter A. Hall, *Governing the Economy* (New York: Oxford University Press, 1986), 169–71; Peter Holmes, "Broken Dreams: Economic Policy in Mitterrand's France," in *Mitterrand's France*, edited by Sonia Mazey and Michael Newman (New York: Croom Helm, 1987), 33–55; Volkmar Lauber, "France and the Economic Crisis, 1974–1987," in *The Politics of Economic Crisis: Lessons from Western Europe*, edited by Erik Damgaard, Peter Gerlich, and J. J. Richardson (Brookfield, Vt.: Gower, 1989), 108–30; David Ross Cameron, "From Barre to Balladur: Economic Policy in the Era of the EMS," in *Remaking the Hexagon: The New France in the New Europe*, edited by Gregory Flynn (Boulder: Westview Press, 1995), 117–57; Jacques E. Le Cacheux, "Fiscal Policy in France: Assessing the Possibilities for Reducing Budget Deficits in the EMU Perspective," *European Economy: Reports and Studies* 3(Fall 1994): 185–218; Jacques E. Le Cacheux, "The Franc Fort Strategy and the EMU," in Flynn, *Remaking the Hexagon*, 69–86.

24. Carlo Dell'alringa and Manuela Samek Lodovici, "Policies for the Unemployed and Social Shock Absorbers," *Southern European Society and Politics* 1(Winter 1996): 172–97; Valeria Fargion, "Social Assistance and the North-South Cleavage in Italy," *Southern European Society and Politics* 1(Winter 1996): 135–54; Stephen Gundle, "The Rise and Fall of Craxi's Socialist Party," in *The New Italian Republic: From the Fall of the Berlin Wall to Berlusconi*, edited by Stephen Gundle and Simon Parker (London: Routledge, 1996), 85–97; Stephen Hellman, "Italian Communism in the First Republic," in Gundle and Parker, *The New Italian Republic*, 72–84.

25. Doreen Collins, "A More Equal Society?: Social Policy Under the Socialists," in Mazey and Newman, *Mitterrand's France*, 81–102; Martin Rhodes, "Labor and Industry: The Demise of Traditional Unionism?" in Mazey and Newman, *Mitterrand's France*, 56–80; René Mouriaux, "Trade Union, Unemployment, Regulation: 1962-1989," in *Searching*

*for the New France*, edited by James F. Hollifield and George Ross (New York: Routledge, 1991), 173–92; Le Cacheux, "The Franc Fort Strategy"; Guy Groux and René Mouriaux, "The Dilemma of Unions Without Members," in *The Mitterrand Era: Policy Alternatives and Political Mobilization in France*, edited by Anthony Daley (New York: New York University Press, 1996), 172–85; Mark Kesselman, "Does the French Labor Movement Have a Future?," in *Chirac's Challenge: Liberalization, Europeanization, and Malaise in France*, edited by John T. S. Keeler and Martin A. Schain (New York: St. Martin's Press, 1996), 143–65; Susan Milner, "Industrial Relations in France: Towards a New Social Pact?," in *The Mitterrand Years: Legacy and Evaluation*, edited by Mairi Maclean (London: Macmillan, 1998), 169–84; Jacques Reland, "France," in *The European Union and National Macroeconomic Policy*, edited by James Forder and Anand Menon (London: Routledge, 1998), 85–104; Henrik Uterwedde, "Mitterrand's Economic and Social Policy in Perspective," in Maclean, *The Mitterrand Years*, 133–50.

26. V. Chiorazzo et al., "Fiscal Development in Italy and Possibilities for Reducing Public Deficits," *European Economy: Reports and Studies* 3(Fall 1994): 219–57; Maurizio Ferrera, "The Rise and Fall of Democratic Universalism: Health Care Reform in Italy, 1978–1994," *Journal of Health, Policy, and Law* 20(Summer 1995): 278–94; Richard M. Locke and Lucio Baccaro, "Learning from Past Mistakes?: Recent Reforms in Italian Industrial Relations," *Industrial Relations Journal* 27 (December 1996): 289–303; Elena Granaglia, "The Italian National Health Service and the Challenge of Privatization," *Southern European Society and Politics* 1(Winter 1996): 155–71; James I. Walsh, "Political Bases of Macroeconomic Adjustment: Evidence from the Italian Experience," *Journal of European Public Policy* 6(March 1999): 66–84.

27. Andrei S. Markovits and Christopher S. Allen, "Trade Unions and the Economic Crisis: The West German Case," in *Unions and Economic Crisis: Britain, West Germany, and Sweden*, edited by Peter Gourevitch et al. (London: George Allen & Unwin, 1984), 147–67; Josef Esser, "State, Business, and Trade Unions in West Germany After the 'Political Wende,'" *West European Politics* 9(April 1986): 198–214; Andrei S. Markovits, *The Politics of the West German Trade Unions: Strategies of Class and Interest Representation in Growth and Crisis* (Cambridge: Cambridge University Press, 1986), 126–46; Edgar Grande, "West Germany: From Reform Policy to Crisis Management," in Damgaard et al., *The Politics of Economic Crisis: Lessons from Western Europe*, Kathleen A. Thelen, *Union of Parts: Labor Politics in Postwar Germany* (Ithaca: Cornell University Press, 1991), 112–46; Dieter Sadowski, Martin Schneider, and Karin Wagner, "The Impact of European Integration and German Unification on Industrial Relations in Germany," *British Journal of Industrial Relations* 32(December 1994): 523–37; Anke Hassel and Thorsten Schulten, "Globalization and the Future of Central Collective Bargaining: The Example of the German Metal Industry," *Economy and Society* 27(November 1998): 486–522; Lowell Turner, *Fighting for Partnership: Labor and Politics in Unified Germany* (Ithaca: Cornell University Press, 1998), chs. 1–5; Reimut Zohlnhöfer, "Institutions, the CDU, and Policy Change: Explaining German Economic Policy in the 1980s," *German Politics* 8(December 1999): 141–60.

28. Sekiguchi Sueo, "An Overview of Adjustment Assistance in Japan," in *Troubled Industries in the United States and Japan*, edited by Hong W. Tan and Shimada Haruo (London: Macmillan, 1994); Robert M. Uriu, *Troubled Industries* (Ithaca: Cornell University Press, 1996), chs. 5–7; Sako Mari, "Shunto: The Role of Employer and Union Coordination at the Industry and Intersectoral Levels," in *Japanese Labor and Management in Transition*, edited by Sako Mari and Sato Hiroki (London: Routledge, 1997), 236–63.

29. Fritz Sharpf, "Economic and Institutional Constraints of Full Employment Strategies: Sweden, Austria, and Western Germany, 1973–1982," in *Order and Conflict in Contemporary Capitalism*, edited by John Goldthorpe (Oxford: Clarendon, 1984), 281–86; Helga Michalsky, "The Politics of Social Policy," in *Policy and Politics in the Federal Republic of Germany*, edited by Klaus von Beyme and Manfred G. Schmidt (New York: St. Martin's Press, 1985), 56–81; Stephen Padgett and Tony Burkett, *Political Parties and Elections in West Germany: The Search for a New Stability* (London: C. Hurst, 1986), 62–163; Martin Hellwig and Manfred J. M. Neumann, "Economic Policy in Germany: Was There a Turnaround?," *Economic Policy* 5(October 1987): 103–45; Andrei S. Markovits and Jost Halfmann, "The Unraveling of West German Social Democracy?," in *Remaking the Welfare State: Retrenchment and Social Policy in America and Europe*, edited by Michael K. Brown (Philadelphia: Temple University Press, 1988), 96–118; Elke Thiel, "Macroeconomic Policy Preference and Coordination: A View from Germany," in *The Political Economy of European Integration*, edited by Paolo Guerrieri and Pier Carlo Padoan (New York: Harvester Wheatsheaf, 1989), 202–30; Douglas Webber, "Kohl's 'Wendepolitik' After a Decade," *German Politics* 1(August 1992): 149–80; Bernhard Blanke and Christiane Perschke-Hartmann, "The 1992 Health Reform Victory over Pressure Group Politics," *German Politics* 3(August 1994): 233–48; Razeen Sally and Douglas Webber, "The German Solidarity Pact: A Case Study in the Politics of the Unified Germany," *German Politics* 3(April 1994): 18–46; Werner W. Pommerehne and Lars P. Feld, "Fiscal Evolution in the Federal Republic of Germany, 1980–1992: Recent Developments and Room for Consolidation," *European Economy: Reports and Studies* 3(Fall 1994): 47–95; Moravcsik, *The Choice for Europe: Social Purpose and State Power from Messina to Maastricht* (Cambridge: Cambridge University Press, 1998), 329–32; Zohlnhöfer, "Institutions, the CDU, and Policy Change."

30. Hiwatari Nobuhiro, "Explaining the End of the Postwar Party System," in *The Political Economy of Japanese Society*, 2 vols., edited by Banno Junji (Oxford: Oxford University Press, 1998), 285–361; Hiwatari Nobuhiro, "Adjustment to Stagflation and Neoliberal Reforms in Japan, the United Kingdom, and the United States," *Comparative Political Studies* 31(October 1998): 602–32.

31. Moravcsik, *The Choice for Europe*, especially ch. 1.

32. Compare Jeffry A. Frieden, "Invested Interests"; Henning, *Currencies and Politics in the United States, Germany, and Japan*, ch. 1; Leila Simona Talani, *Betting For and Against EMU* (Hampshire: Ashigate, 2000).

33. John B. Goodman, "The Politics of Central Bank Independence," *Comparative Politics* 23(April 1991): 329–49; Alex Cukierman, Steven B.

Webb, and Bilin Neyapti, "Measuring the Independence of Central Banks and Its Effect on Policy Outcomes," *World Bank Economic* Review 6(September 1992): 353–98; Alex Cukierman et al., "Central Bank Independence, Growth, Investment, and Real Rates," *Carnegie-Rochester Conference Series on Public Policy* 39(Amsterdam: North Holland, 1993), 95–140; Alberto Alesina and Lawrence H. Summers, "Central Bank Independence and Macroeconomic Performance: Some Comparative Evidence," *Journal of Money, Credit, and Banking* 25(May 1993): 151–62.

34. Cukierman and Lippi, "Central Bank Independence, Centralization of Wage Bargaining, Inflation, and Unemployment"; Hall and Franzese, "Mixed Signals"; Michael Bleaney, "Central Bank Independence, Wage-Bargaining Structure, and Macroeconomic Performance in OECD Countries," *Oxford Economic Papers* 48(Spring 1996): 20–38.

35. See, for instance, David R. Cameron, "Social Democracy, Corporatism, Labor Quiescence, and the Representation of Economic Interests in Advanced Capital Society," in Goldthorpe, *Order and Conflict in Contemporary Capitalism*, 143–78.

36. Roger Gibbins, "Conservatism in Canada: The Ideological Impact of the 1984 Election," in *The Resurgence of Conservatism in Anglo-American Democracies*, edited by Barry Cooper, Allan Kornberg, and William Mishler (Durham: Duke University Press, 1988), 332–50; Norman C. Thomas, "Public Policy and the Resurgence of Conservatism in Three Anglo-American Democracies," in Cooper, Kornberg, and Mishler, *The Resurgence of Conservatism*, 96–136; Paulette Kurzer, "Unemployment in Open Economies," *Comparative Political Studies* 24(January 1991): 3–30; Bruce Campbell, "Restructuring the Economy: Canada into Free Trade," in *The Political Economy of North American Free Trade*, edited by Ricardo Grinspun and Maxwell A. Cameron (New York: St. Martin's Press, 1993), 89–104; John Edwards, "Economic History and Economic Policy: Assessing Paul Keating's Eight Years as Treasurer," *Australian Economic History Review* 33(September 1993): 29–41; John Pitchford, "Macroeconomic Policy and Recession in Australia, 1982–1992," *Australian Economic History Review* 33(September 1993): 96–111; Greg Whitwell, "Economic Ideas and Economic Policy: The Rise of Economic Rationalism in Australia," *Australian Economic History Review* 33(September 1993): 8–28; Ian McAllister and Jack Vowles, "The Rise of New Politics and Market Liberalism in Australia and New Zealand," *British Journal of Political Science* 24(Summer 1994): 381–402; Maureen Apel Molot, "The Canadian State in the International Economy," in *Political Economy and the Changing Global Order*, edited by Richard Stubbs and Geoffrey R. D. Underhill (London: Macmillan, 1994), 511–23; Evelyne Huber and John D. Stephens, "Internationalization and the Social-Democratic Model," *Comparative Political Studies* 31(July 1998): 353–97; Daniel Racette and Jacques Raynauld, "Canadian Monetary Policy 1989–1993: What Were the Bank of Canada's True Actions in the Determination of Monetary Conditions," *Canadian Public Policy* 20(October 1994): 365–84.

# 13

## Globalization and the Squeeze on the Middle Class: Does Any Version of the Postwar Social Contract Meet the Challenge?

*Leonard Schoppa*

In the years since World War II, the nations of Western Europe, Japan, and the United States have all seen the emergence of large "middle classes." The growth of the middle classes in these nations has come to be so taken for granted, in fact, that for twenty years scholars have been writing about the emergence of a new postmaterialist age in which class differences are coming to matter less and less.[1] Income gaps between rich and poor have closed, government policies have cushioned the effects of the business cycle on the overall economy and on individuals, and the extended period of prosperity has created increased opportunities for upward mobility. The amelioration of class conflict that followed from these developments has contributed to the consolidation of democratic rule in nations that only recently have experienced political upheaval, and it has led voters to focus on quality-of-life issues like the environment instead of on economic policy—when they care about politics at all.

In the last several years, however, most of these countries have also seen the growth of what could be called "middle-class angst." Well-paid blue-collar jobs have become much harder to find than they used to be, and even middle managers and public employees have faced layoffs and benefit cuts. Income gaps have begun to grow again, opportunities for upward mobility have been constricted, and government policies aimed at demand management and income support have been cut back or rendered less effective. Although there is little evidence of renewed class conflict on the scale seen in earlier generations, the growing anxieties among those in the middle class about their ability to retain their status suggest that Europe, Japan, and the United States may once again face this challenge.

Everywhere a phenomenon labeled "globalization" is being blamed for causing this renewed anxiety. The growth of imports and exports as a share of all of these nations' economies, the elimination of government and technological barriers to trade (which have made services like telecommunications tradable in ways they never were before), and the free movement of capital across borders have placed more and more low-skilled workers in the rich countries in direct competition with low-wage workers in the developing world. This competition has driven down their incomes even as the expanded world market has created new opportunities for capital and skilled labor to profit from worldwide demand. Globalization has also amplified the effects of disruptions in the international economy on domestic economies, generating recessions that tend to hurt the poorest members of society first. Governments, meanwhile, have been constrained by the same forces from offsetting these unequal effects. Globalization has made it more difficult for governments to use fiscal and monetary policy to smooth out bumps in the business cycle. It has also created fiscal constraints that drive cutbacks in public employment and welfare programs, and it has forced governments to implement additional liberalization measures aimed at improving the efficiency and competitiveness of their economies. By reinforcing the globalization trend, however, these policies expose more and more citizens to the unequal effects of globalization.

In this chapter, I examine in more detail the common challenge of globalization to the middle classes of the advanced industrialized nations, compare the divergent government responses to this challenge, and offer a preliminary evaluation and analysis of the degree to which these divergent responses have been successful in ameliorating the polarizing effects of globalization on class structure. Although economic theory and the history of the previous period of globalization between 1870 and 1913 suggest that globalization ought to have similar effects on *all* advanced economies, increasing the gap between rich and poor and shrinking the middle classes, this time it is affecting nations whose middle-class social contracts have evolved in quite distinctive ways. Whereas the United States has based its contract on the assumption that a rising tide of consumption will lift all boats, European nations have built their contracts around the social protection provided by the welfare state. Japan, in contrast, chose yet another path, basing its contract on elaborate schemes of public-private cooperation and collusion that are captured in the metaphor of a convoy: risk is socialized, so that no one fails and everyone moves up together.

Globalization has placed all three approaches under strain, but the rates at which inequality trends have begun to drive a wedge through the middle classes of these countries have been very uneven. I argue in this chapter that one of these three approaches—the European welfare state approach—has been more successful than the others at holding out against globalization's inequality-inducing effects. The empirical record summarized in this chapter indicates that the United States and Britain (which since Thatcher has adopted a policy profile similar to the American model), along with Japan, have suffered significant erosion in their levels of income equality over the past two decades. Much less affected so far have been the middle classes of continental Europe, where after-tax-and-transfer levels of income dispersion have widened only marginally in some cases and declined in others.

Nevertheless, my conclusions are necessarily tentative. Income inequality is a complex phenomenon that is not a function of trade and investment patterns alone. Demographic and technological change in particular have been identified as additional factors behind recent inequality trends. Although the chapter touches on these other factors in the concluding section, its purpose is to see how far we can get through a focused analysis of the connections between inequality, on the one hand, and globalization and social contracts, on the other. If some nations are doing better at holding out against trends toward greater inequality, and this pattern corresponds to the way in which these nations have organized their social contract, that correspondence provides a useful way of looking at how different versions of the social contract are faring.

Another reason this study's conclusions must remain tentative is that it focuses primarily on a single measure of overall inequality—the Gini index—and consequently neglects important differences in the ways inequality can emerge. Some forms of rising inequality (as when top incomes grow faster but lower incomes grow too) clearly pose less of a threat to middle-class social contracts than others (as when a segment of the middle class is falling into the ranks of the poor). It is possible as well that modest increases in income inequality in nations starting with egalitarian income distributions may be good for these societies in that they create incentives for individuals to make the best of their lives. In focusing in this chapter on the Gini index as the primary measure of income inequality, and in assuming that any increase in inequality from the levels experienced in the 1970s is problematic, I admittedly skirt distinctions of this kind. I assume, however, that whether inequality is a product of movement up or movement down, and whether the erosion still leaves nations with levels of inequality that are lower than those of the prewar era, the nations experiencing increased inequality are likely to see strains in their social fabric.

In the first section, I elaborate the economic theory underlying the prediction of growing inequality in the rich countries as a result of globalization and briefly review the economic history of the earlier period of globalization between 1870 and 1913. That history reinforces worries that globalization may once again widen the gaps between rich and poor and aggravate class conflict. In the second section, I emphasize the differences in the roads that led to middle-class societies in the United States, Europe, and Japan over the postwar period and suggest that these differences should lead us to wonder whether one or another of these models would be better able to accommodate globalization without inducing greater inequality. Finally, in the third section, I review recent trends in levels of income dispersion in the advanced industrialized nations and offer a preliminary analysis of why we might be seeing this pattern.

## Economic Theory and History

Economists tend to worry primarily about *aggregate* economic welfare, and the models they use show that under almost all conditions, increases in trade and capital movements of the kind associated with globalization improve global aggregate welfare as well as the aggregate welfare of each nation participating in the growing volume of exchange. Although these same models show that increases in trade and capital flows can hurt some groups within each of these nations even as they make the population as a whole better off, most economists write off worries about these distributive effects of international exchange by pointing out that they can be mitigated through government programs designed to redistribute a nation's overall gains through side payments that make no one worse off while allowing each nation as a whole to enjoy the gains from trade. The American program of trade adjustment assistance, for example, was designed with this purpose in mind.[2]

Although economists generally put aside concerns about the distributive effects of international exchange in this way, scholars interested in the effects of globalization on nations' class structures have reason to look more carefully at this process. We should be interested first in how the distributive effects of changes in levels of international exchange relate to preexisting patterns of income distribution: do they make already rich capitalists richer and further impoverish poor laborers, or do they reduce the rents collected by rich landlords and bolster the incomes of poor factory workers? Depending on which way the distributive effects work, globalization could reduce levels of income inequality and promote the rise of a middle class, or it could widen preexisting income gaps and lead to a decline in the middle class.

We should also be interested in the degree to which globalization itself may constrain the ability of governments to offset its distributive effects through redistributive programs. If globalization by its nature keeps nations from preventing the poor from becoming poorer, the economists' confidence that distributive effects can be mitigated through policy may be ill founded. Let us look at what the economic models themselves suggest about each of these concerns.

Fortunately, the models used by economists have the potential to shed some light on which direction the distributive effects flow. The predominant trade model used by economists (Hecksher-Ohlin/Stolper-Samuelson)[3] concludes that nations will export goods that are produced through the intensive use of factors of production with which they are relatively well endowed while importing goods that are produced with factors that are in relatively short supply. Increased trade (due to reductions in transportation costs, technological barriers, or tariffs) thus has the effect of benefiting "relatively abundant factors of production," such as the owners of capital and skilled workers in the advanced economies, at the expense of "relatively scarce factors," such as low-skilled workers in these same societies.[4] Given that unskilled workers tend to earn less than skilled workers in developed nations, the economic model described here makes a clear prediction about the effects of increased trade on levels of income inequality in these capital-intensive societies: there will probably be a squeezing of the middle as those who are relatively well off get richer while those who are less well off get poorer.[5]

These models expect direct foreign investment between nations with differing factor endowments to have a similar effect. When manufacturing firms from an advanced economy build factories in nations with abundant low-skilled labor, they are in effect putting workers in their home factories into direct competition with this expanded pool of similarly qualified labor, driving down their incomes. By contrast, the owners of capital benefit by earning higher returns than they might otherwise have earned as they make their investments in nations that are less well endowed with this factor of production. Therefore, these effects of increased international exchange, the models tell us, should be greatest when the exchange is conducted between nations with sharply different factor endowments. Increases in trade and investment between developed and developing nations in particular should aggravate inequality in the developed nations.

A few economists have supplemented this prediction about the distributive effects of North-South trade and investment with the claim that even exchange among similarly endowed nations in the North (for example, Toyota investing in the United States) tends to aggravate inequality by allowing more mobile capital to take advantage of a more elastic labor supply. As Dani Rodrik puts it: "The fact that 'workers' can be more easily substituted for each other across national boundaries undermines what many conceive to be a postwar social bargain between workers and employers, under which the former would receive a steady increase in wages and benefits in return for labor peace."[6] Labor unions are weakened, labor faces greater instability in earnings as it is forced to bear the brunt of economic shocks, and workers are forced to cover a greater share of the costs of benefits and improvements in working conditions.

Although the economic analysis thus far makes quite a pessimistic prediction about the probable effects of increased international exchange on class structure in the advanced industrialized nations, it is still possible that these effects could be mitigated—as noted earlier—through side payments from the globalization winners to the losers. In all of these societies, such side payments are provided at least to some degree through certain kinds of social insurance. Most commonly, this social insurance takes the form of government programs, such as unemployment compensation, trade adjustment assistance, income supports, minimum-wage rules, progressive tax systems, the expansion of (nontraded) public-sector employment, and government subsidies to declining industries. In some places, however, such as Japan, social insurance also takes the form of private-sector arrangements; sometimes organized with the support of the government, these are designed to minimize economic disruptions and pull the losers up with the winners. In both cases, these programs of social insurance also function to provide a built-in countercyclical mechanism (along with other levers of Keynesian demand management, or KDM) to smooth out the ups and downs of the business cycle and dissipate the inequality-producing impact of boom and bust. Finally, corporatist wage bargaining institutions can mitigate wage inequality by raising all wages in a centralized process. Regardless of how inequality is mitigated, the effects of globalization on the class structures of the advanced industrialized nations depend critically on whether globalization frustrates the ability of nations to maintain *and enlarge* these social insurance programs, policies, and networks.

Economic theory suggests that, at low levels of trade and with limited capital mobility, nations can sustain quite elaborate social insurance programs and make effective use of fiscal policy as a tool of KDM, even if these impose heavy tax or private-sector social network obligations on capital and labor. Similarly, even with increased trade and capital mobility, such programs can be sustained as long as the trade flows and capital movements are concentrated within and among nations with similar levels of social insurance and tax systems (especially if exchange rates can be fixed among the primary economic partners, as in Europe). Social insurance arrangements become more difficult to sustain, however, once capital becomes "footloose" and can freely and profitably move to nations that have much lower levels of social protection and lower taxes, and once trade with these nations comes to constitute a growing proportion of the economy. First, capital cannot be taxed (or unduly burdened with social network obligations) because it can relocate in nations that do not impose these burdens. As a result, we should expect more and more of the burden of financing social insurance to be born by labor relative to capital—further exacerbating social inequalities.[7] At the same time, though labor is less mobile and so can be taxed heavily, at a certain point the ability of nations to shift the cost of financing social insurance to this sector will reach its limit. Nations will find it increasingly difficult to raise payroll taxes to the rates necessary to sustain elaborate social insurance programs once more and more of their local industries have to compete in markets with labor that is not burdened with the added costs of social insurance.

It is important to recognize that social insurance programs and social network obligations that provide *interclass transfers* will be squeezed the hardest by globalization. As long as a social welfare program is providing a service that workers need to secure in one way or another—such as health insurance or pensions—labor in countries where these services are provided through the state will not necessarily price itself out of competition with labor in countries where these services are purchased through private markets.[8] British industry *gains* in competitiveness because the National Health Service delivers health care more cheaply (as a share of GNP) than does the American medical system. However, where labor in traded sectors is asked to bear, in addition to the cost of its own social insurance, a disproportionate share of the costs of social insurance and transfers to the lower classes, it increasingly finds itself at a disadvantage in competition with nations where traded-sector labor is responsible only for its own welfare. As a result, the economic logic detailed here leads us to expect that globalization will shrink first those social welfare programs (such as AFDC in the United States) that provide the most direct transfers between rich and poor, leading to a *reduction* in interclass side payments exactly when globalization is creating a need for increases in these transfers to offset its unequal effects on society.

A brief look at an earlier period of globalization, applying some of the insights from economic theory developed here, can help us better understand the effects of this phenomenon on class structures. The last major period of globalization—one with interesting parallels to current trends—spanned the years between 1870 and 1913. During this period, the cost of transportation, which had constituted a major barrier to the trade of bulk commodities such as grains, fell dramatically; for example, the price paid in Liverpool for grain imported from the American Midwest fell from 60 percent above the Chicago price in 1870 to just 15 percent above that price in 1912. This drop in transportation costs ushered in a period of rapidly increasing trade between land-rich, labor-poor areas such as the United States and labor-rich, land-poor areas in Europe. In addition, international labor migrations between the same regions led to a 37 percent surge in the size of the workforce in the labor-short New World, even as the Old World labor force shrank by 18 percent.[9]

Each of these developments, our economic model tells us, should have had distributive effects on the affected societies. Increased trade, as noted earlier, tends to reduce the income of relatively scarce factors while raising the income of abundant factors. Labor migrations have the same effect. During this period, therefore, rapidly increased trade and the migration of unskilled workers from surplus to shortage areas should have had the effect in the New World of reducing the incomes of unskilled labor (the scarce factor) and increasing the incomes derived from land and skilled labor (the abundant factors). In the Old World, in a reversal of this effect, increased trade should have raised the wages of unskilled labor relative to incomes derived from land and skilled labor.

The historical record, the economist Jeffrey Williamson argues, confirms these predictions. "In the New World," he writes, "the ratio of wage rates to farm rents plunged . . . [while] in the Old World the reverse occurred, especially where free trade policies were pursued."[10] Furthermore, the shifts in the ratios were quite dramatic: the ratio of wage rates to farm rents fell to half its 1870 level in the United States, while in Britain and Ireland the ratio rose by factors of 2.7 and 5.5, respectively. Because landowners in both the Old and New Worlds began the period near the top of the income distribution scale, these shifts in the ratios brought on by globalization meant that New World nations like the United States suffered from widening income gaps even as Old World nations, like Britain, Ireland, Sweden, and Denmark, saw reductions in their (still substantial) levels of income inequality.

Williamson sees a possible warning in the record of this earlier period of globalization. This era was followed, after World War I, by a broad retreat from the liberal trading system, owing in part, it seems, to the reaction against growing inequality in nations like the United States. Although the surge in protectionism (and immigration restrictions) that marked the period between 1913 and 1950 did stem the inequality trend in the United States and elsewhere, and perhaps even contributed eventually to the rise of the middle class there, it also helped produce the Great Depression and World War II. This historical precedent makes it all the more imperative that we examine closely the effects of the current round of globalization on the class structure of advanced industrialized nations.

## Globalization and the Postwar Social Contracts

In the early years after the war, the architects of the postwar international economic system worked to create a system that differed dramatically from the one that had existed in the earlier era of globalization. The advanced economies would work to gradually open their markets, but they started with high levels of protection for domestic industries and strict limits on capital mobility. Rather than leaving market forces free to carry economies wherever they might go, they constructed a system of "embedded liberalism" that allowed free trade rules to be bent when they threatened the predominant social purpose: maintaining domestic economic and political stability.[11] Furthermore, as they gradually opened up to trade and foreign investment, the nations of Europe, Japan, and North America developed social contracts that cushioned affected sectors from the short-term negative effects of market forces, providing more citizens with the economic security of life in the middle class. Through these efforts, all of these nations came to experience not only high levels of aggregate economic growth but also improving levels of income equality that reflected the widespread sharing of the benefits of this growth.

By the late 1970s, however, the trade and investment patterns of the advanced economies had begun to reach levels seen during the earlier era of globalization. Just as the falling cost of transportation sharply reduced the cost of trade in bulk commodities during the late nineteenth century, reductions in the tariffs on manufactured goods in developed countries from 40 percent in the late 1940s to 7 percent after the Tokyo Round dramatically lowered the cost of trade in industrial goods.[12] Moreover, liberalization of the regulations restricting capital movements have combined with further reductions in the cost of transportation to lead multinational firms to invest heavily in newly industrializing countries (NICs) in recent years. With NICs incorporated into global production networks, barriers to trade in industrial sectors such as electronics have been virtually eliminated.[13] Finally, technological change as well as moves toward liberalization and privatization (driven in part by the effects of increased trade competition) have led to dramatic reductions in barriers to trade in services such as telecommunications, finance, and insurance.

The result has been a surge in trade overall as well as a surge in trade between developed and developing countries. Merchandise exports grew as a proportion of the economies of industrialized countries from extremely low levels in 1950 (4.4 percent in Germany; 2.0 percent in Japan; 3.3 percent in the United States) to levels that had almost doubled by 1996 (22.1 percent in Germany; 8.9 percent in Japan; 8.2 percent in the United States).[14] Although much of this trade was carried out between developed nations, merchandise trade between these nations and the developing nations, especially the NICs, has surged in recent years. This trade began gaining momentum in the 1970s: the NICs' share of world manufactured exports rose from 1.9 percent in 1964–65 to 8.7 percent in 1983.[15] The greatest surge in imports from developing nations, however, has come only in the last decade: between 1990 and 1996, such imports grew by 60 percent for Japan, 46 percent for the United States, 71 percent for Britain, and 52 percent for Germany.[16]

International competition in service sectors, meanwhile, has expanded to the point that these sectors exceed merchandise trade in some dyads. Finally, the years since capital liberalization began in the 1970s have seen an explosion in the volume of short-term capital movements, with the sum of money flowing through currency markets reaching the level of US$1.2 trillion a day by the early 1990s and the volume of bank loans across borders reaching the level of US$3.6 trillion. Both of these levels were double those of just a few years earlier.[17]

The economic theory summarized here and the historical record of the earlier era of globalization give us good reason to be concerned about the effects of this recent surge in international exchange on the improved levels of income equality that were achieved during the first postwar decades, when international transactions were much more limited. According to the theory, increased trade and investment, especially with developing nations, can be expected to widen income gaps between the rich and the poor in all of the advanced industrialized nations, shrinking the middle class in the process. Unskilled workers (the relatively scarce factor) are predicted to see their incomes decline even as skilled workers and owners of capital (the relatively abundant factors) are expected to see their incomes rise. Globalization, the theory predicts, can be expected to drive a wedge through the middle classes of the advanced economies, pushing less-skilled workers down and more-skilled workers up out of a class that had for a few decades been home to both.

What stands between globalization and these theoretical predictions are the postwar social contracts that were designed to cushion the effects of market forces as economies were liberalized. Before we can explore the degree to which various manifestations of the social contract have been able to ameliorate the polarizing effects of globalization on class structure, we first need to review the differences between the social contracts that helped grow the middle classes in the advanced industrialized countries. All employed Keynesian demand management to smooth out the troughs in the business cycle, and all created some form of social insurance, but the emphases differed enough that we can identify three quite distinct models.

First, in the United States the middle class grew out of a political economy organized around mass consumption. Corporations worked out arrangements with industrial labor unions designed to win labor peace in exchange for high wages, and these wages in turn gave workers the purchasing power necessary to propel growth.[18] Social insurance was largely occupational in the sense that health care and pension benefit levels varied depending on an individual's employer.[19] The state had a minimal role in all of this, using KDM to keep the economy running at full employment so that most citizens could earn their own incomes through work and with a minimal safety net. The elements of that safety net that dated back to the Great Depression, as well as the elements constructed as part of the Great Society project in the 1960s, were designed not so much to redistribute income as to make sure the poor did not starve.[20] The ideology behind the U.S. approach, in fact, emphasized the need to keep benefit levels as low as possible for working-age adults to avoid creating a sense of dependency on the state and to maintain incentives to work.[21] Britain, notably, has moved sharply toward this model since Margaret Thatcher came to power in 1979.

On the continent of Europe, in contrast, the state was much more involved in growing the middle classes by providing, either directly or through mandates, more generous social wages, more universal social protection, and a generous safety net.[22] In much of northern Europe, corporatist networks functioned in such a way as to pull up the wage levels of lagging sectors along with those that were most competitive internationally. The huge proportion of workers employed by the state or working in service sectors sheltered by regulation from market forces were also able to claim generous wage increases and benefits that made them the core of the new middle class. Meanwhile, where the state did not offer social insurance directly through universal programs, it imposed strict requirements forcing firms to provide extensive benefits and job protections. There were certainly important differences in the composition of programs across the European states, but they had in common a universalistic approach to social protection—enforced by the state—that was distinct from the U.S. and Japanese models summarized here.[23]

Finally, Japan, though slow to construct traditional redistributive government programs, gradually converted its system of "convoy capitalism"—built to propel the nation's economic advance—into what functioned essentially as a redistributive support system for uncompetitive and declining sectors of the economy. Internationally competitive firms like Toyota and Toshiba paid higher prices for steel, cement, and flat glass than they could have found on the world market in order to maintain their commitment to domestic business partners. These and other firms paid workers more in order to cover the higher costs of food, consumer goods, and housing that they had to pay in order to maintain employment in agriculture, retail, and construction. And large firms maintained lifetime employment commitments to worker stakeholders even at the expense of profits.[24] Together, these networks made it possible for Japan to maintain extremely low levels of unemployment even during slowdowns and to limit wage differentials between white- and blue-collar labor—effectively redistributing income from the globalization winners to the globalization losers. The state role in all of this, however, was much more informal than in the European model. The state served as a regulator and broker dedicated to helping firms avoid market disruptions so that they could keep the convoy moving steadily ahead, but it provided only a minimal safety net, employed only a relatively small segment of the labor force, and allowed firms to provide benefit levels that differed sharply depending on size.[25]

## Inequality Trends Today: How Do They Differ and Why?

Economic theory and the history of the period between 1870 and 1913 suggest that inequality should be increasing today in all advanced industrialized societies in response to globalization. This time, however, these nations have constructed much more elaborate social contracts designed to cushion the effects of market forces, giving us reason to wonder whether one or more of the three approaches is succeeding in holding out against the tide. In this section, I briefly review the empirical evidence on inequality trends and then offer a preliminary analysis.

Comparing income inequality across time and countries is not a simple exercise. There are multiple ways of measuring income and multiple indices for inequality, the figures often vary sharply depending on which is chosen, and sometimes differences in how governments and scholars keep statistics across nations make meaningful comparison almost impossible. The study that has worked hardest to overcome these limitations is the Luxembourg Income Study (LIS). Unlike other studies that are based on data that exclude substantial segments of the population, the LIS reports comparable income data for *all households*, excluding only those employed in the military, the homeless, and the institutionalized.[26] The LIS also requires all participating nations to use identical definitions of income. Because of the rigorous standards of comparability, however, this database excludes one of the countries of interest to us (Japan) and reports data for only a few scattered years. Nevertheless, the data do show some interesting differences in inequality trends between 1979 and the present (see figure 13.1).

These data show that inequality in household disposable income worsened most dramatically during this period for the United States and Britain, with the Gini coefficient for those nations shifting from 30.9 to 36.8 for the former and from 27 to 34.6 for the latter.[27] These trends have been confirmed by a large number of studies. Frank Levy's study of inequality in the United States, for example, found that the Gini coefficient for household income (before taxes and transfers) worsened from 39.1 in 1969 to 43.1 in 1989 and 45.5 in 1996.[28] Paul Ryscavage, reporting U.S. inequality data for broader measures of income and taking into account the cash value of employee health benefits and capital gains (which worsen the Gini index) along with taxes, transfers, and the cash value of welfare services (which improve it), shows that the trend line worsens on a parallel, if somewhat less unequal, track.[29] Putting these numbers into terms more easily absorbed by those unaccustomed to inequality statistics, Levy concludes that "the middle class" (defined as households earning between $30,000 and $80,000, in 1997 U.S. dollars) contracted sharply from 63 percent of prime-aged households in 1973 to 51 percent in 1996.[30] Other studies have confirmed the LIS observation of a

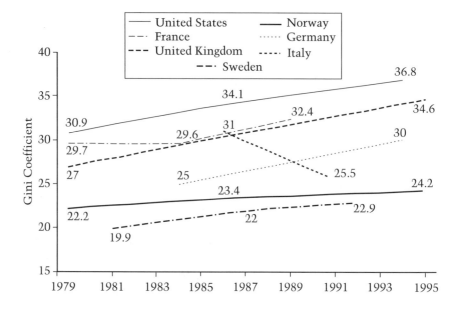

**Figure 13.1**  Trends in Income Distribution of Seven Industrialized Countries, Measured by the Gini Coefficient, 1979 to 1995  *Sources:* A. Atkinson, L. Rainwater, and T. Smeeding, *Income Inequality in the OECD Countries: Evidence from the Luxembourg Income Study* (Paris: OECD, 1995), 49; and Timothy M. Smeeding and Peter Gottschalk, "Cross-national Income Inequality: How Great Is It and What Can We Learn from It?" *Focus* 19 (Summer-Fall 1998), 16. See note 27 for a definition of Gini Coefficient and further information on the data used to generate this figure.

similar trend in Britain. Karen Gardiner reports twelve measures of income inequality in Britain drawn from four different studies and notes that they uniformly document a deterioration since the late 1970s.[31]

The appendix to this volume provides much more detailed data on income distribution trends in the United States and Britain, as well as the other countries discussed in this chapter. Unlike the LIS data featured in figure 13.1, which are limited to just a few years over a span of twenty years—in order to maintain comparability—the national data presented in the appendix cover periods extending back to around 1960, with many more data points. Furthermore, rather than featuring the Gini index, the appendix shows income distribution by quintiles (the share of national income going to families whose income is in the top 20 percent). Measuring income distribution in this way allows us to see whether inequality grew mostly because of a growing dispersion near the middle—not necessarily a problem—or because of movement at the upper and lower ends of the scale. The data for the United States and Britain shows clearly that income inequality in those countries grew mostly because families at the upper end greatly expanded their share of national income while those at the lower end saw their income shares contract.

In contrast, the income distribution data for continental Europe featured in figure 13.1 and the appendix show much less deterioration. Indeed, the LIS data for Italy show an improvement—that is, the nation went from having one of the most unequal distributions of income among the study group in 1986 to a much more equal distribution in 1991. National data sources for Italy presented in the appendix, covering the years 1967 to 1998, confirm that the longer-term trend has been toward an improvement in levels of inequality. They also indicate, however, that there has been a modest deterioration over the past decade. The LIS data for France show that it experienced an improvement too between 1979 and 1984, but that it has since seen a deterioration roughly parallel to that in Britain. Data for Norway and Sweden show a deterioration of 2.0 and 3.0 percentage points, respectively, over this period—much less of a rise in inequality than in the United States and Britain. Peter Gottschalk, manipulating the same LIS data set to focus on the labor market earnings of prime-aged, full-time male workers, found that Sweden experienced the smallest increase in inequality, while France and the Netherlands experienced an increase that was only one-quarter that seen in the United States.[32] Richard Freeman and Lawrence Katz similarly found that wage differentials declined or remained unchanged in France, Germany, Italy, and the Netherlands while growing somewhat in Sweden.[33] Several data sources for a variety of continental European nations thus concur in observing much less of a rise, and in some cases a decline, in inequality.[34]

Japan has chosen not to participate at all in the Luxembourg Income Study, and so data on Japan that are strictly comparable with data for the other advanced industrialized nations surveyed here are not available. Nevertheless, a number of the national studies that have been conducted are consistent with LIS data at least in their definitions and measures over time. The most widely cited data source on inequality in Japan is the Family Income and Expenditure Survey (FIES), but some scholars prefer to use the Ministry of Health and Welfare's Income Redistribution Survey (IRS). Most critically for our purposes, both show that Japan experienced quite a dramatic increase in income inequality over the period 1980 to 1997 (see figure 13.2).

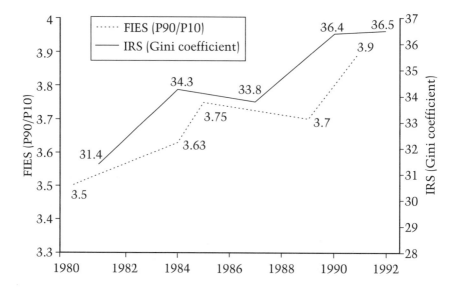

**Figure 13.2** Income Inequality in Japan, 1980 to 1992 *Sources*: Atkinson, Rainwater, and Smeeding, *Income Distribution in OECD Countries*, 70; Tachibanaki, *Nihon no keizai kakusa* (Economic differences in Japan), 5. See the appendix discussion of Japanese data for discussion of indices and data sources.

First, the IRS, which is based on a sampling of a much broader proportion of the total population of households than is the FIES, shows that Japan's Gini coefficient grew from 31.4 in 1981 to 36.5 in 1992. The latter rate placed Japan near the levels of income inequality found in the United States, which according to the LIS had a Gini coefficient of 36.8 in 1994.[35] The trend line documented in this study also placed Japan with the United States and Britain as suffering one of the most severe deteriorations over time. As Tachibanaki Toshiaki and Yagi Tadashi conclude in their analysis of this data, "We would claim that no other major industrialized country had such a drastic increase in inequality of income distribution during such a short period."[36] Although Tachibanaki has not yet published Gini coefficient data based on the IRS data for more recent years, data on the income of the poorest quartile of the Japanese population as a share of average income (published by the Ministry of Health and Welfare and based on the same survey—see figure 13.3) show that the trend continued in the 1990s. Note that in this figure a line sloping downward indicates rising levels of inequality.

The other widely cited measure of inequality in Japan, the FIES (shown in figure 13.2), covers a smaller segment of the Japanese popu-

**Figure 13.3** Income of the Poorest Quartile as a Share of Average Income in Japan, 1985 to 1997  *Sources*: Ministry of Health and Welfare, *Health and Welfare Statistics in Japan, 1995*, 30; and *1998*, 28, cited in Douglas Ostrom, "Rich and Poor in Japan: How Wide Is the Gap?" *JEI Report* 37A, October 1, 1999, 8.

lation than the IRS and generates inequality measures that still place Japan among the more equal OECD nations. The trend over time based on this data, however, is almost identical to that based on the IRS.[37] According to the FIES, the P90/P10 ratio, a measure of income inequality used as an alternative to the Gini coefficient, rose from 3.5 to 3.9 over the decade of the 1980s.[38] The appendix reports FIES data for Japan for the years 1963 to 1998 and shows that, as in the United States and Britain, Japan's recent increase in inequality has been driven primarily by the rise in the income share of top income earners at the expense of those at the bottom of the distribution.

The empirical data on recent trends in income distribution within advanced industrialized societies, in summary, show that these societies have *not* experienced a uniform rise in inequality of the kind we might have expected based on the economic theory and history surveyed in the first section of this chapter. Levels of inequality have risen sharply in the United States, Britain, and Japan, but on the continent of Europe they have remained generally stable, fallen, or risen only slightly. Since it was anticipated earlier that this latest round of globalization might not generate a uniform increase in inequality because of differences in the mix of policies and practices that provide social protection and more equitable distribution of incomes in today's advanced industrialized societies, it is tempting to jump to specific conclusions about the reasons for this pattern of outcomes based on the observed correlation. The ability of European societies to retain previous levels of equality or at least to slow down inequality trends suggests that the mix of activist state policies that are at the heart of European postwar social contracts have proven most effective at mitigating the effects of globalization on inequality. In contrast, the rapid increases in inequality in the United States, Britain, and Japan suggest that approaches relying on consumption-led growth and convoy capitalism have *not* proven sufficient to maintain previous levels of equality.

As noted at the beginning of this chapter, however, the causes of inequality are too complex for us to jump to this conclusion so quickly. Although the pattern is *suggestive,* the correlation on its own does not provide enough evidence to give us confidence that differences in the nature of postwar social contracts across these societies are the primary cause of differences in their inequality trends. First, since it is possible that the contrasting outcomes are due to differences in other factors affecting levels of inequality, we cannot be confident that the nature of the postwar social contract is the critical factor until we more fully explore alternative explanations. Second, the posited conclusion is less convincing absent a more elaborate logic explaining why the European approach has been better able to maintain levels of equality in the face of globalization while the other approaches have not. Finally, that more elaborate logic will require confirming evidence. Although space limitations prevent me from undertaking these tasks here, I conclude this chapter by offering a few thoughts on each step in this research agenda.

### Alternative Explanations of Income Inequality Across Societies

Although most studies of recent inequality trends in the advanced industrialized societies assign significant causal effect to factors related to globalization and the mix of policies and practices we have called postwar social contracts, they also point to the importance of factors such as family living arrangements and technological change.[39] According to studies of income inequality in the United States by Paul Ryscavage and Frank Levy, up to two-fifths of the recent rise in inequality in that nation may have been caused by social and demographic changes such as the rise in female-headed families and the recent tendency of high-earning women to marry high-earning men.[40] Studies of rising income inequality in the United States have also highlighted the role of technological changes, such as the growing use of computers, in generating a skills bias in wage levels.[41]

Although studies of other nations have examined the role played by these factors, the available evidence does not suggest that technology or marriage patterns vary across nations in ways that mirror the uneven pattern of rising inequality described here. For example, Japan has experienced a much smaller increase in female-headed households than the United States but has seen inequality rise just as fast. Similarly, although the United States seems to have been the first to embrace some types of technology (for example, personal computers and the Internet), a technology gap seems unlikely to explain why Japan and Britain have experienced greater increases in inequality than the nations of Scandinavia, France, and Italy. Data assembled under the auspices of the Luxembourg Income Study, supplemented by similar data on Japan, should allow scholars to begin sorting out which factors—globalization, postwar social contracts, or the alternative factors identified here—can best account for variations in inequality trends across nations.

## A More Elaborate Logic Explaining the Relative Success of the European Approach

In the first few decades of the postwar period, the United States, Japan, and the nations of Western Europe all found ways to reduce income disparities and establish relative social peace anchored by large and inclusive middle classes, but the evidence summarized here suggests that the approach adopted on the continent of Europe has been better able to sustain this contract in the face of globalization. Why? The explanation I offer is based on the collective action problem involved in "providing social peace" through social protection and redistribution. These tasks constitute a collective action problem because, although all members of societies that enjoy social peace benefit from it, some segments pay a disproportionate share of the costs to support this effort. Following scholars who have emphasized the role of corporatist wage bargaining in sustaining more egalitarian income distribution,[42] I propose that more centralized processes of redistributing income and providing social protection are more resilient in the face of globalization than those that rely on a decentralized collection of subnational governments, firms, and labor unions.

Even when social protection and income redistribution are provided and managed by nation-states and corporatist bargains are struck at the national level, globalization presents a challenge. Central organizations representing industry, when faced with growing competition from foreign firms operating from countries where they face less of a redistributive burden, are likely to demand that the welfare state and labor market institutions be restructured so that domestic industry is at less of a competitive disadvantage. Tax competition may place states under fiscal pressure to scale back social benefits, cut the salaries of public workers, or accelerate the pace of privatization.[43] As long as these decisions are made at the national level through a political process, however, the pace at which redistributive programs are abandoned is likely to be slower than when key decisions are made by subnational governments or individual firms. When decisions are made politically at the national level, the many beneficiaries of social programs are given opportunities to mobilize to defend the status quo. Nations, moreover, have more flexibility with their finances than do firms.[44]

The American and Japanese cases show us how the process can be accelerated when smaller units are provided with opportunities to reduce their contribution to social peace. The U.S. model, as summarized earlier, relied on firms like General Motors to offer generous wages that provided workers with the consumption power to increase purchasing volume; that increase in turn helped firms maintain competitiveness and earn profits by improving their economies of scale. This approach worked as long as the Big Three automakers all practiced the same strategy and faced few outside competitors. Once Japanese automakers entered the U.S. market in volume, however, each of the Big Three faced pressures to cut costs to compete. Once one began cutting, the others had to follow or face bankruptcy. Their inability to overcome collective action problems when faced with foreign competition thus broke the beneficent circle that had earlier helped improve levels of equality in the United States.

In Japan, equality was enhanced in part because the globalization winners (such as Nissan) redistributed some of their gains by keeping their employees on the payroll in slow times and agreeing to pay higher costs for domestic inputs such as steel, petrochemicals, and construction. The collective action problem among firms was mitigated, furthermore, by lax antitrust enforcement and government assistance designed to sustain the nation's "convoy" approach to capitalism. Nevertheless, the Japanese model remained reliant on *voluntary* redistribution by firms that—especially when whole industries were threatened—could not bear the full burden of a policy serving such a broad social purpose. Once globalization compelled more and more firms to cut costs to remain competitive, even firms that enjoyed much more government protection than their U.S. counterparts had no choice but to scale back the proportion of workers covered by the social contract.

*Confirming Evidence of the Logic Explaining the Resistance of Some Inequality Trends to Globalization*

In the limited space of this chapter, I can do little more than show a simple correlation and put forward a basic logic and a few stories like those just summarized to link the uneven inequality trends of the advanced industrialized countries to differences in how their social contracts have held up in the face of globalization. If I am correct, however, I would expect to find confirming evidence in two places: in a more detailed analysis of income distribution trends, and in a close examination of changes in the features of each nation's social contract. First, I expect that an analysis of income data would confirm a pattern that Gottschalk has already suggested: that wage levels in nations without centralized wage bargaining institutions (most notably the United States, Britain, and Japan) have experienced the greatest degree of divergence in response to greater international competition with low-wage countries.[45] Second, I expect this data to show that taxes and transfers do the most to ameliorate the effects of unequal before-tax incomes in cases where programs are run at the national level (not by subnational governments or firms). Finally, I would expect to find that governments have resisted fiscal and political pressures to cut back on state-run redistributive programs (such as pension programs) more effectively than have firms and industry associations that in the past supported firms and workers in less productive segments of the economy. I cannot explore evidence related to each of these points here, but this list of expectations provides an agenda for further research.

## Conclusion

Economic theory gives us reasons to expect that increased international trade and capital flows, especially when they involve nations with sharply differing factor endowments, will tend to redistribute income in ways that aggravate inequality in advanced industrialized nations. Those individuals who have capital and skills that are in high demand can command much higher salaries in this increasingly global market, even as those with fewer skills face more competition from low-paid foreign workers. Although all of the advanced industrialized nations developed institutions and policies over the postwar period that were designed to provide social protection from market forces like globalization and to moderate the inequalities associated with a market economy, economic theory also tells us that the same global economic forces can be expected to challenge the ability of nations to maintain these social contracts.

This chapter has shown that we have more than just theoretical reasons to worry about the effects of globalization on social contracts. Almost all of the advanced industrialized nations have in fact become more unequal to one degree or another over the past two decades, suggesting that an erosion in the old social contracts or their inability to compensate for the starker distributional effects of growing international commerce is behind this trend. This finding should be a major cause for concern. According to the inequality statistics cited in this chapter, the middle classes in most advanced economies are shrinking. Some individuals are moving up into the upper-middle class, but many are slipping down into the ranks of the poor. Moreover, the institutions and policies that previously worked to grow middle classes and dampen the frustrations of the poor through tax and transfer policies, government- and firm-provided social benefits, and micro- and macroeconomic intervention are not functioning as well as they used to.

Fortunately, not all societies have experienced this trend to the same degree. The sharpest increases in inequality have occurred in the United States, which relied on fluid labor markets and policies designed to maintain steady consumption-driven growth through arrangements like the "treaty of Detroit," and in Britain, which since Thatcher has moved toward the U.S. model. Japan's rate of deterioration is almost as steep, suggesting that its model of convoy capitalism, which relied on government microeconomic intervention to help firms avoid bankruptcy and instability in exchange for their role in maintaining stable employment and subsidizing lagging sectors, is no longer capable of cushioning workers from market forces. In contrast, the rise in inequality has been slower in most European countries, some of which have actually seen improvements. This finding suggests that states may still be able to counteract the effects of globalization if they are willing to centralize the process by which wages are set, run tax and transfer programs at the national level, and rely largely on the state (rather than firms) to redistribute income. Though further work remains to be done to establish more clearly the connections between globalization, social contracts, and inequality trends, the overall correlation holds out the hope that the European approach is a viable way of maintaining social peace in our societies, even in the face of recent economic changes.

## Notes

Japanese names appear with last names first, even in English-language publications.

1.  Ronald Inglehart, *The Silent Revolution: Changing Values and Political Styles Among Western Publics* (Princeton: Princeton University Press, 1977); Daniel Bell, *The Coming of Post-Industrial Society: A Venture in Social Forecasting.* (New York: Basic, 1973).
2.  Judith Goldstein, *Ideas, Interests, and American Trade Policy* (Ithaca: Cornell University Press, 1993).
3.  Wolfgang Stolper and Paul Samuelson, "Protection and Real Wages," *Review of Economic Studies* 9 (1941): 58–773.
4.  Jeffry Frieden and Ronald Rogowski, "The Impact of the International Economy on National Policies: An Analytical Overview," in *Internationalization and Domestic Politics,* edited by Robert O. Keohane and Helen V. Milner (Cambridge: Cambridge University Press, 1996); Jeffrey G. Williamson, "Globalization and Inequality, Past and Present," *World Bank Research Observer* 12(August 1997): 117–35; Adrian Wood, "How Trade Hurt Unskilled Workers," *Journal of Economic Perspectives* 9(Summer 1995): 57–80.
5.  Note that the model predicts the opposite effect in nations that have abundant unskilled labor and a shortage of skilled labor: increased trade should make these societies more equal by increasing the incomes of the poor and reducing those of the rich. See Wood, "How Trade Hurt Unskilled Workers."
6.  Dani Rodrik, *Has Globalization Gone Too Far?* (Washington, D.C.: Institute for International Economics, 1997), 4.
7.  Ibid., 55.
8.  Gøsta Esping-Andersen, "Welfare States at the End of the Century: The Impact of Labor Market, Family, and Demographic Change," in *Family, Market, and Community: Equity and Efficiency in Social Policy,* Social Policy Studies 21 (Paris: Organization for Economic Cooperation and Development, 1997), 71.
9.  Williamson, "Globalization and Inequality, Past and Present."
10. Ibid., 125.
11. John G. Ruggie, "International Regimes, Transactions, and Change: Embedded Liberalism in the Postwar Economic Order," *International Organization* 36(Spring 1982): 394.
12. Williamson, "Globalization and Inequality, Past and Present," 123.
13. William Greider, *One World, Ready or Not: The Manic Logic of Global Capitalism* (New York: Touchstone, 1997), 81–102.
14. Angus Maddison, *Dynamic Forces in Capitalist Development* (Oxford: Oxford University Press, 1991), 327, updated with IMF data.
15. Organization for Economic Cooperation and Development, *The Newly Industrializing Countries: Challenge and Opportunity for the OECD Countries* (Paris: OECD, 1988).
16. International Monetary Fund, *Direction of Trade* statistics. Although these increases have increased the share of imports from developing nations (to 40 percent of total imports in the United States, for example), economists who question whether trade has any effect on wage inequality stress that these imports remain too low as a share of the total economy (5 percent in the United States) to have much of an impact. See Gary Burtless et al., *Globaphobia: Confronting Fears About Open Trade* (Washington, D.C.: Brookings Institution, 1998), 68.
17. Greider, *One World, Ready or Not,* 23.
18. Olivier Zunz, *Why the American Century?* (Chicago: University of Chicago Press, 1998).

19. Martin Rein estimates that 30 percent of total social protection in the United States is channeled through firms in the private sector—three or four times the proportion of protection offered through firms in Europe. See Martin Rein, "Is America Exceptional?: The Role of Occupational Welfare in the United States and the European Community," in *The Privatization of Social Policy: Occupational Welfare and the Welfare State in America, Scandinavia, and Japan*, edited by Michael Shalev (New York: St. Martin's Press, 1996), 14.

20. Margaret Weir, "Ideas and the Politics of Bounded Rationality," in *Structuring Politics: Historical Institutionalism in Comparative Analysis*, edited by Sven Steinmo, Kathleen Thelen, and Frank Longtreth (Cambridge: Cambridge University Press, 1992), 188–216.

21. Gøsta Esping-Andersen, *The Three Worlds of Welfare Capitalism* (Princeton: Princeton University Press, 1990).

22. See Öhngren (this volume).

23. Esping-Andersen, for example, in *The Three Worlds of Welfare Capitalism*, draws a sharp distinction between the Scandinavian social-democratic approach and the conservative-corporatist model found in Germany and much of the rest of Europe.

24. Richard Katz, *Japan: The System That Soured* (Armonk, N.Y.: M. E. Sharpe, 1998).

25. Shinkawa Toshimitsu and T. J. Pempel, "Occupational Welfare and the Japanese Experience," in Shalev, *The Privatization of Social Policy*, 280–338.

26. Anthony B. Atkinson, Lee Rainwater, and Timothy Smeeding, *Income Distribution in OECD Countries: Evidence from the Luxembourg Income Study* (Paris: OECD, 1995), 17.

27. For income figures, see LIS data presented in Atkinson, Rainwater, and Smeeding, *Income Distribution in OECD Countries*, 49, and Timothy M. Smeeding and Peter Gottschalk, "Cross-national Income Inequality: How Great Is It and What Can We Learn from It?" *Focus* 19(Summer–Fall 1998): 16. These figures are for disposable income, after taxes and transfers. The Gini coefficient is the commonly used measure that is based on a nation's Lorenz curve plotting the cumulative share of total income of population segments from the poorest to the richest. The coefficient is the percentage of the area between a straight forty-five-degree line, representing a completely equal distribution of income, and the concave Lorenz curve as a share of the total area of the triangle below the straight line. A large coefficient thus reflects a Lorenz curve that is extremely concave, with poorer segments of the population receiving much smaller shares of total income than the richest.

28. Frank Levy, *The New Dollars and Dreams: American Incomes and Economic Change* (New York: Russell Sage Foundation, 1998), 200.

29. Paul Ryscavage, *Income Inequality in America: An Analysis of Trends* (Armonk, N.Y.: M. E. Sharpe, 1999), 70–72.

30. Levy, *The New Dollars and Dreams*, 162. He defines "prime-aged" households as those headed by an individual between age twenty-five and fifty-four. He found that this spreading out of the distribution of household income involved an increase in the number of wealthier families (those making over $80,000 grew from 13 percent of all households to 20.7 percent) as well as an increase in the number of poorer households (those making under $30,000) from 23.8 percent to 28.3 percent.

31. Karen Gardiner, "A Survey of Income Inequality over the Last Twenty

Years—How Does the U.K. Compare," in *Changing Patterns in the Distribution of Economic Welfare: An International Perspective*, edited by Peter Gottschalk, Björn Gustafsson, and Edward Palmer (Cambridge: Cambridge University Press, 1997), 37–38. Similar conclusions are reached in two other studies of Britain. See Alissa Goodman, Paul Johnson, and Steven Webb, *Inequality in the United Kingdom*, (Oxford: Oxford University Press, 1997), 91–94; Richard B. Freeman and Lawrence F. Katz, eds., *Differences and Changes in Wage Structures* (Chicago: University of Chicago Press, 1995), 13.

32. Peter Gottschalk, "Policy Changes and Growing Earnings Inequality in the United States and Six Other OECD Countries," in Gottschalk, Gustafsson, and Palmer, *Changing Patterns in the Distribution of Economic Welfare*, 29–30.

33. Freeman and Katz, *Differences and Changes in Wage Structures*, 13.

34. Evaluating the evidence for Germany (which, according to the LIS data reported in figure 13.1, experienced a sharp deterioration in levels of inequality between 1984 and 1994) is complicated by the reunification of that nation that took place in the interim. The national data for Germany in the appendix to this volume, examining the trend over time in the area of the former West Germany, show remarkably flat trend lines for the income shares of quintiles in the period since 1970. Though the share of the richest quintile has been rising very gradually at the expense of the lower quintiles over the past ten years, the data suggest that the deterioration in the former West Germany has not been anywhere near the magnitude seen in the United States and Britain.

35. Tachibanaki Toshiaki and Yagi Tadashi, "Distribution of Economic Well-being in Japan: Toward a More Unequal Society," in Gottschalk, Gustafsson, and Palmer, *Changing Patterns in the Distribution of Economic Welfare*, 112–13; Tachibanaki Toshiaki, *Nihon no keizai kakusa: Shotoku to shisan kara kangaeru* (Economic differences in Japan: An examination based on income and assets) (Tokyo: Iwanami shinsho, 1998), 5. Although Japan's IRS data set is not strictly comparable to the LIS, the two data sources are similar in two key respects: both report data for a broad, almost universal, population of households, and both of the Gini coefficients cited in figures 13.1 and 13.2 and in the text are for disposable income (after taxes and transfers).

36. Tachibanaki and Yagi, "Distribution of Economic Well-being in Japan," 113.

37. Ibid., 111–12.

38. This ratio, also based in this case on disposable income, is calculated by dividing the percentage of the median income of a household at the ninetieth percentile by the percentage of the median income of a household at the tenth percentile.

39. These studies generally refer not to globalization in the abstract but to more concrete measures, such as increases in trade, foreign investment, and immigration. Similarly, although none of these studies refer to postwar social contracts per se, they do emphasize more concrete policies and practices, such as government tax and transfer policies and labor market institutions.

40. Ryscavage, *Income Inequality in America*, 124–30; Levy, *The New Dollars and Dreams*, 156–59.

41. Burtless et al., *Globaphobia*, 83–84; William R. Cline, *Trade and In-*

*come Distribution* (Washington, D.C.: Institute for International Economics, 1997), 144–45.

42. Gottschalk, "Policy Changes and Growing Earnings Inequality in the United States and Six Other OECD Countries."

43. See the special survey section titled "Globalization and Tax" in *The Economist*, January 29, 2000.

44. Two observers who are optimistic about prospects for the European welfare state are Geoffrey Garrett, "Global Markets and National Politics: Collision Course or Virtuous Circle?" *International Organization* 52(Autumn 1998): 787–824; and Paul Pierson, "The New Politics of the Welfare State," *World Politics* 48(January 1996): 143–79. More pessimistic are Richard Clayton and Jonas Pontusson, "Welfare-State Retrenchment Revisited: Entitlement Cuts, Public-Sector Restructuring, and Inegalitarian Trends in Advanced Capitalist Societies," *World Politics* 51(October 1998): 67–98. See also Evelyne Huber and John D. Stephens, "Internationalization and the Social-Democratic Model: Crisis and Future Prospects," *Comparative Political Studies* 31(June 1998): 353–97.

45. Gottschalk, "Policy Changes and Growing Earnings Inequality in the United States and Six Other OECD Countries."

# 14

## Europeanization of Social Policy: A Reopening of the Social Contract?

### Bo Öhngren

During the first three decades after World War II, the nations of Western Europe experienced a period of steady economic growth and low unemployment. New forms of the social contract were negotiated and put into force. As earlier chapters have shown, the expansion of the middle classes was both an important product and a key component of that process. These new social contracts varied in important ways from that developed in the United States during the same period. While the U.S. social contract rested to a great extent on the expansion of consumption and an inclusive middle class, the social contract in most of the European states depended not so much on making the middle class inclusive as on increasing working-class incomes and adding social protection. In Europe, the state was much more involved in developing the postwar social contract and took a more comprehensive approach to social protection. In short, this period witnessed the birth of the modern European welfare state.

According to Gøsta Esping-Andersen, the ideal of the welfare state was social citizenship and universal solidarity. Full employment, the redistribution of wealth, and the dismantling of class boundaries were seen as fundamental prerequisites for a stable liberal democracy.[1] However, because of their unique economic and political histories, nations pursued these goals in different ways and provided varying forms of social protection. These structural differences also shaped the ability of each system to adapt to change.

The welfare state had its heyday from the end of the Second World

War until the mid-1970s and early 1980s. Although there had always been those who saw it in a state of crisis,[2] it was not until the late 1980s that the European welfare state was seriously questioned and attacked from the Right as well as from the Left. Social contracts in the European states were in deep trouble, and the debate about their value continues in the political as well the academic arena to this day. New policies are adopted in order to cope with change, and new research is funded in order to provide policymakers with new options. The European Union Fifth Framework Program for Research and Co-operation in the Field of Science and Technology (COST) are at the moment supporting research in these directions.

What ultimately has created the undeniable crisis in the European welfare state? It is not possible to isolate one causal factor; rather it is a myriad of pressures that have led to these calls for reform. The more important of these factors include: the turbulence of labor markets due to new technologies and the globalization of trade and capital; the decline of the homogenous mass worker as a result of new production systems and greater social differentiation; and the steady aging of populations and changing family patterns. Some of these factors are very dynamic and changing constantly, while others, like the demographic factors, change only gradually. At the close of the twentieth century, Europe also witnessed the fall of the Berlin Wall and the first steps toward enlarging Europe eastward. Depending on the speed of the democratization of the east, the welfare landscape of Europe and consequently its social contracts will continue to be challenged. Besides the pace of these changes, their interrelations across countries make it difficult to assess the ultimate outcome in any one country.

Furthermore, assessing these outcomes will take time. Most of the existing analyses are undermined by their short-term perspective. For instance, politicians and the media have been too quick to make statements about the consequences of opening up Europe to the east while ascribing inordinate explanatory power to the vague concept of "globalization." Sweden provides an illustrative example.

At the beginning of the 1990s, the Swedish model, the archetype for the modern European welfare state, was counted out. Inflation and unemployment rates as well as the budget deficit as a percentage of GDP had reached two-digit levels. At the same time, the growth of GDP was negative, and the public sector was in crisis. World leaders were fascinated by U.S. economic success and the country's credo of less government and low taxes. The plight of Sweden was widely viewed as an inevitable consequence of the welfare state.

Today the situation is very different. After some years of astute

fiscal management, carried out with the consent of the political opposition and the trade unions, Sweden began a remarkable recovery in
1998 while maintaining the protections afforded by the welfare state.
Included in the package deal was an increase in personal taxes, with
the silent support of the middle classes, and a so-called shield tax,
which was targeted at higher income brackets. In addition, tough
spending limits were imposed along with targeted cuts in social insurance. Thanks to these measures, public finances currently show a
surplus, unemployment rates have declined and now approach 4 percent, inflation is well below 2 percent, and annual GDP growth is just
over 4 percent. The growth figure is the highest in the European
Union.

Not only is the economy flourishing, but the welfare state is on
strong footing as well. Sweden is a country where the government
consumes nearly 60 percent of the national economy, far higher than
the 32 percent in the United States. When Prime Minister Goran
Persson presented the Swedish budget for 2000, he promised that
Sweden would consolidate its position as a leading welfare nation.

This largely unreconstructed welfare state now is one of Europe's
most vibrant economies, after two decades of sluggishness in which
output per head slumped from third highest to eighteenth, just after
Italy.[3] Sweden's economic success reflects a wider pattern in Europe
and a particularly nuanced reaction to the robust U.S. economy of the
1990s: embracing entrepreneurship and unrestricted competition
while continuing to preserve traditional European social programs.
What lies behind this rebound? One major factor is that Sweden's
political leaders have put the government's budget in order after
tough tripartite negotiations in which the middle classes played an
instrumental role. The measures were painful (reduced sick pay, reduced unemployment pay, reduced baby care allowances, and so on),
but they steadily reduced the deficit and gave corporations some
room to breathe. Another factor is that Sweden moved much faster
than most other European countries to deregulate its markets and foster a more entrepreneurial culture.

At the end of the 1990s, the government started to return to former
levels of social payments. The shield tax for the middle-class income
brackets is still in place, but at a lower level. Sweden is back again as
a leading welfare state, but for how long? Will Sweden, with a population of 9 million, be able to adapt again to new challenges, or will
forces like globalization, the aging of the population, and changing
family patterns once again take their toll?

I have used the case of Sweden to demonstrate how rapidly the
situation can change: in deep crisis at the beginning of the 1990s,

Sweden is now back on track. Can this case also be used to demonstrate that any nation-state is capable of overcoming or resisting unwanted effects on its welfare system of globalization or other external factors? Or is it simply Sweden's particular history and institutional setting that enabled it to adapt? One thing we know is that it is still too early to tell. Although we can describe what is happening in Sweden and other European states, our ability to draw any but the most rudimentary conclusions is limited.

Across Europe, the crisis of the welfare state varies from country to country. Nonetheless, it is true that all over Europe welfare regimes are changing and the middle classes are affected by these changes. The widespread notion of the welfare state in crisis has generated extensive political debate about how to cope with the situation. The EU member states took the first step in the early 1990s of agreeing on a document, *Council of Ministers' Recommendation on the Convergence of Social Protection Objectives and Policies of July 1992.*[4] Later on, in 1997, the European Commission published a communication, *Modernizing and Improving Social Protection.*[5] Both documents focus heavily on employment and unemployment issues. With regard to social policy, the formal situation is different. The Council of Ministers' decision on social policy in 1994 makes it absolutely clear that social policy remains a national issue. However, the EU convergence criteria for public spending may make that position irrelevant as the discretionary ability to spend national funds decreases. Other challenges remain, including the aging of the European population and the issue of immigrant labor. By 2015, Europe will be in great need of immigrants to replace elderly wage earners. These two factors will induce changes in the different welfare regimes that we cannot foresee.

Given these common challenges looming on the horizon and the gradual strengthening of the European Union, it is reasonable to suppose that the answer for most European states lies in a transition to a common European social policy and welfare model. In political terms, will there be a convergence of welfare regimes in Europe? To address those questions, I focus on three important issues: the current absence of a common welfare model in Europe; the impact of globalization; and structural changes and social protection.

## The European Landscape of Welfare Regimes

Our ability to discuss specific welfare programs will be sharpened by adhering to a taxonomic framework, for as Leonard Schoppa so rightly points out in this volume, a number of different social contracts are embodied in diverse welfare programs. One easy way of looking at welfare regimes is to compare rates of social expenditure in different countries. However, a number of problems arise in the analysis of social expenditure data. According to Paul Johnson, expenditure data at best present an indirect and imperfect measure of social security output.[6] Many researchers consider those data, even if disaggregated, an insufficient reflection of overall welfare outcomes. To take account of both public and private activity, Esping-Andersen constructed his welfare regime theory, resulting in a three-way categorization of national welfare regimes based on the concept of decommodification—the degree to which social policies make individuals independent of the market for income and consumption.[7] His three clusters are defined by political ideology—social-democratic, conservative, and liberal—and track the famous distinction made by Titmuss between the institutional, the achievement-performance, and the residual social policy models.[8] Several researchers have also added a southern or Latin rim model, an addendum also used by the European Union itself. We will adopt this scheme.

Each European welfare regime—the social-democratic (institutional), the conservative (achievement-performance), the liberal (residual), and the southern rim—has a different institutional structure or welfare provision. Underpinning each is a different tradition of industrial relations and labor market provisions; accordingly, each has responded to the problem of high unemployment and industrial adjustment in a different way. The distinctions between them are important, not just for understanding their contemporary problems but also for evaluating their prospects and potential for reform. The support of such a taxonomy does not imply, as Robert Cox proposes, a priori adherence to a path dependency theory of causality.[9] Moreover, reform and adaptation to the global economy is contingent on the ability of each country to invest in new technologies ahead of its competitors and to create new means of employment generation.

## The Social-Democratic Model

The social democrats who have dominated the Scandinavian systems created a highly universal and "decommodifying" set of programs. Services and benefits were upgraded to levels expected by the middle classes, and equality was ensured by giving all workers full access to those rights. This model crowds out the influence of the market and creates cross-class solidarity and support for an extensive system of welfare support. Furthermore, the role of public provision is maximized at the expense of private-sector provision. To provide equal life chances to all citizens, the provision of care services has been transferred from the family to tax-financed public services. Private, for-profit health provision has been minimized, and living standards ensured by public-pension, sick-pay, and maternity schemes. The strength of the Scandinavian model lies in its guarantee of full employment: the right to work is as important as the right to income protection. This guarantee is also, however, a source of weakness. Sustaining such a system is very costly and requires that revenue be maximized and social problems minimized.

The Scandinavian welfare model is also of interest from a broader political-economic point of view. The five small Scandinavian countries—Denmark, Finland, Iceland, Norway, and Sweden—also possess the most open economies in the OECD, and their industrialization has depended to a great extent on their active participation in the international markets. At the same time, unions (industrial as well as academic) have managed to maintain political leverage, and they play an active part in more or less officially acknowledged and centralized negotiations to determine wages and working conditions. The Scandinavian model has been based on a corporatist wage formation system and a consensus between capital, unions, and the state on rationalization and technical change.

Having said that, it should be noted that historically there has been a divide between the Swedish and Finnish experience, on the one hand, and the Danish and Norwegian experience, on the other. The Danish road to a welfare society has been more liberal, while the Swedes have taken a more corporatist road. The differences between the Scandinavian countries are also reflected in their different relationships to the European Union. Among the five countries, there are four different formal relationships to the EU. Denmark entered as a full member in 1972, but after numerous referenda (most recently in September 2000), it has so far refused to participate in the monetary union. Finland and Sweden became members in 1994. Finland takes full part in the monetary union. Sweden does not. The most troublesome relationship to the EU is Norway's. Two times, in 1972 and 1993, the electorate (with a slight majority) not only rejected membership but even went against large majorities in the national parliament and the advice of union and employer officials. Together with Iceland, however, Norway is a member of the European Economic Area; thus, the two countries take full part in the internal market but are not represented in the decisionmaking bodies of the European Union.

## The Liberal Anglo-Saxon Model

By contrast with the social-democratic model, the liberal model minimizes solidarity and decommodification and delivers modest benefits through means-tested assistance and modest universal transfers.[10] It caters to a clientele of low-income, largely working-class dependents. Unlike the Scandinavian model—in which the middle classes and their support have been central—this is a more residual welfare state that is increasingly dependent on the support of a restricted class coalition. This is a structural weakness because it creates political space for the anti-welfare pressures brought to bear by people who can afford private-sector health care and pensions provision.

Of all the EU members over the decades, the United Kingdom has shifted its economy the most decisively in the direction of the U.S. model—toward wider wage dispersion, increasing inequality, and the rapid expansion of low-paid, service-sector jobs. As an EU report on social protection shows, the growing dualism in the British labor market has been accompanied by a growing dualism in welfare.[11] More weight is attached to means-testing when allocating benefits, and changes in social security regulations have encouraged higher-income groups to leave the compulsory system and join private insurance schemes. We could say that these changes signal a shift away from the system's Beveridgean origins and toward a low-cost, minimal system of welfare. This shift seems irreversible. To return to a more comprehensive system of welfare will be difficult given the problems of raising taxes once substantial reductions have been conceded. The United Kingdom does not have the kind of institutional and political structures found in the Scandinavian countries that could serve as a forum for negotiations.

## The Conservative Bismarckian Model

The conservative model is also called the continental European model or the Catholic model. The influence of Catholic social teaching is noticeable, and the conservative model is, in sharp contrast to the Scandinavian model, "service-lean" yet "transfer-heavy." According to Esping-Andersen, Austria, France, Germany, the Benelux countries, and Italy all have welfare states with strong elements of decommodification. However, income maintenance and health care are strongly related to employment and family status, as Chiara Saraceno shows us elsewhere in this volume. The Bismarckian insurance principle still determines the distribution of benefits and their funding.

Employers' organizations and unions play an important role in the management of the social insurance funds.

The particular kind of welfare state–family-work nexus that characterizes the continental European model leads to inherent contradictions. Unable to promote employment expansion, policymakers in these states revert to labor supply reduction policies that effectively increase unemployment and pension costs for men and perpetuate the dependency of women on the male breadwinner. For both men and women, this results in extremely high labor costs and market rigidities because the "insiders" are compelled to defend their employment security. The dramatic insider-outsider cleavages themselves pose obstacles to greater flexibility in the labor market.

The continental welfare states are characterized by a combination of three features: a concentration on transfer payments rather than social services; generous income replacements in case of unemployment; and payroll taxes as the major financing source for welfare (two-thirds or more, compared to 40 percent or less in the Scandinavian countries and the United Kingdom).[12]

Germany is the example par excellence of the passive continental welfare state that has maintained its high-wage, high-productivity systems at the expense of employment creation. While labor costs rule out an expansion of low-paid, service-sector jobs, the country's innovation system is partly locked into a Fordist trajectory that prevents the creation of large numbers of high-paid, high-tech jobs as well. It is surprising that recent changes to the system have not been more extensive, as we would have expected in what was once the strongest economy in Europe. The apparent strains in the system seem to be increasing. Germany has already raised the retirement age and reduced the rate of increase in payments of all sorts.

## The Southern (Latin) Rim Model

Many observers call the Southern rim model a subgroup of the continental model, though there is a rich historical and social science literature that considers it a unique welfare regime.[13] The nations of southern Europe have followed a similar path to modernization, and their political economies still share a number of traits.

Southern welfare systems have traditionally emphasized solutions that combine the resources of civil society institutions like church, family, and private charity with those of parallel public institutions, thus providing a rudimentary welfare state.[14] During the last two decades, however, the countries of southern Europe have started to catch up with their northern counterparts in terms of expenditure—

even if, with the exception of Italy, they are still relatively low spenders. Cash benefits play a very prominent role in the countries of this area. Seen in this light, the southern European welfare states constitute an extreme version of the transfer-centered continental model.[15] At the same time, welfare is unevenly distributed, occupationally and territorially, in Spain, Greece, Portugal, and Italy. Except for Portugal, these states are also the only EU members with no national, right-based minimum income scheme for individuals and families with insufficient resources. Another distinct trait is the uneven distribution of protection across the standard risks. These countries tend to overprotect the risk of old age, especially Italy (65 percent of social spending compared to 42 percent for the EU generally), and ignore family benefits and services as well as public housing. These three interrelated elements produce a demographic bias in southern European welfare systems that has serious consequences for their overall performance and stability.

## Globalization and Welfare State Provisions

Given this European landscape of different welfare regimes, it is understandable that the capacity to adapt to external as well as internal challenges varies considerably. One of the most discussed and debated external challenges to the European welfare states is globalization. Is the threat real, and if so, what are the threats to the welfare state?

Traditional analyses of changes in welfare states have very often focused on the national level, but increasingly the focus has widened; there now exists a substantial literature concerned with the impact of economic globalization on welfare states. This literature primarily views globalization as an external force and analyzes changes in welfare states in terms of adaptation to this new exogenous context. It only rarely considers economic globalization as anything but a unitary force. In fact, different manifestations of globalization affect countries in different ways as globalization is mediated through national political and institutional filters.[16]

According to Martin Rhodes, the net results of globalization have been the evolution of a leaner, meaner, arguably more efficient welfare state, as well as explicit or implicit disentitlement.[17] Although globalization may be beginning to erode entitlements, none of these changes has yet undermined the fundamentals of any European welfare system. However, Rhodes is also inclined to support Geoffrey Garrett's conclusion that globalization has had an adverse affect on the Left and its traditional agenda. He therefore fears that the removal of barriers to cross-border capital flows might sweep away the last vestiges of power on the Left, tolling the "death knell" of social democracy.[18] The saving grace, however, may be the political pressures to compensate the casualties of globalization; such pressure could push new forms of state intervention to the top of the political agenda.

Vic George takes a more pessimistic view. He is convinced that internal factors have combined to reinforce the external pressures caused by globalization, with the result that state welfare provisions are being curtailed in all European countries. The responses adopted by different governments vary, but in due course they all resort to reductionist policies. He also stresses the convergent forces of globalization, but he does not conclude that all European welfare states will become the same, since they have all started from a different welfare base, and different internal forces exert their own pressures on welfare development in each state.[19]

In his chapter in this volume, Schoppa is more nuanced with regard to the effects of globalization on social contracts, noting that some contracts are more vulnerable than others. On the one hand, he argues that the advanced industrialized nations have experienced greater income inequality because of the "distributional effects of growing international commerce." On the other hand, he argues that some European countries "have actually seen improvements."[20] His conclusion accords well with my own position with reference to the Swedish case: nation-states are still able to counteract globalization, at least in the short term.

## The Europeanization of Social Policies

Although there has been enthusiastic support from many quarters for a European solution to the employment crisis and a supranational defense of the European "welfare state model," there are serious problems with both ideas. There is no consensus about which of the regimes will be the norm. Will we then witness a convergence to a European mean, indicating either a Europeanization of the Scandinavian model or a Nordification of the other European welfare regimes? Will social policies in the member states be decided by the European Union? As mentioned earlier, social policy is still formally a national issue, but constrained by EU convergence criteria on public spending.

Currently, for instance, there are few indications that the Scandinavian welfare state has been Europeanized, nor have the decisions made in the European Union during the last decade or so had any significant influence on social policy developments. However, this does not imply that the welfare state is hermetically sealed within the nation-state. On the contrary, the Scandinavian welfare model can ultimately be seen as a political-economic model historically developed in response to external pressures.[21] The Scandinavian welfare system is in effect a structural adaptation that territorially confined democratic systems have had to develop to transform volatile external economic dependencies into stable domestic systems of social risk management. This state could conceivably change again in response to dramatic changes in external forces.

Studies of welfare systems have typically concentrated on how the distributive institutions of the nation-state actually work and how they have developed historically, the problems they have encountered, and the effects they have produced on income distribution, life chances, social cohesion, electoral allegiance, work incentives, and so forth. As a general finding, welfare policies in most European countries seem to be sufficiently accounted for by national historical, political, and social conditions. This predominant role of internal factors was corroborated by the findings of a generation of systematic, comparative studies of the development of the welfare states in the years after the dramatic shift in the global economic climate in the mid-1970s. In this period, all national welfare systems were exposed to identical external economic changes but responded in significantly various ways and produced highly different social policy and labor market outcomes.[22] Within welfare research, the logic of industrialism and modernization was replaced during the 1980s by national politics as the dominant paradigm for understanding welfare capitalism. In this context, the notion of a Scandinavian exceptionalism was revived. It has since come to serve as the best illustration that the capacity of democratic institutions and national actors to implement comprehensive distributive policies is far from being totally determined by external factors, even though the economic base of national welfare policy is critically dependent on internationalized markets. And as I have mentioned, the welfare regime itself may have originated in response to external forces.

In fact, these forces have played a major role in the history of Europe during the last twenty years and may yet play a role in Europeanizing national welfare policies. European integration in the mid-1980s gained momentum to a great degree from the growing acknowledgment that a cooperative all-out effort was desperately needed to respond more successfully to increased global economic competition.

Nonetheless, for this momentum to carry over into the area of welfare regimes it must overcome great obstacles. The current constitutional design of the European Union formalizes a division of labor between supranational and national institutions. On the one hand, there is a super-state constraining national sovereignty in economic matters. On the other, there are nation-states individually performing the corrections needed to transform a market economy into socially viable welfare capitalism. The politics of distribution is still the territory of the nation-state, whereas the politics of production is applied across the whole territory of the member states.

All analytical efforts to understand European welfare policies begin in the tension between the politics of production and the politics of distribution, between the competencies of the super-state versus those of the nation-state. The demand for a "social dimension"—a phrase coined by European Commission President Jacques Delors in 1988—rests on the concern that intensified competition in a common European marketplace erodes rather than enhances the capacity of national welfare institutions to pursue their distributional functions. Thus, unless checks on the operation of economic forces are set at an institutional level congruent with the internal market regime, the processes of social dumping, regime shopping, and erosion of national tax bases will gradually undermine the capacity of welfare nation-states to maintain current levels of social security. Another external threat to the European Union and the existing welfare provisions of member states is the globalization of the labor market, which creates the possibility that cheap labor from the developing countries will enter the European arena.

The formal competence of the European Union in developing and implementing social policy is another obstacle. It is limited by the terms of the debate, which at the moment is geared primarily to removing impediments to labor market mobility and promoting health and safety in the workplace. Compared with the broad Scandinavian notion of social policy as redistributive policies based on social rights irrespective of citizens' position in the labor market, the European debate taking place under the rubric of social policy is more concerned with industrial relations than with creating a European social citizenship. This focus is partly due to the limited interventionist powers of the European institutions, but also partly due to the dominance of the continental welfare state tradition. The dominance of the continental model explains why the Scandinavian countries and the new British Labour government are hesitant to endow the European Union with the power to pursue more ambitious welfare policies at a supranational level.

For instance, the significant popular resistance to European integration among Scandinavians is based on their anxiety that participation in a pan-European welfare scheme under the auspices of the European Union implies, in the long run, an erosion of the ability of the nation-state to maintain the extractive capabilities required to sustain present levels of public provision.[23] The high Scandinavian levels of female labor force participation rest on the public-sector provision of care services. The universal system of social rights is to a large extent financed through a general system of income taxation. Seen in this light, the defense of the Scandinavian welfare model coincides with preservation of the nation-state and its unique democratic institutions. To the disappointment of progressive integrationist forces in the rest of Europe, the Scandinavian countries are not reliable allies in the quest for a supranational social policy. New proposals within the EU that more political power be allocated to the larger states do nothing to strengthen popular support from the Scandinavian countries.

Furthermore, Scandinavians feel that it is civil rights, not social rights, that govern activities such as seeking employment in another country, expecting not to lose acquired social benefits and to be treated equally in the labor markets and pension systems irrespective of sex. The Scandinavian states established an internal labor market as far back as 1954 and introduced antidiscriminatory legislation in the early 1970s. Neither of these political interventions was associated with the welfare state or promoted as a social policy reform. Regarding the regulation of working hours, vacations, part-time work, and workers' right to information and participation, the Scandinavian institutional regimes rest more heavily on collective agreements than on formal legislation. The rights granted are generally more generous than the minimum standards demanded by EU directives. Thus, there exist important structural differences between the Scandinavian countries and the rest of Europe, and they present obstacles to a more coherent, Brussels-initiated, European social policy.

Nonetheless, there are signs of change. The egalitarian outcome of the Scandinavian welfare regime crucially depends on private, market-based provisions being kept under tight political control by the welfare nation-state. This system depends on the extractive power of the state staying abreast of demand, and the state now seems to be reaching its limits. The welfare state has encountered severe problems in delivering the quality of services and insurance demanded by increasing numbers of fastidious "customers." Of course, in the Scandinavian countries as well in Europe as a whole, the concept of social rights has changed over time. By implication, the "demand structure" is continually changing as well. Furthermore, the coming demographic transition will exacerbate expenditure pressures; in all Scandinavian countries, the generosity of the core services has already been curbed.

There are also indications that individual retirement savings accounts are growing quite rapidly across all European countries. As Esping-Andersen recently observed, household purchase of private health care has risen in such widely different countries as Sweden and Italy. The trend is valid mainly for middle- and upper-class households. This trend creates a particular dilemma for Scandinavian countries that pursue the ideal of the egalitarian welfare state: for moral reasons of distributive justice, the less resourceful have to be shielded from cuts in welfare services. This conclusion leads those who can afford it to seek private supplements to public welfare provision, but such alternatives can more easily be found at a European level. In this circumstance, and with the current state of the open market, the nation-state cannot restrict the operations of the market providers. As soon as countries make a priority of protecting the poor, the better-off population turns to private groups, further diminishing the regime's egalitarian values. To the degree that the public welfare programs in the Scandinavian countries become less generous to the middle classes, a process of Europeanization is inevitable.[24]

There is a need for more extended public services in many of the EU member states, but the same states are under pressure to curb public financing, unless they increase tax revenues. There is also a trend toward a more pronounced achievement system. This system rewards those who do paid work and maintains the status differences between social groups by preserving their economic situation in retirement. To provide a more service-oriented welfare regime, similar to those of the Scandinavian countries, the other European states are compelled by these trends to negotiate with the insider groups, especially the middle classes.

At the same time, a new, informal, but still visible arena for social policy discourse has emerged at the European level. Besides the reports and communication concerning social protection that have already been mentioned, several action programs, the "Social Charter and Protocol," the "Social Dialogue," green and white papers, research observatories, and other informal networks have made significant contributions to providing a pan-European perspective.[25] However, as long as the legal constitution of the European Union offers no legal basis for a comprehensive social policy, any social policy emanating from Brussels is bound to be facultative.[26]

## Concluding Remarks

The current economic situation in the European Union is somewhat of a paradox. While the European economies are wealthier than ever before, and real income has continued to grow, the demands on social protection systems have risen even more rapidly. At the same time, the forces of economic globalization have put pressure on the European welfare states. State welfare provisions are being curtailed in different ways and to varying degrees in all of the EU member states. Common to all has been the implementation of reductionist policies. Whether this will be an extended process is uncertain. Sweden's experience shows, however, that it is possible to adjust somewhat to the trends, at least in the short term. Active workfare policies, extended public services, and high rates of female occupational participation, coupled with generous child care provision and astute fiscal policies, have preserved the status quo, at least for the time being. But what lies ahead? Fritz Scharpf provides one answer: "In order to cope with their present problems, continental welfare states must find ways to translate a larger share of the incomes earned in the exposed sectors into additional demand for services that are locally provided and consumed, and hence not subject to international competition."[27]

This suggestion implies that there are arguments for a compromise between the Scandinavian and continental (mostly German) models of welfare provision. Having that as a point of departure, it may be possible to create a more general European model of welfare. In many states, social and political processes have brought the middle classes into the welfare state; this inclusion is politically sustainable only to the degree that the welfare state delivers value for money, and only as long as there are no realistic alternatives to public provision. In predicting the future of the welfare nation-state, there is no question that it will have to curb its generosity; what is not so certain is the response of the middle classes. Will they adjust their expectations to what is macroeconomically realistic, or will they increase their demand for private provision?

Finally, the aging population, falling birthrates, and the future demand for increased immigration will no doubt require changes in the European welfare state provisions. Therefore, I do think that European social policy will converge in the long run, either through explicit recommendations from the European Commission or implicitly through sharper convergence criteria with regard to public spending in the member states.[28]

## Notes

1. Gøsta Esping-Andersen, "Welfare States at the End of the Century: The Impact of Labor Market, Family, and Demographic Change," in *Family, Market, and Community: Equity and Efficiency in Social Policy*, Social

Policy Studies 21 (Paris: Organization for Economic Cooperation and Development, 1997), 63–80.

2. Martin Rhodes, "Globalization and West European Welfare States: A Critical Review of the Recent Debates," *Journal of European Social Policy* 6(4, 1996): 305–27; Esping-Andersen, "Welfare States at the End of the Century."

3. Organization for Economic Cooperation and Development, *The Welfare State in Crisis* (Paris: OECD, 1981).

4. European Commission, *Council of Ministers' Recommendation on the Convergence of Social Protection Objectives and Policies* (Luxembourg: EC, 1992).

5. European Commission, *Modernizing and Improving Social Protection* (Luxembourg: EC, 1997).

6. Paul Johnson, "The Measurement of Social Security Convergence: The Case of European Public Pension Systems Since 1950," *Journal of Social Policy* 28(October 1999): 595–618.

7. Gøsta Esping-Andersen, *The Three Worlds of Welfare Capitalism* (Princeton: Princeton University Press, 1990).

8. R. M. Titmuss, *Social Policy: An Introduction* (New York: Pantheon, 1974). Although widely used, the regime theory also has been criticized by many scholars. See Peter Taylor-Gooby, "Eurosclerosis in European Welfare States: Regime Theory and the Dynamics of Change," *Policy and Politics* 24(April 1996): 109–23; Johnson, "The Measurement of Social Security Convergence"; Peter Abrahamson, "The Scandinavian Model of Welfare," in *Comparing Social Welfare Systems in Nordic Europe and France*, edited by Denis Bouget and Bruno Palier (Nantes: Maison des sciences de l'homme Ange-Guépin, 1999), 31–60. According to them, the Esping-Andersen regime theory is more appropriate to the analysis of welfare stability than of dynamic change.

9. Robert Henry Cox, "The Consequences of Welfare Reform: How Conceptions of Social Rights Are Changing," *Journal of Social Policy* 27(January 1998): 14.

10. The terms "liberal" and, more often, "neoliberal" are increasingly used in Europe to describe policies that Americans label "conservative."

11. European Commission, *Social Protection in Europe* (Luxembourg: EC, 1993).

12. Ibid., especially ch. 1.

13. Abrahamson, "The Scandinavian Model of Welfare," 34–35; Stephan Leibfried, "Towards a European Welfare State?: On Integrating Poverty Regimes into the European Community," in *Social Policy in a Changing Europe*, edited by Zsuzsa Ferge and Jon Eivind Kolberg (Frankfurt am Main: Campus, 1992), 253–55.

14. Leibfried, "Towards a European Welfare State?," 253.

15. Esping-Andersen, *The Three Worlds of Welfare Capitalism*.

16. Fritz W. Scharpf, "Balancing Sustainability and Security in Social Policy," in OECD, *Family, Market, and Community*, 211–21.

17. Rhodes, "Globalization and West European Welfare States," 309.

18. Geoffrey Garrett, "Capital Mobility, Trade, and the Domestic Politics of Economic Policy," *International Organization* 49(Autumn 1995): 657–87.

19. Vic George, "Political Ideology, Globalisation, and Welfare Futures in Europe," *Journal of Social Policy* 27(January 1998): 17–36.

20. See Schoppa (this volume).
21. Kåre Hagen, "Towards a Europeanization of Social Policies?" in Bouget and Palier, *Comparing Social Welfare Systems*, 661–90.
22. Esping-Andersen, *The Three Worlds of Welfare Capitalism*; Gøsta Esping-Andersen, *Welfare States in Transition: National Adaptations in Global Economics* (London: Sage, 1996); Göran Therborn, *Why Some People Are More Unemployed Than Others* (London: Verso, 1986).
23. Lee Miles, ed., *The European Union and the Nordic Countries* (London: Routledge, 1996).
24. The Scandinavian countries departed from the Beveridgean universal flat-rate minimum benefits during the 1960s and 1970s by incorporating Bismarckian elements of status-preserving benefits into public schemes. The financial troubles of the last decade have brought the welfare nation-state closer to its Beveridgean point of departure. In this sense, it is not surprising that we can observe exactly what Beveridge saw as an effect of his model—that social protection above a universal minimum should be the responsibility of the individual. But he could hardly have anticipated that an internal European market could be an alternative to the nation-state as the regulatory regime for this. See Hagen, "Towards a Europeanization of Social Policies?"
25. Stephan Leibfried and Paul Pierson, eds., *European Social Policy: Between Fragmentation and Integration* (Washington, D.C.: Brookings Institution, 1995).
26. Wolfgang Streeck, "From Market Making to State Building? Reflections on the Political Economy of European Social Policy," in Leibfried and Pierson, *European Social Policy*, 389–431.
27. Scharpf, "Balancing Sustainability and Security in Social Policy," 218.
28. These and other issues concerning the future of the welfare state are discussed in a special thematic issue of *European Review* 8 (July, 2000). For a recent commentary and discussion concerning the Scandinavian welfare model see, *Scandinavian Journal of History* 26(3, 2001). It is a thematic volume on "The Nordic Welfare States 1900–2000," edited by Klaes Petersen and Niel Finn Christianse.

# 15

Europe from Division to Reunification: The Eastern European Middle Classes During and After Socialism

*Maurice Aymard*

The new situation created in 1989 by the fall of the Berlin Wall and the collapse of the socialist regimes in the eastern part of Europe has been analyzed by most Western scholars, not from a social point of view, but primarily from a political and economic one: the capitalist model won the competition, and the only solution for the former socialists was to adopt, as soon as possible, the rules of the game that have been proven in the West to be superior.

For the experts, the only point of uncertainty was the rhythm of the transition, especially in the economic sector: would surgery be required (as in Poland), or would a more progressive medicine, some series of measures, limit the intensity of the pain even as it extended the length of the treatment? The "treatments" they commonly presented as unavoidable were the privatization of a huge but inefficient public sector, unemployment, quantitative and qualitative restructuring of the overly costly welfare state, limitation of budget deficits, and the generalization, at all levels of the economy and society, of market rules and regulations.

Western scholars did not seriously consider the social acceptability of these measures, because Eastern European societies were not really known, understood, or even studied in the West. The same was true of Eastern Europeans, who, with only some exceptions, had no better understanding of their own situation, but for different reasons. Few social statistics had been kept, and those available were not always reliable. In addition, there had been little serious sociological field research because of the marginal academic status of sociology as a scholarly discipline—a "bourgeois" science by definition. Finally, whatever sociological research existed was undercut by the common use of ideological rather than factual arguments.

All of these factors created the conditions for a Manichaean debate in which a better and deeper knowledge of the Eastern societies was not even considered a prerequisite for evaluating what happened in the past, what was happening in the present, and what could happen in the future. And even if groups of scholars in some of the eastern countries—such as the Hungarians Rudolf Andorka, Erszebet Szalai, Ivan Szelenyi, Agnes Utasi, and Zsuzsa Ferge—had developed in the 1970s and 1980s a critical analysis of their own societies, their research was not taken seriously by the West.[1] Nor did the West look kindly on any kind of opposition or alternative to its program of social and economic transformation of the East. As Zsuzsa Ferge wrote to me in a critical comment on the first draft of this chapter: "Eastern sociologists who knew their countries [felt that] the West had a sure sense of superiority, [and] the supranational agencies . . . applied the one-size-fits-all recipes, mostly ignoring the historical, economic, social, and political differences between the countries."

## From East Germany to the Soviet Union: Redealing the Social and Economic Cards

The conditions of the reunification of the two Germanys can be cited as the extreme example of this strange and, for an industrial and urbanized country, exceptional situation: privatization, parity between the Federal Republic of Germany (FRG) and German Democratic Republic (GDR) currencies, and huge and costly investments by West Germany in its new eastern "länder" were considered sufficient to permit quite automatically the political, social, and cultural integration of the so-called Ossies. On a social level, however, these measures were not enough, and social changes were often quite disruptive and induced discontinuities. For instance, the overpopulated academic and university staffs were submitted to a review that eliminated a large number of teachers of Marxist-Leninism as well as professors in other disciplines who had weak credentials. They were replaced, however, not by local younger scholars but by professors from the FRD, who arrived with their own assistants. The same procedure was followed in many sectors of the state bureaucracy, especially in the populous domains of the middle strata that managed the economic sector. What actually happened in the industrial sector after privatization needs systematic research, but we know that local entrepreneurship (a shorthand formula commonly used in other socialist countries to justify a quick transfer of public enterprises to their former managers) received little encouragement. Instead, priority was given to restructuring and rationalizing production through direct investments of capital from the West. Opportunities were further limited by severe financial cuts in the dense network of nurseries and day care centers. This network had been a precondition of the high rate (relative to West Germany's) of married women with access to permanent jobs, the majority of whom could thus provide a second salary for their family, aspire to a full and autonomous professional career, or be financially independent after divorce.

There is no doubt that this delegitimizing of a large portion of the middle strata of a formerly independent country—including their culture and their self-representation in the process of restructuring—would be a fascinating case-study, even if the former East Germany was an exception among the postsocialist countries. Middle classes base their legitimacy on continuity and upward mobility (through the guarantee of education, patrimonial and cultural inheritance, and social networks), use their accumulated resources and capital to overcome temporary setbacks, and elaborate, for themselves and their children, strategies of adaptation and reconversion. Socialism did not create an exception to this quite general rule. Unlike the process in other socialist countries, privatization in East Germany by a West-controlled administration left the East German middle class few opportunities to appropriate public properties. They lost their dominance of large sectors of the economy, the bureaucracy, and the society and were left with very few opportunities to take direct advantage of the privatization process. Their resources were limited to their education, their professional skills, and the nature of their occupation. For instance, engineers and doctors may have had an easier time adapting than lawyers, who had to learn new public and private laws and new judicial procedures.

The experience was quite different in all the rest of Eastern Europe, including the former Soviet Union, because there was absolutely no external competition for jobs and social positions. Governments changed, and Communist parties lost monopoly power and changed their programs and ideology (except in Russia, Belarus, and some other republics of the new Commonwealth of Independent States [CIS]) to become "social democrats"—a new name that allowed some of them to return to power a few years later. Large sectors of the economy were privatized, but for many years direct Western investments remained much more limited than actually desired by the local governments (even the social-democratic ones). Ruling positions, economic property, and social and political influence were redistributed mostly within the same social groups that had these assets before; they needed only to find a new basis for their renewed legitimization. And those who received the better part of this redistribution were also in the best position to take advantage of new opportunities: from this point of view, Russia and most of the CIS republics would be the other extreme example to oppose and compare to the former GDR.[2] Whoever had a flat in 1989, whether large or small, downtown or in the suburbs, was given the chance to buy it at a very cheap price; to have a flat at all, however, was a privilege that was unequally distributed. Money, higher education, and social influence became the key factors in the new social hierarchies of the transition period. Those who were unable to gain a new position comparable in money and social influence to their old one had to make their way through the risky byways of the new hierarchies the best they could.

## Socialist Europe: An Incubator for New Middle Classes

Ten or fifteen years ago, we could have discussed the topic of the middle classes in industrial advanced societies without taking Eastern Europe into consideration. The omission would already have been an error, however, because the social and economic transformations of the two parts of Europe since 1945 had been parallel and closely related through imitation and competition. A majority of scholars would have argued that Eastern Europe was too different a world to be usefully compared to ours. Exhibiting this kind of indifference and contempt is no longer possible. Differences exist, and they will be long-lasting because they are difficult to eradicate, but we know that Eastern Europe, including the former Soviet Union, is a part of our world, and we hope (and need to hope, in our own interest) that it will develop as such in the future.

That Eastern European countries fostered a middle strata may look like a strange paradox considering that they were ruled for as many as seventy years by regimes and political parties that proclaimed themselves representatives of workers and peasants and instruments of their social and political promotion. Indeed, we can say that the growth in size and power of the middle classes, relative to their position before the revolution, is one of the more impressive and lasting achievements of the socialist period. Socialism did its best to eliminate the "old middle class"—the owners of the means of production, as it is usually defined. But at the same time, socialism provided a "new middle class," defined by education, qualifications, and specific skills, with great opportunities—under the control of the state bureaucracy, which was itself a part of this class. There was strong development in sectors like education, health, research, engineering, services, and management.[3] Some scholars even think that the pressure from the middle classes on socialist governments to meet their economic expectations in the 1970s—that is, to provide both greater access to consumer goods and new possibilities for individual initiative—and their political expectations in the 1980s was a major factor in the transformation and then final collapse of the socialist regimes. Pressure from the middle strata also played a part in the open expression of nationalist claims, which had been kept under control or silenced altogether before 1989 (when they could not be integrated into the rhetoric of the regime, as in Romania with Ceauşescu).

This process also corresponded to what supposedly was known of social transformations in Western societies. Peter Robert points out that "the main determinants of class identification"—that is, of perceptions of social hierarchies—were the same in the East as in the West: "income, occupation, education, and region."[4] With 30 to 50 percent of their population considering themselves middle-class in 1992–93, the Central and Eastern Europe countries had smaller middle classes than the countries of western continental Europe, but larger than in the United Kingdom, where the traditional definition of middle-class has always been much more restrictive.[5] Even if they overestimate the reality, these figures express both a common social self-perception of people at the end of socialism and their expectations for the transition to a market economy.

What we know of the internal history of the socialist countries suggests that even there, as in the West (as Olivier Zunz argues), middle-class expansion has been both an important agent and an outcome of the social contracts, though more in the late 1960s and 1970s in Eastern Europe than in the immediate postwar years.[6] Both Western and Eastern Europeans attempted to blur the distinction between working class and middle class. The main difference between East and West was that this program was never officially formulated as such in the East, for the obvious reason that it would have changed the political and ideological basis of the regime. Nonetheless, the measures taken to develop higher education and welfare facilitated the social stabilization and reproduction of the existing middle class and its absorption of new members from the working class and the peasantry. Moreover, policies designed to improve consumer access to both agricultural and industrial goods also had the unintended consequence of reinforcing the middle class. Just as the Western European governments needed to demonstrate that their capitalist system, in which long-run pauperization was said by their Marxist opponents to be inescapable, could provide the same level of social guarantees as provided by the Communist regimes, the Eastern European governments needed to prove that socialism was able to "overtake and overcome capitalism" when it came to consumption, that it could provide both "butter and guns."

A key element in the success of the democratic and economic transition was not only the existence of the Eastern middle strata but the recognition of them as middle classes on the same order as in the Western countries. Large sectors of these middle classes are subjected today to strong pressures that undermine their opportunities, affecting their wages, jobs, training, positions in the political system and government, and values. The personal status of most members of the middle class was linked to the highly centralized and bureaucratic organization of the society and economy, which has now disappeared or disintegrated. Only a minority of these individuals (and it is extremely important that we gain a better knowledge of the size and composition of this minority) have been able to take advantage of this dramatic change to maintain or even improve their position and that of their family. And the situation is made more complex by the increasing disparities between Eastern European countries. Those that were more developed and advanced before 1940 look to be in a much better position than the others and are likely to be the first to be integrated into the European Union. From this point of view, the socialist period can be seen as a parenthetical interlude.

## East and West: Two Parallel Paths to Modernization

Since as long ago as the late 1950s, the evolution of the Eastern European middle classes can be compared to the evolution of their Western counterparts. There has always been, however, one main difference: the predominance of the state and the Communist Party in the socialist countries made the relationship of the middle classes to political and administrative authorities stronger and more exclusive than in the West, where the private-sector guarantee of personal and patrimonial property provided an alternative. Nonetheless, even in the West the development of the middle classes and their legitimization as social elites—that is, as a class that was able and deserving to take the place of the traditional landed aristocracies—was linked in one way or another to the ambitions of the state. The stronger the relationship of the middle classes with the state during the decades following the end of World War II, the deeper was the crisis and need for an economic and social conversion by the end of the century.

Up to the mid-twentieth century, a sizable peasantry characterized most European societies, both Eastern and Western. A subsistence economy played an important role, keeping in balance both the unemployment or underemployment of the labor force and the low level of agricultural productivity. Even France, with one-third of its population engaged in agriculture, did not produce enough foodstuffs for its urban population and needed to have recourse to imports. In Italy during the Fascist period, the battle for grain was one of the more spectacular aspects of the struggle for economic autocracy. By 1980, the situation had changed completely: urbanization and industrialization had reduced to much lower levels (less than 10 percent in Western Europe) the percentage of the working population engaged in agriculture. The mobilization of these rural reserves of labor, and of production and consumption capacities, became the main factor in economic growth after the reconstruction period. As we can see from France, Italy, Spain, Portugal, and Greece, the expansion of the European unified market played a dynamic role in this process.

This structural transformation was made possible by a wide range of massive transfers that affected all sectors of the European economy and all social strata. These transfers created many opportunities, both direct and indirect, for the development of middle classes, and for a larger range of the population to gain access to goods, to guarantees, and to various other elements of the way of life that had traditionally characterized the middle classes. Emblematic of the ongoing process of homogenization of society, these transfers are mainly evident for:

- *Employment and jobs:* The expansion and diversification of the transfer from agriculture to industry and services led to the global growth of the economy and to the creation of many more skilled jobs that required a high level of education or training.
- *Housing:* With the transfer of 20 to 30 percent of the population, perhaps even more, from the countryside to the cities and their peripheries, a higher percentage of young and prime-age people made the towns (traditional "mangeuses d'hommes") the centers of demographic growth, while the rural population grew older and declined.
- *Economic life:* The monetary sector grew, and the nonmonetary sector and subsistence economy declined. Increasing investments and inputs transformed agricultural production and introduced the structures associated with the industrial sector: mass production

for the national and international markets became the rule. With the decline of the domestic economy and the family as a production unit (but not as a consumption unit), more and more women and young people became direct participants as wage-earners in the labor market.

- *Consumption:* Out of their increasing monetary resources, households spent less on food and more on industrial goods (cars and electrical appliances became the symbol of the new way of life) and services. The "democratization" of consumption became the standard argument of the sociological studies and political speeches that agreed in predicting the end of the gap between the working and middle classes. The "embourgeoisement" of the working classes was commonly described either as a huge success or as a danger for the self-consciousness of the proletariat. At the same time, households could increase their savings, some of which were used to buy a private house or flat. Public intervention supported the development of education and health, which were offered either free or at very low cost, and also large investments in housing, either public (in the East) or both public and private.

- *Organization and control of economic activity:* The patterns of the increasing intervention of the state in economic and social life, as an organizer, a coordinator, a decisionmaker, and an insurer, were different from one Western European country to another, and between West and East. While socialist Europe chose to nationalize all sectors of the economy (agriculture, industry, trade, banking, services) and social services (urban housing, education, health), the Western states limited their intervention to key industrial sectors (mines, energy, steel industry, and so on), transportation (railways, airlines), part of the banking sector, and education, health, and pension systems. Trade and the largest part of the financial sector were never nationalized in the West, and the governments had only limited control of the money market. The Western states also instituted varying systems of intervention to support selected professions, certain sectors of the population (nonworking women, old people, and so on), and regions. The combination of market economies and redistribution by the state administration of a growing part of the GNP (between 30 and 45 percent) became a characteristic feature of the Western European countries.

- *Fiscal system:* The states asked less from their traditional nineteenth-century sources of revenue (land taxes, excises, custom duties) and much more from earned incomes, energy taxes, value-added tax (a French invention, quickly imitated by West Germany and resisted for a long period by the United Kingdom) and taxes paid by the industrial and services enterprises. Thus, their financial capacity to intervene became closely and directly linked to the level and evolution of economic activity. This occurred directly in socialist economies and indirectly, but maybe more effectively, in Western Europe.

- *Education:* Throughout Europe, the major transformations were universal acceptance of primary schooling, an increase in the number of teenagers attending school, and a tremendous increase of the number of students in the universities. Huge public (more than private) investments resulted in an exceptional valorization of human capital. Even if school systems did not succeed in eliminating social and cultural inequalities, they became, for collective representations and expectations, the model and the instrument of a silent and deliberate revolution of social reproduction rules, and particularly for recruitment into, and access to, the middle classes. It became commonly accepted that individual merit could take the place of inheritance and would determine the transfer of position and resources from the older generation to the younger. In a much more mobile social and economic context, upward social mobility could be seen both as a reality (with some limits) and as a target that drove individual and family decisions and strategies.

- *Social security and welfare:* Health insurance, increasing life expectancy, and pensions limited uncertainty and risk for families and individuals. More stable jobs (some of them lifelong jobs) and grants for unemployed people (though not in the East, where unemployment officially did not exist) could give the impression that poverty was a bygone reality. The situation changed in the West from 1973 to 1974, and even more dramatically fifteen years later in the East, a place that had long (officially) boasted of its immunity to what was seen as the consequences of capitalism. Unemployment became the main preoccupation at all levels of society, even if it primarily affected the weaker categories of the population.

Seen from the point of view of the Eastern middle strata, the main differences between East and West before 1989 were "less autonomy in professional work . . . less freedom in private life," less room for personal initiative, less direct control of economic activity, and "centrally leveled wages," which limited an individual's ability to take advantage of the labor market to valorize his or her own professional qualifications.[7] The middle strata experiences a much more limited access to real estate, capital, and enterprises—for which the privileges, both official and unofficial, given by the socialist regimes to their elites and middle classes were a kind of substitute—and experiences a much more limited access to industrial goods and foodstuffs. These two experiences can explain the increased feeling of frustration by the Eastern middle strata.

The transfers outlined earlier had three features in common:

1.  They were not systematically organized or planned, at either the national or the international level, but the general trend was more or less the same in the various countries. Interregional and international migrations equalized the geographical disparities in the West. From the 1960s, fewer southern Italians migrated to the United States and many more went to northern Italy, Germany, Belgium, or France. In the East, in spite of the official proletarian internationalism, political borders were much more difficult to cross; with only a few exceptions (Vietnamese workers in East Germany during the late 1970s), movements of population were limited to internal migrations, which were themselves strictly controlled by the state.

2.  Economic gaps were reduced inside of each of the two blocs, especially in the West, where the less advanced economies (Italy in the 1960s, Spain, Portugal, and Ireland in the 1980s and 1990s) had the quickest rates of growth. But economic transformations finally broadened the gap between the two blocs during the 1970s and the 1980s. Even if the East's Comecon (Council for Mutual Economic Assistance, created in 1949) stimulated an increasing production of consumption goods in Eastern and Central Europe, it never succeeded in becoming a dynamic institutional framework, as did the European Common Market.

3.  There was a gradual but very deep and complex restructuring of society. The proletarianization of former peasants transformed into industrial workers was only one aspect, and perhaps not the main one, of the new social reality: in the West, the true new proletarians were more often migrant workers than local ex-peasants. The so-called middle classes increased very quickly, and the concept of the middle class changed fundamentally. That concept rested on a fluid combination of individuals' professional capacities, the quality and social status of their job, their level of income, way of life, and the emphasis they put on education and culture for themselves and even more for their children. None of these factors, considered individually, were ever the monopoly of the middle classes.

## Social Production and Reproduction of the Elites: Continuities and Discontinuities

Family tradition and wealth and social capital did not disappear as such and indeed continued to have significant influence. Their importance might have been checked in the socialist countries, especially in Central and Eastern Europe, although the elimination or emigration of the former urban and rural elites was much more limited than in the Soviet Union during the 1920s and 1930s, with some exceptions, like East Germany until the construction of the Wall, and Hungary after 1956. As a result, social upheaval was much more limited as well, and the family strategies of continuity and the adaptation of the old middle classes can be studied today in the same way as the upward social mobility of former workers and peasants or their children.

In Hungary, as in the other socialist countries of Central Europe, nationalization of the economy left no place for "the entrepreneurial stratum of the bourgeois middle class," but "its value system and some dominant elements of its style of life" resisted change, and "in the long run society was unable to do without the knowledge wealth of the middle class. Starting with the 1960s, the educated and qualified members of the former middle class gradually regained the opportunity to shape and control the economic and cultural life of society and, as a result, they started to play an increasingly significant role in the state-socialist period."[8] To achieve their goal of rapid postwar industrial development, socialist regimes became aware in the same period, after the death of Stalin and the end of the reconstruction period, that they needed a vastly larger number of trained experts, professionals, and intellectuals. Not only did members of the older middle class find their place in the new economic organization, but their living patterns and values were adopted or imitated by the members of the new middle class being trained, selected, and promoted by the regime.

In the Soviet Union, the renewal of the elites and the middle strata was much more general and systematic during the 1920s and the 1930s.[9] Selection by the party and selection by the education system were the key factors, at least for the first generation. The consolidation of the new social positions was largely a second-generation phenomenon. At this point, access to the best and more prestigious schools became a privilege of the nomenclatura's children.[10] The new middle strata did their best to become a middle class that could control and organize its own selection and reproduction.

The professional reconversion of the old elites and the social reproduction of the new ones look to have been quite common in Eastern Europe, even if we lack the necessary statistics and sociological research to study this phenomenon accurately. These transformations paralleled developments in Western Europe. The socialist regimes preferred to keep a certain level of confidentiality and discretion about phenomena that were not consistent with their rhetoric. Not by chance, the first scholarly information to be published and circulated on these topics came from Hungary (which had been the first to introduce a dose of liberalism in its economy) in the 1970s and early 1980s.[11]

But despite the ongoing role of inheritance and social continuity, it was education that became a key factor for the middle classes everywhere, and the basic factor regulating access to the qualifications and jobs with which the middle classes were identified (and with which they identified themselves). In the selection process for higher education, both positive quotas (in favor of workers' and peasants' children) and negative ones (limiting access for the children of the prerevolutionary middle classes) were introduced and applied in a more or less systematic way. A certain amount of competition is always endemic to education, and competition carries the potential for failure. Uncertainty characterized the early stages of an individual's career. Once credentialed, his or her future was more assured. Economic activities and services required an increasing number of engineers, managers, doctors, and teachers, and public administration required a complex hierarchy of bureaucrats. In Western Europe, the private sector augmented the growing importance of the public sector as a source of jobs. In Eastern Europe, the state and the party controlled first access to all jobs, including the management of the economy.

The conditions of daily life for the Eastern middle classes were the same as for the lives of more than 50 percent of Western wage-earning members of the middle classes. A salary was their primary income (and for more and more married people, their two salaries). Most middle-class individuals could not buy their house or flat, but the rent they paid to the state was very low and quite nominal by Western standards. To be granted a flat was in and of itself a kind of privilege that, as such, could be transferred to children or to close kin—a privilege that could be compared to rent control in France in the decades after World War II. The ability of these middle classes to save and accumulate was limited, but they had the same desire for consumption as their Western counterparts. After 1968, this desire became a kind of political necessity for the socialist regimes. After the 1970s, refrigerators, color televisions, and cars became more easily available on the market, though these products were typically three or four times more expensive (in relation to salaries) than in the West. In spite of this progress, Eastern Europe did not become—or would at best have been very slow to become—a consumer society. There were too many bottlenecks in the production and commercial distribution system. But the same Eastern middle classes had the advantages of job stability, easy access to education, a high level of welfare, and, when they could get it, cheap housing. They also had the guarantee of personal and family security.

## The End of a World and the Difficult Birth of a New One: 1990 to 2000

The situation changed dramatically a decade ago. Only a limited number of former elites (more often the nomenclatura) were in a position to take advantage of the privatization that ensued with the collapse of the Iron Curtain. For the majority of the local middle classes, a market economy meant the collapse of the main support underlying their former security, most often owing to sharp reductions in the purchasing power of their salaries rather than to the loss of their jobs, the declining quality of welfare, and the obligation to pay (officially or not) for their children's university education. This loss of security in turn led to longer working hours, often at several jobs, and a decline in life expectancy. Russian men, for instance, are commonly said to be living ten years less, even though there is no firm statistical evidence for this figure.

The situation today is very different from one country to another, and differences between the former socialist bloc countries have broadened. Poland, Hungary, and the Czech Republic[12] are in a much better position than Romania, Bulgaria, and Russia,[13] which are in a better position than Ukraine, Belarus, and Armenia. But the economic gap between Western Europe and most of the Eastern European countries is much broader than before. The main victims of the collapse of the socialist regimes were the middle classes, which for a long period had enjoyed many perquisites. Only some of the human capital created and accumulated by the former regimes has been put to better and more productive uses, and the future of these middle classes is in jeopardy.

The local middle classes are expected to become the basis of the new political regimes, but their participation is not ensured simply by introducing and stabilizing democratic institutions. The main challenge for Western Europe is to help the Eastern middle classes adapt to the new context of a market economy. A balance has to be found between the public sector, which has lost its dominant position, and the private sector, which has developed very quickly, but in an unco-ordinated and sometimes even predatory way. Moscow offers to the foreign visitor the very surprising (and maybe superficial) impression that it has more bankers and businessmen than industrial entrepreneurs. On the other hand, the vitality of small-scale enterprises is said to have compensated for the crisis of the Gdansk shipyards, al-though we know very little about the reasons for their success. Did the capital come from the banking system, public loans, private accumulation, or the Polish diaspora?

The middle classes of Eastern Europe face many difficulties in finding their identity and their place, but Western Europe cannot forget that any solution to the present crisis lies to a great extent in Western hands. This realization may explain the renewal during the last decade of sociological studies and surveys dedicated to understanding the transformation and perspective of the middle classes in the Eastern countries.[14] Much of this research receives the financial support of Western institutions and foundations. All of them try to evaluate the formation of the new entrepreneurial and managerial strata, which could assume responsibility for the modernization of the economy and replace the former bureaucratic strata as a model for the rest of society.[15]

Does this program have any chance of success? Will the benefits outweigh the costs? Besides national resources and financial capital (a large part of which comes from abroad), support for new economic development in Eastern Europe may come from four sources:

- The existing reserves of labor in the rural sector
- The low cost of labor, a factor that has been underscored by the devaluation of local currencies
- The growth capacities of the internal market
- Educated human capital

The first source of new economic development is still available in some (but not all) Eastern countries where a significant portion of the peasantry has left both the countryside and agriculture. The second source is the direct consequence of the crisis of socialist economies and has already had positive effects on the participation by some Eastern countries in the international division of labor. Romania, for example, competes quite well today with Southeast Asia in the assembly of household electrical goods destined for the Western European market. Western corporations have begun to invest in some Eastern countries to produce cheaper goods more adapted by quality and price to the local market, but also to export some of these goods to the

West. For this reason, the third source is key; new economic development will be possible only if a balance can be found between local
production for the internal market and the necessity to open the
same markets to international competition. The fourth source, educated human capital, will play a crucial role as a precondition of both
economic success and political integration. Are the middle classes
that were produced and shaped by socialist regimes capable of adapting themselves to the new economic, social, and cultural context?
That is now the most important question not only for Eastern Europe
but for Europe as a whole.

Research conducted during the last ten years underlines the very
strong pressures on the local middle strata and the ongoing process of
deep internal differentiation between the middle and upper classes.
Only a limited portion of their members have been able to maintain
their former advantages and convert them into new advantages consistent with the new economic and social system. The more common
experience has been difficulty adjusting to the rules of a new game.

The key factors in successful adaptation seem to be gender (women
are in a weaker situation); age (the East also has its yuppies); education (even when one's training does not correspond to the new field of
activity); family and social networks; place (life is easier in the large
cities and the core regions than in the countryside and on the periph-
ery); and the capacity to combine formal, informal, underground, and
sometimes illegal activities.

Other factors in successful adaptation are one's participation in the
process of privatization and in the international division of labor (it is
always better to work for an international company or for the foreign
market) and the capacity to sell one's professional qualifications in
the new labor market or to take advantage of the privatization process. Foreign-language expertise and financial, managerial, and business knowledge are more easily marketable than other technical
knowledge. Former engineers, professionals, managers, and local bureaucrats with established networks of personal and professional relations have been more successful than the members of the higher state
nomenclatura.[16] In sectors where the number of new, small, technologically driven enterprises and firms created or restructured by the
direct intervention and investments of Western capital is too limited
to counterbalance obsolete factories and mines, information and services are becoming more and more important. They give former state
employees the opportunity to become either full- or part-time entrepreneurs and thus becoming part of a new middle class. The opportunities in these more dynamic sectors bring new hierarchies and in-

ternal gaps to the "new middle class" of wage-earners, whose internal differences were relatively limited during the Communist period.[17]

Everywhere the gap is increasing between the poorer and richer parts of the population, and many members of the middle class have felt their personal situation worsening.[18] This perception may limit their support for social and political transformation, leading to a "new split between the 'old' and the 'new' component" of the middle class.[19]

The social hierarchies of Central and Eastern Europe are clearly being restructured, and nobody knows how or when that process will end, or what its results and consequences will be. Only one thing is sure: the process will be a long one, and social, moral, and ideological factors will play roles as important as (if not more important than) the role of economic factors. Society always changes more slowly than it appears to from the outside; it has to produce its own answers to a new context, but without reliable knowledge of the price that will be paid. From this point of view, former socialist Europe is an exceptional laboratory in which to study the process of social transformation in an apparently peaceful but deeply revolutionary context.

## Notes

1. Rudolf Andorka, *A társadami mobilitás változásai Magyarországon* (Changes in social mobility in Hungary) (Budapest: Gondolat Kiado, 1982); Erszebet Szalai, *Gazdasag es hatalom* (Economy and power) (Budapest: Aula Kiado, 1990); Ivan Szelenyi, *Uj osztaly, allam, politika* (New class, state, politics) (Budapest: Europa Könikviado, 1986); Agnes Utasi, *Eletstilus-csoportok, fogyasztasi preferenciak: Retegzödésmodell-vizsgalat* (Lifestyle groups, consumption, preferences: Stratification model analysis) (Budapest: V. Tarsadalomtudomanyi Intézet, 1984); Zsuzsa Ferge and Jon Eivind Kolberg, eds., *Social Policy in a Changing Europe* (Frankfurt am Main: Campus, 1992).
2. Natacha Chmatko and Monique de Saint-Martin, "Les anciens bureaucrates dans l'économie de marché à Moscou," *Genèses* 27(June 1997): 88–108.
3. Jiri Vecernik, "The Middle Class in Czech Reforms: The Interplay Between Policies and Social Stratification," *Communist and Post-Communist Studies* 32(December 1999): 397–416.
4. Peter Robert, "Middle-class Identification in Hungary: International Comparison and Temporal Changes," in *The Middle Class as a Precondition of a Sustainable Society*, edited by Nikolai Tilkidjiev (papers from a sociological conference in Bulgaria) (Sofia: [AMCD] Association for Middle-Class Development, June 1998), 192.
5. See Savage (this volume). According to a 1992–93 ISSP (International Social Survey Program) study, the percentage of people who considered themselves middle-class was 70.2 in Italy, 60.3 in the former West Ger-

many, 58.8 in Austria, 54.0 in Norway, and 51.6 in the United States. But it was 48.8 in Russia, 42.4 in the former East Germany, 41.5 in Poland, 32.8 in Hungary, 31.8 in (still existing as a political unit) Czechoslovakia, 31.1 in Bulgaria, and 30.4 in the United Kingdom. See ISSP, *Social Inequality II, 1992–1993: Codebook*, ZA Study 2310, 176. To these percentages we can add those of the "subjective" upper working class: 52.0 in the former East Germany (but only 26.0 in the former West Germany), 46.8 in Bulgaria, 44.6 in Russia, 44.3 in Poland (as in the United Kingdom), 41.3 in the United States, 40.9 in Czechoslovakia, 38.9 in Hungary, and 38.2 in Austria. See Robert, "Middle-class Identification," 192–95.

6. See Zunz (this volume).

7. Agnes Utasi, "From the Middle Class to the Middle Strata: The Hungarian Version," in Tilkidjiev, *The Middle Class as a Precondition*, 171–91.

8. Ibid., 172.

9. Daniel Bertaux, "Les transmissions en situation extrême: Familles expropriées par la Révolution d'octobre," *Communications* 59(November 1994): 73–99.

10. Michael Voslensky, *La nomenclatura* (Paris: Belfond, 1980).

11. Andorka, *A társadami mobilitás változásai Magyarországon*.

12. Jiri Vecernik, *Markets and People: The Czech Reform Experience in a Comparative Perspective* (Aldershot: Avebury, 1996).

13. Vladimir Belenkii, "O srednem klasse vo Rossii" (On the middle class in Russia), *Sotsial'no-politicheskii zhurnal* 12 (December 1994): 15–26; Ludmila Beliaeva, "Srednii sloi rossiiskogo obshchestva: Problemy obreteniia sotsial'nogo statusa" (The middle class in Russian society: Getting social status) *Sotsis, Sotsiologicheskie issledovaniia* 10(October 1993): 13–22.

14. Tilkidjiev, *The Middle Class as a Precondition*.

15. Siyka Kovatcheva, "Becoming a 'Businessman' in Post-Communist Europe: Life Careers of the Young Self-employed in Bulgaria, Poland, Slovakia, and Hungary," in Tilkidjiev, *The Middle Class as a Precondition*, 264–72; Raimo Blom, Harri Melin, and Jouko Nicula, eds., *Reformation of the Middle Classes in the Baltic Countries*, Working Paper 4 (Tampere, Finland: University of Tampere, 1995); Chmatko and de Saint-Martin, "Les anciens bureaucrates dans l'économie de marché à Moscou."

16. Chmatko and de Saint-Martin, "Les anciens bureaucrates dans l'économie de marché à Moscou."

17. Utasi, "From the Middle Class to the Middle Strata," 174–77.

18. Petr Mateju, "The Renewal of the Middle Class and Its Political Circumstances," in *Ten Years of Rebuilding Capitalism: Czech Society After 1989*, edited by Jiri Vecernik and Petr Mateju (Prague: Academia, 1999), 207–27; Mikhail Mirchev, "Borderlines Between the Middle Class and the Upper and Lower Classes: Empirical Indicators," in Tilkidjiev, *The Middle Class as a Precondition*, 352–63.

19. Jiri Vecernik, "The Middle Class in Czech Reforms," 402.

# 16

## Upsetting Models: An Italian Tale of the Middle Classes

### *Arnaldo Bagnasco*

Is it possible to bind together economic efficiency, social cohesion, and political liberty? This is a tough nut to crack for societies in this era of economic globalization. For a long time, the social contracts of the postwar years managed to achieve effective combinations along these three dimensions, but now the balance is being upset. In today's world, according to Ralf Dahrendorf, the German model, which combines social cohesion with political liberty, lacks economic efficiency, whereas the Asian small dragon model, which combines social cohesion with economic efficiency, is short on political liberty.[1]

Declaring any country's way of combining the three dimensions to be satisfactory naturally implies subjective evaluation of the options, but it is equally clear that no single best way exists; every form of capitalism has to find its own way of addressing this issue. Many commentators, Dahrendorf included, have observed that Italy has so far achieved one of the best compromises possible, owing in large part to its family firms and small and medium-sized entrepreneurs. This image of Italy may be a trifle overoptimistic and incomplete—the capitalistic practices in question are to be found only in a few regions, accounting for only about one-third of the country—but it does contain an element of truth. It is also interesting that it rests on the role played by the middle classes. Indeed, this assessment suggests that any understanding of the mechanisms whereby economic efficiency, social cohesion, and political liberty combine satisfactorily requires close observation of the distinctive features and actions of a society's middle classes. This is a new way of rephrasing the old observation that the middle classes are society's "connective tissue."[2] Indeed, the social contracts and equilibrium of the postwar years can be seen in different ways to have been directed to the formation of the middle classes and their conditions.

Italy is a country in which the middle classes have always played an important role. Although this is a rather vague concept—it is difficult to establish the collar line, and the actual middle-class status of individual groups can be precarious—figures do exist that support the argument that social "middle-of-the-roaders" are of paramount importance in Italy.

One emblematic statistic is the percentage of self-employed (traditionally considered the "old" middle class): in the mid-1990s, 29 percent of the total in Italy against 9 percent in the United States, 10 percent in Germany, 14 percent in France, and 13 percent in Great Britain.[3] Even more significant is the fact that Italy boasts sixty-eight industrial and commercial enterprises for every one thousand inhabitants, against thirty-five in France, thirty-seven in Germany, thirty-three in Denmark, twenty-eight in the Netherlands, and forty-six in Great Britain. With sixty-nine enterprises for every one thousand inhabitants, Greece is the only European country that bears comparison with Italy. It is vital to remember, however, that Italy is the fourth or fifth most industrialized country in the world and that income per capita in Greece is about one-third of Italy's rate.

Public and private employees (the "new" middle class) now account for about one-third of the working population of Italy. About 6 percent of the population work in the civil service, an intermediate figure in Europe between 14 percent in Denmark and 4 percent in Greece; the commonly held view, however, is that Italy is strangled by red tape.[4] Although not quantitatively true, this impression may derive from the heavy influence that the bureaucracy exerts on society.

Italian society is thus a fertile terrain for exploration of the present and future of the middle classes. My point of departure is the role of the middle classes in how different societies combine economic efficiency, social cohesion, and political freedom. My hypothesis is that in the era of globalization, and at a time when the old social contracts are under pressure, the middle classes form the foundation of an effective compromise among the three dimensions, at least in certain respects, in a number of important regions. It is also possible to extract additional observations from the Italian case. Specifically, as we will see, the Italian case is relevant to the problems examined in this book in part because it also provides a good example of how the middle classes may be involved in mechanisms that lead to poor adjustments of the three dimensions considered.

Many of those engaged in cross-national research consider the part of Italy about which I have spoken as a happy example of the recent "return of civil society"—that is, a more liberal economy supported by traditional cultural resources. This idea envisions a diffuse culture of reciprocal trust—for example, a history of forms of association and all the other traits central to the idea of "social capital." At the same time, the role of politics in planning and regulating social and economic arrangements has been reduced. This analysis contrasts with earlier studies of the regions of Italy that combine to form the Mezzogiorno (the south). This large area—where public spending has been hefty, but major political programs to activate development have failed to produce satisfactory results—is one of the least developed in Europe. Apparently confirming the inefficiency of politics, the case of the Mezzogiorno thus appears to be the polar opposite of the successful "return of civil society" model noted by Dahrendorf in the small-enterprise regions of Italy. More generally speaking, many consider the Italian state, centralized and for many years interventionist in the economy, both expensive and inefficient.

In this chapter, I try to show that the Italian case is a little more complicated than that. It should be clear by now why, at a time when old models are being overturned everywhere, the Italian case is so interesting. It is not that Italy possesses recipes for success, but that its complex, internally differentiated society tends to place both the typical problems and the possibilities in sharp focus. I am not the first to suggest the utility of the Italian case as a touchstone in analyses of other countries. It was only after long studies of the south of Italy and the regions of small-enterprise development that Robert Putnam, for example, sparked a lively discussion on the importance and loss of social capital in the United States. I return to this question later.

## The Postwar Prelude: The Middle Classes and Social Consensus

The Italy that emerged from World War II was a poor, backward country. A large portion of the population still worked in agriculture, though some areas of the north had boasted an industrial tradition since the start of the century. Ten years after the end of the war, in 1955, the country accounted for just 9 percent of total European industrial production. By 1990, however, it had become the fourth most important producer among the OECD countries after the United States, Japan, and Germany.[5] The driving force behind the first stage in its lightning development was big business, especially the mechanical engineering and car industries of the Northwest. Development was export-led, and domestic consumption remained weak. The country was sharply dualistic as the industrial regions of the north attracted sizable numbers of immigrants from the rest of the country.

The distinctive feature of the political system was the presence of the strongest Communist Party in the Western world. The other mass party, the Christian Democrat Party, was always the first in the country, but it never achieved an absolute majority and had to rely on the backing of minor center parties to govern. Unstable, short-lived governments thus became a permanent fixture of Italian politics. One British observer calculated that governments in Italy lasted as long as the gestation period of a mare! Hence an "imperfect two-party" system was eventually established, with the Communist opposition not strong enough to achieve a majority yet also unable to find allies for alternative coalitions. As a consequence, parties whose electoral base was formed by the middle classes held power for decades. The middle classes were treated to special favors and protected and rewarded—with low taxes, economic aid, favorable legislation, facilitation in the granting of licenses, and so on—in ways that were often out of all proportion to their real contribution to the production of national wealth. Other countries saw the decline of the self-employed middle classes, the artisans, peasants, and tradespeople; in Italy, they lived and flourished in their glass house—one that was economically inefficient but filled an extremely useful social control function—and no one threw stones at them.[6] The public administration also grew without any effective check on its efficiency.

Summing up, in the first two postwar decades a populous, differentiated set of middle classes lived in protected political "reserves," which were granted because of their social control functions. Italian society saw the development of "individualistic mobilization" as the middle classes focused on securing jobs and social position.[7] In this way, politics—substantially free, but also largely imperfect—established an equilibrium that ensured acceptable overall social cohesion at a high cost in terms of economic efficiency.

The cost of the system grew evident in the late 1960s, when workers in big factories reached agreements for much better wages and working conditions. Italy was thus moving toward a Fordist-Keynesian system of regulation at the very moment when such arrangements were under pressure everywhere else and even breaking down in some places.[8] Italy's ability to bend with change was thus undermined by these new agreements, as well as by the old compromise that conserved inefficiencies in vital sections of the economy and society. The situation was already extremely critical when terrorism jeopardized the political framework. Yet it was at that precise moment when an extraordinary "coup de théâtre" occurred—the return of small industrial firms. Thanks to these companies, development was able to continue and spread to new regions, which were subsequently to become among the wealthiest in the country. It was thus that some of the old middle classes—now renewed—guided the process of social restructuring.

## The Old-New Middle Classes: A Post-Fordist Surprise

Two of the many consequences of the crisis of Fordism and the process of globalization proved decisive for a number of Italian regions. The first was the return to the economic scene of the small industrial enterprise; the second was the dual process whereby globalization was accompanied by a regionalization of production. The two processes often combined, and in some areas of Italy that combination was an instant success.

A term used to define the post-Fordist form of production is "flexible specialization."[9] In a number of ways, small enterprises are a fundamental ingredient of the new arrangement. True, they sometimes form part of large-enterprise subsupply networks, but the case that interests us here is that of the independent units, or the units interlinked in local small-business systems, in which entrepreneurial initiatives multiply. The Italy of small enterprises does not mass-produce cars or chemical products but specializes in different kinds of low-volume consumer goods, often of high quality, as well as machine tools and associated investment goods.

The return of small enterprises is bound up in the sharp growth in world demand for nonstandardized consumer goods and in improved communications along the supply chain. There has also been increased uncertainty, an acceleration of economic processes (hence the need for elastic organization and low labor costs—at least at the outset and for the simplest manufacturing processes), and an increase in the availability of new elastic technologies, such as numerically controlled machinery, suitable for low-volume production. The availability of these new technologies also explains how small enterprises have been able to follow their own path to modernization, becoming more efficient, profitable, and capable of paying higher wages as they abandon the simplest manufacturing processes.

To describe these local forms of division of labor among small firms, economists use the concept of the "industrial district," introduced by Alfred Marshall in the last century. The new general conditions outlined explain its return to the contemporary economy, and economists are now studying why and how small producers—and ultimately the coordinated division of labor they practice—as opposed to the organizational concentration of large firms, have become so widespread.[10]

In the 1960s, many industrial districts specializing in one or more products appeared. In the most complex systems, a commercial company or medium-sized manufacturer may be the collector or final assembler of relatively complex products either in a traditional sector such as clothes, footwear, leather goods, furniture, or toys or in one of the most technologically advanced sectors, such as mechanical engineering, electronics, biomedical equipment, or investment goods. Other systems are simpler in terms of structure and products. Many enterprises that came into being by imitating others produced similar items, sometimes in competition with each other. Local small-enterprise systems have spread virtually everywhere, but above all in the central and northeastern regions of Italy, from Tuscany to the Marche, and from Emilia to Veneto to Friuli. The question we have to ask is, why have some regions been able to follow this course so much more successfully than other regions?

In industrial districts, the economy appears to be regulated by the free market, and it is easy to hire or dismiss workers. But there is more: below the surface bargaining, the market proves to have a complicated social construction. A closely interconnected fabric of cities and towns have distributed locally what geographers call urban functions: banking, schools, training schools, shopping centers, and services. There is also a fair and relatively efficient local administration, as well as a strong craft and, in some cases, industrial tradition. All these elements are bound together by strong local cultural identities. This social ambit furnishes many people with technical and commercial know-how and fosters relatively efficient infrastructure and services, a shared awareness of the idea and practices of the market, and networks of personal relations. These networks promote reciprocal trust, allowing an easy circulation of information and business dealings. (Economists would speak in terms of lower transaction costs and opportunistic conduct.) Many thus find themselves in circumstances favorable to embarking upon the entrepreneurial adventure. Sometimes it is a family affair. In fact, it is common for brothers and sisters to be entrepreneurs and for more than one member of a family to work for the company.

After the small-business phenomenon caught on, it grew by a process of imitation in medium-sized regional capitals such as Florence and Bologna, as well as in smaller towns, where traditions of commerce, agriculture, and crafts had already produced venture capital and where the activities and forms of organization necessary for the new production were modern offshoots of traditional artisanal know-how. Moreover, the capital needed to set up in business was low and the know-how widespread.

An example may serve to clarify how such an industrial district works. Prato in Tuscany has been famous as a textile production center since the Middle Ages. In the postwar years, it continued to be one of the major European producers of carded cloth, and the average size of its firms remains below ten employees to this day.[11] Prato-born commercial agents operate in London, where they accept any orders, even if they do not know exactly who will fulfill them. They do know, however, that they will find producers ready and willing to do the job in the Prato district. These producers are connected with wool processors and mechanics capable of making the necessary modifications to their machinery. Everybody in the district has known each other for a long time, and they all know that they can trust each other with regard to delivery times and quality.

The urban middle classes initiated the process, interacting with rural areas characterized by a distinctive social structure of autonomous farming families, small landowners, leaseholders, and sharecroppers who often lived in isolated country farmhouses. Companies could thus count on having workers who had learned many trades at home and who, if they were poorly paid to start with or employed only sporadically, could always turn to their families for help. After all, they usually had a house at their disposal and grew food for their own consumption and, in many cases, for sale. Entrepreneurs were not exclusively urban in origin. By combining different forms of income from agricultural and industrial labor, even large peasant families sometimes accumulated enough capital to support the craft or industrial activities of a son who had set up on his own.

Such societies made a selective use of the social and cultural resources of their traditional heritage, investing them in the new economic opportunities that were opening up. To maintain the combination of these resources, production activities were not centered in the leading cities but spread to small towns, which drew from a pool of labor in the surrounding countryside. Hence the development of the so-called urbanized countryside.

There is nothing fundamentally new about small-enterprise industrial districts, whether in Italy or elsewhere. After being superseded by mass industrialization, they have now reappeared in new forms to match changes in circumstances. In Italy, it is interesting to note that the regions of the industrial districts correspond almost exactly to the areas where capitalism first appeared from the Middle Ages to the Renaissance. These areas were not subsequently affected by the Industrial Revolution, and although never inactive, they remained quiescent for a long period of time. The local resources I have discussed here are, to a certain extent, a legacy of that tradition. Some authors believe that a certain original civic-mindedness—or civicness[12]—has been conserved in the social institutions and contemporary policies of these regions, and that this characteristic has generated efficient administrative institutions and supported the form of economic development so prevalent in these regions. The argument is a plausible one, though it is hard to demonstrate. In any event, the civicness in question is part and parcel of a more general legacy. More visible and unquestionably more important are the inherited characteristics that I listed earlier: the distribution of urban functions among several small towns and cities, complemented by an agricultural economy with distinctive social qualities. Today these regions are actively modernizing, keeping in step with the times by constantly improving production techniques and products.

What I have briefly outlined is the Italian capitalism that Dahrendorf says has achieved a satisfactory balance between economic efficiency, social cohesion, and democracy. The small-enterprise areas are now among the wealthiest in the country, and their sizable exports help to balance the national economy. This model continues to show the lowest levels of unemployment—around 6 percent in the various regions[13]—in a country where the average rate is double that, exceeding 20 percent in the southern regions. In general, the model has ensured the diffusion of the benefits of development, the best social services in proportion to national standards, a long-lasting and high level of social mobility, and pragmatic management of social conflict without radicalization.

I might also add that this is a regional development model developed for and guided by the middle classes. Even if small firms are present almost everywhere in Italy, the model is nonetheless characteristic of only about one-third of the country, whose industrialization is due exclusively to the small-enterprise areas. On the other hand, small enterprises have now renewed their position in all of the world's economies, in many cases inducing forms of regional development similar, albeit never exactly identical, to Italy's.[14] In Italy itself, it remains to be seen whether the model can evolve over time and whether it conceals weaknesses and latent costs. I speak about these issues in the final section.

## The Weight of Middle Classes That Have Developed "Badly": Politics and Administration

As I have said, the weight of the public bureaucracy, quantitatively speaking, is not particularly heavy—public-sector employees account for only 6 percent of the population. If we consider, however, that the figure corresponds to about 15 percent of the working population and consists largely of white-collar workers, it is possible to speak in terms of a fairly large public middle class. Its importance, then, is related to the functions it performs and its quality.

The Italian state was born in the second half of the last century as an assembly of smaller regional states that differed greatly in terms of culture, society, and economic development. The process was guided by one of these states, Piedmont—in the northwest of the country—whose local dynasty became the rulers of the unified peninsula.

The different administrations were rapidly unified according to the model of the Piedmontese bureaucracy, with no regard for the diversity of local traditions and needs. Furthermore, a clear majority of bureaucrats were Piedmontese. The bureaucracy was thus flawed from the outset, since the principle of "representative bureaucracy" was not respected.[15] This principle asserts that major differences between the makeup of the bureaucracy and the characteristics of the population call into question the bureaucracy's legitimacy as an impartial tool that reflects common values. In the course of time, this flaw was perpetuated, but with a conspicuous change in the composition of the administration. Today, in fact, two-thirds of civil servants are of southern origin. The reason for this is bound up in the role of the middle classes in consensus mechanisms.

The origins of the relative inefficiency of the Italian bureaucracy also go a long way back in time. This inefficiency was the consequence of a unitary state, which was sharply centralized from the very outset, and of the top-heavy, finicky regulations that it promulgated. These regulations failed to leave room for peripheral autonomy and inhibited the formation of independent initiative. These weaknesses were only exacerbated when the bureaucracy was targeted as a source of new jobs. Since the south is the most backward area in the country, many southerners turned to the expanding public administration for employment. Because the bureaucracy was an important bastion of the middle class, politicians during the postwar years catered to middle-class needs and perpetuated these imbalances. Politicians and members of the administration found themselves caught within a rigid, nonproductive, but lucrative symbiotic relationship.

It would be wrong to think that the Italian bureaucracy owes its characteristics solely to the problems posed by the south, but the fact remains that bureaucratic imbalances have made themselves particularly felt there. Public spending and transfers turned this vast underdeveloped area into a politically regulated regional society. As electoral issues have often demonstrated, in underdeveloped areas investment projects likely to yield long-term results are often shelved in favor of those yielding immediate advantages, which distribute resources to boost consumption.[16] Relations between politics and society in the south have thus been based on traditional forms of "clientelismo," or political patronage, and advantages have been granted and handled in the context of personalized relations of trust. Social cohesion in backward regions has thus ensured the loss of an increasing amount of economic inefficiency and a political climate in which democratic freedoms have sometimes been undermined by criminal influences. The influence of the public middle classes that developed "badly" was thus preserved in the 1960s and 1970s, even as the new small-business middle classes strengthened their position and created a buoyant market economy. The public administration continued to constitute a fertile terrain for individuals in the south searching for permanent jobs.

The bureaucratic middle class, which was born and reproduced in these conditions, was relatively incapable of asserting consolidated professional expertise of its own. It may suffice in this respect to cite an indirect but very eloquent statistic: it has been calculated that in the 1980s and 1990s about 60 percent of civil servants were not recruited through public competition but through provisional recruitments, which were later legitimated by laws.[17] This situation was reflected in the motivations of public employees. International comparisons show that, more often than in other advanced countries, Italian bureaucrats are motivated by the chance to gain a permanent wage and job more than by the idea of contributing to decisions that affect the running of the country. The Italian bureaucrat thus does not possess the impartiality of the legally trained German bureaucrat, or the in-depth training of the French bureaucrat educated in the great French schools of administration, or the authority and motivation of the British civil servant. The Italian bureaucrat tends instead to be inefficient and expensive, greatly hindering rather than advancing the modernization of the country.

## Middle Classes, Economic Efficiency, and Social Cohesion: What Can We Learn from the Italian Case?

Despite their weight in numbers and importance, it would be wrong to see the middle classes as dominant in Italian society. The country's economy has been guided and influenced by an industrial elite that controls a core group of large enterprises; on the other hand, despite frequent changes in government, it is a political elite that managed the compromises I outlined earlier. Having said that, it is also true that the middle classes have begun to play an important secondary role, showing strength, autonomy, and strategic capability. Middle-class individuals seeking to protect their position and other individuals aspiring to a place in the middle classes have made efforts to gain new social positions, and these efforts may have consolidated forms of representation and collective action throughout the society. Research on social mobility has produced very eloquent data on this phenomenon.[18]

What makes Italian society stand out from the many other countries for which comparable data are available is its notable rigidity in terms of relative mobility. The possibility of climbing from the bottom rungs of the social ladder to the top is very low and has not changed over the years; the probability of downward mobility has also remained low. It nonetheless has been calculated that in the growth years, mobility has been so high that today almost three-fifths of the working population belong to a class different from that of their family of origin. At first, this shift was most often seen when the position of workers improved, but subsequently it became more generalized. In fact, Italy has recorded a sharp shift from dependent to independent jobs, and from manual to intellectual labor. The thrust toward mobility has been so strong that, given the rigidity of the existing social structure, it could only have been achieved by broadening the middle rungs of the ladder—that is, by inventing or claiming many more new intermediate positions than had been available in the past.

As we have seen, this mobilization breaks down into two types and eras. At first, political resources produced it. Only subsequently did the *market mobilization* of small entrepreneurs and self-employed workers make itself felt. The two different types of mobilization have also had a variety of consequences for efficiency and solidarity. The double face of development in Italy has turned the country into a sort of sociological experiment on the trends of contemporary capitalism.

After studying the administrative inefficiency of southern Italy and the political and economic development of the central and eastern regions, Robert Putnam explained their differences in terms of civic culture and social capital.[19] He then turned his attention to the United States, where he sparked a lively debate about the risk the country is running of losing its traditional social capital—that is, the fabric of diffuse trust, the networks of association, and the spontaneous interactions that fostered orderly growth in the past.[20] Francis Fukuyama, who shares Putnam's concerns and also relies significantly on the Italian case, has gone even further, arguing that social engineering and welfare state systems have destroyed a great deal of traditional social capital without creating new forms.[21] In his view, the less the state engages in institutional engineering the better. In this model, the market and civil society push politics and policy into a corner. Is this arrangement capable of holding together high levels of economic efficiency, social cohesion, and political liberty in the long term? To what extent can the market and civil society get by without politics? How far can the Italian case support this interpretative model? And in the final analysis, what does the Italian case teach in more general terms?

To begin to answer these questions, let us return to a more general framework. Postwar social compromises were based on a mass-production economy, an increase in wages and consumption for a growing "middle class," and welfare protections, which varied from country to country. In Europe, these protections were strong and part of more complex systems of economic and social regulation, which comprised forms of economic management in partnership with large interest organizations, the supply of public goods, and, in some cases, the existence of state industries. For a variety of reasons, these systems, which for decades had ensured a workable combination of economic development, social cohesion, and democracy, plunged into crisis in the seventies. Everywhere in the world, the globalization of the economy led to greater deregulation of the market, withdrawal of politics, rethinking of welfare systems, and challenges to the forms of regulation negotiated between employees and unions. Problems of social cohesion also grew: where unemployment was low, inequalities increased, and where welfare systems and politics controlled inequalities, unemployment either increased or at least did not drop.

Now taking shape is a new capitalism characterized by the flexibility that comes from outsourcing and networked organizations. Financial concentration is growing, but the large production complexes are laying off employees and establishing networks of suppliers with varying degrees of independence. Market relations are either pure or stabilized by special contracts. Subsuppliers are becoming specialists in supplying elements of more complex products and produce for more than one supplier. Industrial output conforms more closely to a variable, differentiated demand and includes fewer standardized or low-volume products. A new "spirit of capitalism" is taking hold. Fueled more by Joseph Schumpeter's "creative destruction" than Max Weber's "bureaucratic rationalization," the new spirit requires mutual trust among workers and the self-actualization of technicians and managers who are less subject to oversight.[22]

If these are the general characteristics of the new capitalism, in many respects they have been developed and, in some cases, anticipated by Italian small-firm systems. The participants in these systems did not need globalization to teach them the advantages of elasticity, risk propensity, self-control, mutual trust in changing networks, and producing for a variable, differentiated market.

The shift to the global market has been accepted without any difficulty because local society itself supplied the cultural and material resources to take advantage of global opportunities, as well as protection against risk. The market was embedded in a suitable society and defined by all concerned as the right model to allow local society to grow.

One important point must not be forgotten. The project of the old social compromises was to integrate the working class into a large middle class, ensuring security and a progressive rise in wages in exchange for labor in large, hierarchically organized structures. The new capitalism of networks and outsourcing produces a dualization of the labor market: even as leading firms provide well-paid, more autonomous jobs, jobs in subsupply firms are increasingly precarious and the number of weak self-employed workers is rising. This tendency, which may pose major problems for social cohesion, has also become evident in Italy, but to date it would appear to have affected small-enterprise areas less than others. In these areas, long-term unemployment is lower because the production system and local society networks allow workers who lose their jobs to find new jobs. At the same time, information circulates freely, allowing professional skills to be constantly updated.

Putnam and Fukuyama are thus right to say that the case of northeast Italy shows the importance of social capital for the development and proper functioning of administrative institutions. However, they underestimate the role of politics. In small-enterprise regions, in fact, politics has been more important than may appear at first sight, not only at the national level, with measures that favor small-scale ownership, but also, and above all, in regional governments, which are careful to conserve, update, and improve the common resources on which the economy and society can draw. Good local administration, business and community services, the best social welfare system in the country, schools, higher education, and research establishments all provide examples of these interventions. Economic success and social cohesion have been made possible thanks to the interweaving of public action, traditional community institutions, interest organizations, and free business enterprise. Lightweight but effective institutional engineering has thus accompanied and made possible the difficult task of competing on the free market.

Not even the case of the south—where traditional social capital is scarce and institutional engineering has produced unsatisfactory results—proves that the less the state deals in economic regulation the better. In effect, political action in the south—the most important social engineering project in Italy—has failed to produce a local society capable of growing autonomously. It did produce social cohesion, but with a hefty inflow of money for many decades; hence, social cohesion imposed a high cost on the country as a whole and perpetuated inefficiency. Living conditions improved, major infrastructure was built, and production capacity increased. Nonetheless, in 1969 the gross domestic product per capita was only 69 percent of the national GDP, and today the percentage remains roughly the same.[23] This failure is not simply due to perverse long-term effects of top-down economic interventions and generous support for the population. More important is how soon the policy was harnessed to functions far removed from orderly growth prospects. Local political systems based on patronage have continued to redistribute resources rather than invest in the modernization that would challenge their very existence. Clearly, the root problem is one of *bad* institutional engineering.

Similar observations might be made for other aspects of public action in Italy. One important player is state-controlled industry, for a long time an important component of the big-business system. Today the sector is being privatized, a choice made necessary by fundamental and widespread changes in markets. The state-controlled industries in question are weighed down by huge inefficiencies, accumulated as a result of the constraints that government political parties have imposed on their economic action. This was not the case at the outset. In a country with few traditions of large-scale industrial capitalism, the major public enterprises have been decisive in creating some of the basic conditions for development in sectors such as transportation, steel, electricity, and communications. It has only been when these industrial organizations were diverted from their original aims that they came to grief.

The impressive development of the small-enterprise economy certainly proves that civil society can invest resources successfully with actors interacting freely in the new conditions of the contemporary economy. Success encompasses both economic efficiency and social cohesion. Incomparably good results have been achieved in the central and northeast regions without an explicit regional policy, unlike the situation in the south, where an expensive and burdensome regional policy has been implemented. Yet the cultural, material, and social resources available in one regional society may not be available in another. The present thinking is that it might be advisable to capitalize on the resources of local society in the south too, developing more differentiated, bottom-up, spontaneous models situation by situation. In view of the lack of deposited social capital, however, it is difficult to rule out political action as a means of creating favorable conditions. What is under discussion is the character and aims of such political action.

Here we approach the heart of the matter. I posed the question of what we can expect from middle classes that are suspended midway between government action and the free market. I then hypothesized that if we wish to understand the mechanisms through which economic efficiency, social cohesion, and political liberty combine, we have to take a careful look at the characteristics and actions of the middle classes in society. In view of these last observations, everything would appear to boil down to the following question: How can we involve the middle classes in public and private projects of institutional efficiency?

I will try to answer the question by looking at the Italian case from the experience of the United States. My viewpoint on America derives not from Putnam and Fukuyama, however, but from what seems to me to be the more realistic view of Olivier Zunz. As I will demonstrate, the small-enterprise system needs to be consolidated, and the resources it requires go beyond the social capital inherited from traditional society. On the other hand, the underdevelopment of the south continues to be a problem, and that problem could be aggravated in a context of fierce global competition. In the next section, I refer mainly to Zunz's idea of American development. I argue for the type of institutional engineering that Zunz uncovers. I also argue for political change made possible by new opportunities despite hazy political cleavages. In this process, the role of the middle classes is crucial, and indeed, the future of democracy depends on how they carry out that role.

## What About Democracy? The Need for Governance and Hazy Cleavages

Zunz argues that underpinning the American model—and beyond it the "American century"—was an institutional matrix of business corporations, research universities and institutes, government agencies, and foundations that allowed producers, brokers, and users of knowledge to interact fully for the first time and develop together an array of cognitive strategies.[24] This view does not rule out the importance of traditional social capital—mutual trust, the cultural inclination to cooperate, the vitality of civil society, and its capacity for self-organization—but does focus on the institutional and social engineering that could create new organizational social capital for a mass society.[25]

Zunz's matrix posits the growth of a middle class based on technology and a huge increase in consumption. The process of creating a dominant economy is in effect one with the project of expanding a middle class. Overall, this model also shows the importance of political action in creating the conditions of development and in regulating relations between the economy and society. Yet typically this matrix has evolved fluidly, as both public and private actors take part and conserve and develop the self-organizational capacity of society.

If we view Italy from this vantage point, we note a low level of traditional social capital in some areas and a higher level in others. What has clearly been lacking virtually everywhere is efficient institutional engineering capable of creating the conditions for economic efficiency and social solidarity in the interests of modernization. In Italy too, the middle class—whose composition is different from that of its American counterpart—has become a pillar of society. Unlike in the United States, however, the Italian middle class has not been part of a project of institutional efficiency. It is true that the difficulties of institutional and social engineering require that the spontaneous self-organizational capacities of society and the market be called on for help. However, we also have to note the great limitations resulting precisely from the weakness of an institutional matrix, which, in the long term, also jeopardizes the survival of a true capacity for efficiency. For these reasons, in my view, the fundamental question is: How can we involve the middle classes in projects of institutional efficiency, both public and private? Today the question assumes a significance that transcends single national cases, even if the solutions have to be differentiated. It involves not only the social role of the middle classes but also their relationship with democracy.

The problem of institutional efficiency in Italy is a dual one. It involves eliminating the old forms of inefficiency bound up in the consensus mechanism, which I mentioned earlier, and at the same time establishing efficient new institutional resources for development, cohesion, and the free exercise of political rights. Both require major political initiatives as well as institutional engineering. Decisive issues for both questions are the orientation of the middle classes and the political system's capacity to steer and integrate them as part of an innovative institutional design.

The present moment is a delicate one. Social cohesion has not undergone dramatic changes, but unemployment is, on average, high in Italy. There is no balance between regions, and poverty has reached high levels in some areas. The present phase is also delicate in terms of the question of economic efficiency. The old economy of small and medium-sized enterprises was regulated by the free market, which made use of the cultural and social resources produced and made available in traditional local society. The inefficiency of national institutions was felt but could be avoided with tax evasion, indulgent enforcement, or devaluation of the currency to facilitate exports. At any rate, market conditions were very favorable to first-comers in that type of economy. The need for continuous technological innovation, advanced vocational training, investment in research, adequate means of communication, and administrative reliability and speed, however, is becoming increasingly decisive for globalized competition. This makes two things necessary: an efficient central state, albeit with reduced functions with respect to traditional European models, and well-organized local societies endowed with good infrastructure and a capacity for self-government.

Here one positive point needs to be stressed. The political action developed in small-enterprise areas is characterized by pragmatic governance capable of promoting collaboration between public and private actors. This political style is spreading, and new conditions are fostering its diffusion even in the south. The fiscal crisis of the state and the new standards required by the European Union are, de facto, reducing the resources available for redistribution and necessary investment projects with a long-term impact. Because local societies have to count on their own resources more and more, citizens are encouraged to take control of politics. So-called local pacts—projects developed under the joint initiative of local government, interest associations, and single firms—are becoming more common. Through specified mutual pledges, these groups are capable of obtaining government aid.

All this requires institutional engineering, as well as a great deal of sound political action. Over this possibility looms the long shadow of the old arrangements of Italian society: the necessary resource—an efficient political system capable of acknowledging and steering the political demand in society according to these needs—is not immediately available. Hence the past conditions the present to no small extent.

Two points are significant here. The first is in one respect positive: the old party system in general and the imperfect two-party system in particular have collapsed. The reasons are many and various and include the evolution of the international framework following the collapse of the Berlin Wall. The principal reasons, however, are to be found in the political corruption, resulting from patronage and the inefficient management of the national system, that led the country to the verge of financial bankruptcy. A new efficient system of interest representation is still struggling, however, to emerge.

The second point is that Italy needs to dismantle immediately the old, top-heavy institutional arrangements bound up in consensus mechanisms and build radically new ones. Progress in this area has been stymied by hazy political cleavages. Groups with opposing economic or philosophical interests support the same measure. Again, other countries may have this same problem, but Italy illustrates it in a more clear-cut and extreme way.

The problem of indirect political cleavages and anomalous political allegiances comes into play. Entrepreneurs know only too well that they would have everything to gain from a more efficient country and more efficient administrative systems. However, they tend not to trust politicians and may conclude that, given the situation, simply paying a few taxes is the least of all evils. Many of them may thus find themselves on the same side as speculators, for whom total market deregulation is the best prospect. Alternatively, resistance to dismantling part of the welfare state system may be a position shared by progressivists, who support the needs of underprivileged sections of the population, and leading corporate profiteers and entrenched civil servants, who benefit from the old system and are keen to conserve their privileges. Some civil servants are motivated to participate actively and autonomously in the project of forging new institutional arrangements; others cling tenaciously to the old ways. The old Right-Left line does not necessarily capture the divide, and groupings may change as issues change.

With a highly fragmented political climate and a relatively non-institutionalized political system, the balance between efficiency, solidarity, and democratic freedom might deteriorate, especially if generally favorable market conditions were to change. The conclusion is thus that a great deal of initiative and entrepreneurship will be required to maintain this balance, in terms of both political output and political input. Without such a balance, political entrepreneurs might use demagoguery to gain influence and control the rest of society by reducing the space for the "democratic game."

That is why the problem—perhaps the risk—of finding ways to integrate the middle classes into the modernization process has reappeared at the start of the new millennium. In the twentieth century, dramatic forms of middle-class integration were used to bolster anti-democratic regimes in Europe. The middle classes could be used in this way yet again. The "return of civil society" of the last few decades, however, has made it more difficult to manipulate the middle classes by increasing their autonomy as independent actors. This makes a difference. We obviously have no crystal ball with which to read the future, and what we still need today is closer knowledge of the different components of our rapidly evolving world. In the Italian case, however, there are signs that the middle classes *may* also have a positive role to play vis-à-vis the question of democracy.

Many areas with the most dynamic and best-run small firms have been in "red" regions where Communist roots are strong and local governments have been Communist for decades. The fact is less paradoxical than it may appear at first sight if we consider that it was above all in these regions that local government promoted the evolution of the former Italian Communist Party toward social democracy. The process went hand in hand with the growth of the economic and social model that I have described; in that model, the so-called productive middle class was soon considered an ally of the working class.

A second eye-opener has been the role played by small entrepreneurs in the collapse of the old party system. More than the large-scale entrepreneurial elite, small-business people have supported legal action against political corruption, which often consisted of granting favors in exchange for financial support for parties or, more simply, asking for money in return for performing routine functions.

In Italy, finally, two events can be seen as a sort of test of the political aptitudes of the middle classes vis-à-vis the new institutional constructions, the costs that must be paid for them, and the solid prospects for a solution, even if deferred until later. The ongoing reorganization of public finance and Italy's entry into the Euro system have been difficult processes. These two events have triggered skepticism and proven very costly for certain sections of the population, the middle classes especially. However, much to the surprise of foreign observers, the country soon managed to reach the necessary economic parameters and is now maintaining them. This is a sign that a large section of the population, especially the middle classes, is prepared to invest in the future, paying what it has to pay, if the price corresponds to a clear political design. In the short term, for many in the middle classes the price—both directly through taxes and indirectly as a result of the new normative and control standards imposed by the European Union—is by no means low. Politicians who were counting on a negative reaction to these difficulties, however, have been proved wrong.

Fifty years ago, C. Wright Mills concluded his study of the new American middle class by saying that it was up for sale on the political market. He added that no one had yet made "a serious offer."[26] The conclusion I come to is that today we can view the middle class as less passive than it has been in the past and that we can speak, without sarcasm, of its ability to entertain serious political offers and to choose an offer that binds together economic efficiency, social cohesion, and political liberty. The real problem could be a future lack of serious political offers.

---

Translated from the Italian by John Irving.

## Notes

1. Ralf Dahrendorf, "Economic Opportunity, Civil Society, and Political Liberty" (paper presented at the United Nations Research Institute for Social Development (UNRISD) Conference for Rethinking Social Development, Copenhagen, 1995).
2. Another famous image of the middle class is that of society's "vertebrae." Ortega y Gasset said that Spain's historical problem was that it had no middle class and was hence an "invertebrate society." José Ortega y Gasset, *España invertebrada: Bosquejo de algunos pensamientos historicos* (Invertebrate Spain: A Draft of Some Ideas on History) (Madrid: Alianza Editorial, 1988).
3. Evidently, there are important differences between Italy and other countries, but the figure overestimates them. Especially in recent times, corporate outsourcing policies—which I speak of later in the chapter—have led to the diffusion in Italy of new forms of contracts that have pushed many formerly employed workers toward independent labor. Some of these workers find their position ambiguous: though formally independent, they are de facto dependent, and working conditions for many are more precarious and disadvantaged than before. The more traditional activities are flanked, however, by new independent activities with a high professional content, carried out by workers who appreciate the autonomy and flexibility of their new jobs. See Giovanna Altieri and Mimmo Carrieri, *Il popolo del 10%: Il boom del lavoro atipico* (10% People: The Boom of the Atypical Work) (Rome: Donzelli editore, 2000). The figures cited are taken from various Eurostat sources.
4. Alain Claisse and Marie-Christine Maininger, *Fonctions publiques en Europe* (Public Administration in Europe) (Paris: Montchrestien, 1994).
5. Alberto Quadrio Curzio, *Noi, l'economia, e l'Europa* (We, the Economy, and Europe) (Bologna: Il Mulino, 1996).
6. Suzanne Berger and Michael J. Piore, *Dualism and Discontinuity in Industrial Societies* (Cambridge: Cambridge University Press, 1980).
7. Alessandro Pizzorno, "I ceti medi nei meccanismi del consenso" (The Middle Classes in the Mechanisms of Consensus), in *Il caso italiano* (The Italian Case), edited by Fabio L. Cavazza and Stephen R. Graubard (Milan: Garzanti, 1974).
8. By Fordist-Keynesian model I mean an economic system based on large-scale mass-production, high levels of employment, and growing consumption, regulated by policies oriented toward the full deployment of

resources—negotiated with interest representation organizations—and set off by large-scale welfare systems.

9. The development of small enterprises in Italy has given rise to a vast amount of research literature; for background, non-Italian readers might care to refer to Arnaldo Bagnasco and Carlo Trigilia, *La construction sociale du marché: Le défi de la troisième Italie* (The Social Construction of the Market) (Cachan: Les Éditions de l'École Normale Supérieure de Cachan, 1993); Sebastiano Brusco, "The Emilian Model: Productive Decentralization and Social Integration," *Cambridge Journal of Economics* 6(June 1982): 167–84; Frank Pyke, Giacomo Becattini, and Werner Sengenberger, eds., *Industrial Districts and Interfirm Cooperation in Italy* (Geneva: International Institute for Labor Studies, 1990); Frank Pyke, Giacomo Becattini, and Werner Sengenberger, eds., *Industrial Districts and Local Economic Regeneration* (Geneva: International Institute for Labor Studies, 1992). For a definition of flexible specialization, see Michael J. Piore and Charles F. Sabel, *The Second Industrial Divide: Possibilities for Prosperity* (New York: Basic, 1994).

10. Giacomo Becattini, "The Marshallian Industrial District as a Socioeconomic Notion," in Pyke, Becattini, and Sengenberger, eds., *Industrial Districts*, 37–51.

11. For example, in the second half of the 1970s, the fifty thousand people working in the textile sector in Prato, in firms with an average size of five employees, produced 50 percent of all carded cloth in the EEC, as well as other products.

12. See Robert D. Putnam, *Making Democracy Work: Civic Traditions in Modern Italy* (Princeton: Princeton University Press, 1993).

13. In some of these areas—de facto areas of full employment with inflows of immigration—unemployment is lower still.

14. Arnaldo Bagnasco and Charles F. Sabel, eds., *Small and Medium-Size Enterprises* (London: Pinter, 1995).

15. J. D. Kingsley, *Representative Bureaucracy* (Yellow Springs, Ohio: Antioch Press, 1944).

16. This was verified for southern Italy by Luigi Graziano in "Patron-Client Relationships in Southern Italy," *European Journal of Political Research* 1(March 1973): 3–34.

17. Sabino Cassese, "Il sistema amministrativo italiano, ovvero l'arte di arrangiarsi" (Public Administration in Italy, That Is How to Get By), in *L'amministrazione pubblica italiana: Un profilo* (Outline of Italian Public Administration), edited by Sabino Cassese and Claudio Franchini (Bologna: Il Mulino, 1994).

18. Antonio Cobalti and Antonio Schizzerotto, *La mobilità sociale in Italia* (Social Mobility in Italy) (Bologna: Il Mulino, 1994).

19. Putnam, *Making Democracy Work*. The best definition of social capital is found in James S. Coleman, *Foundations of Social Theory* (Cambridge, Mass.: Harvard University Press, 1990).

20. Robert D. Putnam, "Bowling Alone: America's Declining Social Capital," *Journal of Democracy* 6(January 1995): 65–78; Robert D. Putnam, "Tuning In, Tuning Out: The Strange Disappearance of Social Capital in America," *Political Science and Politics* 28(Winter 1995): 664–83.

21. Francis Fukuyama, *Trust: The Social Virtues and the Creation of Prosperity* (New York: Free Press, 1995).

22. The idea of a new spirit of capitalism was developed by Luc Boltanski

and Ève Chiapello, *Le nouvel esprit du capitalisme* (Paris: Gallimard, 1999). In their analysis, the new capitalism of managers supplants that of cadres, the exponents of large organizational "technostructures." In effect, the change affects the whole social corpus, but to different degrees. Although oriented toward flexible specialization, the large tangible-goods manufacturers continue to be organizations that are more hierarchical, rigid, and focused on long-term yields. In contrast, firms that produce intangible goods (such as communications, marketing, and financial services) are the bellwethers of the new mobile capitalism. Small industrial entrepreneurs are, in a sense, suspended midway between the two. One of the most interesting cultural and political cleavages in the near future is likely to be precisely the one defined by this difference.

23. Efforts to understand the reasons for southern underdevelopment have stimulated a long debate stretching back to the unification of Italy and continuing to the present day. At the moment of unification, the south was undoubtedly more economically and socially backward than the rest of the country, and the national policy was to strengthen the nascent economy in the north in the hope that it might eventually spread to the south. This failed to happen, however, and after World War II a regional policy was drawn up for the area. The regional policy produced unsatisfactory results because of its dependence on new local political patronage (discussed elsewhere in the text) and because public spending made the south a sort of protected domestic market for northern industrialists. As an introduction to the literature on the south, see Paul Ginsborg, *A History of Contemporary Italy: Society and Politics 1943–1988* (London: Penguin, 1990); Denis Mack Smith, *Modern Italy: A Political History* (London: Yale University Press, 1959).

24. Olivier Zunz, *Why the American Century?* (Chicago: University of Chicago Press, 1998), xi.

25. This new social capital has arguably compromised old forms of traditional social capital, but for a long period it helped others to survive and also created new ones. After all, it is today—maybe for other reasons—that we are speaking about the loss of social capital, whereas in the past there was no mention of it.

26. C. Wright Mills, *White Collar: The American Middle Classes* (New York: Oxford University Press, 1951).

# Statistical Appendix: Income Inequality in Seven Nations—France, Germany, Italy, Japan, Sweden, the United Kingdom, and the United States

*Derek Hoff*

The figures in this appendix illustrate historical trends in income (not wealth) inequality in seven nations—France, Germany, Italy, Japan, Sweden, the United Kingdom, and the United States—as far back as available data permitted. The data are drawn from nation-specific studies and hence allow for only rough comparisons between nations. The most significant barrier to comparability is that definitions of income differ from one study to the next. While broadly speaking most of the studies report disposable income, they treat government transfers, taxes, capital gains, and benefits from public spending inconsistently. Moreover, though all of the studies examine "household" rather than "individual" income, the definition of the household varies—both in term of who comprises one and how differences in their size are taken into account.

What follows is a brief discussion of the data sources for each country. For the purposes of this appendix, we present data by quintiles, but it is available by deciles for most years for all nations except the United States. Readers interested in retrieving the raw data can consult the following web site: *www.Virginia.edu/~history/projects/zunz/*.

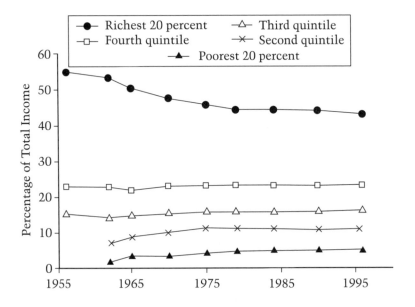

**Figure A.1** Household Distribution of Income in France by Quintile, 1956 to 1996 *Note*: 1956 data for the poorest two quintiles are not available.

## France

*Sources:* Data for 1956 to 1965: Malcolm Sawyer, *Income Distribution in OECD Countries* (Paris: Organization for Economic Cooperation and Development, 1976), 26. Data for 1970 to 1996: Institut national de la statistique et des études économiques, *Revenus et Patrimoine des Ménages* (Paris: INSEE, 1999), 44, table 1. Sawyer also uses INSEE data. For further information on incomes in France, see Thomas Piketty, *Les hauts revenus en France au vingtième siècle: Inégalités et redistributions, 1901–1998* (Paris: Éditions Grasset, 2001).

The INSEE Survey of Fiscal Revenues ("Enquête sur les Revenus Fiscaux") is based on income-tax declarations. Incomes include transfers but are pre-tax, and they are household, not individual, incomes. INSEE has argued that its earliest surveys understated incomes in the lower deciles. See Jean Bégué, "Remarques sur une étude de l'OCDE concernant la répartition des revenus dans divers pays," *Économie et statistique* (INSEE) 84(December 1976): 97–104.

We thank Thomas Piketty of Ens-Cepremap in Paris for his counsel.

## Germany

*Source:* Data for 1962 to 1969: Irene Becker, "Die Entwicklung von Einkommensverteilung und Einkommensarmut in den alten Bund-

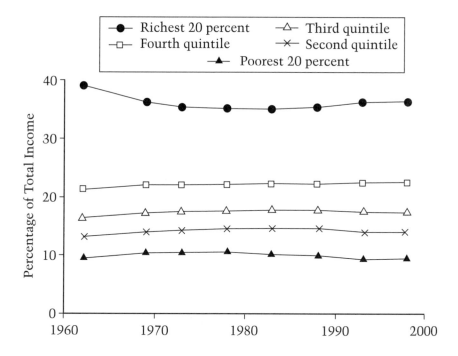

**Figure A.2**  Household Distribution of Income in West Germany by Quintile, 1962 to 1998

esländern von 1962 bis 1988," in *Einkommensverteilung und Armut: Deutschland auf dem Weg zur Vierfünftel-Gesellschaft?*, edited by Irene Becker and Richard Hauser (Frankfurt am Main: Campus, 1997), 47, table 1. Data for 1973 to 1998: Richard Hauser and Irene Becker, *Einkommensverteilung im Querschnitt und im Zeitverlauf 1973 bis 1998*, Studie im Auftrag des Bundesministeriums für Arbeit und Sozialordnung (Bonn: 2001), 89, table 6.1.6. See also Richard Hauser and Irene Becker, "Changes in the Distribution of Pre-government and Post-government Income in Germany, 1973–1993," in *The Personal Distribution of Income in an International Perspective*, edited by Richard Hauser and Irene Becker (Berlin: Springer, 2000), 72–98.

Hauser and Becker constructed their figures from the German government's Income and Consumption Surveys ("Einkommens- und Verbrauchsstichproben"), which are conducted every five years by the Federal Statistical Office. "Income" is household disposable income standardized by the number and age of household members; this weighted per capita income is then assigned to each member of the household. The data cover only West Germany, and for the 1990s only the former West Germany.

For their help, we thank Richard Hauser and Irene Becker of the University of Frankfurt and Alois Guger of the Austrian Institute for Economic Research.

## Italy

*Sources:* Data for 1967 to 1995: Andrea Brandolini, *The Distribution of Personal Income in Postwar Italy: Source Description, Data Quality, and the Time Pattern of Income Inequality*, Banca D'Italia Temi di discussione del Servizio Studi 350 (Rome: April 1999), 70, table B10. Data for 1998: Bank of Italy, "Italian Household Budgets in 1998," 53, table C4; available at *www.bancaditalia.it.*

The data come from the Bank of Italy's periodic Income Survey, which has undergone extensive changes over time. For this reason, figures are not strictly comparable from one year to the next, and the profile shown in figure A.3 must be approached with some caution. Incomes are disposable and by household.

We thank Andrea Brandolini of the Bank of Italy for his advice.

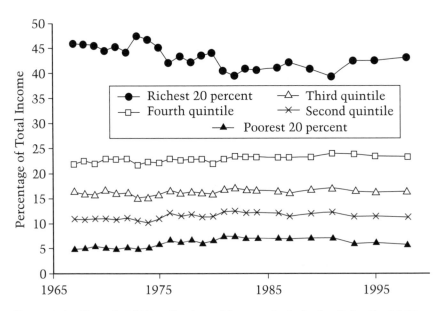

**Figure A.3** Household Distribution of Income in Italy, by Quintile, 1967 to 1998

## Japan

*Source:* Japanese Government, Statistics Bureau, *Annual Report on Family Income and Expenditures* (FIES) (various issues).

FIES incomes are disposable and by household. Note that there are special problems with the comparability of Japanese data. The FIES does not cover the entire population; it excludes agricultural and one-person households, among others.

Another source frequently cited is the Ministry of Health and Welfare's Income Redistribution Survey (IRS). See Tachibanaki Toshiaki and Yagi Tadashi, "Distribution of Economic Well-being in Japan: Toward a More Unequal Society," in *Changing Patterns in the Distribution of Economic Welfare: An International Perspective,* edited by Peter Gottschalk, Björn Gustafsson, and Edward Palmer (Cambridge: Cambridge University Press, 1997), 112–13; Tachibanaki Toshiaki, *Nihon no keizai kakusa: Shotoku to shisan kara kangaeru* (Economic differences in Japan: An examination based on income and assets) (Tokyo: Iwanami shinsho, 1998), 5. These data cover a broader segment of the Japanese population, including single-member and farm households, and show a steeper increase in inequality since the mid-1980s. See the discussion of the alternative data sources and a figure showing the IRS trend line in Schoppa (this volume).

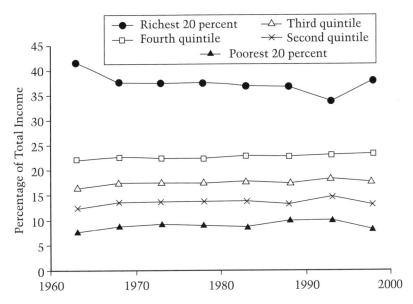

**Figure A.4** Household Distribution of Income in Japan, by Quintile, 1963 to 1998

## Sweden

*Source:* original data courtesy of Kjell Jansson, Statistics Sweden. For comments on differences in Swedish trends, see Ingemar Eriksson and Thomas Pettersson, "Income Distribution and Income Mobility: Recent Trends in Sweden," in T*he Personal Distribution of Income in an International Perspective,* edited by Richard Hauser and Irene Becker (Berlin: Springer, 2000), 158–75. These data build on the Income Distribution Survey of Statistics Sweden (HINK). Incomes are disposable and by household (adjusted to take account of the size and composition of the household). Unlike the data for most other countries, Sweden's include capital gains; this statistical device increases inequality (and helps account for the spikes in the top decile in the 1990s). The household concept, which treats children eighteen years and older who still live with their parents as separate households, also overestimates inequality. Revised 1998 figures (also courtesy of Kjell Jansson), which incorporate a new household definition that corrects for the adult-children problem and which exclude capital gains, give the poorest quintile 10.5 percent of income, up from 8.1 percent in figure A.5, and the richest quintile 33.5 percent of income, down from 36.6 percent in figure A.5.

We thank Anders Bjorklund of Stockholm University for his counsel.

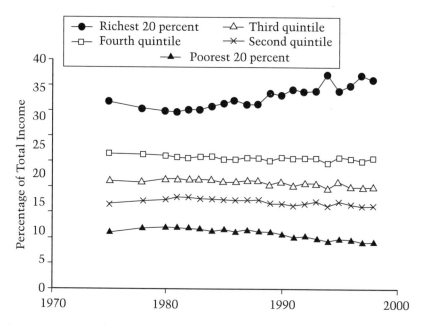

**Figure A.5**  Household Distribution of Income in Sweden, by Quintile, 1975 to 1998

## The United Kingdom

*Sources:* Data for 1961 to 1991: Alissa Goodman and Steven Webb, *For Richer, for Poorer: The Changing Distribution of Income in the United Kingdom, 1961–1991,* Institute for Fiscal Studies Commentary 42 (London: IFS, 1994), A3, figure 2.3. Beginning with 1994, the data include parts of two years. Data for 1994–1995 to 1996–1997: Department of Social Security, *Households Below Average Income (HBAI): A Statistical Analysis, 1979 to 1996–1997,* 97, 150. Data for 1997–1998 to 1998–1999: Department of Social Security, *Households below Average Income: A Statistical Analysis, 1994–1995 to 1998–1999,* 156. Data for 1999–2000 Department of Social Security; *Households below Average Income, 1999–2000,* 101. The most recent edition of the HBAI is available from the Department of Social Security at *www.dss.gov.uk.*

Data for 1961 to 1995–1996 are based on the British government's Family Expenditure Survey (FES). Data for 1996–1997 to 1998–1999 are based on the British government's Family Resources Survey (FRS), which supplanted the FES. (For three years both were produced.) The FES, which covered the United Kingdom, was the smaller of the two surveys. The FRS covers Great Britain; that is, it excludes Northern

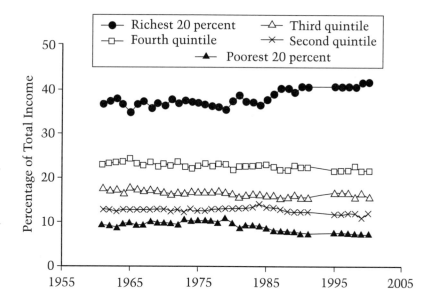

**Figure A.6** Household Distribution of Income in the United Kingdom by Quintile, 1961 to 2000

Ireland. Incomes are disposable and by household (adjusted to take account of the size and composition of the household).

We thank Colin Wilkie-Jones of the Department of Social Security for his assistance.

## The United States

*Source:* U.S. Bureau of the Census, *Historical Income Tables,* table H-2: "Share of Aggregate Income Received by Each Fifth and Top 5 Percent of Households, 1967–2000"; available at *www.census.gov.*

Data compiled from the Bureau of the Census's series *Current Population Reports.* Incomes are by household and include transfers but are pre-tax.

For more detailed discussion of income inequality in the United States, see Lisa Keister, *Wealth in America: Trends in Wealth Inequality* (Cambridge: Cambridge University Press, 2000); Frank Levy, *The New Dollars and Dreams: American Incomes and Economic Change* (New York: Russell Sage Foundation, 1998); Paul Ryscavage, *Income Inequality in America: An Analysis of Trends* (Armonk, N.Y.: M. E. Sharpe, 1999).

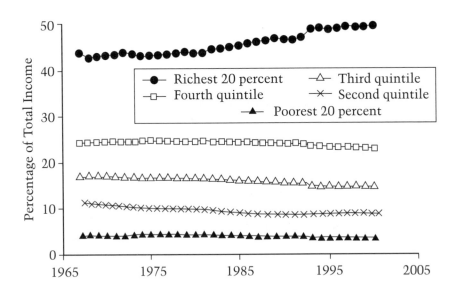

**Figure A.7**   Household Distribution of Income in the United States by Quintile, 1967 to 2000

## Other Sources

For further discussion of income inequality in the various countries, see the following works:

Atkinson, Anthony B., and Andrea Brandolini. "Promise and Pitfalls in the Use of 'Secondary' Data Sets: Income Inequality in OECD Countries as a Case Study." *Journal of Economic Literature* 39(September 2001): 771–99.

Atkinson, Anthony B., Lee Rainwater, and Timothy Smeeding. *Income Distribution in OECD Countries: Evidence from the Luxembourg Income Study.* Paris: Organization for Economic Cooperation and Development, 1995.

Canberra Group. *Expert Group on Household Income Statistics: Final Report and Recommendations.* Ottawa: Canberra Group, 2001.

Förster, Michael, assisted by Michele Pellizzari. "Trends and Driving Factors in Income Distribution and Poverty in the OECD Area." Labour Market and Social Policy Occasional Papers 42. Paris: Organization for Economic Cooperation and Development, 2000.

Gottschalk, Peter, Björn Gustafsson, and Edward Palmer, eds. *Changing Patterns in the Distribution of Economic Welfare: An International Perspective.* Cambridge: Cambridge University Press, 1997.

Gottschalk, Peter, and Timothy M. Smeeding. "Cross-national Comparisons of Earnings and Income Inequality." *Journal of Economic Literature* 35(June 1997): 633–87.

Smeeding, Timothy M. "Changing Income Inequality in OECD Countries: Updated Results from the Luxembourg Income Study (LIS)." In *The Personal Distribution of Income in an International Perspective,* edited by Richard Hauser and Irene Becker. Berlin: Springer, 2000, 205–24.

Williamson, Jeffrey G. "Globalization and Inequality, Past and Present." *World Bank Research Observer* 12(August 1997): 117–35.

In addition, the reader can consult the Luxembourg Income Study (LIS). A division of the Centre for the Study of Population, Poverty, and Public Policy, Grand Duchy of Luxembourg, this ongoing research project facilitates consistency and international comparison of income statistics by gathering microdata from twenty-five participating nations and reorganizing it to conform to common standards. LIS data for most nations exist only since 1979. The LIS web address is *www.lisproject.org.*

# Selected Bibliography

Alexander, Arthur J. *Structural Change and Economic Mobility in Japan.* Report 44A. Washington, D.C.: Japan Economic Institute, November 20, 1998.

Altieri, Giovanna, and Mimmo Carrieri. *Il popolo del 10%: Il boom del lavoro atipico.* Rome: Donzelli editore, 2000.

Andorka, Rudolf. *A társadami mobilitás változásai Magyarországon* (Changes in social mobility in Hungary). Budapest: Gondolat Kiado, 1982.

Andrews, David M. "Capital Mobility and State Autonomy: Toward a Structural Theory of International Monetary Relations." *International Studies Quarterly* 38(Summer 1994): 193–218.

Annan, Noel. *Our Age: The Generation That Made Postwar Britain.* London: Fontana, 1991.

Atkinson, Anthony B., Lee Rainwater, and Timothy M. Smeeding. *Income Distribution in OECD Countries: Evidence from the Luxembourg Income Study.* Paris: Organization for Economic Cooperation and Development, 1995.

Bagnasco, Arnaldo, and Charles F. Sabel, eds. *Small and Medium-Size Enterprises.* London: Pinter, 1995.

Bagnasco, Arnaldo, and Carlo Trigilia. *La construction sociale du marché: Le défi de la troisième Italie.* Cachan: Les Éditions de l'École Normale Supérieure de Cachan, 1993.

Barker, Ernest, ed. *Social Contract: Essays by Locke, Hume, and Rousseau.* London: Oxford University Press, 1947.

Beck, Wolfgang, Laurent van der Maesen, and Alan Walker. *The Social Quality of Europe.* The Hague: Kluwer Law International, 1997.

Bell, Daniel. *The Coming of Post-Industrial Society: A Venture in Social Forecasting.* New York: Basic, 1973.

Bendix, Reinhard, and Seymour Martin Lipset, eds. *Class, Status, and Power: Social Stratification in Comparative Perspective.* 2nd ed. New York: Free Press, 1966.

Berger, Suzanne, and Michael J. Piore. *Dualism and Discontinuity in Industrial Societies.* Cambridge: Cambridge University Press, 1980.

Berkowitz, Edward D. *America's Welfare State: From Roosevelt to Reagan.* Baltimore: Johns Hopkins University Press, 1991.

Bertaux, Daniel. "Les transmissions en situation extrême: Familles expropriées par la Révolution d'octobre." *Communications* 59(November 1994): 73–99.

Blom, Raimo, Harri Melin, and Jouko Nicula, eds. *Reformation of the Middle Classes in the Baltic Countries.* Working Paper 4. Tempere, Finland: University of Tampare, 1995.

Boje, Thomas P., and Arnlaug Leira, eds. *Gender, Welfare State, and the Market.* London: Routledge, 2000.

Boltanski, Luc, and Ève Chiapello. *Le nouvel esprit du capitalisme.* Paris: Gallimard, 1999.

Boucher, David. *The Social and Political Thought of R. G. Collingwood.* Cambridge: Cambridge University Press, 1989.

Boucher, David, and Paul Kelly, eds. *The Social Contract from Hobbes to Rawls.* London: Routledge, 1994.

Bouffartigue, Paul, and Charles Gadea. *Sociologie des cadres.* Paris: La Découverte, 2000.

Bouget, Denis, and Palier Bruno, eds. *Comparing Social Welfare Systems in Scandinavian Europe and France.* Nantes: Maison des sciences de l'homme Ange-Guépin, 1999.

Bourdieu, Pierre. *Distinction: A Social Critique of the Judgment of Taste.* Cambridge, Mass.: Harvard University Press, 1984.

Bourdieu, Pierre, and Lauretta C. Clough. *The State Nobility: Elite Schools in the Field of Power.* Stanford: Stanford University Press, 1996.

Bourdieu, Pierre, and Jean-Claude Passeron. *Reproduction in Education, Society, and Culture.* London: Sage Publications, 1990.

Brint, Steven, and Jerome Karabel. *The Diverted Dream: Community Colleges and the Promise of Educational Opportunity in America, 1900–1985.* New York: Oxford University Press, 1989.

Brinton, Mary. *Women and Economic Miracle: Gender and Work in Postwar Japan.* Berkeley: University of California Press, 1993.

Brusco, Sebastiano. "The Emilian Model: Productive Decentralisation and Social Integration." *Cambridge Journal of Economics* 6(June 1982): 167–84.

Bürklin, Wilhelm, and Hilke Rebenstorf, eds. *Eliten in Deutschland: Rekrutierung und Integration.* Opladen: Leske & Budrich, 1997.

Burtless, Gary, et al. *Globaphobia: Confronting Fears About Open Trade.* Washington, D.C.: Brookings Institution, 1998.

Butler, Timothy, and Mike Savage, eds. *Social Change and the Middle Classes.* London: UCL Press, 1995.

Cain, Peter J., and Anthony G. Hopkins. *British Imperialism.* 2 vols. London: Longmans, 1992.

Calder, Kent E. *Crisis and Compensation: Public Policy and Political Stability in Japan, 1949–1986.* Princeton: Princeton University Press, 1989.

Castles, Francis G., ed. *Families of Nations: Patterns of Public Policy in Western Democracies.* Aldershot: Avebury, 1993.

Chandler, Alfred. *Scale and Scope: The Dynamics of Industrial Capitalism.* Cambridge: Belknap Press of Harvard University Press, 1990.

Charle, Christophe. *A Social History of France in the Nineteenth Century.* Oxford: Berg, 1993.

———. *La crise des sociétés impériales: Allemagne, France, Grande-Bretagne, 1900–1940: Essai d'histoire sociale comparée.* Paris: Éditions du Seuil, 2001.

Chmatko, Natacha, and Monique de Saint-Martin. "Les anciens bureaucrates dans l'économie de marché à Moscou." *Genèses* 27(June 1997): 88–108.

Claisse, Alain, and Marie-Christine Maininger. *Fonctions publiques en Europe.* Paris: Montchrestien, 1994.

Cobalti, Antonio, and Antonio Schizzerotto. *La mobilità sociale in Italia.* Bologna: Il Mulino, 1994.

Collingwood, R. G. *The New Leviathan, or Man, Society, Civilization, and Barbarism* [1942]. Edited by David Boucher. Rev. ed. Oxford: Clarendon, 1992.

Collins, Robert M. *More: The Politics of Economic Growth in Postwar America.* New York: Oxford University Press, 2000.

Cox, Robert Henry. "The Consequences of Welfare Reform: How Conceptions of Social Rights Are Changing." *Journal of Social Policy* 27(January 1998): 1–16.

Crossick, Geoffrey, and Heinz-Gerhard Haupt. *The Petite Bourgeoisie in Europe, 1780–1914: Enterprise, Family, and Independence.* London: Routledge, 1995.

Crouch, Colin. *Social Change in Western Europe.* New York: Oxford University Press, 1999.

Crouzet, François. *A History of the European Economy, 1000–2000.* Charlottesville: University Press of Virginia, 2001.

Cukierman, Alex, Steven B. Webb, and Bilin Neyapti. "Measuring the Independence of Central Banks and Its Effect on Policy Outcomes." *World Bank Economic Review* 6(September 1992): 353–98.

Dahrendorf, Ralf. "Economic Opportunity, Civil Society, and Political Liberty." Paper presented at the United Nations Research Institute for Social Development (*UNISRED*) Conference for Rethinking Social Development, Copenhagen, 1995.

Daley, Anthony, ed. *The Mitterrand Era: Policy Alternatives and Political Mobilization in France.* New York: New York University Press, 1996.

Damgaard, Erik, Peter Gerlich, and J. J. Richardson, eds. *The Politics of Economic Crisis: Lessons from Western Europe.* Brookfield, Vt.: Gower, 1989.

413

Dore, Ronald. *City Life in Japan: A Study of a Tokyo Ward.* Berkeley: University of California Press, 1958.

Eichengreen, Barry J., Jeffry A. Frieden, and Jürgen von Hagen, eds. *Monetary and Fiscal Policy in an Integrated Europe.* New York: Springer, 1995.

Esping-Andersen, Gøsta. *The Three Worlds of Welfare Capitalism.* Princeton: Princeton University Press, 1990.

———, ed. *Welfare States in Transition: National Adaptations in Global Economics.* London: Sage Publications, 1996.

———. *Social Foundations of Post-Industrial Economies.* Oxford: Oxford University Press, 1999.

European Commission. *Social Protection in Europe.* Luxembourg: European Commission, 1993.

Ferge, Zsuzsa, and Jon Eivind Kolberg, eds. *Social Policy in a Changing Europe.* Frankfurt am Main: Campus, 1992.

Finch, Janet. *Family Obligations and Social Change.* London: Polity, 1989.

Fischer, Claude S., et al. *Inequality by Design: Cracking the Bell Curve Myth.* Princeton: Princeton University Press, 1996.

Flynn, Gregory, ed. *Remaking the Hexagon: The New France in the New Europe.* Boulder: Westview Press, 1995.

Fones-Wolfe, Elizabeth. *Selling Free Enterprise: The Business Assault on Labor and Liberalism, 1945–1960.* Urbana: University of Illinois Press, 1994.

Fraser, Steve, and Gary Gerstle, eds. *The Rise and Fall of the New Deal Order, 1930–1980.* Princeton: Princeton University Press, 1989.

Fukuyama, Francis. *Trust: The Social Virtues and the Creation of Prosperity.* New York: Free Press, 1995.

Furner, Mary, and Barry Supple, eds. *The State and Economic Knowledge.* New York: Cambridge University Press, 1990.

Garon, Sheldon. *Molding Japanese Minds: The State in Everyday Life.* Princeton: Princeton University Press, 1997.

Garrett, Geoffrey. "Capital Mobility, Trade, and the Domestic Politics of Economic Policy." *International Organization* 49(Autumn 1995): 657–87.

George, Vic. "Political Ideology, Globalisation, and Welfare Futures in Europe." *Journal of Social Policy* 27(January 1998): 17–36.

Glass, David. *Social Mobility in Britain.* London: Routledge, 1954.

Glassmann, Ronald M. *The Middle Class and Democracy in Sociohistorical Perspective.* Leiden: Brill, 1995.

Goldin, Claudia, and Robert A. Margo. "The Great Compression: The Wage Structure in the United States at Mid-century." *Quarterly Journal of Economics* 107(February 1992): 1–34.

Gordon, Andrew S., ed. *Postwar Japan as History.* Berkeley: University of California Press, 1993.

———. "Managing the Japanese Household: The New Life Movement in Postwar Japan." *Social Politics* 4(Summer 1997): 245–83.

414

————. *The Wages of Affluence: Labor and Management in Postwar Japan.* Cambridge: Harvard University Press, 1998.

Gordon, Linda. *Pitied but Not Entitled: Single Mothers and the History of Welfare, 1890–1935.* New York: Free Press, 1994.

Gottschalk, Peter, Björn Gustafsson, and Edward Palmer, eds. *Changing Patterns in the Distribution of Economic Welfare: An International Perspective.* Cambridge: Cambridge University Press, 1997.

Gottschalk, Peter, and Timothy M. Smeeding. "Cross-national Comparisons of Earnings and Income Inequality." *Journal of Economic Literature* 35(June 1997): 633–87.

Gourevitch, Peter, et al., eds. *Unions and Economic Crisis: Britain, West Germany, and Sweden.* London: Allen & Unwin, 1984.

Greider, William. *One World, Ready or Not: The Manic Logic of Global Capitalism.* New York: Touchstone, 1997.

Guillaume, Sylvie. *La confédération générale des petites et moyennes enterprises: Son histoire, son combat, un autre syndicalisme, 1944–1978.* Bordeaux: Presses universitaires de Bordeaux, 1987.

Hall, Peter A., ed. *The Political Power of Economic Ideas: Keynesianism Across Nations.* Princeton: Princeton University Press, 1989.

Hantrais, Linda, and Marie-Thérèse Letablier. *Families and Family Policies in Europe.* New York: Longman, 1996.

Harris, Jose. *William Beveridge: A Biography.* Oxford: Clarendon, 1997.

Hashimoto Akiko. *The Gift of Generations: Japanese and American Perspectives on Aging and the Social Contract.* Cambridge: Cambridge University Press, 1996.

Hauser, Richard, and Irene Becker, eds. *The Personal Distribution of Income in an International Perspective.* Berlin: Springer, 2000.

Helleiner, Eric. *States and the Reemergence of Global Finance: From Bretton Woods to the 1990s.* Ithaca: Cornell University Press, 1994.

Hirsch, Fred, and John H. Goldthorpe, eds. *The Political Economy of Inflation.* Cambridge: Harvard University Press, 1978.

Hirst, Paul, and Graham Thompson. *Globalization in Question: The International Economy and the Possibility of Governance.* Cambridge: Polity, 1996.

Hobson, Barbara. "No Exit No Voice: Women's Economic Dependency and the Welfare State." *Acta Sociologica* 33(1990): 235–50.

Hout, Michael. "More Universalism, Less Structural Mobility: The American Occupational Structure in the 1980s." *American Journal of Sociology* 93(May 1988): 1358–1400.

Inoue Jun, et al., eds. *Nihon bunka no shakaigaku: Gendai shakaigaku.* Tokyo: Iwanami shoten, 1996.

Ishida Hiroshi. *Social Mobility in Contemporary Japan: Educational Credentials, Class, and the Labor Market in a Cross-national Perspective.* Stanford: Stanford University Press, 1993.

Junji Banno, ed. *The Political Economy of Japanese Society*, 2 vols. Oxford: Oxford University Press, 1998.

Katznelson, Ira, and Margaret Weir. *Schooling for All: Class, Race, and the Decline of the Democratic Ideal*. New York: Basic, 1985.

Keister, Lisa. *Wealth in America: Trends in Wealth Inequality*. Cambridge: Cambridge University Press, 2000.

Keohane, Robert O., and Helen V. Miller, eds. *Internationalization and Domestic Politics*. Cambridge: Cambridge University Press, 1996.

Key, V. O., Jr. *Southern Politics in State and Nation*. New York: Knopf, 1949.

Kidd, Alan, and David Nicholls, eds. *The Making of the British Middle Class? Studies of Regional and Cultural Diversity Since the Eighteenth Century*. Stroud: Sutton, 1998.

Kitschelt, Herbert, et al., eds. *Continuity and Change in Contemporary Capitalism*. Cambridge: Cambridge University Press, 1999.

Kocka, Jürgen. *Die Angestellten in der deutschen Geschichte, 1850–1980: vom Privatbeamten zum angestellten Arbeitnehmer*. Göttingen: Vandenhoeck & Ruprecht, 1981.

———. "The Middle Classes in Europe." *Journal of Modern History* 67(December 1995): 783–806.

Kosaka Kenji, ed. *Social Stratification in Contemporary Japan*. London: Kegan Paul International, 1994.

Koven, Seth, and Sonya Michel, eds. *Mothers of a New World: Maternalist Politics and the Origins of Welfare States*. New York: Routledge, 1993.

Kumazawa Makoto. *Portraits of the Japanese Workplace, Labor Movements, Workers, and Managers*. Edited by Andrew Gordon. Translated by Andrew Gordon and Mikiso Hane. Boulder: Westview Press, 1996.

Kuznets, Simon. "Economic Growth and Income Inequality." *American Economic Review* 45(March 1955): 1–28.

Leibfried, Stephan, and Paul Pierson, eds. *European Social Policy: Between Fragmentation and Integration*. Washington, D.C.: Brookings Institution, 1995.

Lemann, Nicholas. *The Big Test: The Secret History of the Meritocracy*. New York: Farrar, Straus & Giroux, 1999.

Lessnoff, Michael. *Social Contract Theory*. Oxford: Basil Blackwell, 1990.

Levy, Frank. *The New Dollars and Dreams: American Incomes and Economic Change*. New York: Russell Sage Foundation, 1998.

Lévy-Leboyer, Maurice, ed. *Histoire de la France industrielle*. Paris: Larousse, 1996.

Lewis, Jane. "Gender and Welfare Regimes: Further Thoughts." *Social Politics* 4(Summer 1997): 160–77.

———, ed. *Gender, Social Care, and Welfare State Restructuring in Europe*. London: Ashgate, 1998.

Lieberman, Robert C. *Shifting the Color Line: Race and the American Welfare State.* Cambridge: Harvard University Press, 1998.

Lijphart, Arend. *Patterns of Democracy: Government Forms and Performance in Thirty-six Countries.* New Haven: Yale University Press, 1999.

Lubell, Samuel. *The Future of American Politics.* New York: Harper, 1952.

McKibbin, Ross. *The Ideologies of Class: Social Relations in Britain, 1700–1850.* Oxford: Clarendon, 1990.

Maclean, Mairi, ed. *The Mitterrand Years: Legacy and Evaluation.* London: Macmillan, 1998.

Marshall, Thomas. *Citizenship and Social Class, and Other Essays.* Cambridge: Cambridge University Press, 1950.

Mason, Karen O., and An-Magritt Jensen, eds. *Gender and Family Change in Industrialized Societies.* Oxford: Clarendon, 1995.

Matsunari Yoshie, et al. *Nihon no sarariiman.* Tokyo: Aoki shoten, 1957.

Mendras, Henri. *La Seconde révolution française, 1965–1984.* Rev. ed. Paris: Gallimard, 1994.

Merkel, Ina. *Utopie und Bedürfnis: die Geschichte der Konsumkultur in der DDR.* Cologne: Böhlau, 1999.

Millar, Jane, and Andrea Warman. *Defining Family Obligations in Europe: The Family, the State, and Social Policy.* London: Family Policy Studies Centre, 1996.

Murakami Yasusuke, Kishimoto Shigenobu, and Tominaga Ken'ichi. "Debate on the New Middle Class." *Japan Interpreter* 12(Winter 1978): 1–15.

Myrdal, Gunnar. *An American Dilemma: The Negro Problem and Modern Democracy.* New York: Harper & Row, 1944.

Newman, Katherine S. *Declining Fortunes: The Withering of the American Dream.* New York: Basic, 1993.

Nii Kaku. "Sarariiman-ron." *Chūō kōron* 43(December 1928): 39–46.

Nord, Philip. *The Republican Moment: Struggles for Democracy in Nineteenth-century France.* Cambridge, Mass.: Harvard University Press, 1995.

O'Connor, Julia S., Ann S. Orloff, and Sheila Shaver. *Family, Market, and Community: Equity and Efficiency in Social Policy.* Social Policy Studies 21. Paris: Organization for Economic Cooperation and Development, 1997.

———. *States, Markets, and Families.* Cambridge: Cambridge University Press, 1999.

Ortega y Gasset, José. *Invertebrate Spain.* Translated and with a foreword by Mildred Adams. New York: Norton, 1937.

Osawa Mari. *Kigyō chūshin shakai o koete: Gendai Nihon no jendaa de yomu* (Overcoming the corporate-centered society). Tokyo: Jiji tsūshin sha, 1993.

———. "Bye-bye, Corporate Warriors: The Formation of a Corporate-

Centered Society and Gender-Biased Social Policies in Japan." *Annals of the Institute of Social Science* 35(1994): 157–94.

Packard, Vance. *The Status Seekers*. Edited and with an introduction by Daniel Horowitz. Boston: Bedford, 1995.

Patterson, James T. *Grand Expectations: The United States, 1945–1974*. New York: Oxford University Press, 1996.

Pierson, Paul. *Dismantling the Welfare State?: Reagan, Thatcher, and the Politics of Retrenchment*. Cambridge: Cambridge University Press, 1994.

Potter, David Morris. *People of Plenty: Economic Abundance and the American Character*. Chicago: University of Chicago Press, 1954.

Putnam, Robert D. *Making Democracy Work: Civic Traditions in Modern Italy*. Princeton: Princeton University Press, 1993.

———. "Bowling Alone: America's Declining Social Capital." *Journal of Democracy* 6(January 1995): 65–78.

———. *Bowling Alone: The Collapse and Revival of American Community*. New York: Simon & Schuster, 2000.

Pyke, Frank, Giacomo Becattini, and Werner Sengenberger, eds. *Industrial Districts and Interfirm Cooperation in Italy*. Geneva: International Institute for Labor Studies, 1990.

Quadagno, Jill. *The Color of Welfare: How Racism Undermined the War on Poverty*. New York: Oxford University Press, 1994.

Rawls, John. *A Theory of Justice*. Cambridge: Belknap Press of Harvard University Press, 1971.

Rhodes, Martin. "Globalization and West European Welfare States: A Critical Review of the Recent Debates." *Journal of European Social Policy* 6(4, 1996): 305–27.

Ritter, Gerhard A. *Über Deutschland: die Bundesrepublik in der deutschen Geschichte*. Munich: C. H. Beck, 1998.

Robertson, Roland. *Globalization, Social Theory, and Global Culture*. London: Sage Publications, 1992.

Rodrik, Dani. *Has Globalization Gone Too Far?* Washington, D.C.: Institute for International Economics, 1997.

Ruhlmann, Jean. *Ni bourgeois ni prolétaires: La défense des classes moyennes en France au xxeme siècle*. Paris Editions du Seuil, 2001.

Ryscavage, Paul. *Income Inequality in America: An Analysis of Trends*. Armonk, N.Y.: M. E. Sharpe, 1999.

Sainsbury, Diane. *Gender, Equality, and Welfare States*. Cambridge: Cambridge University Press, 1996.

Saraceno, Chiara. "Family Change, Family Policies, and the Restructuring of Welfare." In *Family, Market, and Community: Equity and Efficiency in Social Policy*. Social Policy Studies 21. Paris: Organization for Economic Cooperation and Development, 1997.

Savage, Mike. *Class Analysis and Social Transformation*. Milton Keynes: Open University Press, 2000.

Savage, Mike, and Anne Witz, eds. *Gender and Bureaucracy*. Sociological Review Monograph. Oxford: Blackwell's, 1992.

Savage, Mike, James Barlow, Peter Dickens, and Tony Fielding. *Property, Bureaucracy, and Culture: Middle-class Formation in Contemporary Britain.* London: Routledge, 1992.

Schäfers, Bernhard, and Wolfgang Zapf, eds. *Handwörterbuch zur Gesellschaft Deutschlands.* Opladen: Leske & Budrich, 1998.

Shalev, Michael, ed. *The Privatization of Social Policy: Occupational Welfare and the Welfare State in America, Scandinavia, and Japan.* New York: St. Martin's Press, 1996.

Siegrist, Hannes. "Ende der Bürgerlichkeit? Die Kategorien 'Bürgertum' und 'Bürgerlichkeit' in der westdeutschen Gesellschaft und Geschichtswissenschaft in der Nachkriegsperiode." *Geschichte und Gesellschaft* 20(1994): 549–83.

Siegrist, Hannes, Hartmut Kaelble, and Jürgen Kocka, eds. *Europäische Konsumgeschichte: zur Gesellschafts- und Kulturgeschichte des Konsums (18. bis 20. Jahrhundert).* Frankfurt am Main: Campus, 1997.

Srubar, Ilja, ed. *Eliten, politische Kultur und Privatisierung in Ostdeutschland, Tschechien und Mittelosteuropa.* Konstanz: Universitätsverlag Konstanz, 1998.

Stein, Herbert. *The Fiscal Revolution in America.* Rev. ed. Washington, D.C.: American Enterprise Institute Press, 1990.

Stein, Judith. *Running America, Running Steel: Race, Economic Policy, and the Decline of Liberalism.* Chapel Hill: University of North Carolina Press, 1998.

Stubbs, Richard, and Geoffrey R. D. Underhill, eds. *Political Economy and the Changing Global Order.* London: Macmillan, 1994.

Taylor-Gooby, Peter. "Eurosclerosis in European Welfare States: Regime Theory and the Dynamics of Change." *Policy and Politics* 24(April 1996): 109–23.

Tenfelde, Klaus, and Hans-Ulrich Wehler, eds. *Wege zur Geschichte des Bürgertums: vierzehn Beiträge.* Göttingen: Vandenhoeck & Ruprecht, 1994.

Thompson, Edward P. *The Making of the English Working Class.* London: Gollancz, 1963.

Tilkidjiev, Nikolai, ed. *The Middle Class as a Precondition of a Sustainable Society.* Papers from a sociological conference in Sofia, Bulgaria, Association for Middle Class Development (AMCD), June 1998.

Tsurumi Shunsuke. *A Cultural History of Postwar Japan, 1945–1980.* London: Kegan Paul International, 1987.

Vecernik, Jiri. *Markets and People: The Czech Reform Experience in a Comparative Perspective.* Aldershot: Avebury, 1996.

———. "The Middle Class in Czech Reforms: The Interplay Between Policies and Social Stratification." *Communist and Post-Communist Studies* 32(December 1999): 397–416.

Vecernik, Jiri, and Petr Mateju, eds. *Ten Years of Rebuilding Capitalism: Czech Society After 1989.* Prague: Academia, 1999.

Veltz, Pierre. *Le nouveau monde industriel.* Paris: Gallimard, 2000.

Vogel, Ezra. *Japan's New Middle Class: The Salary Man and His Family in a Tokyo Suburb.* Berkeley: University of California Press, 1963.

Wahrman, Dror. *Imagining the Middle Class: The Political Representation of Class in Britain, c. 1780–1840.* Cambridge: Cambridge University Press, 1994.

Williamson, Jeffrey G. "Globalization and Inequality, Past and Present." *World Bank Research Observer* 12(August 1997): 117–35.

Winkler, Heinrich-August. *Zwischen Marx und Monopolen: der deutsche Mittelstand vom Kaiserreich zur Bundesrepublik Deutschland.* Frankfurt am Main: Fischer Taschenbuch, 1991.

Young, Louise. "Marketing the Modern: Department Stores, Consumer Culture, and the New Middle Class in Interwar Japan." *International Labor and Working-class History* 55(Spring 1999): 52–70.

Zunz, Olivier. *Why the American Century?* Chicago: University of Chicago Press, 1998.

# Index

Boldface numbers refer to figures and tables.